PSYCHOANALYTIC PSYCHOTHERAPY OF

The Borderline Patient

Arlene Robbins Wolberg

1982
Thieme-Stratton Inc.
New York

Georg Thieme Verlag
Stuttgart • New York

Copyright © 1982
Thieme-Stratton Inc.
381 Park Avenue South
New York, NY 10016

VANDERBILT UNIVERSITY
MEDICAL CENTER LIBRARY

JUL 1 4 1982

NASHVILLE, TENNESSEE
37232

Printed in U.S.A.
LC 80-1125
TSI ISBN 0-86577-022-0
GTV ISBN 3-13-613701-9

The names of the author's patients used in this book have been disguised and bear no relationship to their actual names.

To

Michael

Lisa

David

Michael

VANDERBILT UNIVERSITY
MEDICAL CENTER LiBRARY

JUL 1 4 1982

NASHVILLE, TENNESSEE
37232

Preface

Although borderline conditions have been with us for as long as any other emotional ailment, it is only recently that attention has been concentrated on this syndrome. Reasons for this focus are sundry. More and more psychotherapists have become aware of the vast multitudes of patients seeking help who possess a diversity of complaints but who cannot be pigeonholed in any distinctive diagnostic category. Symptoms come and go, fluctuating from evanescent paranoidal projections to obsessive-compulsive maneuvers, to anxiety manifestations, to depression, to conversion phenomena, to distortion phenomena (fantasy defenses), and to temporary psychotic episodes. Moreover, the sadomasochistic relationships established by these patients have made therapy arduous and frequently unsuccessful. The challenge posed by the borderline malady that disables such great numbers of our population has promoted increasing empirical studies and has yielded a vast literature with craftily fabricated theories that espouse many contradictory themes. What is necessary, apart from a critical evaluation of this work, is that systematic and coordinated research in the area of the therapeutic process, difficult as this may be, will hopefully come to pass in the future.

In this volume I have attempted to discùss some of the common elements found in working with a sizable group of borderline patients at the Postgraduate Center for Mental Health in New York City. These studies deal with diagnostic impressions and therapeutic techniques that have proven helpful with many patients, even those who have resisted conventional therapies. I have focused on work with borderline patients over a period of thirty-five years, my first paper on this subject having been written twenty-eight years ago. The thirty-three patients with borderline diagnosis listed in Chapter 9 are those whom I have studied most intensely. Most of these patients have been very successful in their fields. Once they became truly interested in working through their problems, they concentrated on their therapeutic tasks. Their struggles gave me many insights into the dynamics of the borderline personality.

This book is mainly about the treatment process. It is a companion piece to my first book *The Borderline Patient* (1973), in which I primarily considered one technique—the projective therapeutic technique. In this book I shall (1) describe the various theories current in the literature regarding the dynamics of the borderline patient, (2) trace the historical roots of some of these ideas, and (3) show how these theories are applied in the therapeutic endeavor. I shall then elaborate on how I utilize my theory in treatment. I do not employ the id, ego and superego concepts in the sense that Freud defined them, using the traditional developmental theory. Instead I emphasize the defenses of the patient, recognizing that in current theory defenses are defined as *functions* of the ego. My contention is that all patients operate on two levels—a reality level and a neurotic level, the latter being associated with *identification with neurotic parents who have imposed roles upon the patient that are functions of the parents' projections*. It is the identification with severely neurotic, and sometimes psychotic, parents and the *anxiety* that this creates that evokes the organization of defenses and the repressions that are the essence of the borderline patient's "unconscious." Due to intense anxiety, the patient has many denial and projective mechanisms, which with his defensive identification, fantasies, and the acting out of the identification role constitute the main focus around which the treatment process is organized.

I employ no psychoanalytic theory of development, believing that psychoanalysis is not the preferred area where developmental data can best be described and authenticated through research. Psychoanalysis is a theory of neurotic and psychotic behavior as well as a technique for the alleviation of neurotic and psychotic disorders. It seems quite possible to me that the structural theory will have to be augmented, enriched, and reorganized as the continuous flow of information comes from the developmental field. A much more rational theory of interpersonal relations within the field of psychopathology will have to emerge.

I predict that Freud's simplification of the instinct theory and his nebulous concepts about the id, describing the representation of instincts in the mind, will undergo even more revision in the future due to the information we now have and will undoubtedly continue to acquire through the efforts of the many investigators in the behavioral sciences.

In this book I have described some early papers that never before have been reported in modern literature as well as the various theories that have more recently been suggested to account for borderline conditions and the ways these theories have influenced present-day treatment methods. Throughout the book I contrast my ideas with the ideas of others and have attempted to illustrate through summary and illustrative sessions some of the techniques I use in relating therapeutically to the borderline patient.

Psychoanalysis is basically involved with how neuroses and psychoses develop as well as with the treatment of these disorders. We are interested in the dynamics of learned responses of a neurotic nature and particularly the dynamics of identification. We cannot as psychoanalysts and therapists encompass all that is "internalized" in our explorations; we thus must be content with understanding how and why identifications with the neurotic parents occur and how the "internalizations" that have to do with these identifications affect the life pattern of the individual. We have available to us data concerning these identifications from the patient's dreams, symptoms, and fantasies. Both the patient's "conscious" and his repressed ideas and feelings ("unconscious") are represented in the dreams and fantasies since the patient operates simultaneously by (1) attending to reality and (2) denying and distorting reality in selective ways as a means of defense.

We have much to learn about the treatment of the borderline case. I have presented a four-part treatment outline that I believe will help to organize and integrate the material one hears and observes in sessions. It is my hope that this book will stimulate more thinking and work on the treatment of the borderline, this interesting yet elusive patient.

I wish to acknowledge with gratitude the grant from the Postgraduate Center for Mental Health in support of this work.

I must also thank several staff members at the Postgraduate Center for their help in collecting data in regard to borderline patients. I am especially indebted to Ellen Baumwoll for conducting the study of the personality characteristics of the sample of patients as seen by the therapists. Lee Mackler, our librarian, was of inestimable help in compiling the bibliography. Typing and editing could never have been done without the assistance of several experts, particularly Ann Kochanske and Frances Guss.

I appreciate the opportunity to work at the Postgraduate Center and the cooperation of the many colleagues who have made my studies of the traits of borderline patients possible. I should like to name a few who have been especially helpful. In a 1958 study, Max Geller, Ph.D.; Oskar Guttmann, M.D.; Benjamin Fielding, Ed.D.; Thomas Aiello who was then M.S. but is now Ph.D. During the last four years I have worked with Leah Tolpin, M.S.S.; Eileen Toban, Ph.D.; Michael Glazer, Ph.D.; Marsha Wineburgh, M.S.W.; and Barry Weiner, Ph.D.

Arlene R. Wolberg

Contents

PART I

Historical Background

CHAPTER 1

Early Papers: Present-Day Implications

The psychiatric literature reveals that the borderline patient was a focus of interest as far back as 1884 and 1890. The word *borderline*, however, was not used, although from descriptions, patients that we think of as borderline today seem to have been included in case studies. This chapter will set forth briefly the views of some of these early writers and examine them in reference to current theories.

Charles H. Hughes and Irving C. Rosse

In his book co-authored with Werble, Grinker (1977) refers to two papers in the bibliography, one written by Charles H. Hughes of St. Louis, lecturer on nervous disease, St. Louis Medical College, and another by Irving C. Rosse, of Washington, D.C., professor of nervous disease at Georgetown University. In reading these papers, I found cases that might now be classified as *borderline*. Hughes wrote of patients whom he had seen in 1878 and 1882 who had obsessions (almost to the point of delusions). Morbid ideas, he said, dominate the mind of a person who may eventually have a psychotic attack, but in some cases this could be avoided by certain interventions. One man had developed a symptom of not being willing to eat potatoes after he observed workers in the field spraying potatoes with Paris green, an insecticide. This obsession generalized to "all things green." When he was a child, someone had fired a toy pistol in the patient's ear at the same time that the patient had seen the workmen spraying. The patient improved slightly, over time. The other patient whom Hughes described, developed symptoms "on the left side" after having been struck a violent blow on the head with a cane. He had a rapid pulse, constant headache, and a green spot before his eyes that gradually widened until he could see nothing else; also he had numbness, impaired vision, and a roaring in his head. All symptoms disappeared after a few months of treatment, which consisted of "cephalic galvanization" (the rubbing of electric sparks on the skin) and the taking of "bromides and arsenic with occasional courses of quinia." These men were considered to be cases of "partial or limited insanities." According to their description, we might now classify them in the borderline category if illnesses, with an emphasis on obsessive and hysterical symptoms.

Rosse (1890) wrote of "borderland insanity" cases, i.e., individuals whose minds were "trembling in the balance between reason and madness, not so sane as to be able to control themselves, nor yet so insane as to require restraint or seclusion."

What is interesting about these reports is that the patients received short-term treatment, and symptom relief was attained in a considerable number of instances. While the symptoms in some situations did recur after a time, in most instances they did not come back. The question we may ask is, Why for some did relief persist? Was it tension alleviation? Certainly that helped. These early therapists used suggestions freely. For example one patient was advised to take a sea journey, which seems to have given him freedom from tension. In another case the individual was a "work-a-holic," and telling him to take a trip to Europe was liberating for him. This may have reduced the guilt that was driving him. The primary symptom for these patients seemed to be one of an obsessional type with hysterical tendencies. Apparently, medications such as bromides were used in those days to relieve worry and anxiety. In each instance the individuals had motivation to get better. They realized something was wrong; most feared insanity; all were amenable to suggestion. Even one man with paranoid trends had insight of a certain kind.

The borderlines whom we see today are not so well organized around one symptom as these patients seemed to have been. Today we see the characteristic *shifting of defense* that was noted by Hoch and Polatin (1949) in their "pseudoneurotic schizophrenics." The same kind of speculation, however, goes on today, where we see symptoms disappear as in Hughes and Rosse's day. What was it that produced the symptom relief? We tend to credit these short-term techniques to a kind of behavioral modification or to a certain degree of psychoanalytic understanding. Some analysts feel the "cure" is due to a partial resolution of the oedipal situation and the idea that the patient "identifies" with the "healthy" analyst rather than the "unhealthy" parent. The fact is that while many so-called obsessional symptoms are an overlay of a basic schizophrenic problem, the symptom can apparently be overcome in the majority of cases with short-term procedures.

"Cure" or relief of symptoms is due certainly to what Alexander and French (1946) called a "corrective emotional experience." Usually this means a nonpunitive experience with the therapist, who does not attempt to control the patient's behavior. The treatment person is thus a different type of individual from the parents—one who is more flexible, less demanding, and not demeaning. Experience today with such patients shows that they respond to brief methods using behavior techniques, hypnosis, and relaxation exercises. The best results occur, however, when a dynamic theory is used as a basis for the employment of these measures with the recognition that transference and certain kinds of resistance must be interpreted in common-sense terms within the therapeutic relationship. Interpretation is applied to the patient's here-and-now concerns, in the interpersonal context of his daily life where he understands the problem to be operative.

One patient reported by Rosse (1890) was a prominent, middle-age businessman who had suffered from "obstinate insomnia" for many years. During that time he had developed a "bromide habit." He expressed hypochondriacal ideas and morbid fear. He was impotent and had a suicidal impulse. He "complained of general languor and debility; of a clawing pain within the head; of inability to concentrate his thoughts; of loss of will power; and a fear of insanity." He took enormous doses of bromides daily, but he had managed, over time, to decrease the dosage slightly. Rosse was about to give up on this patient when a colleague told him that he had treated a similar case by "prescribing a solution of chloride of sodium," the dose of which is gradually increased, "the bromide at the same time being gradually decreased until a few minims is reached, when the patient breaks off the habit on being told that he is taking nothing but common table salt." This plan succeeded until, during Rosse's summer vacation, the patient accidentally learned from the druggist what he was taking. He immediately canceled the prescription, and his symptom reappeared. On his return from vacation, Rosse "in a fit of desperation" directed the patient to eat large quantities of grapes, "the object of which was explained to him," and within a week there was a "salutary change." The patient's "psychical depression" was reduced, and the craving for the bromides was nearly gone. Soon after, the habit was broken. The patient was able to sleep; he regained his virility; and he was rid of his morbid impulses. Rosse described other disturbed individuals who recovered their stability with a type of short-term directive therapy and placebo.

Montague D. Eder

In 1914 Montague D. Eder, in England, wrote a paper with the word *borderland* in the title and *borderline* in the text. About this time Freudian ideas were being studied, and Eder recommended the use of such concepts in understanding the "dynamics" in the diagnosis and treatment of psychiatric cases. Freud's paper "On Narcissism" (1914) had appeared in which he referred to certain patients as a "third type of paraphrenia" (Freud, S.E.

14:86-87; Wolberg, A., 1968). Such a patient did not withdraw from objects completely; or if he did so, "he reestablished himself with the object again . . . after the manner of a hysteric in dementia praecox or paraphrenia proper, or an obsessional neurosis (in paranoia)." In this passage Freud recognized the type of patient who has withdrawal tendencies yet remains related to objects and who has paranoid trends and symptoms that at times resemble hysterical complaints and at other times obsessional traits.[1] Eder in his paper did not specify which dynamic concepts he thought were especially important. Freud emphasized in his group of patients the withdrawal into fantasy yet the maintainance of a relationship with objects. This led him eventually to consider "character traits" as opposed to "neurotic symptoms" (Freud, S.E., 1915, 1917). The types Freud delineated in his essays had what we would call today passive-aggressive characterological patterns. According to his descriptions, they had sadomasochistic modes of relating, but when he wrote of sadomasochism in the essay "A Child Is Being Beaten" (1919), he pointed out that this was an oedipal problem. The narcissistic neuroses were seen as preoedipal—borderline schizophrenia being one of those preoedipal disorders. The essay on narcissism was meant to describe the development of the ego in the early phase of life when difficulties began for these patients.

W.A. Jones

W. A. Jones described a passive-aggressive personality in a paper published in 1918 in *Lancet*. The writer had no knowledge of psychoanalytic concepts, but he noted certain character traits in these patients. He stressed particularly their "neurasthenic" symptoms and remarked that one must surely differentiate between those who do indeed have a physical condition and those who do not because the former could often be cured immediately by medical means; the others he felt pessimistic about, showing a most unusual kind of negative attitude toward such patients. He called those who did not have a physical condition "vampires" who are enslaving, captivating, and destroying. Thus he saw the acting-out symptom of these patients with the concomitant aggression.

---

[1]Kety has called these types of cases borderline schizophrenia, and there are estimates by him and some of his colleagues of genetic factors being involved ranging from 8 percent to 44 percent, depending upon which investigator makes the calculation (Goldstein & Jones, 1977; Kety, Rosenthal, Wender, et al, 1971).

The paper by Jones demonstrates the extreme countertransference problems that a naive therapist may have in relating to the more difficult patients. Of these "impossible ones," Jones wrote of the woman with "wiles and witcheries", of patients who are "intellectual but not necessarily intelligent (those who are "bright but act stupid"), the "sweet babylike vampire," the "selfish vampire," and the "ugly vampire" who rules with a rod of iron. Of the vampires, he said, "These people can and do cause many heart-rending situations and are able to upset, not only individuals, but communities" (the term "acting out" had not become popular at this time). "There is unfortunately very little to do for these people, as killing them is still considered a crime. . . . They look ugly, and they are ugly in mind and body, and yet there is no help for us other than complete annihilation." The reaction to the patient's aggression and hostility would render Jones useless as a therapist, I would think. Jones could see the hostility in these patients, but he did not recognize their masochistic traits.

There is no doubt that borderlines and certain other types of "passive-aggressive personality" do create disgust and dismay in people and desperateness when they have interpersonal contact with them. There is in the Jones paper, however, a lack of distinction between borderline patients and paranoid people. The latter do not have obvious delusions and hallucinations but are, in many and varied ways, acting out their destructive impulses and concealing their paranoid pathology by being purists, such as people who fight constantly against the sins of others. Jones did see, without understanding the dynamics, the sadomasochistic person with hypochondriacal symptoms who forces others to care for him and who makes others feel guilty because of all the disasters that the patient has been through, due primarily to his own self-destructive behavior. It is to be noted that the "borderland" patients whose acting-out qualities were not comprehended by these early therapists often had suicidal ideas. Those who were obviously acting out impressed these doctors as hostile, destructive, and ugly. In the current literature there is a paper by Eigen (1977) relevant to the reactions therapists may have to such patients. One might make the point that it is not only the therapist who may feel disgust for these patients; the individuals themselves often feel self-disgust, but they defend against this by trying to make others feel guilty, often projecting blame onto people outside the family who have had no real role in the development of their problems.

L. Pierce Clark

L. Pierce Clark began discussing the *borderland* case, which he also called the *borderline*, in 1919. His writings show an extraordinary astuteness in working with these patients, and he delineated tactics that we are rediscovering today. Even though his work was influenced by Freud's theory of narcissism and is tinged with many of the misconceptions of present-day psychoanalytic thinking, some of his suggestions for treatment are worth considering. It is obvious from his writings that Clark considered the borderline patient to be passive-aggressive and sadomasochistic. He spoke of the necessity of going "carefully over the conscious and foreconscious settings of the patient's difficulties, especially those which seemed to act as precipitative causes . . . not until then did I take up a strictly psychoanalytic approach." He found the dream productions of such patients "for the most part engrossed in quite adult settings," and they were "not so latently obviously sexual" as in cases of the neuroses. He considered it necessary in the interpretation of dreams to ask the patient for "memories of actual experiences . . . a more or less common-sense reformulation of their life problems" being essential. The analyst himself uses analytic insights but does not interpret these to the patient in the regular analytic way except in commonsense "dynamic terms." These ideas may not seem so revolutionary today. However, at the time, coming from a psychoanalyst, they were most unorthodox, and they are particularly relevant in treating character problems of the passive-aggressive type—the typical characterological makeup of the borderline patient. Whitehorn and Betz (1960) have documented Clark's approach to borderline patients. Shows and Carson (1965) duplicated their experiments.

The unorthodoxy of Clark's ideas can be seen when we realize that the developmental psychosexual concept in relation to the instinct theory was in vogue in his time and the "unconscious" was considered more important than the "conscious." Student analysts were being told not to let the patient talk about "reality" or what was going on in the actual life situation. The analysis centered about the "id derivatives," early Freudian ideas having given way to the topological concept, infantile sexuality, and the defenses against the instincts of sexuality and aggression. The notion of a constitutional factor and "a weak ego" in the more distressed patients was also very important in this period as was the concept of "defective development." Freud, however, did speak of "ego modification," a concept that seems more adequate than that of "ego defect" since the word *modification* connotes *a certain kind of ego organization*. But the word *ego* itself is a polygot melange since it includes almost all that the individual says, thinks, and does. Its breadth, consequently, renders it useless as a scientific tool. (If we are more parsimonious in theory, and less global, we shall do ourselves a great service.)

Clark's idea in treating his patients was that psychoanalytic knowledge is important in understanding how the patient behaves and that therapists should use this knowledge to explain the patient's here-and-now problems, anxieties, and feelings. But the interpretive language, he emphasized, should consist of everyday words and concepts; thus the type of interpretation employed in traditional psychoanalysis should be avoided. Clark thought that the therapist should not try to pierce the patient's protective armor (his defenses). He should make no demands upon the patient and have a noncritical attitude, a kind of "casual wondering why may sometimes be necessary."

Like Kohut (1971) today, Clark felt that the analytic situation with the borderline is similar to an early mother-child relationship of the preoedipal type. The goal in the beginning, said Clark, was to help the patient work through his preoedipal problem so that he could, through identification with the analyst—"the perfect mother"—attain a higher level of ego organization. The initial relationship with the analyst is on a "narcissistic level," and "primary identification" is the aim in the beginning. In this respect, Clark's orthodoxy was manifest, and he was following a psychoanalytic ego concept that many analysts still use. Actually, in analysis we must *resolve the patient's identifications with his parents and his tendency to identify with the therapist, an activity that is a denigration of his own propensities and qualities.* Freud recommended the dissolution of the identification as an aim in treatment, but at the same time, in his ego psychology, he introduced the concept of identification as a normal motif in "ego development." Most analysts then assumed that due to the patient's "defects" an identification with the analyst (the good mother as opposed to the bad parent) was the nub of the curative process.

According to Clark, the analyst, like an ideal mother, must be "a complete ally to the patient's efforts to get well. . . . An ideal mother is a noncritical mother, a staunch friend." While the analyst does not accept the patient's neurotic attitude toward reality (the patient fears reality and feels the environment is inimical), he is, nevertheless, not critical or punitive. He does not question the patient's attitudes, but he may generalize about some of the problems the patient says that he has. For example, he may question the patient about why the patient believes certain people (with tendencies similar to those of the patient) act the way they do. Both the analyst and the patient work together to investigate "the critical attitudes of the environment." (This is a projective technique.)

The analyst may have to do more of the talking in the beginning, said Clark, but the patient will understand through this that the process is a "talking treatment" covering a wide range of problems. There is no interpretation, at first, of the oedipal or preoedipal problems of the patient; rather, the concern is *people in general and the way that the environment affects people.* [2]

What Clark was suggesting can be said to be an *interpersonal or group principle*. Discuss what is happening in the patient's here-and-now situations with others—his interactions and methods of relating. Clark advocated taking into account the patient's social or group contacts as the patient's neurosis was acted out in interpersonal encounters.

Clark thus proposed that the analyst have a noncritical attitude full of enthusiastic support for "healthy attempts" as expressed in social situations so that the patient begins to feel that it is an "easy process that makes him get well."

The similarities between Clark's suggestions and the findings of Whitehorn and Betz (1960) can be seen in a report by Betz. In a series of studies focused on resident psychiatrists and their schizophrenic patients, Betz (1962) sought similarities and contrasts among the doctors with respect to styles of clinical transactions as related to personal characteristics. Comparisons were made to reveal any differential effects on patient outcome. The research indicated that some therapists consistently had high success rates with schizophrenic patients and others did not. In one study the five top-ranking doctors (designated *A* doctors) were compared with the seven low-ranking doctors (designated *B* doctors). The *A*s had an average success rate of 75 percent with their 48 patients, while the *B*s had only 27 percent with their 52 patients. A detailed analysis of the individual case records revealed differences in clinical style between the *A* and *B* doctors. The *A* group more frequently *grasped the personal meaning of the patient's behavior beyond mere clinical description*: they more frequently aimed at *modification of adjustment patterns and constructive use of assets* rather than merely symptom decrease or correction of faulty "mechanisms." They *set realistic limits in their goals in therapy*; they *avoided passive permissiveness*; their *interpretations of behavior were never given in an instructional manner*. The study was cross-validated on an independent sample of 18 residents and 109 schizophrenic patients.

The symptomatology, the Betz study revealed, became meaningful when it was recognized that the patients manifested a special orientation toward "authority as external and imposed" with feelings of suspicion and distrust (fear and hate) toward the self and others.

The findings of Whitehorn and Betz concerning *A* and *B* doctors implied a sadomasochistic problem in schizophrenia with projective defenses. One finds this also in the borderline patient. The patient, they avowed, does not act from "inner leads," but at the same time he is wary of leadership in-

---

[2]Two interesting papers have been published recently in which the authors advocate a similar technique approach—"The Role of Didactic Group Psychotherapy in Short-term Psychiatric Settings," by Andrew B. Druck (1978) and "The Rationale for the Use of Group Psychotherapy for Borderline Patients on a Short-term Unit" by H. D. Kibel (1978).

itiated by others. In studying borderline patients, however, we may say that the patient does act from "inner leads," but he projects and often denies his inner feelings ("internalizations" of his problems) that are defended against by *repression* and *denial*. He sometimes acts as if his identifications are outside himself. The defense is against thoughts and feelings that were initiated by experience with parents, and the "inner problem" is that of the *conflict over the identification with parents*, now represented in the *fantasies*, which are, in fact, *identification fantasies*. In treatment when projection is operative in the borderline patient, one should not suggest ideas in the sense that Freud (1937) proposed in his essay on reconstructions in analysis, but one should use preconscious material from the patient's productions to outline the patient's everyday problems and conflicts in *common-sense terms*. The projected material should be employed by using *the projective therapeutic technique in interpretation* (Wolberg, A., 1952, 1973), that is, using the "other" in the relationship the patient describes, since in projection the material is too highly defended by denial and repression to make direct explanations. The rationale for this kind of interpretation is that the patient's projection is actually a *projected fantasy depicting his identification*, and he has indicated that he wishes to talk about this problem, albeit denying this at the same time. The most extreme forms of the projected identification fantasy are the delusions and hallucinations seen in schizophrenia. The borderline patient has a loosely defined delusional system that is not solidified and rigidly organized as in schizophrenia, thus it is not a motivating factor in the patient's everyday existence (Wolberg, A., 1952).

The projective orientation is a formidable obstacle to the therapist who in treatment is striving for a "trusting relationship." The sadomasochistic personality is oppositional. A trusting relationship is difficult to establish, as important as it is in the therapeutic involvement.

"Insights" about "morbid pathology," Clark pointed out, are not essential in the first phase of treatment and do not help to cement a trusting relationship. This is because the patient, in the beginning, treats such interpretations as an assault. Betz said that comon-sense interpretation "brings about relaxation of the barrier between the patient and therapist." She reported that "when this barrier is lifted," the symptom of "clinical schizophrenia" seems to disappear. (This would suggest that "clinical schizophrenia" is a *defense against anxiety* and that as the anxiety lessens in the establishment of the kind of relationship where the patient feels *accepted and understood*, his fears and feelings of "danger" are reduced and he can relax his projective/delusional defense.)

Clark's proposal of a noncritical attitude and enthusiasm for "healthy attempts" is similar to Kohut's "mirroring" to give the patient self-assurance, to correct his denigrated self-image. Although this may not be solely a "mothering response," and one would not recommend that the analyst be "supportive" in the appeasing sense, encouragement for "normal" or "rational" behavior is an important element in any interpersonal process including that between patient and therapist. For one person to take note of the contributions that the other makes to positive constructive thinking and acting is one of the marks of a "normal" relationship. "Positive feedback" is another way of looking at this process. This principle has been considered in psychoanalytic literature to be an aspect of an identification process where the patient takes the analyst as an ideal and thus makes his first step toward "object constancy," that is, a separation of self from object and a primary move toward the formation of a superego. The theory today, according to many psychoanalysts, is that the borderline patient has not moved in this direction in his life with the members of his family, so he must accomplish the task in therapy.

It is true that the analytic situation evokes a new kind of intimate experience due to the differences between the analyst (therapist) and the patient's parents. The analyst's involvement with the patient's positive contribution (in effect agreeing with him and his constructive ideas), however, is different from the patient's identifying with the analyst's ideas since identification means thinking and acting like another person. (This happened with his parents.) When we agree with a patient's idea, we simply see the idea as reasonable and commendable. It is for the patient to act upon his own ideas if he is to change his behavior. The analyst in this kind of agreement does not act like the patient, and the patient does not act like the analyst; there is a consensus of opinion, a group dynamic that eventually leads to action and change in a particular group member, the patient. This group dynamic occurs in groups of two (the so-called one-to-one situation) as well as in groups of three or more. The parents gave positive signs when the child identified with their neurotic behavior. The analyst agrees when the patient expresses constructive notions.

With the borderline patient there is one reservation in the beginning phase of treatment: supporting too avidly his positive ideas may be too anxiety provoking due to the patient's fears of change and his tendency to denigrate his own constructive thoughts. A move toward a different autonomy away from his sadomasochistic life pattern is excessively guilt provoking. (The sadomasochistic life pattern is a result of his identification with the neurotic ways of his parents, as we shall discuss later.) The use of a projective therapeutic technique is helpful in relation to this problem. Thus the analyst may use himself as a projective instrument for the patient's positive wishes and potential moves. Although I have formerly described this technique (see Wolberg, A., 1952) as "positive ego construction," I see it now as a means of counteracting the patient's masochism. The analyst should try to take the responsibility for the patient's positive ideas: "I see that you might like to take some courses at the university, to enhance your interest in sociology, but you hesitate to do so. It seems like a good idea and I would advise it. But first we should try to understand your anxieties about it, I might almost say guilt, because you look guilty and fearful when you talk to me about it." Another way of thinking about the guilt problem in relation to positive moves is that the analyst, as Clark phrased it, must help the patient reduce the effects of his "punitive superego"; that is to say, in this particular way we help to correct the devaluated self-image, which is a function of the patient's masochism. Eventually we show how the patient has "internalized" (identified with) the controlling or restricting attitudes of the parents, thus creating inhibitions and a condition of being boxed in. The technique is used in relation to forward moves that the patient might have made himself, activity that he would have liked to engage in as he was growing up had it not been that such rational behavior caused anxiety for the parents and they forced him, due to their anxieties, to inhibit these "healthy attempts." As Clark saw it, we enable the patient to "identify" with the "analyst-mother" and to feel that the analyst is a friend. The "ego ideal" can then take form out of this "talking relationship." The analyst is accepted as an "object of identification." The identification with parents evoked neurotic behavior while the identification with the analyst would produce normal behavior.

The concept of the "ego ideal" was considered to be extremely important in psychoanalytic circles when Freud presented it (1914) in the paper on narcissism, in which he also mentioned "ego libido" and "object libido." This was one of Freud's first metapsychological attempts to discuss the effects of interpersonal relations in terms of "internalization." What was thought to be so important was that this was a kind of forerunner of the idea of the "super ego" (this idea had been touched upon in the early concept of the "censor"). Actually, Freud had for several years been considering group process and its effect on the ego. The problem of understanding mental functioning and mental structure and the dynamic influence of the environment upon the individual in relation to ego functions was the core of the matter. How to conceptualize "systems of the mind" as well as "functions of the ego" and "internalized interpersonal relationship" were matters that Freud had been pondering over the years. The development of an ego ideal obviously depended upon group dynamics, and it provided a connecting link between ego and superego and between the ego and the object. While the ego ideal was a manifestation of group process, Freud regarded the organization of the ego idea as the instinct seeking an object in the service of development rather than the idealization being the function of an interaction between two behaving objects.

Today we have Kohut, who believes that the "ego ideal" is the "internalization" of the "idealizing self-object," and this provides the basis for the formation of the "cohesive self." (We shall discuss the self-object later.) Idealizing is thus a necessary step in the formation of identification and the development of the ego and the superego. The way Freud talked about his own father, whom he obviously idealized, may be one clue to his insistence that idealization must precede the organization of a superego. Freud thought that idealization occurred with respect to people that the individual either loved or feared. (One can see that in idealizing fear, hate and envy are the main emotions so that it is an appeasing or masochistic kind of mechanism, actually a defense rather than a developmental phenomenon.) Kohut (1971, 1977) says that as a first step the infant "internalizes" the functions that the mother performs. This is called "transmuting internalization" and is the foundation of "ego structure."

The concept that the analyst must act as a female parent and repeat the mothering responses in a different way from the original mother so that the individual can make up the "lacunae" or "defects" in his ego and superego is open to criticism. It is a theory used by many current writers on the treatment of the borderline. The theory came from Freud, by implication, and Clark used the idea as Kohut does today. But Freud admonished, in spite of his earlier theoretical formulations, against the analyst's thinking of himself as a model or ideal when he wrote: "However much the analyst may be tempted to become a teacher, model and ideal for other people and to create men in his own image, he should not forget that it is not his task in the analytic relationship, and indeed he will be disloyal to his task if he allows himself to be led by his inclinations. *If he does, he will only be repeating a mistake of the parents who crushed their [child's] independence by their influence and he will only be replacing the patient's earlier dependence by a new one*" (Freud, S.E., 1938, present author's italics). Neurotically, this is precisely the kind of role that the patient tries to establish. The therapist, however, should not fall into this trap. A few paragraphs later in the same essay Freud says, "The therapeutic successes that occurred under the sway of the positive transference are open to suspicion of being of a suggestive nature." (I would think of the positive transference as masochistic or appeasing in nature as Freud himself had suggested earlier.)

"Wanting to be like the parent" may simply be the compulsive need to succumb to suggestion, a masochistic trait in the patient that has been conditioned in him by the parents' authoritative, punitive, and controlling attitudes, brought about by their own anxieties. This is the source of the "punitive superego," a masochistic need in the case of the borderline patient. In the beginning of treatment, however, the sadomasochistic stance is the only way the patient has of establishing a relationship that can be used to advantage. He knows only sadomasochistic modes of relating. The masochism must be interpreted to the patient at appropriate times, in every-day language; it is related not only to the need to receive sadistic treatment (i.e., to be beaten, humiliated or degraded), but it is also a function of the guilt the patient has in stepping out of his sadomasochistic role into a more constructive use of himself. The patient feels guilty when he seeks psychotherapy, and whenever he improves, he also develops guilt and anxiety. Clark certainly recognized the sadomasochistic pattern, but he had a simplistic idea concerning these dynamics.

It is much more acceptable to the borderline patient in the beginning of treatment to discuss (1) guilt when he seeks psychotherapy and (2) anxiety in relation to some of his normal impulses than to probe his denigrating attitudes and the need to be injured that are associated with the sadistic fantasies that the patient has and often acts out. It takes a long time before the patient will discuss sadism in a meaningful way.

Clark wrote that the analyst must realize initially that the "harsh superego of the narcissist" must be dealt with. The resistance is amplified by severe repressions and "dependence on parental attitudes," the patient's entire personality having been inhibited in its chance for free development. Apparently Clark saw the influence of family members as an important aspect of the patient's problem. He assumed that the patient had a superego but that he would have to develop a new ego ideal in the course of treatment and modify his existent superego. Many analysts today contend that the borderline patient has neither an ego ideal nor an identification system and, therefore, has to develop these. Others say that he has a superego but that he must discard what he has and develop a new one in his relation with the therapist. Clark said that the patient's "inability to maintain a real aggressiveness constantly allows the superego to take the drive of the destructive impulses and to use their violence in further punishing restrictions against the ego." A reduction of the effects of this "punitive superego" must be attained. (This, I believe, is simply another way of describing the patient's sadomasochistic pattern, particularly the masochism. This was imposed on the child by the parents due to their own anxieties and neurotic problems and their unconscious insistence on identification.)

Although Clark did not conceptualize the problem as I do, he, nevertheless, felt that the sadomasochistic pattern had to be taken into account early in the analysis. I believe that we must understand the dynamics of masochism as a function of the "punitive superego" and its relation to depression as a damper on aggression, realizing that the masochism and depression must be reduced first before a meaningful working through of the sadism can begin. The session with James Weber (see Chapter 11), a young psychologist, the son of a physician, illustrates the kind of sadomasochistic pattern that is established, in transference, not only with the analyst but with others as well. When James talks about his girlfriend, the teasing quality in his relationship is typical of borderline patients. This quality has been attributed to the oedipal situation, which is obvious in this session, but it is also a characteristic, I believe, that has its origin in a preoedipal phase where the controlling parent has the child in a bind. James felt "bottled up" and "in a vise." His father was a "nervous tyrant," a compulsive person who had to have his own way about everything. He was easily irritated if James, an only child, or his mother "stepped out of line"—that meant doing something that would irritate the father who was very easily upset. The mother would plead with James "to be good" because if he weren't the father would "take it out" on her. Being good meant, for example, washing the car but doing that in exactly the precise way that the father wanted and not swerving in any way from the explicit directions the father gave. The father would "go to pieces" if his instructions were not followed to the letter. These rules were to be observed not only when James was a small child of 2 years but also when he was older—all through his teens and even when he was in graduate school. In analysis James revealed fantasies of being a wealthy man who could wield power over a country. He could actually act out his hostility only by withdrawing, teasing, and pitting one person against another. In one session with me he used the example of Kleinian theory to tease because he knew that I did not support such a theory. He liked to pit one teacher against another. Originally, James had wanted to be a physician, but he had flunked out of medical schools three times, and not because he lacked a brilliant mind.

The "punitive superego" (identification with the aggressor) supports the sadism that is in part turned inward, a consequence of guilt over the hostility and revenge feelings that the patient has toward the parents, part of which he displaces toward others. The conflict is over the parents' controlling tendencies and their consequent inhibition of certain of the child's "normal" impulses, inhibitions that are "internalized" by the patient. In other words, the patient learns to perpetuate the inhibitions as a result of his identification with the parents, and this is the source of the operation of the "punitive superego" that keeps the patient in a trap. Frustration evokes aggression. Certain of the child's "normal" impulses originally created guilt and anxiety in the parents, and now, through identification, guilt and anxiety are mobilized in the child, who eventually becomes the patient. On the other hand, no inhibitions shadow those areas of behavior that were not considered dangerous or did not arouse concern or anxieties in the parents. Certain types of aggression are encouraged, for example.

The permitted aggressions of the patient are initiated by signals the parents give through their verbalization and their projective defenses, which enjoin the child to act out the parent's aggressive needs in some form or another. Szurek and Johnson (1952, 1954) and their colleagues found this kind of dynamic to be the source of the acting-out patterns of delinquents (both in sexual and nonsexual forms of delinquency). In my opinion this is the dynamic in all acting-out patterns—whether they be delinquent patterns in the judiciary sense of the word or destructive kinds of behavior in any form, self-destructive or destructive to others, sexual or nonsexual.

While "identification" and the development of an "ego ideal" do not describe all that is actually taking place in the therapy between the analyst and the patient in the first phase of treatment (other activities such as problem solving do take place), there comes a time in this early stage (which with borderline patients can last anywhere from one to three years) where the patient, as Clark said, begins to feel understood, and he enters into a more cooperative relationship with the analyst. Obviously this occurs as a result of the common-sense delineation of those aspects of the patient's problem about which he can tolerate disclosure without intense anxiety and concerning which he can take positive steps to correct. In the beginning the positive moves are minimal and goals are limited. The patient recognizes that the analyst understands his self-defeating patterns and his anxieties and that the analyst does not participate with him in his neurotic aims. The use of generalizing and the projective technique will allow the patient to select those areas of the problem that he can bear to discuss. The relationship then becomes one that the patient feels is special and into which he can enter more freely. Although the relationship is still narcissistic, according to Clark (in my opinion, sadomasochistic), the patient's participation in the analytic situation at this point involves more of "secondary narcissism." The patient has begun to "give something" into the analytic relationship. The analyst is still "maternal and protective," but he has now a leverage with which to work since the attitude of the patient is more favorably inclined. Kohut (1971, 1977) believes that in this process the analyst, acting as a mother, provides the milieu in which missing ego functions may be produced. "Gaps" are filled, and defects in the "self" are overcome. The mother "mirrors" and "praises" and "agrees." She gives the child a positive conception of self. Is it not possible that the action or behavior stimulated by the patient's positive or constructive ideas are what give him a feeling of coping and managing, and it is this that allows the patient to develop a feeling of self-confidence? The analyst merely encourages the patient to behave in the way that the patient feels might be important, since he agrees with the patient's constructive ideas.

Clark in 1919 recommended "in the talking" it is possible to elicit a more and more elaborate description of incidents. The therapist (analyst) should also inquire into some of the patient's "subjective feelings." The material should be discussed in carefully phrased questions. In my paper in 1952 I expanded upon this. In asking questions and elaborating on situations, the therapist should have as a goal the outlining of certain aspects of the defensive systems that operate between the patient and the other persons with whom the patient is interacting. This first step is to designate the defenses and how they operate in interpersonal relationships. This is a precursor to analysis of the identification pattern (the "introjects," the "not mes," the "ego states," the "false selves," the "pathological object relations"). When one works with borderline patients, a confrontation concerning the defensive patterns used in interpersonal relations is not desirable at the beginning when resistance is high. One merely outlines the behavior in detail with no comments; if necessary, one uses a projective technique to delineate the patterns. The "talking technique" is employed to define the behavior, but the therapist should speak no words that the patient can use masochistically. For example, one might proceed as I did with Maurice Belk (see Chapter 11). In my early paper (1952) I called this technique "attitude therapy." Actually, I like Don Jackson's (1957) interpretation of this type of situation: it is working with a slice of the patient's social existence as it is reflected in his relations with the therapist and with others. I believe, expanding on Clark's suggestion, that the therapist should interpret the masochism in terms of the "positive" (appeasing) transference, as it is acted out in the session with the therapist and as it exists on the interpersonal level with others. The sadistic side of the transference is referred to initially as it is reflected in relation with others. One points out first that the masochism stirs up anger or sadistic feelings toward others, in view of the self-contempt it evokes.

We can see in many of Clark's suggestions items that Eissler (1953) later considered in his paper on "parameters," or modified treatment techniques. Clark said that even though more detailed incidents are elaborated by the patient, the therapist still does not offer "regular"-type psychoanalytic interpretations and does not make particular inquiry into childhood experiences—indeed, this is avoided. (I suggested this in 1952, not having heard of Clark at the time.) Kernberg (1975) apparently does not explore genetic origins in his early technique with the borderline. It is hoped that, as Clark pointed out, the patient will himself recall childhood experiences on his own and recognize their connection to later experiences and reactions. (This is indeed the outcome of the technique of exploring defenses, situations, and attitudes in interpersonal relationships.)

Clark insisted that in taking the role of the "perfect parent" the therapist can dilute the severity of the critical superego. The therapist supports the ego. As this is done, a questioning and investigative attitude toward "parental dictates" is to be encouraged rather than a "cringing acceptance." Here Clark made a most important point. Reducing the effects of the "punitive superego" (that is, the burden of sadomasochism and particularly guilt, anger, revenge feelings, and the fear due to the "identification with the aggressor") is a most important function of the therapist, right from the start of treatment. This must be accomplished, not by confronting the patient initially with his sadism, but by attending to several facets of the patient's problem simultaneously. We gear our technique to the understanding that masochism is functionally related to sadism and guilt. Dealing with the sadomasochistic defense at any level is one of the major problems in the therapeutic program with borderlines and involves the therapist and patient almost from the first day of treatment until the last. The problem of guilt is related to self-defeating patterns (masochism); at the same time, as the therapist will point out, anger, reactions to anger, and self-contempt (also associated with guilt) are related to masochism as well. The borderline patient, unlike most neurotics, acts out his sadomasochistic identifications.

Clark believed that "working through" could not take place until the patient was able to do his part in the analysis, which could only be produced by adequate mothering. It is my contention that working through can begin with the first session, that is, if we look at the process as (1) the stating of some small aspect of the general problem; (2) the description of that aspect, (3) the discussion of a possible means of its solution, and (4) encouraging initial steps to be taken to change behavior so that this aspect of the problem can be solved. The goals in working through are modest in the beginning. They amount to no more than a simple clear statement of a tiny aspect of the patient's total sadomasochistic problem and consideration of what can be done regarding this small aspect. In the total psychoanalytic situation small gains are subgoals and are the only kinds of goals possible for many years.

From the point of view of "working through," the therapist must stress the masochistic modes of behavior with people (the acting out) and begin this process as soon as possible, realizing that masochism, as we have mentioned, is also a function of the low self-esteem, self-denigration, and failure in relationships. It masks to a great degree the sadism, which is a function of *revenge feelings*, the *jealousy of others who are more conflict free and successful*, and the *fears* associated with acting out the aggressive wishes of the parents. As one speaks with the patient about his anger and his fears of his anger, the situations that arouse his aggression and the way that it is expressed, one delineates the patient's patterns. *The actual working through of the sadism that is connected with the aggression* is extremely difficult for the patient to tolerate; therefore, this can come later after the masochistic pattern has been broken. While Kohut (1971, 1977) does not see the sadomasochistic pattern in the same theoretical frame of reference that I do (I do not use a "gap" or a "defect" theory, and I see the sadomasochism as a *defense related to the identification with parents*), nevertheless, it seems that in working as Kohut does with the "good mother mirroring technique," he is actually attending to the patient's masochistic pattern. At the same time that

he points out the denigrating qualities and equates these with some of the patient's attitudes, he also emphasizes the positive, constructive side of the patient's productions and stresses its importance.

Guilt and fear of acting out coexist with the need to act out, for in one
sense action brings a temporary relief of anxiety. The acting out, however,
creates another kind of anxiety as these patterns further the self-defeating
mechanisms. Kohut feels that working with the narcissism, i.e., reinforcing
or establishing the patient's self-esteem, reduces the aggression. This seems
in line with what Clark believed, and it appears to work out that way in
practice. My feeling is that as the therapist acknowledges the patient's constructive trends, acting out is reduced, and the need for exercising the sadism
turned against the self and others is lessened. The identification with the
sadistic or punitive side of the parental projection is partially directed
toward the self in masochism and partially directed toward others in sadism.
Denial of the identification pattern in the narcissistic neuroses is, I believe,
what Kernberg (1975, p. 23; 1976, p. 44) has called the "dissociated identification system." I find this pattern in borderlines too. Clark could see that
in lowering the effects of the "critical superego" it would then be more possible to have a "questioning and investigative attitude" toward the parents'
dictates.

Clark alleged that "the narcissist" may come upon material that may be
so painful that he will return to earlier attitudes of aloofness, withdrawal,
detachment, and distancing. This is the kind of resistance that necessitates,
according to Clark, "modification of psychoanalytic technique." When the
patient uses these withdrawing and masochistic defenses in the session, the
therapist should realize that he has given the patient a premature interpretation or has spoken of something that creates an inordinate amount of anxiety. This kind of defense has been called "regression." What is termed regression, however, is actually *defensive masochistic behavior*; it is an acting out
and a nonverbal way of saying, "Look, I am nothing; I am a child, an infant. I have done wrong—I have sinned." The defense is a self-denigration
before the idealized image, an appeasement due to fear of aggression if the
patient were to complain of the anxiety he feels as a consequence of the
premature interpretation. When the patient does complain, either he does so
in a masochistic way, trying to make the therapist feel guilty for having "attacked," or he himself uses attack in defense against the therapist. Both attack and withdrawal can be a demonstration of hostility. But these
maneuvers have their masochistic side, for they are meant to drive the
therapist away from the cooperative relationship, which, on one level, the
patient knows he needs.

When the individual, continued Clark, shows that even passively "he will
drink in ["oral libido," Freud's sexual theory] what he needs from reality,"
then one may say that there is some possibility of his tolerating a modified

technique in analysis. Clark felt that the prognosis is not at all favorable unless there can be some formation of this "secondary narcissism." The more the individual shows that he is "willing to project his libido outward in order actively to gain what he seeks in the way of love and assurances," the more possible it is that he will be capable of meeting the requirements of the second stage of analysis. He must have contacts with people and be able to relate to the analyst (therapist) and work in the analysis in a way that will "win the analyst's approval." Thus, the libido, while conditioned by narcissistic needs, is directed toward objects, and at the same time "the less these efforts have been motivated by the need for reward to the ego, the more hopeful the prognosis." One wonders, Does the patient improve or work in the therapy to please the analyst or is it because his positive moves have given him satisfaction, which is a reinforcement of his desires for further positive moves? What is meant is that in order to be in a constructive relationship, the patient will have to give up some of his withdrawal tendencies to the extent that he can work in a positive way with another person. He will also have to give up some of his masochism and acting out. To say, psychoanalytically, that the patient should renounce his "narcissism" (withdrawal tendencies), "giving love for the sake of giving," and mean that the patient, in doing this, would not expect rewards from the relationship is being unrealistic. It is true that in a "normal" situation one must take the other person into account, but there is no relationship where the person does not expect some pleasure or reward from the other. The patient must give up withdrawal tendencies to the extent that he can cooperate in a problem-solving endeavor, and he must venture a give-and-take attitude with the analyst, asking for help when he needs it, realizing that the analytic situation is for his benefit. Still another way of looking at this matter is to say that the analyst must have techniques suitable to deal with the kind of anxiety that the borderline patient manifests in interpersonal relationships, so that the analysis can proceed in a manner to resolve the patient's anxiety problems, and his defenses. (Letting the patient determine the area of problem solving is an important step in developing a therapeutic relationship.)

Clark implied that the more the patient can cooperate with the analyst in the treatment or "narcissistically use" the analyst in a way to promote his development, the more likely he is to succeed in working through his problem. It is only when the patient can say, "I see that I am doing this" or, referring to the other, "I see what we are doing" that the analysis begins to move from the projective to the direct method of handling the transference. It may be a long time before the patient will make such admission, for it does not come easily. Prior steps involving exploration of relationship between the patient and other persons reveal their attitudes toward each other, i.e., what their verbal and nonverbal behavior indicates through their attitudes and feelings. It reveals the acting-out patterns, a defense related to identification. The exploration of relationships is an uncovering technique that is implemented prior to the analysis of sadomasochistic patterns. In my opinion, the analyst is able to reveal the defensive patterns in the very beginning of therapy by asking what happened between the patient and another person, and he seeks answers to questions about the feelings and attitudes of the two people—with no other comment (see Wolberg, A., 1973, pp. 195-206). First we reveal that patterns do exist in the patient's interactions so that later the patient can say, "I am doing this" and "He is doing that." Still later he can say, "I see what we are doing." Even in the initial interview, one must explore areas that the patient is willing to discuss, areas where he has partial insight that will lead to further exploration of the problem and delineation of the defensive patterns as they operate in interpersonal relationships. Letting the patient lead in this process is an important principle.

According to Clark, the analytic probability is increased as the patient is able to give "object-love toward the analyst," for then the transference can eventually be worked through. (Here Clark is more hopeful concerning the outcome and the possible eventuality of successful analysis with the borderline patient than Kohut, for example.) If the patient begins to show some ability to face issues, to fight them and not the analysis, and to work through real experiences, then, Clark contended, there is hope for eventual insight. Too docile and cringing an ego is a handicap. The more the compensatory substitutes (the fantasies? the symptoms? or both?), the less one can face issues. The stronger the ego in these matters, the better. Clark recognized the failings of a masochistic attitude and how it interferes in any cooperative relationship. A sadistic attitude is similarly an impediment. In either case, one must in some way undermine the masochism before the "ego can gain strength." Grandiosity and self-centered attitudes were considered by Clark as narcissistic impediments to a relationship. The individual arrived at this sadomasochistic mode as a result of long-standing and persistent training on the part of the parents and other important figures.[3] It is not

---

[3]I believe that we shall have to recognize that neuroses and psychoses are not made in the first and second years of life as some therapists currently suppose; rather they develop gradually over a number of years. In the therapeutic session, even as the patient defends, he describes his problem and indicates his "compensatory substitutes," as one can see by the patient's statements in my initial interview in *The Borderline Patient* (1973, pp. 195-206), where the patient James tells me that he is rigid and has obsessive-compulsive mechanisms and tends toward hysterical (or psychotic) reactions and that his resistances are strong even when he is asking for help. He has great anxiety and fear about uncovering how he feels toward his parents; consequently, it will be a long time before he will be able to work through those feelings. This is indicated by his worry about what the *school* may have done to him. He is highly defensive using the school as a projective defense. This is not to say that the school was perfect and may not have done him some harm. He also describes his sadomasochistic patterns with his girlfriend. His fantasies interfere with his work and with his relations with people.

clear in Clark's paper whether he is using the term "compensatory substitutes" in the same sense that Kohut speaks of "compensatory structures" (Ornstein, 1978, p. 99), but this seems likely. The road into grandiosity, for example, is not seen by Clark as a sadistic defense but as a regression and a substitute for love and respect in the developmental sense.

As the objective trend ("the observing ego") develops more and more consistently and strongly, said Clark, the projections toward the analyst can be more precisely and fully understood. In describing the dynamics of the borderline patient, Clark presented a number of criteria. He alleged that the patient had not received enough "narcissistic gratification" and that a barrier had arisen between him and objects, so that interpersonal participation was difficult. Eventuating symptoms then represent forms of "substitute-gratification of narcissistic libido" (an idea that seems to be similar to Kohut's "compensatory structures"). In the psychoanalytic language of today there are attempts to redefine what is meant by "fantasy," "symptoms," and "defenses." Many investigators attempt to differentiate between these; in my mind they are all connected. Kohut distinguishes between "compensatory structures" and defenses. (I believe he means compensatory due to defects in the ego or more precisely the "self," which has a separate line of development from that of sexuality.) Masterson (1976, pp. 38-39, 55-56, 77-80, 100-112) speaks of a "structural defect," which is similar to what Kernberg (1975, p. 22) means when he speaks of "nonspecific ego weakness." Kernberg lists "ego defects" in the borderline patient as follows: inability to perceive reality, inability to differentiate object from self, inability to integrate good and bad in a single person, inability to repress aggression. Masterson would add to Kernberg's list the intensification of feelings of abandonment and acting out the wish for reunion. One might also add that Kernberg says that the borderline has an inability to identify with others; thus he has no true identification system, no ego ideal, and no object constancy, no observing ego.

Emotional energy in the patients we classify as borderline is not directed into the usual life activities but has been "impounded within the ego," said Clark. Excessive tension was created, the neurosis then being necessary for its release. Moreover, the neurosis was a flight or a "regression" from "higher levels of development" to "a more infantile plane" where impulses might be gratified in disguised forms by means of symptom formation. The disguised forms are in Kohut's terms "compensatory structures," which are a manifestation of the ego line of development. Thus compensatory structures mean "a system of ideals and of correlated executive ego functions" as opposed to defenses (Kohut, 1971). An example of one would be obesity: metapsychologically speaking, a "pleasure-seeking oral stimulation" of the erogenous zone; clinically speaking, a "depressive eating," to be seen as a reaction to the unempathic self object, an "interpersonal consequence" rather than a "drive" or a "compulsion to eat." (We can agree that symptoms are due to interpersonal relations.) The "unresponded to self" has not been able to transform its "archaic grandiosity" and its "archaic wish to 'merge' with an omnipotent 'self-object' into reliable self-esteem, realistic ambition and attainable ideals. The abnormalities of the drives and of the ego are the symptomatic consequences of this central defect in the self" (Kohut 1971, pp. 81-83). Kohut (1971, p. 85) also assumes a concept of a "group-self." The symptom is a reactivation of an incompleted developmental task (the Zeigarnik effect). The idealized self-object (Freud, S.E., 1921; Kohut 1971) would be a completion, according to Kohut, of that particular task. It was Breuer who advanced the idea that in treatment we give the patient the opportunity to talk about the experiences that he did not complete adequately (Wolberg, A., 1973, p. 22). In treatment he said that the individual has a second chance to deal with a traumatic memory by "recalling with affect" or by effecting an abreaction. I suggested (1973, p. 4) that these "incompleted tasks" are probably what enables a patient to engage in therapy. Kohut (1971) suggests that it is an incomplete developmental task that provides the impetus for the patient's need to be relieved of his symptoms. The symptom, Kohut asserts, is a reintensification of an attempt to "fill in" a specific "structural defect." Sexualization of the transference, encountered in the early phases of some analyses, is another example of a compensatory structure.

In my experience, these "compensatory structures" have a definite relation to *identifications with the parents* or parental figures. The few cases of obesity I have worked with were definitely a consequence of such identifications. One of my patients, Frances Krasmire, had a running dialogue with her mother and father about eating and what to eat. Her mother was chronically on a diet; as soon as she went off the diet, she gained back all the weight she had lost. She was involved with Frances over a period of many years (until Frances was an adult) in inculcating a similar diet pattern, which Frances adopted in her early years. Frances was the "bad one" in the family while another sister was the "good one." (This pattern of "bad" and "good" seemed to be typical of families where borderline and schizophrenic patients exist.) Both the father and the mother were obsessively interested in Frances. Geraldine Girard, another patient, also had a weight problem. She identified with her mother who was "fat" and was in and out of sanitaria, for both health and weight reasons, all of Geraldine's young life. Geraldine was the only child of her father's second "late" marriage. She always thought of her father as a grandfather. The mother was beautiful but "sickly," much younger than the father. As she grew older, the mother became overweight. Mother was completely preoccupied with herself. A half sister, a child from a former marriage of the father, was both "mother" and "father" to Geraldine, her own parents having partially abdicated those roles. Geraldine often thought of her mother when she was overeating. Geraldine ate to relieve depression, which was usually associated with anger, sexual sensations (maturbatory equivalents), and a feeling of having been demeaned.

The patients I have seen who sexualized the therapeutic sessions when talking of their compulsive behavior were patients who had definite sexual encounters with their parents or parental substitute over periods of time. Some were symbolic, but most had certain physical contacts, not always direct intercourse, but stimulating and teasing physical events. Identification with the seductive object was one basic dynamic in those cases. It is true that many patients have sexual feelings when working through the transferences. They transfer to the therapist erotic images that they had with their parents but images that they repressed. In transference the patient is working through identifications with parental figures. Those patients who tend to sexualize *most sessions*, I have found, are homosexuals or are individuals who are about to break through to a homosexual or schizophrenic adjustment. Borderline patients do not have this persistent kind of sexualizing in sessions, although like the homosexuals and other schizophrenics they have sexual and aggressive thoughts in relation to transference feelings.

Whether "compensatory structures" or "compensatory substitutes" are similar phenomena seems to be answered in the affirmative when illustrations are given, for these appear to mean symptoms, defenses, and fantasies. The meanings attached to symptoms and fantasies can be quite different, however, depending upon the general theory of borderline that is being used. One of the problems in defining these terms is founded in the nature-nurture controversy and in the individual-group concept. One is asked which of these opposites is more important in the development of neuroses and psychoses? The answer, of course, lies in the fact that they are intertwined, one does not exist without the other. The symptom is not without its mental and neurophysiological components. We are talking, of course, of neurotic symptoms. If we take for an example a derealization episode, we find that in the dream structure that is intrapsychic and "structural" (i.e., containing elements of id, ego, and superego) the memory of the incident might show up in the form of "people who are mere shadows" or the patient might say, "I was there but not part of it," a defense of denial. We see in the manifest content that the mental event has a relation to an interpersonal or group experience. The mental event includes the defense. The dream represents a need of the patient to blot out the memory of a situation that occurred in the past, a memory that is being revived by some situation in the present. In order to repress the memory in the face of the current stimulus, the patient resorts to a derealization maneuver in the dream. If we pursue this symptom (defense), we shall find that the defense is against the memory of a sadomasochistic event, or more likely a series of sadomasochistic events, and will have a relation to the ego ideal in that there has been an idealization of the parents, since it was they who originally evoked a sadomasochistic milieu. Rickman (1926) felt that the superego was a way of *maintaining object relations*, presumably with the parents. This is a little different idea from that of Freud, who felt the superego was a way of controlling bad instincts by way of identification, a precoursor of which was the ego ideal. (My concept is that the id should refer to the autonomous behavior.)

Freud (1921) associated symptoms with identification and the oedipal problem and considered the stimulus for identification to be derived from an "inner urge" (derivation of the id?) on the part of the child to oust the parent of the same sex and take the role of that person with the parent of the opposite sex. (There were occasions, of course, when the child took the parent of the same sex as object.) The symptom, Freud thought, was a punishment, a kind of atonement for the oedipal wish. Often the symptom is a punishment, and in my terms it is associated with the hostility and revenge feelings that the child develops over time when he is controlled and forced into the identification with the parents.

Identification, in the neurotic sense, then, would mean that the stimulus comes from the parent who is using the child as a projective object and in defense presses upon the child an identification role. The frustration and inhibitions that are created as the child gradually conforms to the parent's pressure for the identification evokes the tension and anger and finally the aggression and revenge feelings that are syphoned off in the acting out of the identification role. The paranoid trend is the poignant need of the individual to deny (1) the implications of his bondage in the sadomasochistic position, which eventuates out of the adoption of the identification role, and (2) the aggression that has been evoked in his interpersonal encounters with his parents, which one might call a derivative of the id.

One might also consider the aggression to have an ego factor in that it is a reaction to an actual situation of which the individual has conscious feelings. It is correct to speak of "identification roles," for both father and mother project roles as functions of their defensive patterns. They have a neurotic need for the child to act out the roles. As a matter of fact, the father and mother come together on the basis of their neurotic needs, which I stressed in my 1960 paper when speaking of the "the parents' interlocking neuroses" and which I now specify as an *interlocking defensive system*. The identifications of the child would then be based on what Rickman (1926) called the need to maintain object relations through the ego ideal or superego, which really is a masochistic defense in the face of the parents' pressures for the child to accept the acting-out roles (Wolberg, A., 1973, p. 49). Identifications are the basis for the patient's acting-out patterns. In our example of derealization one can find both oedipal and preoedipal characteristics if we look for them in the associations to fantasies. The symptom when represented in the dream can be of a person who is considered to be cold, and unapproachable—a father. For example, one of my patients, Daird, would have a *fear* instead of *representing a memory* in his dream; at other times he would deny that a particular session was of any importance (Wolberg, A., 1973, p. 182), this being a kind of depersonalization and derealization at the same time, of both himself and the analyst and of our relationship. One must obtain associations to discover the context of the derealization. At the same time one must obtain associations to discover the context of the interpersonal situations that the symptom connotes, but one can assume that the individuals in the interpersonal or group interactions that are blotted out contain the essence of the sadomasochistic memory and that the people in the dream have in some way reflected the patient in his identification role and the parent in his evocative stance. When the patient discusses the setting of the dream, it is obvious that his identification with his father is the important conflict in that particular session. When a symptom is represented in the dream, one is tempted to think of character problems, but when an interpersonal situation is represented, one tends to think of oedipal problems. As a matter of fact, it can be one or the other or both that is the preoccupation of the patient at the time.

The aim of treatment, according to Clark, must be (1) to remove the barriers which made it impossible for the patient's release of energy to convert to rational performance; (2) to encourage the socialized use of the tendencies already present (the developmental tendencies); and (3) to reinvoke developmental trends so that the cruder impulses can be modified and be more acceptably discharged in reality. To estimate the prognosis, we must decide, said Clark, which factors point to the greater probability of the aims being realized. The *barriers* that blocked acceptable emotional discharge were to be found (1) in the outer world, (2) in the individual ego and superego, and (3) in the nature of the impulses themselves. At first psychoanalysis could have little effect except to favor passively the environment in which the patient functioned most happily. *Within the individual himself we should attempt to strengthen the ego by reducing or softening its harsh superego (the hostility and its "categorical restraints").* It thus would become a more kindly guide for conduct. A weak ego required a powerful and despotic superego. The ego must be strong in order to maintain a friendly superego. Alexander and French (1946) stressed the importance of *reducing the hostility and categorical restraints of the "harsh superego."* This can be done best by outlining the dynamics of the *masochism* and eventually showing that the "harsh superego" is in fact an internalization, that is, an identification with the parents' hostile and denigrative attitudes. When the patient threatened the parents' defenses by certain types of normal impulses and behavior, he was made to feel guilty.

Clark did imply that the parents had some responsibility for the borderline patient's dilemma even though he used the theory of narcissism and the preoedipal concept as his underlying theory of borderline personality. Apparently he felt that identification and the formation of an ego ideal had to take place in the therapeutic situation so that the patient could go on with his development.

In treatment we encourage the individual to seek contacts with the outer world, Clark said, but we must realize that when we say "direct contacts" with the outer world we mean also the quality of these contacts. The decisive question must be not only how much the ego directed the instinctual energies into contacts with the outer world but also what kinds of contacts the ego maintained. Contact with the outer world is not necessarily synonymous with objectivity and the meaning and solving of realistic problems. When the ego can meet obstacles by redirecting itself rather than regressing into withdrawal, timidity, masochism, or narcissistic absorption, then we may say that the ego is strong rather than weak, and we may estimate progress by whether the ego is capable of doing the former. (I have found that it takes years for some borderline patients to move away from neurotic companions, but they often progress during that time in other ways.)

Stressing the need to keep in mind the characteristics of an exteriorizing "object-libido," Clark pointed out that the giving of interest and effort to the object without the expectation of return creates a satisfaction in the doing, quite apart from autoerotic pleasure or the narcissism of accomplishment. It is something by which only the object gains in any substantial way. The object is distinctly separate from the subject, something outside himself toward which he must go. In my opinion, "satisfaction in the doing" without any expectation of return simply does not exist. Indeed, why should it exist? Clark realized that complete altruism was scarcely possible since "clearly no one ever attains complete objectivity in any particular activity or relationship. What we are estimating is a component, a partial quality, not an absolute or independent factor." Clark adds: "Whenever there is a sadomasochistic reaction to the failure to gain a return it clearly indicates the narcissistic element in the projection. The degree of sadomasochism would be a measure of the need for return, and hence an indication of the low level of objectivity."

When Clark wrote of sadomasochism as regression, presumably it was because the "sadomasochistic instincts," according to psychoanalytic theory, are supposed to put in an appearance at the age of 18 months to $2\frac{1}{2}$ years, in the anal period. The "ego" is then required to tame these instincts.

When this does not happen, it is due to "ego defects" as a result of poor mothering, or to heredity, or to some of each. Mahler, Pine, and Bergman (1975, p. 211) and Kernberg (1966, pp. 250-252; 1975, pp. 25-30) say that splitting is the first defense due to projective identification, and normally the defense of "splitting" drops out at the end of the second year when the infantile hostility toward the parent is submerged by repression, leaving only a minimal degree of ambivalence.

In reporting Clark's ideas, I do not wish to overstress the use of the term "narcissism," primary or secondary, as applied to the developmental process, for I believe these concepts to be largely speculative. Modern infant research clearly refutes postulations such as that of narcissism (Wolberg, A., 1977). For example, the defense of withdrawal in a child should not be considered a disorganizing, infantile "narcissistic" trait since under certain circumstances it is a very adaptive method of coping. In the analytic or therapeutic situation such withdrawal would then be a transference reaction. It is difficult to embrace the idea of "infantile fantasies" and "regression" if we mean by regression in the borderline that the adult goes back to ideas, thoughts, and feelings he had as an infant from 4 to 16 months of age in the "narcissistic" stage where he was "fixated." Usually what is meant by "regression" is a withdrawal into fantasy, at least when a given author describes what he means. If one believes that the original mental state of the infant is a fantasy semipsychotic (id) state, then regression means going back to that state; but the presumption of such a state is an esoteric idea. Fantasy is, in fact, a sophisticated way of dealing with anxiety rather than a primitive mental form. It is an advanced form of symbolization. Searles (1963) speaks of "transference psychosis" but apparently does not suppose it to be a reflection of "regression to an autoerotic level of development."

We know that children do have fantasies when they imagine that something "bad" outside the family is menacing their existence. The hope is that the family is "good." We can say from experience with children that a protective fantasy, a projection, begins after the age of 2½ or 3, whenever a child begins to experience fear associated with shadows on the wall representing animals or creatures that are "dangerous." It is the fear of parents that makes the child project the object or, in more precise terms, use denial and projection, idealizing the real family members.

A most valuable part of Clark's treatment seems to have been the emphasis on the patient's constructive capabilities along with analysis of some of his neurotic behavior patterns.

The psychiatrists before Clark and Eder had no knowledge of dynamic concepts; yet they treated patients both on long-term and short-term bases with good results for the most part. We would think that the main vehicle for their success would be the kind of empathic relationship they established with their patients since the measures they used in their symptomatic approach were of no great significance. These early psychotherapists, however, noted a great deal about the behavior of their patients. Eder (1914), Clark (1919), and Stern (1937) seem to be the earliest observers in the psychoanalytic field aside from Freud (1919) regarding the borderline patient. Stern emphasized the importance of the mother in the child's emotional quandary.

CHAPTER 2

Early Psychoanalytic Concepts Concerning Borderline Conditions

Between 1937 and 1954 , beginning with Adolph Stern, very few papers were written on the borderline patient (about 25 were published including my own first paper in 1952). One of the major findings relating to the borderline during the late 1930s came from the psychologists who worked in the testing field, particularly Rorschach and others who employed projective testing. They discovered that on structured material the borderline did very well, but with the unstructured material the patient showed anxiety and pathological responses.

Adolph Stern

Stern read a paper before the New York Psychoanalytic Society in the spring of 1937 expressing ideas that were published in 1938 in a treatise entitled "Psychoanalytic Investigation of a Therapy in the Borderline Neuroses." The paper contained descriptions of many essential features of the borderline group of patients as well as interesting information concerning their families. Stern stated that regular psychoanalytic procedures were not effective with "neurotic characters" who made up a large number of borderline patients. While he had "handled thoroughly enough the object libidinal phenomena" when treating these patients, they, "nevertheless, remained sick." He listed a number of symptoms typical of borderlines (though not all specifically confined to borderlines):

1. A narcissistic neurosis
2. Psychic bleeding
3. Inordinate hypersensitivity
4. Psychic and body rigidity
5. Rigid personality
6. Negative therapeutic reactions
7. Seemingly rooted feelings of inferiority
8. Somatic insecurity or anxiety
9. The use of projective mechanisms
10. Difficulties in reality testing, particularly in personal relationships

We shall consider each of the symptoms, then examine Stern's thoughts on the effect of the home environment on the borderline, and conclude our examination of Stern with a discussion of his approach to the treatment of the borderline.

Narcissism In the history of borderline patients Stern found that adverse factors were present in early childhood affecting narcissistic development. In at least 75 percent of the group Stern treated, the mothers were neurotic and some had had psychotic episodes. Practically all of these mothers were deficient in demonstrating affection, many being over-solicitous and overconscientious. Some were meticulous about food habits and behavior but lacked a wholesome capacity for spontaneous affection. In the families there were many quarrels and bursts of temper between the parents, also anger directed at children. (I would judge this to be anger, displaced from both marital partners based on their identifications with their own parents—the projective identification defense.) Some parents had been divorced before the patient was 7 years of age; thus a "separation experience" for the child took place. All of the children in Stern's group had remained with the mother, "not one of whom was an adequate mother from the point of view of affection." Actual cruelty, neglect, and brutality by the parents over a period of many years were common factors. (Today we call such children abused or battered children.) In reality, neglect can more precisely be defined as rejection. Consequently, these patients suffered "affect hunger" (Levy, 1932) or what Stern called "narcissistic malnutrition." Defects in narcissistic development seemed to be the cause of the symptoms and personality problems in this group of neurotic patients. The self-esteem was low. Prevalent were (1) insecurity, (2) lack of adequate affective relationships, and (3) disturbances between father and mother. The research of Grinker seems to bear out the validity of these three factors in the lives of borderline patients (Wolberg, A., 1973, pp. 149-150).

Psychic Bleeding Instead of a resilient reaction to a painful or traumatic experience, the patient, as described by Stern, "went down in a heap," appeared to be immobile, in a deathlike collapse instead of a rebound. In other words, the reaction was a sort of "playing possum" (a phrase used also by Laing [1970]), showing paralysis rather than fight or flight. This is obviously a flight reaction in the form of a masochistic maneuver with hysterical features. It is also a hostile controlling maneuver in the adult to make others feel guilty and do for the patient what he should do for himself. On another level it is a defense to protect the "object" from the patient's aggression.

VANDERBILT MEDICAL CENTER LIBRARY

Inordinate Hypersensitivity Excessive hypersensitivity seemed to serve as an exquisite receptive apparatus or instrument *to detect danger.* The patients were constantly being insulted by trifling remarks and occasionally developed mildly paranoid ideas. [Can it be that their parents displayed paranoid traits not only in relation to their controlling, monitoring tendencies, but also in their denial of their deceitfulness, which is a part of their defensive systems (a source of the "double bind?"). The parents "remake reality," which is a defense—in simple language, they lie as an aspect of defense. The patient, as a consequence, is characteristically on guard with others expecting a similar kind of behavior as evidenced by my session with George Frank Quinn (see Chapter 7).]

Psychic Rigidity Stern connected psychic rigidity with insecurity. It was "almost of a reflex nature" like the rigid abdomen or, in the extreme, like the catatonic with his shifting, watching, alert eyes and the rigid posture of his body. Such rigidity begins in the early years, before age 4 or 5. This kind of "alertness" is perhaps the same trait that Rosenfeld (1965) talks of in his concept of the superego quality that is "omnipotent," "omniscient," and "omnipresent." It is an indication that the parents, over the years, were excessively controlling, watching every movement of the child, monitoring, so that he would not step out of the identification mold they proclaimed for him. This "superego quality" in the patient is learned from the parents' rigid, punitive, and cruel restraining watchfulness. The phenomenon is depicted in the man and woman drawings of my patients Harold Hemple and Harriet Hamburger (see pp. 238-249). At the time that Harold sought therapy he was 32 years of age, single, and employed in a very good job with an adequate salary. He had a kind of paranoid feeling, i.e., a distrust of the motives of others. This originated in his experience with parents who also had this attitude and who denied or lied about what they were doing to the patient. In projection, this wariness was a transference manifestation toward others.

In the case of borderlines, and schizophrenics as well, the patients have been deprived of adequate peer relationships by the neurotic and/or psychotic parents *who have bound them in a family interlocking defensive relationship.* Fear of others together with a lack of experience in getting along with people and of feeling accepted makes the relationship with peers a stressful experience. This becomes a source of intense anxiety at school or at work. It is also a factor in the sexual realm and in treatment. (Harold had dreams and fantasies of cringing before others. He would not allow himself to become aware of his grandiose feelings and his "wariness" until the fourth year of his seven-year analysis.)

The "watching" and "wariness" can also be related to the sexual problem that develops because the parents have not accepted their own sex roles —thus they experience anxiety when their children act sexually and normally toward either parents or peers. In addition, the parents themselves use their children in secretive ways to satisfy their own sex needs through perverse modes. These controlling, punitive, and abusive parents frequently express their perverse trends by staring at parts of the child's body, developing in the child obsessive patterns concerning certain organs (Wolberg, A., 1973, p. 42).

The road to good relationships with peers is blocked by these many problems, and there is the constant guarded alertness to see what the other will do. This excessive attentiveness began in the family, the child trying to decide what the parent wanted or would do next. "Watching" is also based on a fear of what will happen. In the session it is as if the patient is always wondering, "Will the other pierce my defensive armor?" The patient realizes his inadequacies in his relationships with others and is often rejected for them. He sometimes is ridiculed by other children for his rigidities, his fears and his need to control, his sensitivity, and his apparent frailty.

Emotional closeness is a threat to the borderline patient's parents, so that the individual learns to use hostility and withdrawal to give himself distance in his relationships with his parents, and thus with others. In spite of all that has gone on, however, I do not find that the borderline patient stays away from the opposite sex. Rather he relates to the opposite sex in a sadomasochistic way.

Negative Therapeutic Reaction Readily aroused anger, discouragement, and anxiousness, said Stern, are responses by the patient to any interpretation deemed injurious to self-esteem. Interpretive activities are seen by the patient as evidence of lack of love or appreciation on the part of the analyst. One reason that I suggest *generalization* in discussing problems and the use of the *projective therapeutic interpretation* in the beginning of treatment (in fact at any time where denial and other defenses are in use) is that at these points direct interpretation will fall on deaf ears, and the therapist will stir up defensive maneuvers in the patient. A negative therapeutic reaction (NTR) often means that a premature interpretation has been made and the patient will "get even" by trying to make the therapist feel guilty. This is an aspect of the complicated defense of projective identification and the sadomasochism that is inherent in the defense, which includes revenge attitudes. The masochistic aspect of denying the reality of the confrontation is a way of putting off the therapist. It is as if the patient is saying, "Look you have injured me! I cannot tolerate this closeness!" It does no good to point out this defense directly at first, since this only increases the patient's paranoid mechanisms and projective maneuvers to make the therapist feel cruel and guilty and thus to desist.

Stern's "psychic bleeding" is a masochistic trait of this same nature. It appears often in the treatment situation and must be interpreted at first projectively, using "others" to point out the maneuver. When direct interpretation is made the first time, it should be approached in general as follows: "When I talked of the possibility of the meaning of your behavior, this stirred up anxiety in you and your reaction was to feel hurt." The strategy to make the therapist feel guilty—a devise often used with the patient by his parents—must be discussed at a later time. Interpretations must be done step by step or piece by piece, so to speak, eventually fitting all the parts together and always referring to the patient's anxiety as the stimulus for his defensive behavior. This piecemeal technique is used in the face of denial, taking into consideration what the patient is willing to tolerate at any given point in time. We judge this by listening to his productions, asking for his dreams, and focusing on the area of least anxiety. The negative therapeutic reaction can be a pervasive masochistic reaction with great fears on the part of the patient that his defensive armor will be destroyed, and a "flare-up" of the kind where symptoms appear usually means that the patient cannot tolerate the anxiety. The patient also can have the opposite kind of reaction, using a counterphobic attack against the therapist employing verbal abuse or teasing.

There have been many suggestions in the literature as to what causes the negative therapeutic reaction (NTR), and each may be correct in any given case. Already noted have been the general masochistic stance in all cases and the feelings of guilt. Revenge feelings (sadism) account for some of these reactions: "I will never let you help me even if I frustrate you forever." This is the help seeker who refuses to let you help. His reaction, of course, is masochistic at the same time that it is sadistic. Envy has also been suggested as a motif for revenge. In my opinion it is the sadism of the parents that creates the envy and the revenge feelings; then in denial these are projected or displaced. One finds that the negative therapeutic reaction, in the early stages of treatment, is usually related to the passive-aggressive character pattern of the patient—the need to feel no pleasure from attainment, even in treatment. This negative or antagonistic feeling is related to "oppositionalism," and to the patient's perverse feelings. It creates a kind of sexualizing at times in the therapeutic relationship, a type of masochism, a function of an excited or somewhat elated mood, a defense or counteraction to the depression. The borderline patient has mood swings (not, of course, such severe swings as manifested by the manic depressive) related to what I have described as a twelve-step cycle (Wolberg, A., 1952, pp. 696-699). In treatment a depiction of these various facets of the sadomasochistic cycle should take place before the mention of envy, jealousy, and sadistic feelings. Such delineation helps to reduce the negative therapeutic reactions. The envy often is a function of the passivity that the patient feels and his poignant wish to be more assertive as he sees others being assertive (see Wolberg, A., 1973, the session with George Frank Quinn—named George Adler in my first book—pp. 216-219, and the session with Elizabeth, pp. 246-251).

Freud (1913) referred to the patient's inability to enjoy his attainments (or to deny that they exist) as a pre-obsessional factor and he connected this with sadism (Wolberg, A., 1973, p. 95, note 15). There is often a negative therapeutic reaction when the patient denies pleasures in attainment. I believe that this is a characteristic also of perverse sexual feelings which are an aspect of the revenge motif. My patient Elizabeth had this problem (Wolberg, A., 1973, p. 244). She would often say she could not *feel* during the sex act, but mostly she would begin to feel and then lose the feeling (turn off); finally she would burst into tears. On one occasion I was able to elicit from her a fantasy she remembered while having intercourse, of her father taunting her.

Feelings of Inferiority Stern described feelings of inferiority as pervasive feelings. Even when borderline patients are highly successful, they insist they are inferior, almost in a delusional sense. Such feelings of inferiority are used to overcome anxiety whenever action or thinking is required that might demand what could be called "adequate functioning." In the therapeutic session the feelings of inferiority serve the patient against being active, and thus he hopes to bring out the parental role in the therapist. (This is one way that transference is expressed in the beginning of treatment.)

"These mechanisms, even when analyzed, are so tenacious that they have little effect on the patient who continues to remain sick." It is my impression that in such a case the "feelings of inferiority" have not been considered as acts of masochism and appeasement, covering anger, rage, contempt, sadism and the fear of ridicule. If these feelings are recognized as masochistic defensive maneuvers, then one has a different attitude toward this behavior than if one thinks of the behavior as "ego weakness," "lacunae," or "defects." When the patient is saying "I am inferior" or he is acting inadequate, he is really telling the therapist that the therapist by contrast is perfect and that he, the patient, is nothing.

The expression of inferiority, verbally or nonverbally, has been mistaken as the patient's inability to perceive the situation as it really is; actually, it is the acting out of a transference maneuver, or what I call the *pantomimic transference* (PT), a sadomasochistic act. The patient is dimly aware of his behavior, but he represses the idea that he is acting toward the therapist as he had to act with his parent or as the parent acted with him.

For such patients interpretation must be made over and over again since inferiority feelings are deeply ingrained. The therapist must use a special type of interpretation, if an adequate point is to be made with the patient. The therapist needs to point out that the patient's self-denigration is the acting out of a masochistic role for purposes of appeasement. While the patient is aware of *what* he is doing, he blocks the reason *why* he assumes this role. The *why* is left for the future, and we, as the therapists, ask the patient to observe the pattern in his everyday life, suggesting that he take note of the situations that precede his acting out this role, much as we might ask a patient who has a headache to give attention to the kind of situations that precede the onset of symptoms. Some patients will not win at a game, even though they could at times do so. Some patients will act inept, for example, at particular tasks they may have to do, such as anything mechanical, anything creative, anything mathematical (see the description of the behavior of Gertrude Belan in Wolberg, A., 1973, pp. 78-79).

Masochism It is usually very clear, said Stern, how masochism fits in the borderline personality as a defensive or protective phenomenon. Masochism is present and obvious. Self-pity, self-commiseration, and the presentation of being a long-suffering, helpless, and injured one (a kind of wound-licking) are regularly seen. There is no doubt that these patients have suffered much, and among their symptoms we see mild depressions. They hurt themselves in all effective relationships—business, professional, social and others. But, said Stern, it seems futile to say that masochism in the borderline is entirely defensive or protective.

It is necessary to have a clear concept of the myriad forms of sadomasochism as defensive behavior if we are to treat borderline patients successfully. Many of Stern's stated characteristics of borderline can be seen as sadomasochistic. Self-defeat is a form of sadomasochism, for it is related to revenge behavior, anger, oppositionalism, and the NTR which can come from guilt that has not been sufficiently explored in the sessions. Masochism continues as a factor in the therapy with the borderline patient almost throughout the therapeutic process—masochism associated with anger, revenge feelings, fear, and guilt as illustrated in the session with George Frank Quinn (see Chapter 7). Anger turned on the self is often projected in a subterfuge as if the other had done the projecting. This is typical of the defense of projective identification except that we must realize that the anger is not a "primary instinctual anger" that occurs without provocation as Melanie Klein proposed: it is a *reactive anger* that began in relations with parents and accrued as time went on, eventually becoming associated with revenge fantasies and techniques. When aroused, the patient's projection and the displacement to a third person is a transference reaction, a way of handling intense anger at the "other," and reflects the strong impulse to demean the "other" as a representation of the original parental object.

Many therapists regard this kind of negative therapeutic reaction as a manifestation of an inability to integrate the "good" and "bad" of the object. The inability to integrate good and bad, they explain, is a characteristic of two factors: (1) a constitutional defect of excessive aggression which creates (2) a defect in the defensive system preventing the individual's progression from "splitting" to the next stage of defense—repression. Actually, rage that takes the form of feelings of revenge, when confrontation occurs, is accompanied by the patient's transferential wariness of the therapist or others whom the patient fears are bent upon breaking up his defenses, a fear that is groundless if the therapist is handling himself in an appropriate manner. (The question of fantasies and an understanding of their importance and their dynamics in relation to this problem is discussed on pp. 126-127.)

Self-demeaning is another aspect of sadomasochism. It is a defense against the wish to violate or hurt the "other," often physically (see Wolberg, A., 1973, pp. 210-211, 216-219). When the patient "goes down in a heap" after an interpretation and asks for directions, acts helpless, says he cannot figure out what to do and the like, he is employing the masochistic defenses used with parents. Therefore, they are transferential with the therapist. The therapist must respond, not by thinking that the patient is "defective," but by recognizing that he is acting in a self-demeaning or masochistic way, using the analyst as an idealized figure. Such behavior is an example of *pantomimic transference* (PT). The PT is a sadomasochistic act—an attempt to hide the sadism of controlling others, making them "help" and then frustrating them by not letting them succeed in the helping process. It is a mechanism used in the negative therapeutic reaction as well as an expression of guilt over possible success, an undoing, so to speak.

In response to the patient's self-demeaning behavior and helplessness, the therapist must interpret in language such as the following: "I know that you have behaved this way before and you are now, for some reason, presenting yourself to me as someone devoid of reasoning powers. I guess something or someone must have made you very angry or very anxious, or both. Perhaps we should examine what happened in more detail so that we can understand your anxiety." The therapist should not ask why or query "What does your part in this exchange mean?" or comment "You are doing it again."

This kind of patient reaction is also related to what Kohut might call the "idealizing transference" (in my terms, pantomimic transference), not verbalized but acted out nonverbally; in other words, "I am weak; you are great. Tell me, all-wise seer, what to do." This behavior is often mistakenly taken to be a manifestation of dependency rather than of the sadomasochism that it actually is. Kohut (1971) views it in an entirely different way—as an indication that the patient is trying to make up a developmental deficit. For Kohut, the patient is attempting to get from the therapist what he could not get from the mother so that he may experience self-esteem. He wants praise and he is idealizing the parent-therapist as a step in developing an ego ideal and an identification with an adequate object. In my opinion such behavior is an act of masochism and the opposite of grandiosity, which the patient often feels. When it is translated, it means, "You, the therapist, are a worm! I have you!" Historically, the parent has indeed told the patient what to do and has behaved in the role of "all-wise seer" and the all-encompassing authority, acting as if the patient were "a nothing." Particularly when the child violated the defenses of the parent, he was made to feel guilty for not keeping to the neurotic code and the commitment to the identification that is so important to the parent in relieving his own anxiety and his fear of losing control of the child and thus of his own defense. What the parent has communicated to the child is that the child must perform a sadomasochistic and self-destructive role to relieve the anxiety of the parent. The child's (or patient's) grandiosity is a counterphobic measure, a way of dealing with his fear of destruction, a defense against fear of the aggressor—the parent.

Is the patient's masochistic reaction due to fear, based on an original fear of abandonment, as Masterson (1976) and others have suggested? Or is it a fear of *annihilation* based on the fears of parental aggression and the humiliation of being used by the parents in the interests of their own defenses? The patient's fears are actually multidetermined. They are, for example, the reactions (as a child) to the parents' fears of having to face their own aggression and their sadistic feelings toward their children. They are the parents' fears of facing the reason for their depressions, a fear of recognizing guilt, a fear of facing up to the lies and deceits needed to maintain the projective defenses, fears of expressing autonomous and constructive behavior, sexual fears, a fear of challenging the ideas of their own parents and ridding themselves of their identifications with their parents, fears of losing controls, fears of losing their children as projective objects, the fear of having to acknowledge their overt cruelties toward their children. In turn, their children who become borderline have fears of exposing their parents and themselves by various confrontations.

The borderline's original fears of the parents began between the ages of 3 and 5 when the child's defenses were, in part, to project from the family onto animals in fantasy. Other symptoms appear as well in what has been called the "infantile neurosis" through manifestations such as panic attacks, tics, rigidities or obsessional patterns (more precisely, repetitive patterns to control the fears and change the meaning of the events in the environment), inhibitions, intestinal disturbances, temper tantrums, fears of the dark, fantasies of being hurt, and so on. Freud tended to categorize such symptoms as "constitutional defects" that prevented the child from reacting rationally to the ordinary stress situations that occur as a consequence of normal maturation as a child plows through the "psychosexual phases of development." It is much more probable that these manifestations are due to (1) fears of the parents' aggressive behavior as parents cope with their own anxieties and (2) fears of the counteraggression felt by the child himself.

Masochism and sadism, its concomitant, are still much misunderstood phenomena in treatment, and masochism in some forms is not obvious as Stern thought. In the borderline patient "fear of abandonment" is considered a "regressive" fear and is attributed to a "separation anxiety" such as a child might have when the mother is out of the room. This fear has sometimes been called a masochistic symptom. Melanie Klein suggested that such fear is due to the child's own aggression, which he somehow recognizes in the period (age 3 to 12 months) when he is defending against "innate oral aggression." If one explores the abandonment fear, however, one finds that the patient will "feel lonely" without another, "cannot tolerate to be alone," will experience a "rejected" or a "poor me" feeling, or will be "jealous of others who have someone." Some patients express "fear of what they will do if alone." Actually, they fear facing their own aggressive feelings, which they can discharge if they are with someone, but when alone they are deprived of the projective vehicle. In that case they sometimes fear they may turn on themselves in a suicidal fit. Group therapy has been considered advisable as a vehicle for the borderline patient so that he can dispel some of his anger by projecting it to several individuals. It is my thought that also in the group the sadistic concomitant of the masochism can be interpreted as a defense against the self-demeaning pattern.

For many years most psychoanalysts refused to consider group therapy a valid instrument for helping patients.[1] It, however, became a technique with the more difficult patients out of the desperation of therapists who were willing to try any method that might yield results. In psychoanalytic practice a family group process was considered advisable in the treatment of young children in the light of Freud's developmental theory. The "preoedipal

---

[1]Most of the papers on group therapy with the borderline and schizophrenic patients speak of the patients' regressions to earlier phases of development. A great mass of essays have been printed consequently that interpret group process in terms of the structural theory and Freud's concept of infant development. Family therapy as a system concept is a later contribution to treatment literature.

phase" of development was treated via the mother-child relationship while the later oedipal period was handled within the confines of the group of three, that is, mother, father, and child. Interaction dynamics were neglected for adults in psychoanalytic circles, however with some exceptions (Wolberg, A., 1977). Jackson was a pioneer in this area.

"Abandonment" fear is considered to be an oedipal concept, thus a group concept. I believe it is a fear of losing the object upon whom rage can be displaced. It is the fear of losing the substitute for the parent before the patient has worked out counteraggression and hatred for the parent to a tolerable degree. Interpersonal relationships are contaminated by this fear. Abandonment is a fear, however, that is much more complicated than the fear that an infant feels when the mother goes out of the room. It is a fear that belongs to a later phase of life than the so-called "narcissistic" stage. The basic fear is of *annihilation* in the face of parental aggression, but this fear comes after the child has accepted an identification with the aggressor and thus has begun a sadomasochistic mode of life. The pattern can begin as early as age 3 under extreme pressure from parental figures, as was evident in the case of Roxanne Felumero (Wolberg, A., 1973, p. 12). Roxanne did not accept or "internalize" the identification although she lied (distorted reality) before a judge as her mother told her to do. She had not yet, however, at the age of 3 accepted the identification, internalized it, and repressed the ideas related to the abuse she was receiving, nor had she yet idealized her mother. She was fighting against this process. Just when such identifications are internalized and the repressions and denials do set in, I do not know. The periods probably differ with different situations and children. The time period is, I believe, much later than is currently supposed. This does not mean that repression or other defenses do not occur earlier, but we are speaking of the identifications induced by the trauma of parental behavior when the parents are sadistic and brutalizing.

Abandonment fears come only to children and their parents who have been punished in childhood by sadistic authorities threatening to leave or to force the child to leave if the child steps out of the neurotic sadomasochistic role. There are nonverbal indications of "leaving" even when the parent is present—for example, withdrawing, not speaking for days, looking at a person and using facial expressions of disgust, and the like. This is PT behavior of an inverted nature. Out of anxiety, the individual takes the role of the feared person and uses the other as himself, heaping scorn, sarcasm, contempt, and aggression upon the other. It is one of the mechanisms in *projective identification* (PI). In my opinion the borderline's fears are more of *punishment* and *annihilation* than abandonment in the beginning, due to the punishments they actually do receive when they temporarily give up the identification roles projected onto them by the parents. Later the fears are mixed with fears of anger over the frustration the child felt in succumbing to the parents' neurotic needs, and still later the frustrations are associated with revenge feelings—and perhaps with abandonment as a punishment.

Borderline patients are angry and hostile, but I have never worked with a borderline who did not have a picture of himself or herself as a beaten, passive, helpless depressed person from early childhood on. In the formative years the patient was in the clutches of punitive and sadistic parents, but at the same time that the parents are described as cruel, abandoning, threatening, neglecting, detached, and so forth, they are idealized and defended. Usually, one parent is felt to be less punitive than the other, the less punitive one being considered to be under the thumb of the more punitive.[2] What is denied is that *the patient has identified with these sadistic characteristics of the parents and is now, in this sadistic respect, like the parents.* Even though he describes the parents as sadistic and often alludes to his own sadism, denial and negation are especially strong when the patient is confronted with his own statements (see the case of Lisa in Wolberg, A., 1973, pp. 208-209). As the identifications solidify, not only does he defend against remembering the traumatic experiences that helped to create the identifications, but now he defends his own behavior that is a consequence of the identifications. In a session with the therapist, the information about the parents and the identification role is given in a disjointed and often dissociated form, which is an aspect of the denial mechanism.

With respect to the sadistic qualities of the parents, those parents whom I have known do indeed have sadistic characteristics. The patient is not projecting his own innate sadism onto the parents. They are sadistic. The patient acts out his transference responding to others as he did with his parents out of his neurotic necessity. Thus he projects not his raw aggression but his *reactive hostility* onto others. As a counterphobic measure he will act out the role of the parent with others. This is a PT maneuver in view of his identification with the aggressor (IA).

The borderline patient often hangs on to feelings of having been cheated in life by the parents, but he defends against revealing these thoughts. His explosive reactive rage and revenge feelings against the important people for whom he wishes to feel love in spite of everything that has happened are cause for guilt. Many therapists do not recognize the more subtle forms of the borderline's guilt in relation to his masochism and sadism, and thus they

---

[2]This is revealed in the patient's associations to man and woman drawings, the bigger figure being more controlling and threatening. See the drawings of Harriet Hamburger and Harold Hemple, pp. 238, 249, 255.

often miss the opportunity to interpret this phenomenon. "Wound licking" for example is a way of trying to make the other person feel guilty. It is part of the projective identification defense, which is a sadomasochistic maneuver. It is a form of acting out (i.e., a PT experience) based on rage and guilt combined—rage at having been abused and neglected and guilt for the feelings that have been aroused in the patient as a result of life with the parents.

Somatic Insecurity or Anxiety   The psychosomatic apparatus, asserts Stern, has been conditioned in the direction of tense and rigid preparation against ever present traumatic assaults. Chessick (1977, p. 220) has commented on the tendency of the borderline patient to develop psychosomatic symptoms, and he has suggested that therapists should always encourage the patients to be examined by a physician when such symptoms occur. This is important advice. It has been my observation that somatic symptoms do occur frequently in these patients. This is due to the anxiety and accompanying physical tenseness that the patients experience daily and even hourly, no matter how detached and withdrawn they may appear. The bodily tensions are great, and the organ systems (circulatory, gastrointestinal, and so on) are undoubtedly affected. Stern said that these patients do not complain of anxiety. In fact, they do not seem to have anxiety as a constant symptom. They often present a stolid physical and mental equanimity and at times they do not seem to be disturbed by their situation. (Stern seems to speak here of the patient's pervasive detachment.)

An inordinately strong system of defenses has been established so that the therapist must be careful to undo as little of the defenses at a time as possible, since these patients are capable of releasing unpleasant and sometimes dangerous quantities of anxiety in the course of therapy. Clark (1919) too thought it unwise to "pierce the patient's armor," and I feel that such penetration must be done very gradually, using projective techniques in the process. In treatment the deep, underlying insecurity is revealed, said Stern. Insecurity (masochism!) seems always to have existed. Periods of security were evanescent rather than more solidly established through growth, maturity, and experience.

These individuals, stressed Stern, express an all-out reaction to events or no reaction, which is similar to Kernberg's concept of the "all-good" or "all-bad" self and object images. (These patients, I find, have intense anxiety, but their detachment and withdrawal tendencies help conceal this fact. It is true they do not always complain of anxiety per se; but they often speak of being tense, and they have many inhibitions due to fear. The patient looks and acts anxious, however. Stony detachment is more likely to be a symptom of schizophrenia rather than of a borderline condition.) In childhood, Stern continued, these patients have been inordinately submissive and obedient through fear and need. *They cling to parents and substitutes in the desperate manner of the greatly endangered.* (Clark thought that in analysis we must help the patient "have a questioning and investigative attitude toward parental dictates rather than *cringing acceptance.*") Harlow (1962) has observed that the more rejected his baby monkeys were, the more they clung or, more precisely, the more they tried to wring from the mother what they needed in their development. This aspect of human behavior in infancy has erroneously been taken to mean that the child is "symbolically tied to the mother," but in my opinion such behavior is *self-actualizing behavior, an assertive attempt to gain what is needed from one or the other* of the parents. Usually, however, it is doomed to failure due to the emotional problems of the parents. Children do try to get what they need, and even try to protect themselves from the aggression of the parents. They complain when they do not get what they need, but they are often made to feel guilty for their complaints. The mother of Harriet Hamburger, one of my patients, said that as a child Harriet "urinated through her eyes," meaning that she cried and whimpered a lot. This was meant to say to Harriet "Look what I had to suffer from you" to cover the mother's guilt in not being able to give Harriet what she needed. The concept of symbiosis, which includes the idea that the patient considers himself one with the mother rather than a "separate person," is used constantly to explain these different kinds of masochistic behavior in the borderline.

The chronic anxiety and insecurity of the patient, I believe, comes from the basic rejection received in relations with parents. The patient cannot feel wanted, for he is used and demeaned. Finally, in turn, he does the same with others. It is this kind of interpersonal experience that evokes the sadomasochistic pattern. The anxiety is often somatized, taking the form of worry about the body—a worry that occasionally borders on delusional fear. The identification with the aggressor (the parent) is partially converted to self-contempt in the face of the tension and anxiety the patient feels as he copes with these conflicts. Some of these conflicts are related to the perverse use of the child's body by the parents, that is, their manifest concern about the child's body parts (Levy, 1932). A parent's obsessive interest in body parts (his own or his child's, or both) may be a manifestation of the sexual perversity of the parent and the source of the child's preoccupation with himself. This is a more plausible explanation of hypochondriasis than speculation that oral aggression in an early narcissistic stage has gone awry. The "clinging" Stern spoke of is better understood if we think of Harlow's battered monkeys (1962, 1975) and the fact that the infant tries to make the unwilling parent or a substitute object give what he needs. (The parents are "unwilling" due to the fact that they themselves were rejected and denied what they needed in the way of protection and warmth in family relationships.) Later the child's rational demand is fused with the sadomasochism that arises not from some instinct that automatically makes its appearance in the "oral" or "anal" period along with envy and other esoteric feelings assigned by certain theorists to the first few months of life, but from sadomasochistic patterns that develop gradually through experience with "battering," brutalizing, and cruel parents. There is much "mental battering" due to the parental aggression in the form of repetitive parental use of their children, in defense, as projective objects (a conditioning process, over time) entailing displacement of those aspects of their identifications with their own parents that they deny in themselves (Wolberg, A., 1968, pp. 108-109; 1973, pp. 2-11, 12-13, 25, 55 [note 7], 92-93, 102-103, 148-149; 1977).

Stern noted that in early childhood in the relationship with parents there was "cruelty, neglect and brutalization by the parents." He did not mention how this can be corrected with sexual feeling. The perverse behavior using the child as object is a consequence of the parents' sexual problem. "Love" for these children is sadomasochistic in nature since sexual feelings are bound to arise in the general course of events and some disposition of these feelings must be made. [3]Obsessive talk is one way that the parent has of "letting off steam" or of handling anxiety. This "talk" centers around the areas of anxiety, sometimes sexual, sometimes nonsexual (see Wolberg, A., 1968).

There is enough favorable feeling in the relationships with parents, however, so that borderline patients do not become isolated as is the case with many battered children.[4]

The Use of Projective Mechanisms   Stern thought that the common use of projective mechanisms is one of the phenomena that links borderlines with psychotics. The "immature narcissistically needy person" protects himself from what he considers a hostile environment through defensive measures, such as the development of a rigid personality, introversion, psychic and physical withdrawal, a mild delusional system.

I feel that we must picture this "immature narcissistically needy person" as an individual who was deprived and frustrated, over time, and "used" by his parents as a projective object in the course of their defensive aims. This individual was forced to identify with those aspects of the parents' iden-

---

[3]See A. Wolberg, 1973, pp. 155-161, for a description of the effects of parents' oedipal problems.

[4]See JAMA, January 5, 1979, Vol. 241, No. 1, regarding the results of continued physical battering in children.

tifications with their own parents that the parents needed most to deny. My conception differs from the view that the individual is a defective whose ego functions are "missing" due to an early "fixation" in the period of 10 to 18 months. Our "needy person," the borderline patient, develops a revenge feeling that he acts out with others, and with the therapist, hoping to succeed in using these objects to satisfy his reactive hostility against which his projective mechanisms are partly used. He does have ambivalent feelings toward the therapist; he has good feelings that show up occasionally, but in general he tries to keep them hidden. These feelings are to be distinguished from the appeasing positive transference feelings that are masochistic in nature and that take so long to unravel and to analyze. The ambivalence is what creates the obsessiveness of the borderline patient—the "yes-but" symptom related to the patient's reticence about making clear-cut decisions.

Difficulties in Reality Testing　Borderline patients, Stern stated, accept a fantasied role of the therapist as god-magician *as if it were a reality.* The ungratified and ungratifiable narcissistic needs are responsible for the demand that the therapist be "the greatest." This psychic and physical image is of utmost importance to the patient. Here we recognize the masochistic role the patient assigns to himself and the grandiose role or, to be more precise, the sadistic or controlling role, assigned to the therapist, a transference reaction. The patient does reverse these roles in transference, however, shifting from one to the other, and this becomes disconcerting for the therapist. The idea of a grandiose person in the therapist, I have found, is a projection in one sense; in another sense, it is a masochistic wish (sometimes called a passive-dependent wish) that the therapist be not just the helper but the "rescuer." Underneath this wish, which is masochistic and passive in nature, is a hostile and paranoid-like reaction or defense. The patient feels that he should be able to "act out" the wish to relieve his neurotic anxieties, including his perverse wishes. Others, including the therapist, are assigned the role of undoing the self-destructive mess that his acting out of self-contempt has entailed. There is hatred and revenge attached to this wish. The patient feels that he has been cheated by the world, and the world, in the person of individuals whom he can manipulate, must pay for his misfortune—pay, and pay, and pay. The patient has been manipulative from childhood, once he understood that he was not getting from his parents what he needed. This was a way of survival, and it becomes one of the most difficult transference reactions to analyze. Reality testing is intact, I believe, but in periods of intense anxiety defenses against reality are used.

Home Atmosphere　The mother holds the key to the home environment, stressed Stern. Conceiving the world as dangerous, she imparts this to the child: "The apprehension is in later life a fertile source of so-called un-motivated anxiety." Stern contended that although the father's influence is important, it does not play the chief role until a later date. Stern saw the mother as the dominant figure in the early life of the child. It was she who set the atmosphere in which the child must learn to survive. He saw the mothers of borderlines as neglectful, beastilizing, self-oriented, and unable to perform a mothering role.

In the homes of his patients Stern observed that the parents were non-protective, dehumanizing, laissez-faire, and often overtly cruel. His patients came from upper-middle-class homes; thus there was no poverty to "distract" the parents. It was the emotional tone in the interpersonal relationships between family members that was of a sadomasochistic nature. Occasionally there was physical battering. In Stern's opinion the mothers could not or would not take an adequate parental role. It was obvious that there was much discord between the parents, for a large number of the parents from his particular group of patients were divorced.

My observation is that *parents who have a disturbed, tumultuous home keep the child from forming adequate relations with peers because of their paranoid feelings and their need to hold on to and use the children as projective objects.* This is true of *both parents* in the case of the borderline patient. These parents often have a fear of strangers and of people invading the privacy of their sadomasochistic defensive system. The problems of the parents frustrate the child in finding companions and keep him in the sadomasochistic bind. "Clinging" is one response to this situation, but I believe that anger and rage come first. *The "clinging" is first a repetitive asking for what the child needs. Later appeasement is part of the defense against the anger and rage.* It is also a new way of "asking." In some instances, the neglect and the beastialization of the child by the parents has made the child act in ways that are obnoxious to people around him. Such patterns discourage forming relationships with "adequate" companions. These same patterns also often militate against therapy since many therapists refuse to treat these patients.

Treatment   Stern wrote that in working with borderline patients "supportive" measures are called for. The relationship is as one to a "corporeal magician." (Kohut would call this the mirror transference attributing it to an unrequited early developmental phase at which the individual is now fixated.) The patients do not admit that there is something strange and odd in this attitude, said Stern. When the godlike fantasy is disturbed, the patient develops intense anxiety. "One can easily picture the anxiety, the depression and defensive anger, when the naively accepted love-giving object becomes hostile in the patient's eyes." Interpretations must be given very carefully in this situation, advised Stern. Illusory improvements occur on the basis of positive transference. The rise in self-esteem at what the patient interprets as approval, commendation, or preference of him by the therapist, the magical figure, is marked. (This is a typical reaction of the borderline patient. The patient's defense is "I am not rejected, I am preferred," and this is an aspect of the transference. The lack of proper peer relations make it important for group therapy to be included in the treatment regimen of the borderline patient at an appropriate time [see Wolberg, A., 1960; 1973, pp. 251-255]).

The handling of negative reactions to interpretations, according to Stern, lasts for a considerable period. "When some familiarity with the unpleasant material should have come about through reiteration, and some acceptance should have resulted, the patients for a long time react as though it were novo." (This is the defense of denial in operation.) The anxiety of facing the reality situation has been avoided at the expense of pain, for example, a depressive reaction. To achieve a successful performance means a violent suppression of neurotic inferiorities and the assumption, which can sometimes be detected, of the role of some highly envied omnipotent image. Freud understood this reaction correctly when he attributed it to obsessive characteristics and anger—I would say anger turned into rage.

A negative therapeutic reaction, Stern pointed out, can be discerned in the patient's taking interpretations as an attack. As we have mentioned, this reaction often occurs when the analyst makes a direct interpretation that is premature. The reaction is a defense. With the borderline, I have noted, direct interpretations must be related to preconscious ideas rather than to more remote unconscious material that one might deal with in the case of the neuroses, although I suspect that the former type of interpretation is wise also in the neuroses. One should not make "deep" interpretations to the borderline patient at first, for through his defenses he has "chopped up" his concepts, so to speak, into pieces and parts. This is what Freud referred to in his concept of "compartments" in the obsessive personality. We interpret the pieces and parts later, putting them into a series of wholes. The borderline patient should not be considered naive, as Stern suggested, but *wiley* in the sense that he tries to control through the defense of idealization or appealing to the grandiosity of the other person. This is an aspect of the defense of projective identification. When guilt overcomes the patient as he takes the part of the powerful person (what Stern has said is the role of some highly envied "omnipotent image"), he then attacks himself (the "suffocating superego" is operating).

As a result of frustration, Stern wrote, the borderline evidences insecurity. As children, borderlines have stronger "affective fixations," oedipal and preoedipal, than those who have experienced understanding and love. During therapy their character traits are the main sources of emerging problems that are "clinically so stormy and so difficult for both patient and analyst." Once the "affect hunger" is recognized in the transference, "many other phenomena group themselves about it and become at least comprehensible even though not always accessible as we would wish." "Affect hunger" is, as I have pointed out, a characteristic of the frustrated individual, but this trait persists because it becomes fused with the individual's later revenge feelings and sadism. We deal with an "insatiable person" who is an "angry person" fired by revenge feelings rather than being "needy" as an infant, or "fixated in the oral stage of development" ("fixated" or "arrested" in development). The passive trait of "neediness" has turned into active exploitiveness and an acting out of the revenge motif.

Stern ended his treatise by saying that in treatment the positive transference is limited by the poor capacity for object love. The analyst, therefore, cannot play a passive role. If these patients lie on the couch, they maintain their accustomed withdrawn, detached states interminably; they remain protected against transference involvement.[5] Most of these patients' early activities in treatment, according to Stern, are aimed at "winning over the analyst." Another way of looking at this is that the patient tries to control the analyst through the "winning-over" mechanism. Actually, the patient tries to get the analyst to act out with him and become involved in a sadomasochistic pattern while at the same time he wants the analyst to fight against the control. Above all, the patient hopes the analyst will *not* indulge in a tug of war for this will reduce the patient's chance to be treated.

"When the patients were silent, I attempted to explain as best I could the significance of their silence," said Stern, "but this did not always help . . . I came to realize that these patients did not need to learn, that in fact they already knew a great deal about which they were *guilty or terrified"* (present author's italics). They needed an "easier relationship with me." What they needed from the analyst, asserted Stern, was *help in lessening their guilt and fear* so that they could reinvest their thoughts with more appropriate emotion. How to give them this help was the problem. (In my opinion, this can be done only by working through the masochistic pattern using consistent and varied interpretation of the transference in the patient's contact with others and finally with the therapist, eventually connecting these with the patient's relationship with parental figures.)

It was important, Stern continued, that the analyst bring about a *reality-oriented relationship*, essentially different from the original parent-child relationship. In this way these patients might obtain more assurance and

---

[5] This is a defensive masochistic stance and can be minimized in the borderline patient by having individual sessions once or twice a week using the sitting position (see Wolberg, A., 1952). Excessive defensiveness must be reduced before an extensive working through of the hostility can take place.

courage to face their painful affects. This is like the "corrective experience" later suggested by Alexander (1940, 1948) and Alexander and French (1946); it also correlates with the ideas of Clark and Kohut and the findings of Betz and Whitehorn (see pp. 9-10, 288). In stressing "reality factors," however, we are referring to discussions of the patient's defenses, his fears and angers, the way in which his *current situation* is affected by his sadomasochistic attitudes. We are not referring to a discussion of how he distorts reality, confronting him with his distortions. We must remember that distortion of reality is a function of *conflict, anxiety, and defense*— not a sign of missing ego functions. Stern equates the projection of the borderline with difficulty in reality testing. (Does my patient Harriet Hamburger not see me as I really am? I believe that she does, even though she acts toward me as if I am somebody else when she calls me twenty minutes after the session to see if I am "all right.")

Stern noted, as I have often seen, that when the borderline thinks of independent action, anxiety is created that is not easily handled. The anxiety, I believe, is related to sadism. On the one hand, the anxiety is motivated by the desire to outdo someone by way of secretively expressing revenge feelings which originally related to the parents; on the other hand, the anxiety is evoked by *guilt* in anticipating the stepping out of the neurotic role and thus to change by way of the therapeutic process. (See the sessions with Daird and Kurt Blau in Wolberg, A., 1973, pp. 183, 215, 221.) The usual pattern in making forward moves is to engage in obsessive behavior in order to defend against anxiety associated with guilt and revenge. Some patients use *action* to quiet their anxieties in dealing with feared authority figures—a kind of counterphobic mechanism mixed with the need to employ control mechanisms to express the "self" or "I" as opposed to the authority. The action employed is constructive sometimes, but usually it is oppositional in nature, even though on the surface it appears constructive. The oppositional behavior is a statement, so to speak, of the individual person as opposed to the authority who tries to control. Passivity as negativism also gives the individual a sense of *being someone* and of *having power* as a separate entity. Especially in the first three years of long-term treatment, I have recommended that independent action be discussed with the patient in advance of his attempts at such actions, with emphasis on the anxiety and guilt that it may create. In order for the patient to reach autonomy separate from the sadomasochistic interlocking defensive patterns, he must recognize how his oppositional tendencies, in whatever form they take, create a transference problem in the treatment and hinder him from attaining his therapeutic goals (see Wolberg, L., 1980).

During the sessions the patient will talk on incessantly, said Stern, and if interrupted by an interpretation he will, as a rule, become angry and anxious. (This is the patient's use of his oppositionalism creating the negative therapeutic reaction so that the analyst cannot pierce the patient's defenses.) It is essential to control the transference, admonished Stern, keeping at a minimum its negative or disturbing aspects. Stern is correct here. One interprets anger in the beginning only by raising the possibility of its existence as if the patient felt that he *should not* or *could not* express the anger. The therapist can mention that many people typically express anger indirectly in some way. One must realize, however, that to incite the patient to express anger, or to ask *why* he expresses anger, is merely to stir up and to create the need for further defense. If the patient responds with anger when urged to do so, this merely provides catharsis. When the anger is openly expressed, without urging, the problem is even more difficult since this is a spilling over of rage that must be leveled at any target. It has been called "raw instinctual rage"; this rage is complicated, however, since it is a paranoid reaction and, therefore, a projective defensive reaction.

The paranoid reaction is, in reality, an obsessive use of rage to fend off closeness in the treatment, which is frightening to the patient. The relationship is sadomasochistic. A "warding off" creates frustration for the therapist and "sadistic pleasure" for the patient. At times the session is sexualized, but unlike certain homosexuals and some schizophrenics, the borderline patient does not sexualize the majority of his relations with the therapist. The sadomasochistic pattern is associated on the sexual side with the patient's perverse pattern and on the nonsexual side with distancing mechanisms, acting out, and revenge feelings when the therapist is seen as stepping out of the "good-person" mold. Even though there are these paranoid-like reactions, the borderline patient in his sexual life retains a relationship with a member of the opposite sex. The male patient may have periods of abstinence and impotency, or the female patient may be frigid. The derivation of these perverse patterns, as I have said, are to be found in the sexual use of the child by the parent. The patterns are sadomasochistic. The question of perverse sexuality was not developed by Stern in his writing concerning the borderline. As a matter of fact, there is little on this subject in any of the current literature. Stern's observations were concise and seem to be similar to those made today. In his writings he did not expand on therapeutic techniques as Kernberg and Kohut have attempted.

Freud's Concept of Perverse Sexuality

We have to return to Freud to find any suggestion as to the dynamics of perverse sexuality, and Freud was vague as to the derivation of certain of these problems. He did associate impotence and frigidity with seduction, but he apparently gave that up—but not quite, for later in his writings on female sexuality and on the development of the male libido he alluded to the possibility that servants might be responsible for the heightening of the sexual impulse in preteen years. He never took the step that would lead to an interaction theory as the basis of the child's neurotic patterns, with the parents as contributory partners. His object relations theory was one that emphasized the instinct seeking objects, the hapless object being a responsive but usually benign influence. It is my thought that symptoms such as impotence, frigidity, and others that Freud encountered initially in his patients had a perverse element. In his early studies he credited these patterns to hysterical phenomena; indeed, we see the same hysterical patterns today. There has been no consideration of the possibility of these patterns having a perverse side because in Freud's work he stressed only the obvious perversions: homosexuality and fetishism, for example. Later when he developed his preoedipal theory and began to write of the "self" or the self-preservation instinct and the development of the "early ego", he conceived of the concept that "somatic symptoms" were somehow connected with hypochondriacal ideas. They were an outcome of the preoedipal phase of development, particularly the early autoerotic phase (Wolberg, A., 1973, p. 15), which would mean the "libidinalization" of "part objects." The concept that Levy (1932) suggested would be a use of the child (object) on the part of the parent in the latter's gazing or wandering with the eyes over the child's body, whether the child was dressed or undressed, and this would suggest a peeping perversion. We know, of course, that peeping is never connected solely with eye meandering and that an acting-out pattern is usually associated with it as well. It is interesting that Freud touched upon the dynamics of this kind of perverse behavior that is associated with masochism and with sadism. The bodies of children have many and varied meanings to neurotic parents, and for borderlines this meaning pattern is important in the analysis of the perverse sexual behavior.

Freud wrote that the origin of perversion is in the oedipal situation (Freud, S. E., 1919, pp. 192, 196). His interest in sexuality began early in his psychoanalytic career and continued throughout his writings. The sexual problems of his patients were what stimulated his curiosity in the beginning and accounted eventually for his developmental theory. He recognized that the rearing techniques have a great deal to do with sexual life, that is, the way in which the original sexual stimulations occur, the way in which the mother handles the child's body, and so on. In the end, however, Freud seemed to put as much importance, if not more, in his theory of a bisexual constitution, which he regarded as an element in all people. He seemed willing to attribute active sexual seduction to nursemaids and servants but not to the parents themselves. Freud proposed that the psychological aspects of bisexuality could be seen in the child's identifications with each parent during the oedipal period. As a matter of fact, Freud assumed two meanings in his concept of bisexuality: (1) an actual biological or constitutional bisexuality, using his concept of *active* and *passive* relating to male and female trends in all people, and (2) a relation to sadomasochism (never made clear) where every person's character had some connection with the stages of sexual development through which the individual had to pass. According to this theory, we all have male and female characteristics, psychologically speaking, as we all attempt to resolve our developmental problems. Also, we all have sadomasochistic instincts that weave their way through sexual development and are resolved for practical characterological purposes during the oedipal period when the superego begins to take form. An interaction theory such as I have proposed would implicate the parents in the organization of the neurotic pattern, a pattern that would not be *set* in infancy but would be conditioned *over time* by the neurotic needs of the parents and their behavior relating to their efforts to relieve the anxieties associated with those needs. The defenses of the parents of borderline patients are such that they contribute to the borderline's main defensive pattern—*projective identification*. As I interpret projective identification, it is a defense that is organized over a long period of time before it is finally consolidated. Perhaps in metapsychological terms we should speak of the identification part of the ego as a dissociated part when it is seen in the borderline patient. We would say *dissociated*, not in the sense that "splitting" is a defense in infancy prior to the institution of repression and in the borderline, therefore, a preoedipal phenomenon, but in the sense of its being a hysterical phenomenon, an internalization of the neurotic experiences with the parents, a persistent phenomenon related to acting out of the roles that the parents not only project onto the child but over time condition him through punishment and reward to accept. The acting out can take many different forms depending upon the parents' problems, the environmental situation at home, and the conditions in the community where the home is located. Projective identification, as a process, however, is much more complicated than simply an acting out of roles and internalization of these roles; it also includes the defenses that surround the identification roles— denial, dissociation, repression, and displacement. Symbolization and distortion are included in the projective aspects of the defense.

Freud thought that the oedipal problem per se is to be considered only as the child works through his conflict with the parent of the opposite sex, but in projective identification we see conflicts with both sexes and perverse behavior as an identification with both male and female parents. Freud's main works on perversion are "Sexual Aberations" (1905) in "Three

Essays on the Theory of Sexuality," "A Child Is Being Beaten" (1919), and "Fetishism" (1927). It is perhaps not sufficiently understood today that various forms of impotence in men, and certain aspects of frigidity in women, may have a definite relation to a sexually perverse trend. The masturbatory activities of these patients or the masturbatory equivalents are factors in the perverse sexual life of the patient. This can be detected through the fantasies, the dreams, and the patient's associations, as the sexual conflict with parental figures unfolds. In his theory of sexuality Freud placed emphasis on constitutional factors in relation to perverse trends.

The working through of the anger that is associated with a paranoid trend, and thus with a perverse sexual pattern, is a difficult process. It includes an understanding on the part of both the therapist and the patient of the psychodynamics of sadomasochism and the recognition of its defensive nature. If the patient shows a denigrating attitude toward the therapist, this is a defensive maneuver and a transference reaction that has a perverse quality. The patient is acting toward the therapist as if he were the parent and the therapist the guilty child. This is an *acting out*, however, and makes direct interpretation of the transference ineffective. *This acting out represents, in part, a conflict over the feeling toward the parents' perverse nature, and in part it is a conflict over self-assertion when to act as one would wish goes against the parental mandate.* The acting out is also a counterphobic maneuver to overcome the guilt and certain inhibitions inherent in accepting the parental admonitions. Freud (1909) touched on such conflicts in one paper where he discussed the case of the young man who wanted to marry a woman "different" from the one whom he had been "in love with." The second woman was more to his liking. He interpreted his preference of the second woman as a possible aggression against his father (who was dead). The patient said that if he chose the woman he wanted, some harm might come to his father. The patient had to determine whether his choice was free or, in fact, based on anger and revenge. The patient's conflict was related to an early but unresolved problem with his controlling father. When anger and aggression are actually worked through, the revenge and sadism are exposed and recognized. This cannot be done with the borderline patient until late in the analysis. Interpretations, in the treatment of the borderline, are repeated over and over in various forms, at various times, with various meanings, until these patterns are crystal clear. In the need for repetitive interpretations as the patient acts out the patterns representing the derivatives of early experiences, patience is the watchword. The tendency of the borderline patient to somatize makes it necessary to proceed carefully and do nothing in the way of interpretation that will cause undue stress, such as deliberately trying to provoke or frustrate the patient. Premature interpretation creates the need for further defense, which, in turn, creates more tenseness. When the patient is in conflict over a solution to a problem that he must work through, the therapist should not attempt to protect him from emerging anxiety, but neither should the therapist try to evoke more anxiety.

Geleered (1944) studied borderline children and presented a paper describing 7-, 10-, and 12-year-olds who had a symptom of temper tantrums. All exhibited the need to control situations and to be in relation with a woman (a mother figure?) whom they felt loved them or had regard and respect for them. When they were not sure of the "other," they would break out into what appeared to be a psychotic attack, yelling and striking out, and they would verbalize what seemed like paranoid feelings. They contended that they were being abused, harm might come to them, and they might be killed. The need to control for fear of annihilation was great. They experienced fantasies of being the most powerful person in the world. A delayed reaction to events and the displacement of anger was evident in these cases (Geleered, 1944, pp. 241-242). It seemed to me that these children had great fears of authoritative, controlling, ridiculing attitudes in other people and fears of their own counterhostility. Their fantasies were sadomasochistic.

It would be interesting to know whether temper tantrums are always present in the early childhood of those who later become borderline patients. It is certain that these patients report feeling humiliated and controlled in early childhood, and they have beating fantasies or their equivalent. Freud felt that the beating fantasy meant that the father was always represented as the beater (in the case of both boys and girls). He thought that these people showed a great irritability and sensitiveness toward anyone whom they might think of as father and opined that we might some day find that a perverse wish toward the father might be a dynamic in the "delusional litigiousness of paranoia." Freud at first felt that masochism was derived from the "sadistic instinct." Later in "Beyond the Pleasure Principle" (1920) he was of the opinion that there might be a "primary form of masochism" since he could not see how masochism could be pleasurable if it depended solely on the pleasure-unpleasure mechanism. If masochism were an instinct, it could not be attributed to interpersonal experience, and thus such a "defect" in sexual development was of a constitutional nature. In the beating fantasy the problem with the father would be in fantasy rather than due to experience. When in transference the patient was irritable with father figures, the patient would evoke hostility in the figure. This would then create a milieu where his fantasies would be realized.

Kurt R. Eissler

We have mentioned that many of Kurt Eissler's ideas were similar to Clark's. Eissler (1953) wrote about *modifications* in treatment, stating changes are necessary in analytic technique in order to deliver adequate therapy of delinquents and borderline patients. Eissler defined certain "parameters" that appeared to follow some of the same lines as Clark had earlier. The effect of a parameter (a deviation from standard technique), said Eissler, must be such that it does not interfere with the working through of the transference. The parameter might be related to giving encouragement or altering or reducing the frequency of interviews according to the patient's particular kind of problem or to the life style of the analyst. Such modifications do have an impact on the mode of relating to the patient. (Eissler pointed out that the therapist may be involved with meetings, lectures, and the like and thus may find it necessary to cancel sessions.) Another type of parameter might be that the patient would ask questions that the therapist might answer, as opposed to interpretation and this procedure would be a repetitive tool of treatment. Or the therapist might set limits if the patient is prone to act out. Or the therapist, for one reason or another, might refer the patient to another therapist before the treatment is finished. Other parameters used are education of the patient in the dynamics of the problem (Freud used this technique), explaining a defense or a symptom (i.e., the dynamics of a symptom), and having the patient sit up rather than lie on a couch. All of these modifications are important in the treatment of the borderline patient. In 1952 I suggested sessions once or twice a week for the borderline (Wolberg, A., pp. 701-702)—particularly in the first phase of treatment—and the use of the sitting position. I also advocated explaining to the patient the dynamics of defense against certain reality factors (Wolberg, A., 1952, pp. 706-707).

The use of the couch in the first phase of treatment of the borderline, I find, tends to propel the patient into a masochistic position and thus toward the use of excessive withdrawal into sadomasochistic fantasy. Since fantasies are easily elicited, even when the patient is sitting, there is no advantage in the therapist using a technique that forces the patient into a more extended defense than he ordinarily has. As a matter of fact, the goal of therapy is to help the patient let up on his projective defenses, thus reducing rather than increasing his anxieties and his withdrawal tendencies, which in psychoanalytic terms have been called "regression." The early psychoanalyst spoke about "regression" as a necessary ingredient of the treatment process. Regression obviously was meant as a retreat into fantasy, thinking of fantasy as a "primitive" form of expression, but the early analyst did not observe or take into account the detachment and the withdrawal tendencies that increase as the patient "regresses." (As a matter of fact, the whole concept of regression is one of the many mystiques that continue to clutter the thinking of many analysts. A rational way of looking at the phenomenon designated as regression is to understand it as withdrawal into fantasy, an aspect of the defensive system.)

Eissler, like other writers, pointed out the need for caution in the employment of parameters. He warned of the great temptation to cover up inadequacies (of the therapist) by their introduction since they can, if used inappropriately, represent "one's own inability to use properly the interpretive technique." Eissler's idea of introducing parameters has been criticized by numerous people. They point out, for example, the risk that a resistance has been temporarily circumvented without having been properly analyzed. Defenses, these critics say, are necessary, but the person may have paid too high a price for a defense. They turn to Sigmund Freud's "Analysis Terminable and Interminable" (1937) and Anna Freud's *The Ego and the Mechanisms of Defense* (1930) to buttress these opinions. In replying to these critics, Eissler suggested that the deleterious effects of defense on the ego should be called "ego modification," a concept of Freud's concerning certain kinds of defenses, particularly the *projective defenses* used in the "narcissistic neuroses" and the psychoses. It is precisely to deal with "ego modification" (a term used by Freud to mean almost exclusively projection that tends toward delusion or that becomes delusion) that a deviation from standard technique is needed. The borderline patient can have psychotic episodes (mini episodes), and in working with such cases the treatment process may be stretched out for years. While these instances are rare, they do exist. One of my patients, Harriet Hamburger, was one such long-term case, having finished analysis after being in treatment for twenty-two years. After a tumultuous early life and unsuccessful marriage, she is now happily married and is employed in satisfying and lucrative work. Lydia Ranson, who was not my patient but whom I followed through supervision, was another such individual. Her acting-out patterns were dangerous to herself and so persistent that she failed in her therapy with two very good analysts who gave up, feeling that she was a hopeless case. Persistence and help from a sister over a long period of time and analysis with a third analyst who was sympathetic to years of treatment, with group therapy as an adjunct, produced great changes in her. She had the additional problem of being an alcoholic at one point, and with the help of a friend, also an alcoholic, and her sister, she became a member of Alcoholics Anonymous. Today she is a changed person having continued her studies in a university (she had in her early years been a dropout from college), receiving a diploma. She now functions as a trained counselor working with children and adults who have alcoholism as a problem. She uses music therapy as an adjunct with some of these patients. She has been abstinent from alcohol for years. Characterologically, she is almost completely reconstructed.

Eissler contended that when "ego modification" takes place "the whole process [of analysis] is conducted in the face of most strenuous opposition." He referred to Freud's essay on "The Loss of Reality in Neurosis and Psychosis" (1924), and he emphasized that the *the ego of the psychotic must defend itself constantly against the perception, recognition, and acknowledgment of objective reality which precipitates great anxiety.* This need to defend against "objective reality" is an important point that many therapists do not understand. It is one of the reasons that some patients take many years to work through their problems.

Eissler emphasized that reality is ever impinging and that confrontation with reality is an ever present threat so that the struggle is against the pain that could result in the recognition. One is reminded here of a statement attributed to Ovid, "We are slow to believe what hurts when believed." This is an important statement to keep in mind when treating certain borderline patients, for resistances or defenses are extremely strong, having been organized because reality did indeed hurt the patient. The need to defend against certain aspects of reality is a dynamic in all neuroses, character disorders, and psychoses, but the defenses in each of these cases should be thought of as on a continuum of increasing complexity. In the neuroses projection is present but not as persistent as in the character disorders, and in the character disorders the projections are not as complicated as in the borderline cases. This pertains to all of the defenses (i.e., denial, displacement, repression, undoing, and so on). As distinguished from the psychotic, the borderline patient does not have persistent and chaotic defensive distortions of reality, i.e., delusions, hallucinations (Wolberg, A., 1952).

Eissler pointed out the need of the psychotic person to hang onto hatred and never to reveal the tender side of his nature (1953, pp. 130-131). The borderline, too, has this characteristic to some extent. Both Searles (1963) and Kohut (1971, 1977) have stressed this fact. This use of aggression explains why the "schizophrenic ego" is a masochistic or self-destructive one, Eissler contended. My impression is that the borderline's excessive aggression, like the schizophrenic's, is a reaction to the aggression of the parents— that is, their controlling tendencies and punitive attitudes, particularly the projections of their own aggression and guilts to the child that the child finally adopts, becoming aggressive through his frustrations. Freud (1938) felt that holding back aggression leads to illness. Originally this was thought to be a problem in the hysterias (Freud, S. E., 1893). "Recall with affect" was considered important in reducing symptoms, the "affect" being tinged with a certain amount of anger (Wolberg, A., 1973, pp. 10, 16, 22-23). It is certain that Freud did not mean that one should express aggression freely. Rather he meant (1), as Breuer had suggested, insults from others if not responded to in some direct way left the individual in a state of "mortification" (Kohut would say lowered self-esteem), and (2) self-assertion, which Freud, like many others, often equated with aggression, was a manifestation of the ego instincts or the "selfish instincts" as opposed to the love instincts and in treatment these must be fused, or more precisely, sublimated.

Clark seems to have equated self-assertion with aggression when he spoke of the "ability to maintain real aggression," by which he meant self-assertion. Actually, in defense anger and revenge feelings often are fused with the desire for self-assertion, for when one has been belittled or insulted or disregarded, one often feels angry. The child is in no position to retort when the parent is the chronically demeaning person so he must resort to defense, which is a less satisfactory but necessary mode of adaptation. Freud said that "necessity" was the educative element that had to do with some of the reactions of the individual. By this he meant the exigencies of the environment caused the individual to react in particular ways and thus had an effect upon the character of the ego. Here Freud seems to have contradicted his basic thesis that heredity was more important than environment.

The "observing ego" in certain patients including the borderline is, Eissler claimed, weak or nonexistent (this seems to be the opinion of Kernberg also). As an example, he cites one individual (obviously a psychotic) who remarked, "I could rather believe that you or the world around me do not exist than assume that the voices I hear are not real" (Eissler, 1953). He refers to Waelder (1934) as being in agreement with his own idea that the schizophrenic "has lost the ability to differentiate between the possible and the real in certain sectors of reality." It should be pointed out that if one looks at the patient's production in that manner, then one's response would be different than if one feels that the meaning of the remark is that the patient *can* distinguish fantasy from reality. Denial, repression, and distortion mask the observing ego (see my session with Maurice Belk, in Chapter 11)— *but it is there.* And it is for this reason that projective therapeutic techniques are so important at particular times. *The skill of the therapist in determining the least defended areas of the patient's productions is the clue to keeping in touch with the observing ego on the preconscious level. The ability to understand when the patient is speaking of a particularly anxiety-provoking problem that he verbalizes but cannot face, yet wants on some level to discuss, is the key to disclosing the observing ego as the patient defends with the mechanism of projective identification. In the latter type of situation the projective technique is most useful and essential, for it is through this technique that the patient realizes that his problem is being understood.*

Understanding is revealed in the projective interpretations. The patient "knows" he is communicating with the therapist, even though he is denying and protesting against this at the moment. In my interview with Maurice Belk in Chapter 11, Maurice talks of his son's acting out, referring to the behavior not as neurotic or impulsive, but *as behavior that he can understand*. He can also understand the attitude of his son's doctor. He does not delve deeply into the relationship, for his message to the therapist is that he must act out, otherwise he cannot live. He scolds the therapist for not listening to this communication.

The interview with Belk could be thought of as a disjointed and fragmented session, a session where the patient jumps from one subject to another, a session that leads nowhere. Actually, the session tells a great deal about Belk, his anxieties, his patterns, and how he handles his relations with people. Even though it seems disorganized on the surface, there is a theme and a communication that is clear and expressed, albeit by using the "other" (in this instance his son) as the projective vehicle through which to express his thoughts. The patient's protest that "they don't listen" applies both to himself and to the therapist. He is in essence saying, "You are not listening to what I am telling you. You are talking in another way, and about something else." With Belk I handled this protest by referring to people who do not listen, people who are talking with each other but at cross-purposes. I also described the way that some people feel that they must act out. It relieves their tensions, and they do not believe their tensions can be relieved in any other way, except perhaps by pills.

The explanation to Belk might be thought of as the use of parameter. I believe it is a form of interpretation since I was relating my remarks to communications I received from Belk in the sessions. Before we can make connections with the childhood experiences of borderlines, we must establish (1) what the patient accomplishes and feels about acting out, (2) what the acting-out patterns are like, and (3) their relationship to the identification fantasies and behavior. Interpretation must be made in common-sense terms. Prior to this we have to outline the *interlocking defensive system* that the patient sets up with others. And this I did with Belk.

Eissler explained that the patient's incapacity to use his observing ego to pull himself out of the context of defensive phenomena makes the technique of treating severely ill patients essentially different from that of treating neurotics. Thus one extends the treatment parameters to the treatment of *ego modifications* (Eissler, K., 1953, p. 241). We know that the borderline patient's defenses do not extend to fixed organized delusions and hallucinations (Wolberg, A., 1952), nor are these patients excessively and obsessionally bent on a pattern of destroying some person or group as in the case of the paranoid. Therefore, we understand that the borderline uses a more attenuated defense of projective identification than the psychotic, and a projective technique employed by the therapist is a recognition of this fact. I have introduced projective technique to recognize the presence of the patient's *ego functions* and his *observing ego*, albeit in the context of defense. I illustrated (1973) that one explores the situation that the patient talks about and then elaborates on incidents that the patient describes and verbalizes, discussing the latter in the context of the "other" keeping in mind the patient's denial and the projection of his identification images (see the sessions with Lisa in Wolberg, A., 1973, pp. 208-210). I do not consider the projective therapeutic technique a parameter; rather I consider it an analytic procedure that allows the discussion of the patient's problem in dynamic terms through the use of the "other" with whom the patient is identified while he is denying the identification. The observing ego is ever present, just as the capacity to understand reality is extant (Wolberg, A., 1952, 1960).

The projective technique (Wolberg, A., 1973) can be used simultaneously, in the same session, with other more direct psychoanalytic methods. When the patient's productions show preconscious awareness, we can employ a direct statement for interpretation or emphasis; but when the material is highly defended, we use the projective technique. As a matter of fact in the early stages of treatment, we use both direct interpretation and indirect interpretation (projective interpretation as an aspect of the projective technique) alternately in the same session. We also use the technique of reinforcement of the patient's positive ideas in both direct and indirect ways.

Annie Reich

The work of Annie Reich illustrates that psychoanalytic concepts regarding the narcissistic disorders have changed little since she wrote her paper in 1953 entitled "Early Identifications as Archaic Elements in the Superego." And much of the current theory continues to be the same as it was in Freud's day. The new information that is available today on these disorders has had little effect on the mainstream of psychoanalytic thinking.

Reich's (1953) paper is a psychoanalytic interpretation of what we might now call narcissistic or borderline personality. Reich distinguishes between the *superego* as a later and more "reality-syntonic" structure and the *ego ideal* as the predecessor of the superego or a more "narcissistic superego"— the distinction between (1) "identification with parental figures seen in a glorified light based on the child's longing to share or take over the parental greatness in order to undo his feelings of weakness" and (2) identifications resulting from the breakdown of the oedipus complex. The former represent the ego ideal; the latter, the "true superego."

In this formulation, as in Freud's ideas, the impetus for the identifications come from the child as one of the automatic behaviors associated with growth and development. Actually, these are compensating devices as described—or, what I would call, defenses. Freud, however, considered the "ego ideal" and identification necessary and "normal" phenomena in the development of the ego. In my opinion the young infant or child would not "normally" have such feelings of inferiority with the need to identify with a strong parent; rather, the young infant or child "normally" would feel secure. The identifications with a powerful figure would come at an age much later than 4 or 5 months, or, when the unresolved oedipal symptoms are presumed to begin, and they would be a defense against the neurotic need of the parent for the child to take over some of the characteristics of the parent, i.e., the neurotic roles that the parent wishes to deny. The child would resist this as long as possible, but he would eventually have to "give in" and adopt the role the parents project onto him as they communicate their need. The identifications would not be sought as a means of growth and adaptation; rather they would be accepted under protest, causing anxiety and anger, resentment, and despair, thus providing the basis for the individual's future neurosis.

Reich believed that identifications leading to superego formation are related to the oedipal problem and are identifications with the moral side of the parent that are used for repression of oedipal strivings. Identifications can be positive (do what your father or mother does) or negative (do not do everything that your father or mother did). Such activity as aggression toward the objects is eliminated by "putting oneself in the objects' place," and it is in this way, Reich thought, that character traits of parental figures are taken over that are no longer connected with the task of instinct mastery. By this simplistic formulation and mystical circuitous route, using the litany of psychoanalytic early-phase doggerel, Reich arrives at a description of symptoms related to the narcissistic personality. But in her model she has circumvented the complicated family dynamics involving the struggle that takes place over a number of years as the child fights against becoming the projective object for the parents, i.e., identifying with the parents and acting out the neurotic roles (identifications) that will relieve the parents' anxieties. In Reich's neat little world aggression accruing through frustration by the parents is resolved by "putting one's self in the place of the other." True, identification is a defense. It does not, however, entirely reduce the aggression, for the aggression is needed both by the parents and by the child and is absorbed in the sadomasochistic (passive-aggressive) character pattern, which evokes acting out at certain points.

Freud, according to Reich, insisted that the choice of identification used for the formation of the superego is determined by the degree of bisexuality

present and also by the pregenital history. The "instinct restraining" identifications, whose task it is to hold back incestuous genitality, become
fused with earlier identifications against "pregenital indulgence"; the identifications that substitute for the parents as objects of love or aggression
become fused with the more primitive ones, and an integration takes place.
Early identifications are with "parental qualities" that are envied or admired, and thus they help to undo a narcissistic hurt.

One must realize that "narcissistic hurts" do not a neurosis make, unless
these hurts are practiced by the parents over a period of years and in a
persistent obsessive manner with punishments for certain normal behaviors
when these interfere with the child's adoption of the neurotic role that the
parents wish him to play. Lack of self-esteem does not derive from mild
ordinary everyday punishments that are aimed at not letting the child hurt
himself or that protect him from other kinds of harm. Normally, the child
does not "long to be like the parent"—why should he? In identifications
he is forced to be like the parent, or, more precisely, he is forced to do
what the parent wants of him as the parent forces him into the passive-
aggressive sadomasochistic neurotic role.

Even though early identifications, said Reich, come about because of
feelings of inferiority, helplessness, and envy of the power of the adult and
later as a consequence of oedipal strivings and even though they represent
a "normal longing" to be like the parent, an idealized parent, these early
identifications may lead only partially or not at all to personality traits.
These "longings" must be described as "ego ideals." Self-esteem depends
upon them. In the early preoedipal stage the ego ideals restore injured
narcissism by expressing themselves predominantly as imaginary wish fulfillment, i.e., "narcissistic fantasies." In these fantasies the child sees himself as big, powerful, a genius, and the like. These can be elements in a
masturbation fantasy. They may become a permanent part of the personality against which the ego is measured. In the phallic period, for example,
the child may experience a trauma (sudden threats to narcissistic intactness)
and cause the main part of the libido to be withdrawn from love objects and
become concentrated upon the ego. This leads to the use of "grandiose ideals
and fantasies." The grandiosity is used to "ensure phallic intactness."

My interpretation of grandiose fantasies is that they are defensive; they
depict the interpersonal relationship between the parents and the child in
disguised form, that is, that aspect of the interpersonal relationship that is
chronically traumatic for the child. When the parents need a particular kind
of relationship to appease their neurotic needs, they project the role onto
the child and force him through punishment and reward to enact the role
that is similar to the parental role (neurotic) that the parents wish to deny in
themselves. The relationship thus becomes sadomasochistic over time, and

the grandiose fantasies develop as defenses against the anxiety aroused in the sadomasochistic relationship. Grandiose fantasies develop out of fear of being overcome or destroyed by the aggression of the parents, who punish repeatedly for normal behavior when this creates anxiety in the parents.

Reich thought that the early identifications were superficial in the sense that they are not associated with trauma but are identifications that occur when the infantile ego is weak and when fusion with strong parental objects ("a magic taking over of the strength of the parent due to the insufficiency in the child") is necessary. These are "transient and changing," (now thought of as "self-images" and "object images"). Reich said that in this circumstance the child simply imitates whatever attracts his attention momentarily in the object, and these imitations express (in a primitive way) "that he is like the object." A definite wish to be like the object precedes the formation of the grandiose fantasy. It also indicates a "realization of the differences of the self" and the "object." As these "passing identifications" develop slowly into a real assimilation (internalization) of the object's qualities (a partial identification because the child can never be like the parent in all respects), we see a type of "normal ego ideal." This will lead to attempts to bring about a realization of the identification aims as soon as the growing capacities will permit. The identifications and the ego ideals divested of the earlier grandiose forms, i.e., the unrealistic aspects, are then "reduced to human proportions." A clinging to the earlier form represents a "fixation" or a "regression" to the early stage of ego development. In pathological cases the "imitation identifications" persist, and there is not even an impulse to translate these fantasies into reality. The step from fantasy to reality cannot be taken because the ability to achieve this goal is not present. There is no capacity to stand tension, to wait to accomplish the goals of this display of fantasy and the adoption of reality. Reality testing may be partially relinquished, and "a state of partial or temporary megalomania" may prevail. A state of inferiority is present, and varying states of depression can be seen. Sometimes these "narcissistic ego ideals" become conspicuous only in adolescence or at puberty. How this all comes about is not explained by Reich; Freud thought that this circumstance was due to constitutional defects rather than interpersonal relations in the family.

In repression, Reich asserted, object-libidinal strivings are replaced by identifications of the early infantile kind. These "archaic elements" show in the inability to distinguish "good" and "bad." In the "narcissistic nonpsychotic state" narcissistic ego ideals prevail. In certain circumscribed areas the individual does not discriminate between fantasy and reality. Objectivity toward the "self" is lacking. In the "good" and "bad" identifications with the love objects there is no fusion, and this facilitates mood changes between megalomania and deeply self-critical periods. "The sick suffering pregnant mother" identification in one of Reich's cases was counteracted by the "nonreality-oriented omnipotence" ascribed to the mother. The "sadistic father identification" was counteracted by "good deeds"— the opposite of the father. The narcissistic core of the superego in this case was seen in "narcissistic ego ideals," also: (1) reality testing giving way under certain conditions, (2) infantile feelings of inferiority, (3) megalomania, i.e., an inner feeling or conviction of one's own greatness,[6] (4) the undoing of the separation between "self" and object, (6) depression and mania (not extreme as in manic depressive illness), (7) fear of being inferior, (8) overconcern with other people's thoughts about oneself, (9) sadomasochistic fantasies, (10) oral concerns, (11) sexualization of parent-child relations, seen later in patterns with the opposite sex. I would say that the identifications are pictorialized in the patient's dreams and fantasies and that these are sadomasochistic in nature. The sadomasochism arises, however, not through the automatic appearance of instincts around the age of 2 to 3 years, nor even later at 5 to 6 years, but through the traumatic relations with parents who project their own unwanted (guilt-producing) neurotic activities onto the child and force him to react in kind over a period of years. This causes anxiety, frustration, fear, anger, and resentment in the child, which then must be handled by the defenses Reich has outlined. Much later in adolescence, the resentment is tinged with revenge feelings, which are acted out in a variety of ways.

We shall now consider in Part II current papers that present ideas concerning borderline patients and discuss these from the theoretical and treatment points of view.

---

[6]In reality, Reich's patient had graduated college summa cum laude.

Current Theories and Their Implications for Treatment

CHAPTER 3

Comments on Current Theories

The dynamics and treatment of the borderline patient have been examined extensively by Otto Kernberg, James F. Masterson, and Richard D. Chessick as well as the present author. In this chapter their theories will be the focus of the discussion. In addition, we shall consider Heinz Kohut, for although he writes primarily about narcissistic disorders, he assumes that his theory concerning narcissistic personalities and some of his ideas regarding schizophrenia cover the main facets of the borderline syndrome. Other researchers who have contributed to the literature of the borderline or whose research is pertinent will be included where their writings are relevant to the theory being reviewed.

While there are broad areas of agreement among Kohut, Kernberg, Masterson, and Chessick, there are also, as might be expected, wide differences in their interpretation of the same phenomena. To complicate matters, in some of their writings the technical vernacular at times is difficult to decode. Therefore, when the chief concepts of these writers are presented, the original phraseology is retained to a great extent, but terms that might be regarded as cryptic will be clarified.

Each of these authors utilizes a developmental theory to explain the dynamics of the borderline patient in accordance with the presently accepted psychoanalytic version of development. Therefore, we shall start our review of these theories and treatment techniques by examining the concepts of "self-object" and "splitting," two popular ideas of primary importance in the thinking of Kernberg and Kohut based on Freud's, Melanie Klein's, Mahler's, and Erikson's postulations. While each author may have differences in approach, the main tenet is that the pathology of the ego, which begins in the first year of life, is a basic problem in the development of the borderline syndrome. The thrust of Kohut's theory of early onset is that the mother's personality is the main cause of the problem of the infant who will become the borderline patient. Kernberg puts more emphasis on constitutional factors, which are basic in his theory.

The "Splitting" Phenomenon and the "Self-object"

Kohut originally wrote about "the ego" (1959), but modified this at an early period (1963) by alleging that he analyzes the "self" in line with Hartmann's theory of the subdivisions of the ego (the "self," the "self-represen-tation," and so on), a concept related to narcissism. *Following a developmental motif*, Kohut (1975) believes that the analyst must function as a mothering person so as to help the patient make up the developmental deficits in the "self", a support that the depressive or withdrawn real mother could not provide. The "self-object" is the focus of treatment. Self-objects are objects that are not experienced as "separate and independent from the self," an idea deriving from Freud's "anaclitic state." In my 1952 paper I expressed similar ideas, but I have changed my concepts since then.

Kernberg, too, proposes a "self-object" concept (using some of Hartmann's ideas) in an "object relations theory" modeled after Melanie Klein, with some modifications (1975, pp. 26-27). He says that the patient has *developmental defects present in the defensive system*. There is an interference with the patient's synthesizing capacity characterized by an early division of the ego into "good and bad objects" i.e., aggressive "self-" and "object" images. This division is due to a constitutional defect, genetically determined, expressing itself in an excessive amount of oral aggression that has to be defended against by projective identification, the main feature of which is "splitting," i.e., dissociation. Kernberg (1975, p. 25) considers the "splitting phenomenon" a distinctive mechanism in borderline cases (others find this mechanism in other types of cases). Splitting is connected with a "compartmentalization of contradictory ego states." A patient, Kernberg says, may at one moment manifest outlandish sexual or hostile impulses while at another time may swing to an opposite stance, conveying highly moralistic, virtuous, and compassionate sentiments, acting as if he never had engaged in the original impulsive behavior at all. The patient may project his own impulse-laden motives onto the therapist in transference or onto other substitute objects. This is the patient's way of preserving his equilibrium.

Kernberg (1966) illustrated this phenomenon by citing a borderline male patient in his late 30s with a paranoid character structure who, in the third interview, vociferously accused Kernberg of rejecting him by passing him by on the street. The patient felt that he was being held in contempt by his analyst. Kernberg considered this a manifestation of a beginning need for a dependency in the relationship with the analyst. On subsequent occasions the patient voiced gratefulness and intense positive feelings toward Kernberg, but a few weeks later he shifted back to angry outbursts. During the period that he manifested gratefulness, Kernberg considered these feelings to be sentiments of "closeness and longing." (I would think of this as an appeasing masochistic attitude in transference.) When the patient was feeling good toward the analyst, he seemed oblivious to the fact that he had evidenced anger, in spite of remembering that he had possessed feelings of such an opposite nature. "It was as if there were two selves, equally strong, completely separated from each other in their emotions although not in his memory, alternating in his conscious experience." Kernberg could not discern this pattern in the patient's activities at work, his behavior there being socially appropriate.[1] Whenever Kernberg attempted to question either state of unrealistic emotion in its presence, the patient would elicit anxiety. This, Kernberg felt, pointed to the fact that the "splitting of the ego" was "not only a defect in the ego but also an active, very powerful defensive operation." Kernberg postulates that certain mechanisms of defense operate differently in the borderline than in other patients, particularly the mechanisms of *isolation* and *denial* (Kernberg, 1967, pp. 669-671; see also Wolberg, 1973, pp. 130-131).

Kernberg (1967) believes that the borderline patient has a "constitutional defect" that prevents the normal mode of integration of perceptions. He accounts for this in the following way: Object relationships involve drive derivatives, affects, emotions, wishes, fears, images, and fantasies. Introjections are the "earliest point of convergency of object relationships and instinctual drive representatives" and "may be visualized as an essential 'switch,' bringing the ego into operational readiness." Splitting is the normal defensive operation in this early stage of development. There is an undifferentiated phase of development (Hartmann, 1939, 1950), a common matrix to the ego and the id (Freud's concept); and there is a specific stage in which the ego may be considered for the first time as an integrated structure, i.e., the 3-month period (Spitz, 1951).

Another defect in the borderline, according to Kernberg, is "a constitutionally determined lack of anxiety tolerance." This interferes with "the phase of synthesis of introjections of opposite balance," i.e., the phase from birth up to 8 or 10 months. The "quantitative predominance of negative introjections" stems from "both a constitutionally determined intensity of aggressive drive derivatives and from severe early frustrations." Kernberg says that in the borderline patient a constitutional defect interferes with the normal mode of integration of perceptions. This perpetuates the "splitting" that normally occurs in every child, due simply to the inability of the child in the first few months of life (before the id/ego differentiation takes place) to integrate the contents of his mind. The consequence is that, as a child, the future borderline never does give up the splitting, and it, in turn, creates a problem in the development of the autonomous ego functions. Kernberg attributes the *destructive mental images* in splitting to derivatives of the instinct that have not been handled owing to

---

[1]Freud had a theory that a patient could have two attitudes existing side by side without influencing each other. This was described in a case of fetishism and in the amnesias.

the constitutional defect. (I would conceive of the aggression as stemming from a family situation where the parents are unusually frustrating.) Kernberg calls the aggressive images nonmetabolized ego states or introjects.

Freud thought of these fantasies as id representatives. Kernberg's idea is reminiscent of Breuer, too, who spoke of "hypnoid states" and felt these to be due to a constitutional inability of the individual to hold together the contents of his mind. In my view, Kernberg is describing a sadomasochistic defense when he speaks of these opposite "ego states."

The constitutional defects and the early frustrations create painful types of object relations. As a consequence, "all-out negative valence" increases anxiety and produces the need *to project aggression, which is taken back in the form of negative introjections*, which then become "bad internal objects." But the need to preserve "good internal objects" leads not only to excessive splitting, but also to a dangerous "predepressive idealization"; in other words, the external objects are seen as totally good in order to make sure they cannot be contaminated, spoiled, or destroyed by the projected, bad external objects. When idealization of the parents occurs, it creates unrealistic all-good and powerful object images and, later on, a corresponding hypercathected, blown-up omnipotent ego-ideal, which is quite typical of borderline patients.[2]

Kohut has a different concept of the idealization of the parents, based on the child's "normal" need to be "merged" with an omnipotent person who provides him with a feeling of worth and self-estem. Meyers (1978, p. 135) says that this corresponds "in development" to a situation where "little Johnny might fall hurting his knee and crying." His father, "whom he admires," would pick him up and then Johnny would feel "calm and secure in his powerful arms, as if he and father are one" (Mahler's symbiotic period and Freud's anaclitic state in the age of id/ego undifferentiation).

The question of the origin of the "splitting tendency," the predisposition of the ego toward it, and how other defensive mechanisms such as repression, introjection, and identification are related to it, encouraged Kernberg

---

[2]Some theorists may question the concept of an ego-ideal as inconsistent with Kernberg's idea that the borderline patient has no true identification system on the "higher level." Others see no problem, they believe the identification process, which is seen as a pivotal factor in ego and superego development, can be acquired in the therapeutic process. Kernberg accepts introjection as a form of identification. Since in the psychoanalytic frame of reference identification is a developmental necessity, the patient after working through his oral and anal stages will automatically identify with the analyst, and the oedipal dynamics will begin to unfold. The analysis itself is a developmental process. In view of this idea that the borderline patient lacks a "higher level" identification system, Kernberg (1975, p. 89) proposes that transferences in the patient do not always reflect experiences with parents. In light of the self-object concept the borderline has no "observing ego" and the "lower level" borderline have no guilt (Kernberg, 1975, pp. 79-80, 19 respectively). These are severely masochistic characters.

to formulate a tentative model which fused theoretical concepts from classical psychoanalysis, Kleinian psychoanalysis, and the schools of ego psychology: Hartmann (1939, 1950), Jacobson (1954), Erikson (1946, 1950), Klein (1946), Fairbairn (1954), Segal (1950, 1956).

Kernberg contends that interpretation is a futile way of stopping the contradictions of the patient's behavior. Since splitting is not dependent on repression, efforts to deal with the pathology by delving into repressed, unconscious material yield barren results. To avoid anxiety, the individual will try to maintain the barrier between contradictory states. For this reason an active attack on the mechanism of splitting as a defensive operation must be made. This will stir up anxiety and help mobilize new defensive operations. In this way intrapsychic change may be brought about. *Repeated interpretations of the defensive dissociation which exists between contradictory states, or between lack of impulse control in a specific area and the patient's usual behavior, may mobilize the conflict in transference.* When regular psychoanalysis is attempted, says Kernberg, reality testing becomes defective and what eventuates is a transference psychosis (loss of reality testing and appearance of delusional material within the transference rather than transference neurosis). This indicates that there is a tendency to act out "instinctual conflicts" within the transference as a way of gratifying pathological needs. Yet efforts to treat borderline patients by supportive approaches merely serve to reinforce defenses and leave the patient where he was before. In spite of the effort to avoid transference emergence, negative transference is prone to erupt in an insidious way: it is split up by acting out, both outside of treatment and, with emotional shallowness, within the therapeutic situation.

Kernberg (1968, pp. 601-602) outlines seven procedures in a "modified approach": (1) Systematic elaboration of the manifest and latent transference (without relating it extensively to early genetic origins) inside the therapeutic situation while elaborating the negative transference as it occurs in the patient's relationships with others. (2) Confronting and interpreting pathological defensive tactics that foster the negative transference. (3) Structuring the therapeutic situation (such as the setting of limits to nonverbal aggression) to block the acting out of negative transference. (4) Utilization of environmental resources, such as a hospital or day hospital for these patients whose acting out outside of therapy is too disturbing or so gratifying as to prevent progress. (5) Focusing on defensive operations that weaken the ego (splitting, projective identification, denial, primitive idealization, omnipotence, reduced reality testing). (6) Fostering those postive transference manifestations which help the therapeutic alliance with only careful partial confrontation of the patient with such manifestations. (7) Encouraging a more appropriate and mature expression of sexuality where necessary, to free it from its entanglement with pregenital aggression. These techniques, Kernberg feels, fall under the rubric of psychoanalytically oriented psychotherapy rather than formal psychoanalysis.

The borderline patient, according to Kernberg, uses "splitting" because of an inability to handle ambivalent feelings. He has not developed repressions because these are related to *conflict* and an ability to regard the "object" as *separate*. The borderline has a consciousness of "good" and "bad" but not at the same time. That is, he experiences relationships in terms of "black and white," so to say, blotting out the one when the other is in the foreground. This is different from *denial* where there is *no consciousness in the disavowal.*

It is my impression that in all of the defenses mentioned by Kernberg— *dissociation, denial, disavowal,* and *repression*—there is, indeed, a rejection of mental content *due to a linkage* not with just one vague memory or the dim memories of a few experiences from 4 to 10 months but *with many memories of relations with parents over time that created conflict.* There is an accumulative effect over a period of years that necessitates defenses against the understanding of the conflict. It is a matter of the intensity of the conflict over what has been called "cumulative traumas" as to whether such mechanisms as denial and dissociation are used. As a matter of fact, denial is a necessity in a dissociative process, and *there is no denial and no dissociation without repressions.* The resolution of the conflict comes about through the organization of fantasies, the development of symptoms and acting out, (i.e., a return of the repressed), and the consolidation of a passive-aggressive, sadomasochistic personality brought about by relations with parents. Acting out is a function of the patient's identification with parental figures, denied and projected.

Aside from the fact that there may be no such thing as dissociation in the early stages of infancy, we must have a more precise usage of the term. We should reserve the term *dissociation* to refer to the kind of defenses evident in the amnesias, the fetishes, and the various forms of multiple personality. Dissociation is fleeting in depersonalization and derealization and more lasting in the amnesias than in fugue states. But all of these defenses are based on *conflict* derived from relations with parental figures and *the attempt to avoid the anxiety in the conflict aroused by thoughts and feelings stimulated by current events.* The current events set off anxiety when the individuals in the interpersonal relations behave in a manner that is in any way reminiscent of the parents. The borderline patient projects onto these individuals the parental characteristics with which he is identified. Kernberg resolved the matter of defenses and their relation to identification and acting out by simply contending that the borderline patient has no identification system and therefore has no feelings of "real love" or "regard" for others and no true superego values, especially *guilt*. The borderline's acting out is the acting of "raw instinctual aggression."

Kernberg believes that the "ego defect" of the borderline is in the defensive system, and from the point of view of development the patient has not passed through the separation/individuation phase (Mahler's elaboration and modification of ideas suggested originally by Freud, Rank, and others). The patient remains with the primitive "splitting" defense. The defenses are against his "primitive rage" and the expression of "raw aggression," which Kernberg sees as the source of the patient's acting-out tendencies rather than that the acting out is due to identifications with parental figures over which there is conflict. Kernberg is of the opinion that the borderline patient has not reached the stage of development where identification can form, the so-called period of "object constancy" beginning about 16 months. The borderline is "fixated" in the 4- to 12-month period.

The theory regarding "splitting" as a defense preceding repression, developmentally speaking, has been criticized by many psychoanalysts and psychiatrists as not being demonstrable (Gunderson, 1975; Gunderson, Carpenter, & Strauss, 1975; Gunderson & Singer, 1975; Heimann, 1966; Mack, 1975; Pruyser, 1975; Robbins, 1976; Wolberg, A., 1973, 1977). In my opinion identification is an important factor in all neuroses and in all psychoses; therefore, we cannot use Freud's or Mahler's preoedipal system as a guide (Wolberg, A., 1973, pp. 11, 135, 137-138).

Kohut (1971), too, uses the concept of splitting prior to repression, proposing a "vertical split" in the ego by "disavowal" (Freud's phrase). For Kohut, however, the "split" (the dissociation) results from a developmental phenomenon related to the "self." There is an early period when the "grandiose-exhibitionistic self" is operative. The future borderline is unsatisfied at this stage by the deficient mother so that part of the "self" becomes fixated, denied (disavowed), and converted into fantasy. Bifurcation, as Freud called it, takes place when in the case of neurosis part of the libido is split off to become fantasy. Modern theorists apply this principle of Freud to ego formation as well as to the instinct, and the effects are seen in the form of derivates. In the "vertical split" there is a *consciousness* of the "grandiose self," while at the same time the individual is aware that he is not an important or "grand" person. In *disavowal* both aspects of the ego are conscious, but one part is *unaware* or *ignores or disregards* the other. Kohut uses a concept similar to that of Kernberg but in relation to the development of the *"self"* aspect of the ego rather than to the *defensive* side of the ego. Chessick (1977, p. 56) says that there is disagreement as to whether *disavowal* ought to be called a splitting of the ego or a splitting of the "self" in the service of defense. In any case, "splitting" presumably happens before the "repressive barrier" is formed. This theory derives from Freud's ideas of schizophrenia, applying data to concepts of narcissism and regression.

Freud theorized that the schizophrenic patient did have identifications, resolved and integrated in the ego, but that in the process of "regression," which was a systom in schizophrenia, the ego was broken up due to "splitting." It was a kind of disintegrating of the ego into parts so that what was present was the "abandoned identifications," which were then remade or distorted. It could be considered a "going-back-in-time" concept, or an undoing of an integration, throwing the "introjects" into a fantasy—or more precisely a delusion—as a disavowal of and a remaking of reality. Actually, it seems to me, *the delusion is a form of integration*, a fantasy that takes on a more rigid and permanent type of organization while disguising the root of the acting out by projecting certain memories of the original figures (the parents). These memories have to do with the identifications in the form of defensive fantasies, for example, voices and ideas that require a particular kind of action. These are defensive maneuvers to exculpate the parents as the "batterers," or the "persecutors," or the "manipulators." The borderline, however, does not become motivated in his behavior by an organized delusion; rather he has fleeting paranoid ideas and a loosely defined delusional system that is activated in times of intense stress.

Narcissism and Its Relation to Self-objects

Kohut postulates a stage of narcissism in which a "normal primitive self" has a "separate line of development" from that of sexual development. In the ordinary course of events an "idealized parental image," which is a "self-object," is formed as an aspect of development (a precursor of identification and the superego). According to Chessick (1977, p.64), Kohut consideres this "image" to be in the nature of a "transitional object." Therefore, it is a residual of the period before the id/ego differentiation takes place, antedating the period of "object constancy." Kohut refers to narcissism as developing "side by side with object love." The analyst is a "self-object" in the patient's eyes, and a self-object is a need-fulfilling object, as Meyers (1978) says, "not experienced as a separate independent being having its own needs" etc. but "experienced as part of one's self, like one's arm." The "self" has two parts: the *grandiose self* and the *idealized parental image* and both evolve from a stage of primary narcissism. Goldberg (1978) has explained that one can expect maturation of the self to progress along one line and sexuality along another "rather than conceiving of narcissism as developing into object love."

Clark (1919) used Freud's concept of the infant emerging into a state of secondary narcissism, getting into this state by being able to "identify" with the object and thus having feelings of empathy for the object. Kernberg (1976, pp. 57, 63, 64) uses a similar idea. The mother is a self-object to the infant, according to Kernberg. The mother is also "one" with the child according to Mahler et al (1959). Spitz (1965) thought that there is an absence of an "inner organizer" in the child's mind in the first three months so that the adult has to serve as a buffer, and this is why the mother and child are "one." It is only when "object constancy" is achieved that separateness can be discerned by the child (from 16 to 24 months). This theory, as we shall discuss later, should be discarded in the light of modern infant research.

There has been a tendency to equate "object constancy" with the ability to hold the object in memory when the object is not present. Kohut uses an idea similar to Schaffer's (1958) in relation to object constancy. He contends *it is part of the process of internalization.* This process begins, according to Kohut (1977, p. 86), when the infant or child is "anxious" and the mother comes to comfort him: he feels the mother's touch, hears her voice, and the like "as if this were his own." The following is the order in which the event is experienced: there is mounting anxiety within the self— the signal; the self-object (the mother) performs; this is followed by calmness and absence of anxiety. The "psychological disintegration products that the child had begun to feel when his anxiety increased disappears when the self-objects" (i.e., the mother) performs. Stabilization then begins to take over and the "rudimentary self is reestablished." These are need-satisfying activities performed by the mother, the self-object. The event is and "empathic merger" of the self and the self-object.

Kohut feels that interpretation in psychoanalysis follows a similar pattern —it is a means of relieving anxiety by explanation in the context of empathy. *The analysis is a way of examining "self-development" and "self-experience" in relation to "intrapsychic development."* The analyst joins the patient in self-experiencing; i.e., he becomes the mother rather than remaining neutral as Freud suggested. The mother and child are "fused" in the infant's mind, as in Mahler's symbiotic phase or Freud's anaclitic relationship. As the infant experiences the failures of the mother to respond as he would like (i.e., to fulfill his every need and wish), he gradually "internalizes" the functions that the "self-object," the mother, has performed. This is called "transmutting internalization" by Kohut rather than introjection or identification. Kohut believes that "ego structure" is built up in this way. He postulates a developmental line for narcissism through an "ego ideal" that is the "internalization" of the "idealized self-object," and this provides the basis for the formation of a "cohesive self." The preoedipal phase is then followed by an oedipal period. In this period further structure is acquired to form the ego and superego, the ego ideal being absorbed, so to speak, in the superego. The borderline patient due to his genetic defects and his experience with an inadequate mother does not develop this "cohesive self"; consequently, he does not go on to the object constancy stage.

When the self-object has not performed properly in the child's infancy and the child has been deprived of "merging experience," he will not be able to build psychological structures capable of dealing with anxiety in an adequate way. In the normal course of developmental events the infant gradually takes over the functions of the self-object. Where this is not possible, the child has a lack of normal tension-regulating structures (a weakness in the ability to tame affects), and this results in an inability to curb anxiety. The acquisition of faulty structure then leads to the propensity toward active intensification of affect and the development of states of panic.

Object Constancy, Narcissism, and Early Development

The period of *object constancy* makes its appearance at different times according to different authors. Between 16 and 18 months of age the child has a "sustained mental representation of the mother" so that the child uses his memory and his fantasies to soothe himself, having "internalized" the soothing behavior of the mother. Prior to this he may use an object, i.e., a blanket or a toy animal for this purpose. The theory is, however, that "libidinal object constancy" requires another year.

Some modern theorists, in contrast with classical theorists, say that memory is established by 3 months (Caplan, 1973, pp. 82, 85-87). De Casper (1979, p. 227) seems to have done experiments to indicate that *learning and memory are present at birth*. Object constancy is supposed to be established when the infant can "remember" the object when the object is out of sight. This does not happen, according to psychoanalytic postulations until 16 to 18 months. The theory is that the age at which the child will take "anyone as mother" extends to about 7 months; thus it is up to this point that the mother and child can be considered in Mahler's terms as "an omnipotent symbiotic unity" (Mahler et al, 1959, p. 822). This means that the child does not distinguish between himself and objects so far as his "need-satisfying requirements are concerned." This idea, however, does not conform to recent experiments in development (see Caplan, 1973, pp. 85-91). Mahler says that object constancy is not complete until the beginning of the third year. She describes a crisis in the infant's life associated with the "rapprochement phase" as the child begins to internalize certain events (Mahler et al, 1959). This idea of "crisis" follows Freud's concepts in that he proposed that walking makes the "omnipotent infant" acutely aware of his helplessness and as a consequence he develops "separation anxiety." The mother is then seen as powerful, and the infant feels weak. Mahler states that as the child begins to realize the separateness of himself and the mother, his omnipotence is reduced. Too sudden deflation of this sense of omnipotence and control, however, tends to evoke the grandiose view of the self and idealization of the omnipotent parent. This, according to Mahler, is similar to the *narcissistic defense* described by Kohut (1971). As I understand it, Kohut does not see the "grandiose self" as a defense but as a normal developmental phenomenon. It is Kernberg who thinks of the grandiose self as a defense. If thwarted, this grandiose self remains, says Kohut, and becomes a defect of the "self," due to the deficiencies of the mother and the lack of "transmutting internalizations."

Settlage (1977) contends that we must understand the difference between *object permanence* (Piaget) and *object constancy*, a psychoanalytic concept. In addition to *cognitive representation*, which is inherent in object permanence, object constancy includes the intrapsychic representation of the human love object in "libidinal" and "affective" terms. Caplan (1973, pp. 83-92) reports that the child relates in an "affective" way at 2 and 3 months. At 3 months the baby is beginning to have an image of different people and of himself. Most theorist presume that "absence of the object" and then "presence of the object" or "anger toward the object" and then "good feelings toward the object" mean in intrapsychic terms that the "images of the object" are loving and disapproving, are "good" and "bad," "loved" and "hated." The opposites begin to be registered. Current research tells us that the infant in the first month is able to react to stimuli of both people and objects, but he shows preferences for people over things when people are present (Caplan, 1973, pp. 53-55).

Kohut (1971) writes that normally the "idealized parental image," which is at first undifferentiated from the self, is finally integrated through identification, and separation takes place as the infant begins to experience approval from the mother. At this point "object constancy" has been achieved (12 to 18 months). "Integrated images" are essential, says Kohut, in the formation of object constancy, which is a precursor of the ego ideal and the superego. In the period of object constancy, not only can the child tolerate some separation from the mother, but he can also experience good feelings for the mother, not clinging to her simply as a "need-satisfying object."

The self-object, according to Kohut, is different from how Kernberg (1975) conceives of it; it is the source of the later pleasure we feel when we "obey the dictates of our conscience." This stimulates our need to "live up to our own ideals." Originally, the self-object, as the "grandiose self," is a precursor to the infant's desire to please the parents and to gain approval for them, a forerunner of the capacity to identify. According to Kernberg, the ability to achieve object constancy comes from the infant being able to overcome his aggression through the defense of projective identification and thus to develop some good feelings toward the object. The aggression is tamed through the process of projective identification as delineated by Melanie Klein, and object constancy is finally achieved, during which the infant can begin to identify with the object. The first step is the development of empathic feelings; the second step is an appreciation of what the object does for the infant. Kohut feels that the infant gains self-worth by receiving praise from the mother. He loses self-worth if the mother is depressive and ungiving or disapproving.

Masterson (1972) embraces certain aspects of the theories of Kernberg and Kohut and has a notion based on some of Fairbairn's ideas that he schematizes in relation to the individual's response to an "exciting object," which is also a self-object. He comments on the patient's *fear of abandonment* as a factor in the building of defenses. He believes that true separation from the mother does not take place in the borderline patient. Chessick also emphasizes the patient's fear of abandonment, citing Odier (1956) who speaks of the patient's "neurosis of abandonment." Chessick mentions the patient's oscillations between love and hate, security and insecurity, dependency and paranoia, this latter described by Leuba (1949) as fear of penetration, fear of deception and betrayal based on "overfeeding" and "pseudogiving" accompanied by a "hidden stream of demands." Chessick cites certain ideas of Modell (1963; 1975) regarding the persistence of primitive object relationships as the narcissistic defenses against the "illusion of self-sufficiency" as opposed to a sense of object love and security based on real experiences in a "holding environment" such as is envisioned by Winnicott (1965) to be necessary for the health development of the individual. Chessick also sees value in Winnicott's (1951) concept of the "transitional object phase," the stage of primary narcissism when there is "no object" and the anaclitic or "clinging" stage where the mother becomes the object. Chessick mentions the "intrusiveness of the mother" (Heinmann 1966; Mahler et al, 1975) as an important idea, and he considers that the patient has identifications "of at least some adaptive properties," with "some parental or grandparental figures," stating that sometimes the identifications do not occur until adolescence. He says that up and down the ego axis there are "inherited styles of defense and primary autonomous functions."

Kohut is of the opinion that the borderline is one form of schizophrenia and that the same types of transferences are manifest in the schizophrenias as in the narcissistic character, although schizophrenia is a separate syndrome and possesses tranferences of a different quality. Each represents a "fixation in narcissism" due to the inability of the mother to provide the necessary emotional support for the child. As frustrations occur normally, the child tries to preserve his omnipotence by assigning it to the *grandiose self* and the *idealized parental image*. As the child gradually is able to perform some of the functions that the parent performed, he "internalizes these functions" and they become a part of the "idealization of the self." The self-objects are then given up, and a "structure" begins to form in the individual's mind. There are "self-representations" in relation to the *id*, the *ego*, and later the *superego*. As structure forms, the agencies of the mind are solidified by the "repression barrier" that surrounds each. Expressions of the transference are based, first, on the "grandiose exhibitionistic image of self," a "self-object" which derives from relations with the mother and emerges in treatment as the "mirror transference" and, second, on the "idealized self," also a self-object.

Kohut focuses on the developmental aspects of the "self" and targets his analysis on *self-esteem* in contrast to Kernberg. Kernberg tackles the *defensive operations on the ego*, with special attention being paid to "ego strength," "structural characteristics," and the "pathology of internalized object relationships." He sees the patient's ego defects as (1) an inability to perceive reality, (2) an inability to differentiate object from self, (3) an inability to integrate good and bad in a single person or in the self, and (4) an inability to repress aggression.

Kohut does not specify which "functions" of the ego are missing in the borderline, but he says that the way in which the self-object develops is a vital factor in the formation of the *self-system*, i.e., the manner in which the individual regards himself. *Poor self-esteem* is the main defect in the borderline ego evolving from the relations with a mother who cannot fulfill the role of a caretaking person. Patients lacking in appropriate self-esteem have been *unduly frustrated* by parents lacking in empathy, and they tend to have the following traits: (1) insufficient ego cohesiveness; (2) hypersensitivity; (3) feelings of emptiness; (4) poor tension regulation; (5 hyperexcitability; (6) lack of initiative; (7) problems with aggression; (8) perverse sexual patterns; and (9) search for an anchor. These traits are due to *fixation at the narcissistic stage* that causes the individual to have a tendency toward fragmentation of the self and a perpetuation of the grandiose self rather than a more mature development. *The analyst must create self-esteem* since this has a pivotal function in the emergence of the ego and the superego. Kernberg says that "introjections" are the earliest point of convergency of object relationship and instinctual drive representations and are the essential switches bringing the ego into operational readiness.

It is possible that when Kernberg speaks of "good" and "bad" introjects and of "pathological internalized object relations" in borderline patients, he may be describing in his terms what I refer to as the "identification system"—or, more precisely, the *identification fantasies*,—since I define identification as a defense basic in all neuroses and in all psychoses. I would not use the term "introjection" as applied to the early stages of infant development, nor would I think of the early infant as being able to "identify." In descriptive terms "identification" implies a learned behavior pattern determined by the communications of the parents; in terms of neuroses and psychoses it means a *neurotic behavior pattern provoked by the parents in the service of their own defenses*. When the child adopts the identification pattern, he does so *in defense* so that the patterns, in fact, are an aspect of the child's defensive system. After the behavior becomes a chronic pattern, projective defenses are employed in order to deny the implications of the interlocking defensive family identification system. This process takes time, and the total defensive picture may not be complete before early adolescence. Then the behavior is often erroneously, I believe, considered to be part of the "oddities" that occur in adolescence.

In Melanie Klein's terms, projective identification is a "normal defense" of infancy that sets in motion the process whereby an instinct such as aggression is projected onto another person (the mother) and is then introjected as a "bad object." Later this projection spills over to the father. Since I consider learning to be a different process from what is presumed to be introjection and/or identification and since I do not embrace Klein's formulation, my idea of the dynamics of identification differs from those presumed in the current ideas of borderline pathology just discussed. Identification, in my terms, is the adoption by the child of roles actively projected onto him by both parents; the roles and identifications that they represent are, of course, learned.

It is due to the patient's denial mechanisms that the concept of "splitting" has been introduced, but the concept of "splitting" as a characteristic of the defensive structure of the infant seems to be an esoteric concept. I conceive of splitting as dissociation and therefore an hysterical phenomenon. The infant does not develop hysterical mechanisms although he can "tune in" and "tune out" stimuli (Caplan, 1973, p. 28), and this capacity may be instinctual. This, like certain other characteristics, such as fear and the capacity to imitate, may belong to the self-preservation potentials of the individual, utilized as an element in the implementation of a defense. "Tuning in" and "tuning out" may be related to the "isolating technique," which has a neurophysiological base and which will be discussed later. These together may make it possible for hysterical defenses to be organized. A paper by Kagan (1979b) is of interest here since it speaks of certain behaviors that "emerge" as part of the developmental process and are thus genetically evoked, while other behaviors are "psychologically" determined, i.e., are products of experience in this world. My thought is that whatever the genetic base of the self-preservative behavior, the content both emotional and cognitive is related to experience in this world; thus the psychological significance of the behavior is built out of experience and learning in the life span of the individual.

The concept of "self-object" does not appear to be consonant with the dynamics of infant development as we know it to be today (Wolberg, A., 1977). The infant's "mind" is an organized entity shortly after birth, perhaps before birth, and he not only relates to objects in a most meaningful way, but his behavior demonstrates that he has memory for the effects of his experimentation with the environment (Caplan, 1973).

The conceptual basis of the idea of a "self-object" so prominent in Kernberg's and Kohut's theories derives, first, from Freud's idea of the "anaclitic" relationship and, second, from Melanie Klein's object relations theory, which purports that the "instinct" becomes an "object" in view of the projection of the infant's own aggression and an introjection of the aggression as an object. The instinct is "incorporated" or taken back into the infant's psyche as an object—more precisely a "part object" (Segal, 1964), —by the "normal" process Klein described as projective identification. This is obviously a different approach than the one in my concept of the dynamics of projective identification. The idea that the infant has a symbiotic relationship with the mother (Mahler), or what Freud called the "anaclitic" or "clinging" relationship, implies that the mother and child are a closed system. This is not so in any family. A problem with the concept of "self-object" is that it is modeled after Freud's idea of an "undifferentiated state" where the infant and the exclusive mother are "one." The "undifferentiated state" does not take into consideration the infant's complex autonomous behavior that is present at birth and continues in more and more complicated form as the first year proceeds; nor does it take into account the infant's emotional relations with several others besides the mother in the family and what he learns from these contacts.

I believe that in the borderline we should look at what is being called "pathological internalized object relations" as a phenomenon that in reality is a nest of fantasies (the identification fantasies) sadomasochistic in nature that reflect the sadomasochistic relationships the borderline individual has had with the parents, *over time*, the fantasies disguising the traumatic aspects of the relationships in defense. Part of the conflict of the child is over the "good" and "bad" parts of the parents. It is difficult for the infant and young child to tolerate the "bad" parts because they are life threatening. The neurotic parent is "bad" out of anxiety and the need to maintain a neurotic equilibrium. His "badness" is a controlling mechanism and, in addition, constitutes a way of projecting his own hostile parts onto the child. The parent needs the child to act out a destructive role in order to deny his own destructive needs. Denial is a necessity for the parent. The child does not deny at first; instead he confronts as a self-preservative pro-cess. But he is made to feel guilty and is punished for this confrontation, and soon he sees that he too must deny. This conflict is threatening to him, and he is full of insecurity and anxiety.

The borderline patient projects his identifications because when he acts them out, they are destructive to him. His self-destructive tendencies are based on his identifications with the hostilities of the parents. This is what Freud used to refer to as the "punitive superego," but he interpreted this phenomenon as an internalization of the parents' attempts to control the aggressions of the child. In my view the aggressions do not appear auto-matically; they are evoked by the hostile and inhibiting behavior of the parents due to their neurotic anxieties. The parents use the child as a pro-jective object, as a defense, or, in other words, as a means of expressing their own identifications with their own parents which they wish to deny (Wolberg, A., 1960). The punitive parents force the identifications on to the child. Through shame, and sometimes physical battering, and through sexual seduction (or what Freud might have called incestual impulses) the identifications are played out and finally adopted by the child. This is be-havior that is *learned* rather than the adoption of defense to control bad instincts.

Freud (1923) spoke of "libidinal dangers" that create a reaction of the fear of being overwhelmed or annihilated. These would include the controlling be-havior of the parents. Most authors do not consider the father in this early picture, as I do. According to my understanding of the dynamics of border-line patients and of projective identification, the father is intimately involved along with the mother as an integral part of the family's defensive system, and the infant is a family member at birth, immersed in a group process with all members as well as with relatives and friends. The infant is a mem-ber of a social system, right at the start, and relates to many people and many things, and learning begins a few hours after birth (Wolberg, A., 1977).

Apparently Freud's pleasure-unpleasure principle has validity with re-spect to psychologically, more precisely, environmentally determined (learned) behavior, including identifications with people. We find that nor-mal objects evoke "affects" of pleasure and unpleasure in the infant and that the neurophysiological apparatus receives these messages. Indeed "af-fect" is present from birth on (Caplan, 1973, pp. 54, 71). But "good" and "bad" as ethical concepts meaning "danger" become factors only when there is real danger from the parents' aggressions. The fear reaction, which is phylogenetically determined, appears between 8 and 12 months so that when actual danger is present, anxiety and tension are coupled with fear. How long does it take before fantasies are organized as part of the defense against danger? Perhaps these appear around the age of 2½ or 3 when the child begins to defend against the parents' controlling tendencies and punishments by projecting danger from shadows on the walls, and so forth. As he begins to conceive of "good" and "bad" stimulated by (1) the admonitions of the parents and (2) his own understanding of the reality situation, the superego thus begins to form and is "split," so to say, due to these two elements. The defenses of the parents help them to deny the reality, while the child sees the reality. But the parents insist that the child deny too; so the child resorts to what Geleerd (1965) has called "denial in the service of the need to survive," or what I believe to be the development of identification with the parent (the aggressor) and denial of the identification. The identification would be learned over time, but it is not a function of the learning process itself.

The child begins to defend in this situation by having fantasies that depict his problem of "giving in" to the pressure of the parents to distort reality. He develops sadomasochistic fantasies then, and we find phenomena such as Freud (1919) described in his essay "A Child Is Being Beaten." These fantasies represent the child's "internalizations" of the sadomasochistic experiences with parents and are based on the anxieties associated with the identifications that are beginning to form. They contain the meaning of the child's conflict, which can be ascertained through associations as one would analyze a dream. We give the word "internalization," therefore, a special meaning, distinguishing it as a special kind of learning associated with the process of identification to differentiate it from all other kinds of learning. It is related to defenses against anxiety and the neurotic resolution of conflict. Here we have an instance of the superego as influenced by the parents being "bad" while the id or the phylogenetic schedule aids the self-preservation aspects of the child's behavior. It seems that Kohut's list of symptoms or "traits," while they are descriptive, do not apply across the board. The borderline patient may be "hypersensitive" (somewhat paranoid?), for example, but not in every area; he may "lack initiative," but he can be very successful in his work while being very unsuccessful at home or with friends. These traits operate in selective ways.

Kohut believes that while "narcissistic personalities" can tolerate the transference in treatment, borderlines, due to their particular defects, cannot. In the narcissistic personalities the two main transferences—(1) grandiose or mirror and (2) idealizing—can be worked through because of a certain "cohesiveness of the self," but when these transferences occur in the borderlines, who because of their defects do not have this cohesive self, the threat of "ego shattering" or fragmentation makes the task of working through difficult, if not impossible. The lack of stability in the self is due both to genetic defects, which Kohut does not specify, and early untoward experiences with the mother.

With "narcissistic personalities," as has been mentioned, the inappropriateness of the grandiose fantasy must not be mentioned, says Kohut; therefore, the transference reactions are met by supporting measures. In the grandiose transference "regression is set in motion" by the analytic situation, and the goal is to establish a "narcissistic equilibrium," which the patient feels as "boundless power and knowledge" and as "aesthetic and moral perfection." These attributes are more or less undifferentiated in the therapeutic regression, which leads to "very early fixation points." Just as there is a "cohesive therapeutic revival" of the "idealized self-object" (introject) in the "idealizing transference" in the narcissistic neuroses, "the grandiose self" is therapeutically reactivated in the "mirror transference."

Kohut's grandiose (mirror) transference, I believe, is an aspect of the sadomasochistic pattern (the sadistic side) and has no relation to ego deficits as linked to perception and learning. It does, however, have a definite function in the patient's low self-esteem, his defensive system, i.e., his sadomasochistic interpersonal relations, particularly the masochistic aspects of the personality. If we must talk about an "ego," then we might say that the patient has a sadomasochistic type of ego organization as revealed in his fantasies rther than that he has ego deficits. In a book edited by Goldberg (1978, pp. 227-245) there is a case that is a reminder to those who work with borderline patients that the patterns in acting out are not merely reflections of an early unpropitious environment. It is obvious in the report of this case that even while the patient was attending college, he had a very neurotic relationship with his parents that was sexually tinged. He reported back to them by letter his sexual exploits, writing to them practically every day. (This would be a form of sexual seduction on the part of the parents and an identification on the part of the patient with the parents' sexual perversions.)

In narcissistic personalities (and in borderlines) the "grandiose transference" takes three forms, according to Kohut: (1) the "archaic merger," (2) the less archaic "twinship," and (3) the still less archaic form, the "mirror transference." Kohut believes that grandiosity may be tinged with delusion and that some people, who have special gifts of intellect, in spite of their grandiosity, may succeed in life on the basis of these gifts. The average person who manifests grandiosity, however, may not be able to accomplish this. Kohut refers to Freud and Goethe as people with special gifts. In this context, he cites Eissler (1963) who commented on Freud's paper "A Childhood Recollection" (1917) and who also mentions Goethe's autobiography *Dichtung und Wahrheit*.

Kohut believes that as the analyst helps the patient acquire the missing elements in his ego, the aggression abates and the analysis of aggression becomes easier. The "mother is a "longed-for object," an object with whom the patient desires "fusion." During psychotherapy the object is not only longed for, but also is *needed* in order to develop the ego functions that were not established in childhood. Kohut is correct in assuming that if one works with the low self-esteem (the masochism) first, the aggression will reduce somewhat. The anger will still have to be analyzed and the revenge patterns with which the anger is finally associated attended, but this can be done at a later date. This tactic seems to be in line with the findings of Whitehorn and Betz (1960) and Betz (1962).

Kernberg (1975, p. 226) disagrees with Kohut regarding the origin of the *grandiose self*, which Kernberg refers to as a "pathological self-structure," also a "self-object," and which he says is the same as Rosenfeld's (1965) "omnipotent mad self." Kohut regards the "mad self," or its equivalent, as a *fixation* of the "archaic normal primitive self." Kernberg, however, considers it a reflection of a *pathological structure*, clearly different from normal narcissism in early normal development; he views the "grandiose self" as a *structure that is defective and different from birth* in the borderline case (Kernberg, 1975, pp. 133-134).

Kohut's activation of the grandiose self to help the patient achieve full awareness of it, is, according to Kernberg, an "emphasis on libidinal conflicts with an almost total disregard of the vicissitudes of aggression." This, in Kernberg's opinion, interferes with a systematic interpretation of the defensive functions of the grandiose self.

Kernberg argues that initially the patient must be made aware of his need to devalue and depreciate the analyst as an independent object, which, as Melanie Klein insisted (1946, 1950), he does in order to protect himself from retaliation. According to Kernberg, the aggression is a "projected sadistic reaction" that stimulates fear of retaliation in the patient activated by "real or fantasized frustrations" from the object. Fear, because of the patient's attack on the analyst as a primitive "giving" or "ungiving object," is an important "mother transference" against which narcissistic resistance has been erected. This transference needs to be explored and interpreted systematically, right at the beginning. Kernberg views the hatred of the mother as a projection of the infant's own excessive oral aggression, and this is extended to the father as well (Kernberg, 1975, p. 41). Thus the aggression is irrational, and genetically determined.

Aggression in my viewpoint, as already stated, is evoked in the child by the parents who are projecting their own aggression onto the child. The parents' aggressions, however, are defensive and are connected with identification fantasies. These fantasies are not only defenses in themselves, but are at the same time depictions in symbolized form of the identifications the parents had with their own parents, representing the *interpersonal relations*, sadomasochistic in nature, that produced the identifications. Projective identification, therefore, has to do with a son or daughter's denial of hated identifications with parental figures, parents who in reality through sado-masochistic interpersonal encounters, over time, demanded the identifications in the interests of their own neurotic defenses. In turn, when these sons or daughters become parents, they project their unwanted identifications onto their children and others with whom they are ordinarily related. There seems to be a consciousness on the part of the patient to act out sadistic impulses. My patient Mabel Claire, for example, had the idea that she might act with hostility if she had children, and she did. Another patient, Flora O'Toole Levy, had similar feelings, and she acted out over the years in hostile ways with her sons. There is, in the evocation of projective identifications, three elements: (1) the parents use of each other as projective instruments, (2) the parents use of their children as projective objects enmeshing them in their defensive needs and (3) the parents use of "others" as projective objects. In the case of their own children, parents can control the situation through punishment and reward and eventually, over time, stimulate the kinds of roles they need. In the case of "others," they do not have this control. It is possible, of course, to find others who will engage in the sadomasochistic encounter, but usually this occurs only when the individual settles into an intimate relationship where the pattern can be used coordinately for neurotic purposes. Those who do not fit into these patterns do not have intimate relations with borderlines, but the borderline may project onto and act out his neurotic needs toward these "others" in any case.

The "ungiving projection" that Kernberg refers to in transference is, in his terms, a manifestation of oral aggression. This is an unrealistic picture of what the parents are like and thus is not a manifestation of identification. In my way of thinking, while not an exact duplicate of a real experience, this "ungiving projection" is a symbolized reproduction of the kind of relationship the child actually had with the parent. On occasion the patient may try to duplicate real experiences, as the patient who detailed his sexual exploits to his parents seems to have done (Goldberg, 1978, pp. 224-245). We may talk of this phenomenon as being a mother or a father transference or a fusion of both since both parents at times were ungiving and hostile.

Grandiosity, in my opinion, is a defense, but it is a defense that is organized much later in life than in infancy; it is a defense that helps the patient submerge (repress) some of his feelings of self-contempt as well as his anger and revenge feelings. I agree with Chessick (1977, pp. 112, 115) that the sophistication attributed to the infant at ages 6 to 7 months is highly speculative. That the infant actually "envies," is full of "oral aggression," possessed of "fantasies of power and beauty," "grandiose and controlling," "filled with love and hate," and so forth are projections of adult ways onto an infant.

The popular ideas that the infant's mind has no organizing capacity and is unintegrated due to aggression appears also to be an error. The infant learns from birth; he has preferences; he sees patterns of objects as wholes; memory is firmly established; he communicates right from the start in various ways—eye contact, crying, withdrawal by falling asleep, gesturing, and smiling. Apparently in later papers Kernberg has had second thoughts about aggression saying that the infant "seeks love as power" but it is the adult who "seeks beauty" equating it with security.

According to Kohut (1971, pp. 56-66), the personality of the "mother" in the early phase of development is more important than gross environmental events such as separation from the object by such contingencies as death or divorce. In normal development "firming and buttressing of the psychic apparatus," especially in the areas of the establishment of "reliable ideals," takes place during latency and puberty (8 to 12 years) with a decisive final step in late adolescence, i.e., during the period of "object loss." "However crushing this may be," the object loss will be tolerated by the firm ego, but where the mothering person has failed in her functioning, the resultant ego lacunae do not permit a "firming." This is the case with the borderline patient.

Chessick (1977) has written an excellent summation of the various developmental systems presented by Mahler, Kohut, Kernberg, and others. These systems do have a relevance to understanding the borderline patient, but they do not reflect, in my opinion, what actually happens in infancy. All follow the modern practice of transferring some of Freud's ideas of sexual development into nonsexual terms and relating them to the ego. This has not helped to clarify psychoanalytic theory. Freud's brilliance is not reflected in this concept of ego development. It is a fact, however, that they have repeated his errors in the face of overwhelming evidence that some of his speculations could not possibly be true. Freud did recognize an "innate schedule" in development, but his concept of what appears as a consequence of the genetic code, such as sadomasochism and aggression, does not always coincide with what modern theorists are advancing as aspects seen in infant and early behavior (Kagan, 1979b). The "innate schedule" does unfold regardless of what happens to the child as a result of environment, and there are thus appearances of certain behaviors at certain periods. Sadomasochism, however, does not seem to be one of those innate factors, and aggression will appear only after a great deal of frustration. *Sadomasochism seems to be a learned response after much conditioning in relations with neurotic parents.*

In psychoanalysis the assumption is that the theory of infantile sexuality is correct, and any proposition ritualistically must fit into this aspect of the libido concept (even when the theory does not make any sense); otherwise the individual who is practicing is not considered to be a psychoanalyst. This is a problem for many who treat borderline patients since the current idea among most analysts is that the borderline syndrome is a preoedipal problem, the "fixation period" occurring in the first year—or at the most the first year and a half. Within this framework there are many mystical ideas that have thrown psychoanalysis off balance in its efforts to be scientific. The grandiosity of the infant is one such idea, and the theory of primary and secondary narcissism with their accompanying primary fantasies is another divergent side step. In actual fact the infant is very busy learning and can be said to be preoccupied in the first few months after birth with getting movements organized in a way that will make it possible to cope with the environment. As a means toward this end, the infant is a social being right from the start.

Freud actually discovered, early in his studies, the relation of identification to parental and neurotic behavior, but when he realized that his insight meant that the parent had to play a primary rather than secondary role in the development of the child's neurosis and particularly his sexual problem, he could not accept the idea. Freud resolved his dilemma by making identification a developmental phenomenon as well as recognizing that at times it could be a defense. It is my opinion that the parents' sexual use of the child is the source of the child's sexual problem and that it is the basis of the perverse traits that we find in borderline patients. Milton Klein has written a paper (in press, *Bulletin of the Menninger Clinic*) that discusses seduction as a factor in the neuroses and psychoses.

Psychoanalysts have been preoccupied over the years in their efforts to understand identification with questions such as whether the infant "loves" since love for another person is a "high-level emotion" or whether the infant merely engages in "object relations" with empathy or with some small regard for the "other" as a precursor to identification. Sometimes the arguments pro and con regarding love remind one of the old philosophical discussions about how many angels can dance on the point of a pin. The problem of early development is contaminated with various concepts of how the individual emerges from his "narcissistic state" to feel some warmth or "love" for other people. There are many points of divergence among psychoanalytic writers concerning the transition from "pure narcissism" to the state of "object relatedness." Actually, the infant is "object-related" a few hours after birth. He is "related" and he "emotes" over his relationships with objects. Those authors who agree that the borderline patient has no identification system and therefore is not a person who can care for another and that he has a split ego and therefore is fragile also agree that the transference is a "narcissistic" one rather than one that would be the consequence of identification. The fact is the patient is self-centered out of anger and rage, but he is also "identified" with parental figures.

Kohut contends that the borderline's fragile ego makes the patient psychosis prone due to the lack of a *cohesive self*. According to Kernberg, the borderline is psychosis prone due to a lack of ability to integrate "good" and "bad" introjects. Narcissistic injuries in the borderline, says Kohut, may usher in a regressive movement which tends to go beyond the stage of archaic narcissism, beyond the forms of the cohesive grandiose self and the idealized parental image. This leads to the stage of "autoerotic fragmentation" and the threat of psychosis (an idea based on Freud's developmental concepts and his notion of regression). The individual acquires a schizoid "defense" (Kohut, 1975, p. 27) which is the result of a "preconscious awareness of his fragile ties," but this does not come from the patient's inability to love. Kohut makes a distinction between (1) the "admiration and/or contempt transference," a "lower level transference" with respect to ego organization, being preoedipal in nature where there is not yet true love, and (2) the "love-hate transference" as in the case where the patient has a "well-delimited cohesive sense of self, associated with a massively introjected internal replica of the oedipal object" and thus a "higher level" ego structure. The borderline patient has the admiration/ contempt transference; because of this, Kohut believes, he cannot tolerate psychoanalytic procedures.

Kernberg uses a similar idea when he says that the "low-level" borderline patient has no identification system since this assumes some "love" for the object. Kernberg, however, apparently does feel that the borderline patient *can* respond to psychoanalytically oriented procedures with supportive measures added. Kohut believes that the patient is capable of empathic feeling, while Kernberg doubts this. Kohut recognizes that in treatment the therapist may feel "tyrannized" by the patient's expectations and demands; he calls this a manifestation of the therapist as a "narcissistic object" for the patient. I would think that this is obviously a hostile transference based on an identification with the aggressors (parents) who have fostered this type of identification over time. Tyrannization is the sadistic side of the patients' sadomasochistic transference where the patient is acting out the role of the controlling parent (the obsessive anxiety of the parent) and using the analyst as if he were the guilty child. Kohut contends that in neurosis the adult personality is "impoverished," and realistic activities are hampered by the breakthrough and intrusion of the "archaic ego structure," which is related to the suppressed and unintegrated "grandiose and idealizing selves," the two transferences that must be analyzed. While Kohut speaks of "selves" that have not been integrated, Kernberg considers that there are two "ego states" that have not been integrated. They are "nonmetabolized introjects" that provide the stimulus for the transferences. I believe that the transference is based on the sadomasochistic pattern that develops in the relations with parents, as the parents, in defense, use the child as a transferential object, that is, they use the child as an object of displacement while communicating the kind of roles they wish the child to act out, denying this all the time and demanding that the child also deny that such an identification process is occurring. The borderline patient always acts out the transference in some particular way in the beginning of therapy.

Kernberg considers the aggression that Kohut describes as "tyrannizing" or demeaning to the therapist as "oral." This type of transference does not lend itself to immediate analysis. An example of how patients displaying such transference attempt to involve the analyst in a sadomasochistic pattern at the start of therapy can be seen in the case previously cited in Goldberg (1978, pp. 224-245). The patient tries to interest the analyst in his sexual acting out as an observer, or perhaps one might more accurately say as a kind of Peeping Tom, a role that his parents obviously played out with him. The patient in the beginning of treatment was not engaging in analysis but was trying to seduce the analyst into a sexually perverse game that would knock him out of his therapeutic role.

Many types of patients relate to the analyst in the beginning phase of therapy by playing a sadomasochistic game of some kind, trying to involve the analyst in an interlocking defensive system as he himself was involved by his parents. Many analysts do not understand this kind of acting out in the transference, and when the patient acts toward the analyst in an aggressive way or in an appeasing way to induce him to respond defensively, the analyst's reaction is countertransferential. In the case just mentioned the analyst obviously let the patient know that he was not particularly interested in playing the role of Peeping Tom by listening to the patient's sexual exploits and reading his erotic notes. This was a valid response. The analyst did so in such a way that the patient could understand that he was not being rejected, even though he was acting out a sexually perverse pattern. The relation to the parents was not particularly stressed since this was a beginning phase of treatment. The case was discussed, however, in the Goldberg text in the light of Kohut's theory and the transference was said to be an aspect of the "grandiose self." The implication was that the patient's sexual provocations were really a residual manifestation of a developmental phase, the grandiose exhibitionistic phase, that had been unrequited in infancy. The analyst *should* have reacted as the mother, it was said. I believe he acted correctly in the first place, different from how the real mother acted, not only in the patient's early childhood but how she was still acting when the patient was an adult and out in the world earning his own living. The father, it appeared to me, was in an interlocking defensive relationship with the mother, an aspect of which determined the patient's preoccupation with sexual matters. Thus the transference could be seen as a combination of mother and father projecting onto the analyst.

Mahler accepts the concept of splitting as a defense in the early stages of infancy, and she supports the Kleinian concept. She believes that splitting drops out toward the end of the second year of life when the major part of the infantile hostility toward the parent is submerged by repression with only a "normal degree of ambivalence" as a factor representing "good" and "bad" internalization of the object. The borderline patient, according to Mahler, has not reached this stage. According to Kohut, in the latter part of the preoedipal period there is a point where the "repression barrier" is formed, between the relatively structured ego and the id. It is during what Mahler has called the oedipal period that the superego is formed, then the repression barrier normally surrounds id, ego, and the superego. For Kohut, Kernberg, Mahler, Masterson, and others the borderline patient has not reached this stage of repression.

The formation of the repression barrier between ego, id, and superego Kohut calls a "horizontal split." He goes on to say that the narcissistically disturbed patient has a "vertical split," which means that the archaic grandiose exhibitionistic self and the archaic idealized self-object are walled off from consciousness (by fixation), i.e., by dissociation, and *denied* as opposed to the repression acquired normally at the end of the preoedipal period. In "fixation" the idealized object is still fused with the "self" and does not become absorbed in the ego as in normal developmental procedure. The self-object remains as a separate entity expressed in fantasy that interferes with healthy "narcissistic development." As a consequence of the "fixation," the "grandiose exhibitionistic self" and "archaic or voyeuristic idealizing self-object" are evoked in treatment in the transferences projected onto the analyst. Kohut states that actually this is not transference in the ordinary neurotic sense of the word *since the analyst is a self-object*, part of the patient's "self." It is as though the analyst were a "body part," having no separate existence. The "mirror transferences," such as (1) the merger—"the self-object with the grandiose self"—and (2) "the twinship" —the alter ego of the "mirror" in the narrow sense of the word, functionally are to be understood in the developmental sense in ascending order. The transference proceeds from the "mirror type" to the "idealizing" phase, and there are alternations of the two. The analyst acting as the good or perfect mother gives the patient the opportunity to experience the normal developmental phases that the patient missed, as an infant and young child, thus enabling him to absorb the bifurcated "selves" into the *real self* and further develop the ego, removing the "vertical split" and transforming the primitive narcissism into the more mature forms. Apparently, this can happen only with the narcissistic personalities and not the borderlines. The latter remain "split" and cannot tolerate the analysis of transferences (Kohut, 1971, p. 220). In analysis the "primary defect" in the structure of the "self" is healed by the acquisition of new structures through "transmutting internalization."

Kohut believes that in childhood borderlines try to cover up their depression through erotic and grandiose fantasies. They try "self-stimulation" when the appropriate kind of stimulation is not forthcoming from the mother. I believe that the parents do stimulate the child sexually through their perverse habits and that there is a sexual response on the part of the child. The parent's stimulation or sexual use of the child changes as the child grows older, and the projections or the displacements seen in the sexual acting out with the child take many and varied forms. There is also a nonsexual use of the child, that also leads to acting out of an identification role, a denied role. There are various forms of projection in both types of transferential use of the child (a projection is a denied form of transference). For the borderline patient there is both verbal and nonverbal communication to indicate the kind of role that the parents project. There is, for example, the monster, the idiot child, the pervert (and there are various forms of this perverse behavior), the girl who acts like a boy, the boy who acts like a girl, the liar, the cheat, and so on and so on. The results of these projections are particularly noticeable in homosexuals (who tend to sexualize most relationships), in patterns of excessive masturbation, in fantasies of pederasty, and so forth. The mental defenses against these acted-out patterns are found in romantic ideas, in demanding notice from others, in fantasies of weakness, in hypochondriacal fantasies.

Internalization, Psychic Structure, and Character Structure

The problem of understanding how experience becomes registered in the mind, how it relates to development, and how this influences the possiblity of "good" or "bad" relations with others has been explained in many ways from the psychoanalytic point of view, but the basic premise involves the processes of *identification* and *internalization*. There is presumably a "normal" form of identification. In the earliest phase of development this process has been conceived of as "incorporation," in the next phase as "introjection," and finally as "identification." The most confusing concept in this theory is that of incorporation, a special form of introjection. It is a taking into the mind the attributes of another person in the sense of "orally engulfing these and swallowing them." A change in personality occurs, and the person becomes like someone else by "fantasied oral consumption" (Moore & Fine, 1968, p. 52).

The theory of how the "external" (experience) becomes a mental representation is delineated in the concept of *internalization*. There are two definitions of internalization, a very broad one and a more narrow concept that is, in fact, similar to a conditioning process (Moore & Fine, 1968, p. 57). Each has a basic tenet, however, a concept of relationship with objects and the idea of substituting or incorporating "inner for outer controls." Spitz (1966) spoke of the "no-yes" phenomenon as being an important first step in this process, which involves the mother and her permissions and prohibitions, an idea similar to Kohut's. The concepts, on the group level, of survival of the species, social institutions, and interpersonal relations and, on the individual level, of memory, symbol formation, decisional phenomena, thought, fantasy, isolation, and projection are all involved in the broad definition of internalization. Thus there is a plethora of concepts and a great confusion of ideas. As a result, information from one discipline becomes misapplied in another. It is also in this area that the individual versus the group becomes a conceptual difficulty. The developmental system and its various universes (physical, mental, genetic) have been translated and retranslated into various "scientific" schemes. Social institutions are conceived of as being in the broader "no-yes" category representing the guidelines of society with respect to cultural norms. Such an idea is only partly correct, for not all social institutions represent the best norms for behavior in the society. Like fathers and mothers, social institutions can be "good" or "bad" or a mixture of both good and bad. Durkheim introduced the concept of "collective representations," social institutions being one aspect of the entities that are in toto the "culture" of a given society. When Freud decided that psychoanalysis could explain society as well as the dynamics of emotional disorders and the treatment thereof, he went into speculations that sociologists and anthropologists could not accept.

According to Schaefer (1968, p. 9), internalization means all those processes by which the subject transforms real or imagined regulatory interactions with his environment and real or imagined characteristics (of others) into "inner regulations and characteristics." One can see that the autonomous behavior, the creative process, problem solving, or learning by one's self are not stressed here; what is favored are imitation, conditioning, and identification. Learning from repetition through the admonitive behavior of others seems to be the essence of Schaefer's concept of internalization. Schaefer first alleges "object" and "self" are one. Then from 8 to 13 months of age (at 7 months the infant has left the period where he will accept anyone as mother) the mother becomes the focus of the infant's "object relations." As yet, the infant has not established a lasting memory of the mother in a way sufficient to soothe him when the mother is not there, but he has transitional objects (people and things) that he can use as her substitute. Around 15 months (the first part of the rapproachment sub-phase) change that has been gradually accruing over time is seen in force in the child who tries to feed the mother and give her gifts, acting toward the mother as the mother has acted toward the child. This process began in rudimentary form between 8 and 13 months in the "no-yes" process (in Piaget's Stage IV [1954] and Mahler's separation-individuation phase [1971]). When the mother leaves the infant and comes back and when she says "no" and "yes," these experiences make him understand some of his separateness; he begins to say "no" and "yes" to others.

Various writers have placed the capacity to experience or recognize self from 2 months to 2 years. Spitz proposes that in the "no-yes" period, identifications begin, both identification with the "aggressor" and identification with the "good object" so that the "good" and "bad" object concept takes form. Identification means acting like the mother with regard to behavior related to "yes" and "no." Some modern experimenters, on the other hand, believe that self-awareness begins at 3 months (Caplan, 1973, p. 85).

Kohut, as has been indicated, also emphasizes the importance of the character of the mother rather than the instincts of sexuality and aggression as do Klein and Kernberg. They place little emphasis on the characteristics of the mother or the influence of the environment; they stress, instead, the infant's own defenses, or lack of them, against the instinct of aggression.

We have mentioned that psychoanalytic developmental theory emphasizes the change that occurs between 7 and 15 months of age. According to the theory, this includes the important transition from a feeling of omnipotence that the infant has as the mother administers to him in his "need satisfying period" (i.e., the period when the infant conceives of his mother as an extension of himself) to the "separate" but "weak feeling" that develops as the infant recognizes his helplessness and develops a high consideration for the object. Around the eighth month the child has begun to suffer some "separation anxiety," but he is able to soothe himself with "transitional objects," (such as a teddy bear, or toys, or a blanket) and with brief memory or fantasies of the mother. Some analysts utilize Piaget's idea of Stage IV (around 8 to 13 months), where the infant will look for a toy if it is shown to him and then hidden, to establish the age when separation begins to take place. It is not until the end of the sensorimotor stage (18 months), however, that a true sustained mental representation of the mother is presumed to be present, according to Piaget (1954). In the period up to 18 months the child has learned to soothe himself by substitute objects and fantasies. Piaget puts the beginning of the "appearance-disappearance" phenomenon at 8 to 13 months. In the beginning the infant will look for a toy if it is hidden, but it may be only at 13 months (perhaps 12 to 15 months) before he will actually find the toy. When he is able to locate the toy, this will mean that he will have reached a state where he can keep the memory of the toy in his mind long enough to search and discover. This, then, ushers in the period of object constancy and object permanence.

Some authors believe that the period that leads to object constancy also is the beginning of the secondary stage of narcissism. It is perhaps important to remember that it is at this 8 month period also that the phylogenetically determined fear response is said to come into operation.

The borderline, Kernberg insists, is different from birth by virtue of his aggression. Anger is his basic emotion. He is unable to *relate* to people due to his aggression, but it seems to me that the capacity for relationship is a "given." By the age of 2 months the infant is immensely aware of human beings when they are in his presence. We do not know that the borderline patient is any different from other children in infancy. Actually, shortly after birth the infant relates and is emotional in the relationship with others. Plutchik (1962, 1970) has been working on a phylogenetic theory of emotion. In the case of aggression he uses the word *destruction*. A low degree of this emotion would be "annoyance," a more extreme form "anger," and the most extreme form "rage" (Kellerman, 1979, pp. 32-33). I believe that the aggression has an instinctual base, but as Harlow (1976) and Eibl-Eibesfeldt (1974) suggest it must be stimulated by external forces. We must remember that in the most final stages of defense "rage" becomes converted into *revenge feelings* in the borderline condition. The individual gets back his self-respect through revenge. It is the degree of frustration-aggression that is stimulated in the situation that is the basis for understanding these various degrees of aggression. One of the most distressing effects of aggression is in the symptoms of masochism. Masochism may be attenuated if the individual is able to strike out actively at someone else. The young child, however, will hit at himself if he is restrained from striking at a person in his anger, and this reaction can be encouraged by parents who are defending against or denying their own aggression.

It is my belief that the more restricted definition of "internalization" refers to identifications with *parental figures*, which in the case of the borderline patient, are aspects of the parental neurosis that are projected onto the child as a role which he is impelled through punishment and reward to accept. The "internalization" is a learned response to the neurotic needs of the parent. This is a special case in learning. All other internalizations, I believe, should simply be called responses to the environment or *learning*, which includes all that the person absorbs in relations with others or with any type of "object." In psychoanalysis we are interested primarily in the learning that has to do with developing neuroses and psychoses and with the autonomous behavior that helps to resolve these difficulties. In masochism one finds a great deal of "self-reference," the opposite being the grandiose feeling of self-importance, associated with sadistic impulses.

Self-Reference What is called *self-reference in interactions with others* and a need to be admired and loved is considered to be an "unmetabolized" aspect of a primitive self-object, a residual of what Kohut sees as a normal development gone wrong due to the deficiencies of a neurotic and/or psychotic mother. Kernberg attributes the problem to a genetic defect evidenced by a split in the mind which deprives the patient of the ability to integrate the good and bad of objects, the patient having haughty, grandiose, and controlling behavior toward those from whom he expects little and an idealizing attitude toward those from whom he expects most. The haughtiness and grandiosity are defenses, according to Kernberg, against paranoid traits that emerge due to the projection of innate oral rage. The main defenses against oral rage are splitting, denial, idealization, and omnipotence. There are also periods of derealization and depersonalization that are frightening to the patient because they blot him out, as well as his surroundings, for brief periods.

It seems to me that "self-reference" means, "Bring the focus back to me." This furthermore means, "Let me control the situation; otherwise my defenses will be penetrated and you will harm me." Also "If I lose my control over you, I will have to face myself, which I do not wish to do. You must play the game my parents played with me for this is how I survived." There are fears of engulfment if these defenses are disturbed. If the individual gets into a close or intimate relationship, he will have to be submerged in the other person as he was with his parents. He defends against that possibility. *Twinship*, as Kohut uses the term, apparently can mean identifying with the illness of another person; or it can indicate a normal relationship. Being "submerged" is interpreted to mean that the borderline patient has not left the symbiotic stage of development. To me, "submerged" means that the individual has, over time, accepted the sadomasochistic position and he finds he cannot, due to his guilt, step out of that kind of role. His anxiety would be too great if he were to act in a more normal or rational way. It is not that he is not "separate," for he acts in many ways as a separate individual. It is that his conditioning is sadomasochistic, and even though he wishes to give up the pattern, his guilt causes him so much anxiety that he hesitates. Coming for therapy, however, is a first step in the effort to relinquish the sadomasochistic pattern.

"Self-reference" is associated with fear, suspiciousness, paranoid feelings, fears of engulfment, counterphobic mechanisms, inhibitions, and so on. These are the kinds of characteristics that Chessick, Modell, Odier, and Leuba describe. The implication is that the patient has been so disappointed by the parents and their lack of regard, their lying, and their deceits that he is suspicious of everyone. These traits would be associated then with transference feelings. The patients would not trust anyone suspecting that everyone would be like their unreliable parents. It has been my experience that borderline patients are not so suspicious as to remain aloof from people. They do have relationships and primarily with members of the opposite sex. They are not loners, or isolates, although their relationships are of a sadomasochistic nature.

Revenge   There are many ways that the borderline patient acts out the revenge problem in the transference with the analyst. The patient also has *fears* of acting out revenge. Daird (see Wolberg, A., 1973, p. 174) was afraid he might attack a child sexually, and George Frank Quinn (p. 172) feared he might strangle his girlfriend. Revenge can be evident in passivity and "spoiling" (undoing?). For example, one patient (passively) made innumerable mistakes as an editor and let books be printed with errors in the hundreds. There are certain patients who confront the analyst with their open aggression from the beginning: they deride, taunt, attack, and demean. I am inclined to view such overt attacks as symptoms of schizophrenia rather than of borderlineness. Such patients have definite paranoid trends that are persistent rather than fleeting, as in the case with borderlines. There are certain patients who express the idea that they wonder if the analyst can "take it," i.e., can survive their aggression. If one believes, as Melanie Klein did, that the mother must "withstand" the infant's aggression if both are to come out of the parent-child relationship intact, then one could see a parallel between the "battering infant" and the patient who as an adult beats verbally at the analyst; but Klein's idea seems farfetched and unrealistic. It is the parent who projects aggression onto the child rather than the infant who reacts with raw innate irrational rage.

Fears of Annihilation and Abandonment in Relation to Aggression
The patient's efforts to hold onto his "grandiose self" (I consider this an aspect of his sadism or revenge feelings) and his efforts to avoid acknowledging the analyst as an independent autonomous person, according to Kernberg, consistently reveal his defenses against (1) his "intense envy," (2) the feared relationship with the hated and the "sadistically perceived mother image" (his projection), and (3) his dread of the sense of empty loneliness were he to be separated from his object, a contingency that the patient feels would create for him a world devoid of meaning. Behind the "disappointments" in the parents is the "devaluation of the parental images." Devaluing the analyst in an effort to eliminate him as an important object who would otherwise be feared and envied because the patient is so

dependent and so desperately needs to rely on an object is a characteristic function of the rage reaction, according to Kernberg. It would be my thought that the patient would hang on to his rage in order to defend against his masochism, which is a function of devalued self-esteem. In this way he can avoid the feeling of having been *used* and therefore *rejected* as a person in his own right by his parents; he can seek out a sadomasochistic relationship with the analyst (in transference) and with others to help sustain yet contain his anger and revenge feelings. The patient fears being alone, according to my view, for he will then turn his aggression on himself. It is true that the patient has envy, but this is envy of others who do not have the *inhibitions* that he has or who are not driven by revenge feelings and sadism. I do not agree with Klein's proposition that envy is a function of an early stage of infancy.

Masterson (1972, 1976) has written several books on the borderline patient. He has elaborated his ideas about adolescent borderlines as well as the adult patient. His general thesis (Masterson, 1976) is that the mother is threatened by and is unable to cope with the infant's emerging individuality due to her fears of abandonment; therefore, she clings to the child to prevent separation, discouraging moves toward other individuals by withdrawing her support. In relation to this idea, he has a scheme based on some of Fairbairn's concepts (1954) concerning a "withdrawing object relations unit" (WORU) and a "rewarding object relations unit" (RORU) and the transferences expressed in the service of the relations to these objects. Fairbairn spoke of (1) the tantalizing mother, (2) the rejective, angry, authoritarian, antilibidinal mother, and (3) the emotionally neutral, morally idealized mother. "Ego splitting" was a reaction to the experiences with these mothers. (The same designations I find can be attributed to the father although each parent has his own unique combination of these characteristics.) The idea of special relation with the mother is reminiscent of Kohut's idea that the mother reacts either positively or negatively to the infant's "grandiose self" and that this has a relation to high or low self-esteem. This seems a rational thesis, but I believe we should include the father as well in this picture. It is not the mother, per se, but the *family group and its defensive system, including the special rearing techniques used, that are the important conditioning factors.* Is it not possible that the parents fear abandonment due to their need for an object upon whom to express and project their rage and revenge feelings? Does not denial occur because of the fears the child has of the parents' aggressions and his own counteraggressions, and the dangers these pose?

Like Kohut and Kernberg, Masterson considers the borderline patient psychosis prone and cites the kind of situation that he believes might "throw" the patient over the border. He says, for example, that a patient might attack the therapist by projecting on him the WORU image of the mother. If the therapist is passive, as in classical psychoanalysis, the therapist's action will "so correspond to the patient's projection of his withdrawing maternal part-image that the patient will not be able to distinguish between his WORU projection and the reality of the therapist's behavior. Consequently, he may enter a transference psychosis. This will activate the RORU unit which the patient has denied and experienced as egosyntonic so it will produce resistance and therapy will stop" (Masterson, 1976, p. 108).

Unlike Fairbairn, Freud could not credit parents with "blame" for the child's emotional ,problems. Most analysts today "blame" the mother for the borderline's difficulties. The only passage in Freud's writing I have discovered that refers to the possible hostility of the parent and the counterhostility of the child, is in the essay on "Female Sexuality" (Freud, S. E., 1931, p. 237). There is no reference to the "unconscious hostility" of the father. Fear of the parents may well be the sourse of the child's first projections and displacements, and it is certainly the basis for his identifications, especially those that impel neurotic behavior. But I believe that the projections or fantasies of the father must be considered as well as the mother's fantasies, recognizing the interlocking defensive system between the parents (Wolberg, A., 1960, pp. 170-184; 1973, pp. 102-114). The *fantasies* become a stimulus for the acting-out patterns of the borderline patient, and they are activated in situations where the individual has felt demeaned.

Fenichel (1945) suggested that the neurotic person has a fear of *annihilation*. This seems a likely possibility in the borderline since it is the *aggression* (the patient's own as well as the parents' and the aggression of others) that creates fear and the need for defense. Before the destructive tendencies are worked through, the borderline patient dreads being alone with his own destructive fantasies since he fears turning on himself, or running out to find another person (a stranger) with whom to act out. Turning on the self (displacement) in the absence of another figure is a mechanism that may be genetically determined and related to frustration. When birds are frustrated, they turn to displacement behavior; the same is true of animals. When infants and small children are frustrated from expressing anger, they turn on themselves in fury (see Wolberg, A., 1973, note 2, pp. 123-124). Harlow's (1976) frustrated monkeys showed these tendencies, too. Freud mentioned this kind of reaction on the part of children.

It may well be that the child fears annihilation from the parents as they express their aggression, especially in the early years (from 1 to 5), and that is why fears and aggression are exaggerated and disguised in dreams and fantasies. The feelings of annihilation, according to some psychoanalytic theorists, are due to fears of separation from the mother. I suggest that such a fear is based on the knowledge that the parents' aggression is dangerous and certainly forthcoming if the child steps out of his assigned identification role, just as Roxanne had need to fear but, nevertheless, tried to save herself, even at the age of 3 years (see Wolberg, A., 1973, pp. 12-13).

In my opinion, the child's feelings of danger are based on fears that love is a tenuous and feeble matter and is no safeguard against annihilation by aggression. Freud thought that every type of fear is related to anxiety and that all anxieties are based on an original prototype of danger, but the *content* of the fears of danger change as the individual advances in age. "Loss of love" inspires guilt feelings in the child. One who does not receive love is a hated person, thus a "bad" person who does not deserve love. There is ambivalence, however, in the borderline patient, for he is not completely rejected. He is sufficiently rejected, nevertheless, to arouse not only fear but also rage and revenge. And he fears his own rage. Thus, my patient James Weber, a psychologist, feared he might not be able to function with patients due to his withdrawal and detachment defenses and his impulse to tease and express aggression (revenge feelings). He was correctly seeing these traits as a detriment in establishing a working relationship with patients and with other people as well. At one moment he felt he could never be free of these traits and thus would need a supervisor for the rest of his life if he were to become a therapist. The supervisor would protect his patients by keeping him in line. He often attempted in the analysis to make me into his supervisor rather than allowing me to be his analyst. At other moments he felt capable on his own.

Masterson (1976) speaks of the "reunion fantasy" as an aspect of the RORU transference. Kohut has a "reunion" concept in his "fusion" and merging idea. Kohut sees the "reunion" as fulfilling a need that has been unsatisifed—it is expressed in a longing for a mother who can help create the needed ego functions. This is related to self-reference and narcissistic feelings. While it is true that the borderline patient's mother interferes with the child's autonomous and self-actualizing behaviors due to her conflicts and anxieties, the father does this as well. In each case the parents interfere either by activity or through default or by both kinds of behavior. On the surface it might appear as though the parents need a substitute figure for their parents in the child. But, this "need" is not like a need that is carried over from infancy due to some ego defect; rather it is the consequence of the fact that the parents require a sadomasochistic relationship (defense) with the child in order to perpetuate their neurotic homeostasis by projecting aggression and revenge feelings and acting them out. The parents do not wish the child to get beyond their grasp. The child not only represents the projected identification with the parents' mothers but *with their fathers as well.* These "images," I think, are not "infantile images" that are "unmetabolized"; they are reflections in fantasy of the kind of relationship the mother and father had with their parents over time. This means, as a rule, throughout infancy, early childhood, and adolescence and often into young adulthood. The "images" (fantasies) represent among other considerations, the acting-out roles (identifications) that have been demanded by the parents.

Masterson makes a salient point in saying that *activity* is an important aspect of treatment with these patients. I believe that the activity must be geared toward certain goals: (1) asking questions that lead to a delineation of the interlocking defensive system, (2) outlining the identification roles, (3) depicting the guilt-ridden, masochistic attitudes that are always present when the wish for normal pursuits occurs. Later questions should refer to revenge, sadism, perverse sexual feeling, and the fears of giving up neurotic relationships. We find in borderlines fears of making new kinds of relationships, fears of abandoning people the patient has known and been close to (i.e., fears of hurting people by giving them up), and fears of retaliation from people who may not wish to be abandoned. In dreams giving up attachments to neurotic parents is often depicted as killing someone or some animal, or perhaps watching someone else kill, or perhaps knowing that someone is going to be killed. Giving up the sadomasochistic relationship is *felt* as an aggression (or perhaps it is *feared* as an aggression), as a blow to the parents. The "reunion" would then be a return to the sadomasochism out of fear of giving it up.

Thus when Masterson speaks of the "reunion fantasy," he is really talking about a sadomasochistic fantasy of passivity. It takes place after the patient has experienced fear in associating with others due to his own feelings of aggression or after he has had to deal with aggression in others. It is a return to the masochistic role similar to the one he had with the parents rather than a mother-child type of reunion due to a fear of separation such as the child might experience in the 12- to 16-month stage. A masochistic feeling (a feeling of humiliation and low self-esteem) usually precedes an acting-out episode, as was illustrated in my session with George Adler (Wolberg, A., 1973, pp. 216-219). When I pressed George to go on with his fantasy, he said he had a fantasy of choking his senior colleague, who seemed to be in competition with George at inappropriate times. (It was fear of choking his girlfriend that brought him into treatment.) At that time he was locked in a relationship with a girl who was quite sadistic and tantalizing due to her own problem, particularly her fears of sex. The "reunion fantasy," I believe, is actually a form of the *identification fantasy* and a defense against acting out murderous feelings either against others or on the self. The person feels that the other is teasing or being sadistic. George Frank Quinn had this feeling about his senior colleagues; the colleague was teasing, being controlling and hostile, like his parents. He had this feeling in transference. When he went out from a session, he sought a homosexual partner (a person he did not know) so as to act out a revenge motif.

The reunion fantasy is a sadomasochistic bind that is being acted out. In relations with the parents the patient is a projective object in order that the parents may express their aggression in various forms, in this way avoiding feelings of anxiety that they would have were they forced to face their real feelings about themselves and their children. If the mother feels "abandonment," then it is due to the *anger* and *depression* she would have to face and analyze in a confrontation of her own neurosis if she did not have the child as a foil. I would see what Masterson calls "fear of abandonment" and the "reunion fantasy" as a need to retain a defense against aggression due to a feeling of humiliation. The mother would have to admit, in a confrontation, the fact that she is using the child in a neurotic way and that there are sexual (perverse) as well as nonsexual aims in the behavior. The same would be true of the father. The patient would have to face his identification pattern with the parents. The sessions with James Weber (see Chapter 11) are illustrative of these problems, and his resistance to working them through is typical of the borderline who has a need to hang on to his aggression to protect his identification. The anxiety is often so great that the individual fears he will "go to pieces" if he cannot express his aggression.

We have mentioned that Kohut believes the borderline patient cannot be analyzed because of his intense anxiety and fear of collapse. Some patients do collapse; that is, they have a psychotic episode rather than face the facts of their sadomasochism. *The psychotic attack is thus another kind of defense* and one that puts a stop temporarily to the therapeutic endeavor except insofar as hospitalization can become an aspect of the treatment procedure.

In his paper "The Question of Family Homeostasis" (1957) Jackson wrote of the need for the parent to bind the child *so that the parent would not lapse into a psychotic episode.* Apparently, the parents did not mind if the child became psychotic and had to go to the hospital. The child could escape into psychosis. But if the parent became psychotic, the burden of guilt would be on the child for not doing as the parent wished. In such cases I feel that the psychotic episode is in the nature of a temper tantrum and revengeful act. The parent is angry because he has lost control of the other and can no longer receive the bounties of the sadomasochistic position. In the case of the child, punishment and guilt create the aggression that is defended by the psychotic episode.

Intrapsychic Symptoms   Chessick (1977) has made some comments on the work of Kernberg and Kohut in contrast to his own ideas. He asserts that the borderline patient has an *intrapsychic defect* (rather than developmental arrest) grounded on massive failure in the maternal environment. His internalization of objects and thus his narcissism and introject formation are related to setting up his own *substitute structures* in order to deal with aggression and other drives so that he can achieve some kind of adaptation to life. One could say that Chessick agrees in part with Kohut and in part with Kernberg. I suspect that the term "substitute structure" refers to fantaies, which in the context that Chessick uses the phrase would mean the same as what I call the "identification fantasy." Chessick believes that the patient's fantasies are later elaborations; they are attached to ideas and feelings that occur after infancy (Chessick, 1977, pp. 111-112). This seems a factual way of looking at matters.

Chessick distinguishes between the borderline syndrome and the narcissistic personality disorder by saying that the latter has achieved some *internalized psychic structures*, although these are primitive. The former, on the other hand, has an *intrapsychic defect*. (Here again, we see similarities between Chessick and Kohut.) The narcissistic personality is responding to a failure in the maternal environment that is more subtle than that experienced by the borderline patient. Disillusionment with the mother, according to Chessick, is the central factor leading to substantial "developmental arrest" in the area of narcissism. I have found that the borderline patient is disappointed in both parents. The child has hoped for rescue. If the mother is more controlling and sadistic, the child hopes that the father will rescue, and if the father is more punitive and rigid, the child hopes for rescue from the mother. Since both parents are locked in a sadomasochistic defensive relationship, true rescue comes from neither side.

The treatment for *intrapsychic defect* should be different from that for people with *developmental arrest*, contends Chessick. We must not confuse *defensive structures*, he says, with *"pristine or archaic psychic structures"* as they manifest themselves in the personality and behavior of our patients. Chessick's phrase "intrapsychic defect" in a borderline must be a way of considering a problem within the context of the structural hypothesis, in relating to the early stages of organization of the id, the ego, and the superego. "Developmental arrest" seems to refer to the idea of *fixation*, and yet all of these authors (Chessick, Kohut, Kernberg, Masterson, to name a few) speak of fixation in the borderline patient. Fixation, however, seems to imply the presence of a basic psychic structure as in developmental arrest, while intrapsychic defect means something is missing mentally.

Fixation is a nebulous concept. Moore and Fine (1968, p. 47) suggest that there are "unknown constitutional reasons" for fixation such as "inherent differences in the functioning of various erogenous zones" and in "ego givens." In fixation there is an *immature ego* that can be overcome by "too much stress." Kohut (1971, 1977) has explained this difficulty by means of his social psychological theory concerning the conditioning of the child in his relationship with an unresponsive mother. There is no "quieting internalization" possible, for the mother has not comforted the child in times of stress. In defining fixation, Moore and Fine (1968) also speak of "arrests of development" in both instinctual and ego-superego organization. These "arrests" cause primitive ways of relating to people and a form of defensive reaction that was used in what were considered to be early dangers. The defenses are later outmoded but are still used. "With disturbances of subsequent development and conflicts over contemporary functioning" the individual may *regress* to the "remnants of earlier functioning" that are "fixed in the psyche." Kohut's theory states that the child "internalizes the functions" that the mother performs. In this interchange the infant "idealizes" the object (the mother) that he both loves and fears. As the infant "idealizes," the ego ideal begins to form. Mahler (1971) agrees with Freud saying that the impetus for idealization stems from the infant's experience in walking. As he begins to walk and realizes that he needs the object for this period, he loses his feelings of omnipotence, which are gradually replaced, and the infant now feels helpless. This causes him to develop an idealization of the parent, whom he now conceives of as strong. He begins to overcome his helplessness by identifying with the strong person and by internalizing the controls that the parent was forced originally to impose.

Chessick comments that Kernberg has referred to "pristine structures" as "substitute structures" in the form of fantasies of power, wealth, and beauty that compensate for the experience of severe frustration, rage, and envy— the compensation being idealization of the object by a fantasy of an ever loving and ever caring mother in contrast to what exists in reality. As I have said, it is most improbable that infants have fantasies of power, wealth, and beauty: these are obviously concepts that refer to the desire to control others in particular ways. The concept of an "ever loving mother" is, in reality, an idealization of a mother who binds the child in a sadomasochistic way, constituting a defense in the face of a parent who does not rescue. My interviews with James Weber touched upon this problem (see Chapter 11).

The relationship between the child and each parent is sadomasochistic as a result originally of the problems of the parents. Both the parents and children are bound together, psychologically speaking, out of fear, guilt, and rage—not from willingness to love or to be helpful to one another. In this type of relationship there is hostility and a sadomasochistic game that is played out in the family. The parents know that they should love and often they accomplish what Chessick speaks of as "pseudogiving," i.e., they give out of guilt or they overprotect. This kind of interaction with parents is denied and idealized. Distinctions can be made between the father and

VANDERBILT MEDICAL CENTER LIBRARY

mother transferences as they repetitively crop up in the treatment situation, once the working-through process is well under way. In treatment there is an analysis of the fantasies so as to have eventually a confrontation about the reality situation that existed and that still exists with others.

If one were to summarize Chessick's concepts, one might say that the borderline has no true identification (in the positive developmental sense according to Freud's idea of the composition of the ego) with the parents and hardly any introjects (Kernberg and Erikson) in the early stages of development so that he utilizes fantasies (substitute structures) that take the place of what is lacking in the form of early ego and superego formation. He incorporates his experiences with his parents into his fantasies at a later stage and can develop identifications of a kind in this later period. He can differentiate self from object at later periods. Chessick here differs from Kernberg, Kohut, and Masterson. They seem to feel that the borderline patient has no capacity for "separation" because emotionally he has not passed through the developmental stage of "object constancy" where it is possible to have some rudimentary forms of interpersonal empathy and some early indications of superego structure. The latter has to do with what Clark called "secondary narcissism" and what both Clark and Mahler refer to as a relationship based on some consideration for the "needs of the object." Chessick believes that the "unmetabolized aggression" is an interference with an adequate way of coping with life and relating to people and that analysis requires an emphasis on the *intrapsychic defects* as reflected in the fantasies. The id, ego, and superego are defective or have deficits, that are seen as "archaic psychic structures." Idealization is one kind of defect, and rage is another defect. Grandiose fantasies are also indications of a defect that prevents a resolution of the rage and idealization.

According to Chessick, the borderline patient's "primitive affect" is founded upon the development of enormous "undifferentiated primitive rage." However, he says that in the borderline patient we see this represented through ideation that is organized in a later phase of development at a time when there is adequate cognitive capacity, including the capacity to form, retain, and represent self- and object images, but the enormous undifferentiated primitive rage (affect) disrupts the development and the smooth functioning of the psychic apparatus. The negative affect is later attached to and appears clinically in fantasies and projections of destructive, archaic, bad, unintegrated self- and object images. Both "intrapsychic defect" and "developmental arrest" are due primarily to lack of strong positive identifications that neutralize and modify aggression. (It is certainly true that anger and rage prevent the individual from responding adequately in an interpersonal relationship. This can be seen readily in the interpersonal encounters within the therapeutic relationship. One sees anger as inhibitive both in the case of the patient, and counter-transferentially on the part of the analyst if anger is evoked in him. In this latter case when anger is stimulated, the analyst is often not able to understand the negative therapeutic reaction.)

Chessick contends that the borderline uses his fantasies to deal with his *innate aggression and other drives* so that he can achieve a form of adaptation. Are the fantasies then a substitute for a rudimentary ego? Or are they *defenses* while at the same time *they contain reality concepts that form the basis of the ego?* I would think that these fantasies would contain forms of *defense*, forms of escape, forms of dealing with anxiety, forms of denial, and distortions of the reality against which the defenses are utilized. *Reality concepts do exist in the fantasies.* (Actually, reality constructs are present in the infant's mind even at the age where Kernberg conceives of a defense of splitting, 1 to 24 months.) Freud mentioned that fantasies could be a denial of the feelings of danger concerning the parents, the fantasies being substitutes for the parents. I think of the fears in the fantasies as *precursors* to later identifications with aggressors (the parents). As the individual gets older, the fantasies become more complicated, and so in the mind of the borderline, as we have repeatedly stressed, they represent the sadomasochistic relationship with the parents. The fantasies represent the disguised reality of the sadomasochistic relationship the patient has throughout his life with other people, but they are also defenses against the reality (traumas) of the interpersonal relationships with parents.

We have noted that Kernberg has proposed that the pathology that "fixates splitting" and prevents its replacement by "more mature defenses" is the consequence of "nonmetabolized early introjections which later come to the surface, not as 'free floating' internal objects but as specific ego structures into which they have crystallized." Fixation occurs in the period from 6 to 14 months. Apparently the "ego structures" to which Kernberg refers are the fantasies of "power, wealth and beauty," which would be related to grandiose mechanisms. In my opinion these fantasies would have to be later elaborations, as Chessick suggests, since the infant would know nothing of control by such factors. The beginnings of such fantasies would be the fears of unknown things or of animals. Much later the idealization of the fearful objects can be seen in dreams. *Actually idealization is a form of "remaking reality,"* but this too would be a later elaboration, at 5 years or older, when the "family romance" would be organized. Prior to this, one finds the "beating fantasy" (occurring first about the age of 4), which then persists in one form or another throughout development and into adulthood.

The timing of the crucial period of fixation at which the borderline pathology precipitates has been a subject of controversy and debate among different authors. For example, Chessick says that Masterson and Rinsley

(1975) agree with him that Mahler's rather than Kernberg's timing is more attuned to the facts. Kernberg places this time in the period of 4 to 12 months, while Mahler favors fixation at 16 to 25 months coinciding with the period of the "rapproachment subphase." Kernberg considers his Stage III the period of fixation (6 to 14 months) before the period of "object constancy."

When Chessick says we must not confuse *defensive reactions with pristine or archaic psychic structures*, I take this to mean that he has in mind psychic structures formed in the period of 2 months to 16 or 18 months that correspond to the period of what has been called "the oral triad" (Moore & Fine, 1968, p. 68), which is described as a *developmental phenomenon* that can be related both to the *self* (the ego) and to the *instincts*. Psychic structures, according to this way of thinking, are different from defenses: they are *representations of the instinct and of the self* that become attached to ideations in early periods and they are found to be present presumably in later periods when the id, ego and superego became solidified, as postulated in the structural hypothesis. The theory is, for example, that when the teeth begin to erupt, it constitutes the psychological basis for *oral aggression* or *oral sadism*. The appearance of the teeth ushers in *oral drives* that are motivated by the *aggressive instincts*, which express themselves in chewing, biting, and spitting. When problems arise in the so-called "oral stage," they are said to be the forerunners of later character problems, such as greed, demandingness, restlessness, as well as forerunners of traits that are completely opposite, such as generosity and penuriousness, dependency and independence, and so forth. Practically speaking, eating and later chewing are normal activities that have no intrinsic relation to aggression and sadism. Anal activities are prominent and present at birth as well as oral activities, and they create as much need for maternal attention and pose as much possibility for relief of tension and pleasure as feeding. "Oral activities" are also forerunners of the later abilities for speech and facial expression, important communication functions.

When Chessick says that narcissistic personalities have "developmental arrest" while borderlines have "intrapsychic defect", this seems to mean that *arrest in development* implies "fixation" which can occur in the ego-superego formation and thus in the development of the "self" (this would require *defense*) while in the borderlines the *structural process is defective* so that the id, ego, and superego do not form a composite organization or do not reach an equilibrium. The latter has to be achieved in therapy. Both Kernberg and Kohut, on the other hand, feel that in the narcissistic disorders there is a "cohesive self" (Kernberg would say "ego") and therefore there must be basic intact archaic psychic structures. Kohut says that the *self* is the mediating factor or the "switch" that puts the ego into operation.

The borderline's ego and the substructure *self* are defective; that is, they do not have cohesion or an organization because the *fantasies (at 16 months?) do not hold down the aggression to a point where the individual can get along with others without gross symptoms.* What are these symptoms? Grandiosity and low self-esteem, according to Kohut and Kernberg.

Chessick discusses similarities and dissimilarities of various authors who concerned themselves with developmental phenomena by reconstructing these, as Freud did, from psychoanalytic data. For example, he finds that the "no-self-object differentiation" of Modell corresponds roughly to Freud's stage of "primary narcissism" and is the same period as Mahler's "symbiotic phase" (2 to 6 months). Chessick also points out that Freud's phase of "object love" is like Mahler's "separation-individuation" phase (6 to 24 months). (We know that Freud postulated overlapping phases. For example, the oral phase extended to 18 months, but the "object love phase" was included in the latter part of this stage. The stages of primary and secondary narcissism were included in this time span as well.) Chessick reminds us that Kohut sees the development of primary narcissism as occurring from 6 to 10 months, and it is during this period that the "grandiose self" and the "idealized parental image" emerge. These are *developmental phenomena*, not to be confused with *defensive reactions*, and they appear later on in the transference of borderline and narcissistic personalities due to the conflicts and unresolved difficulties of this 6-to-10-month era.

These concepts of early infancy are difficult to accept. I believe that the infant *"feels good" about accomplishment*, even at a very early age, and *even if no one responds.* When the infant is by himself, his learning is a pleasure for him. When he accomplishes something, he coos, he is excited. He also responds to people. He smiles at them, he "talks" to them (see Trevarthan, 1974). The infant under favorable conditions experiences "pleasure" both alone with his own accomplishments and with others in an interpersonal encounter so that Kohut's idea of a "self" during this early period with respect to pleasure and unpleasure is completely conceivable. Perhaps this should not be called a "grandiose self"; nor is the pleasurable experience completely dependent upon the mother's responses. Grandiosity is a much later phenomenon that has defensive connotations and is related to more advanced social constructs than those of the infant. The grandiosity is actually associated with fantasies. It would seem that fantasies of power, strength, and beauty indicate a contest, and there does seem to be a power struggle in the family of the individual who becomes borderline, a struggle that is sadomasochistic in nature. The experiments by Asch (1952) and Milgram (1973) are relevant to this issue. They indicate a *trait of susceptibility to suggestions* or commands that we find is a characteristic of the borderline stemming from the experience of giving in to rigid, demanding, and controlling parents who urge acting out. The demands are sometimes acceded to through passive behavior and at other times resisted by way of aggressive acts. However, the aggressive acts are sometimes stimulated by the parents. Unraveling the dynamics of the sadomasochistic problem with the paranoid feelings and anger related to it is a tedious and long drawn-out procedure. The first two sessions with James Weber reported in Chapter 11 are a beginning stage in an attempt to work through this problem.

Freud spoke of "giving in to the other" as a trait in homosexuality. It is also a trait of the borderline. There seems to be a need to act out homosexuality in a sadomasochistic way when some borderline patients feel belittled and wish to get revenge. This trend can be expressed as a fear of acting out in a homosexual episode for those patients who have never had homosexual experiences. The trait of susceptibility seemed apparent in my patient Harriet Hamburger, who felt she had to give in to the demands of female co-workers. She had the same feeling about males, but at work she was afraid of males and kept a distance. She would feel suspicious of both males and females, but she could form friendships with women and could feel close.

Harriet had a fear of homosexual acting out, and for three years she spoke frequently of her homosexual trend, although she never did have homosexual experiences. Her fears were related to transference feelings, which she was not able to work through until many years later. Her mother who ruled the family through hysteria and other controlling mechanisms was very competitive with Harriet, always telling how she was sought after by men. Harriet was never able to form relationships with boys in her teens. The mother also had a repetitive fantasy of her husband being unfaithful to her, but Harriet felt the father never did have affairs and was completely under the mother's thumb. The mother's sexual fantasies were "purely in her own head." The father was a kind of "dandy" and did smile at women, but the mother's fantasies and accusations were groundless. In Harriet's case any references to any possible hostility to the analyst was complete unacceptable to her, but her identification with the analyst's work was evident in her behavior. She became interested in writing for a paper that popularized psychiatric concepts, which she did for several years. This acting out meant that the patient had ambivalence toward the analyst that could not be worked through but was acted out. "I am better than you are; I am smarter than you; I can interpret better than you; I have contempt for you." On the other hand, she admired the analyst, but she was obsequious for the most part.

Freud would call this transference problem an aspect of the oedipal problem, the analyst representing the mother with whom the patient competes. Current bordeline theorists might see this situation with the patient as an aspect of the "split ego," and Kernberg in this kind of analytic relationship might advocate confronting the patient with her "polarity" in accepting and rejecting the analyst. Kohut might see this maneuver as an attempt by the patient to obtain appropriate mirroring from the analyst. I saw this as competition, a fear of "giving in" to the competitor, a fear that was acted out (a pantomimic transference) rather than talked out. When I attempted to discuss the problem, I met strong resistance and deep detachment. Therefore, I would wait until she herself brought up the matter, even if it had to be a period of years. The good feelings I took as appeasement (masochism). The competitive feelings were, in fact, sadistic in nature, with strong defensive resistance to interpretation. Accepting interpretation would be a "giving in," a manifestation of her trait of susceptibility, a masochistic move which she did not want to admit that she was fighting. Her behavior was in a sense counterphobic, and yet she was highly competitive. Harriet had no conscious wish to "merge." She had contemptuous feelings toward the analyst, but unconsciously she wanted to be near the analyst. She wanted to be special, to be smarter than other patients. She would look upon each interpretation with wonder, saying that the analyst was "so astute," "so sensitive." Such attitudes require special treatment techniques.

In the next chapter we shall discuss some research papers and some of the writings on special problems related to the borderline syndrome.

CHAPTER 4

Special Problems

This chapter is a review of selected papers on the borderline condition. Except for the research papers, one finds the authors utilizing current theories to explain particular problems that arise in the treatment of this patient. In anticipation of the discussion of modern developmental theory in Chapter 5 and the critique of Freud and Mahler's developmental systems, I am suggesting in this chapter other alternatives that I think may be useful to the therapist who is working with the borderline patient.

Research

The main research data on the borderline comes from several studies—Grinker and Werble (1968, 1977), Gunderson and his colleagues (1075a,b, c) and Spitzer and his associates (1979). The information is mainly descriptive. Gunderson, Carpenter, and Strauss (1975b) compared 24 borderline and 29 schizophrenic patients. The results showed that 45 percent of the borderline patients displayed depressive delusions; 45 percent, paranoid delusions; 60 percent, dissociative symptoms (derealization episodes in 20 percent, depersonalization in 40 percent); 20 percent, hallucinations and 7 percent, delusions (organized and motivating). I am of the opinion that when organized delusions are present and are motivating the person, the diagnosis is schizophrenia rather than borderline. In the Gunderson study depression was the most frequent affective symptom. Anger and anxiety were also present. For the schizophrenic patients anger was less a problem than depression and anxiety. (Depression is probably a defense against intense anger.) The borderline patients themselves reported anger as a symptom, but the interviewers noted more anxiety and depression. Grinker's study showed anger to be a central emotion.

Gunderson et al found that the borderline patient led a "frenetic stormy life style" punctuated in some instances by unusual or occult experiences. While the borderline patients had some psychotic symptoms, these were "circumscribed and experienced by the patient as alien." The borderline patients "showed significantly fewer psychotic symptoms than the schizophrenics." (In my 1952 paper I noted that some borderline patients have what seem like hallucinatory experiences with religious or ecstatic states, but these are fleeting. Kety has suggested that borderlines can be placed on a continuum, at one end nearer to psychotic and at the other end nearer to neurotic. (Interpersonal difficulties were acknowledged by most of the borderline patients in the Gunderson study. Suicidal threats, doubts of self-worth, somatic complaints were quite common. In the year before admission these patients had worked three-quarters of the time, had met with their friends about once every three weeks, and among the unmarried had dated fairly regularly. Prognostic variables of known importance to schizophrenia were in the moderately favorable range for the group of borderlines.

Depression

Authors who use current psychoanalytic developmental theories feel that the borderline patient does not have depression but rather has an apathy. We have mentioned that the implication is that apathy is a state related to the "separation-individuation phase" (occurring from 12 to 16 months of age) i.e., a preoedipal phenomenon, while depression is a state accompanying "oedipal anxieties" and guilt; thus it is a factor in the developmental stage in the 3-year-age range. These concepts are based on Mahler's refinements of Freud's developmental scheme where "higher and lower" stages of mental or "ego" development are presumed.

Following current ego theory, some authors consider the analyst, in the treatment process with patients who are "fixated" at this early stage, to be an *auxiliary ego* (Mahler), or an *auxiliary superego*, or both, while others suggest that the analyst is a *"transitional object"* (Winnicott). There are those, such as Boyer and Giovacchini (1967), who say that the analyst is an object with whom the patient may "identify" in order to change "harsh punitive introjects" into "good and kindly ones." And some analysts, as we have seen, feel that the analyst must function as a mother. Those who follow Kohut's theory separate sexual development from the development of self-esteem; these are two distinct lines of development, but the question of guilt is not emphasized. However, Melanie Klein's concept of early envy is used. When Freud (1915-1916) was developing the libido theory and expanding on his concept of narcissism and his ideas about the ego, he suggested that there are two kinds of instinctual development out of necessity. Also he proposed two kinds of identification: (1) the hysterical kind and (2) the narcissistic kind (Freud, S.E., 1917, 16:428). He posited autoerotism as the original physical state of the infant (1917, 16:416) and megalomania as the "feeling state" (16:415), which he compared to a later overevaluation of the object in "normal erotic life." Narcissistic identification had something to do with a "lost object." It was a compensation, so to speak, for the lost object. It is my thought that the object is "lost" due to the rejection of the child by the parents and the strongest identification is that with the most rejected parent (Wolberg, A., 1968, pp. 105-107). The sense of rejection can begin early in the child's life, and idealization of the object is a defense accompanied by a feeling of unworthiness, which is the beginning of a later persistent feeling of low self-esteem the defense against which is grandiosity or megalomania. Freud had the idea that a "narcissistic identification" is projected onto the ego (1917, 16:427). Perhaps he thought that the idealization of the lost object was somehow taken into the self, becoming the megalomania of infancy. It is difficult to understand just how Freud did conceive of the dynamics of this early phase of life. Although Freud suggested two lines of development, he nevertheless, unlike Kohut, considered that these were fused or at least that they were eventually in harmony. The ideas that Freud expressed in his lectures 22 and 23 (see Freud, S.E., 1916, 14:311-331, 1917, 14:239-258) dealt with these metapsychological schemes, and in lecture 24, he returned to these ideas again (1917, 16:7; 412-430). We shall see in Chapter 5 that these concepts of early development are slowly but surely being questioned and refuted.

It is the loss of object or more precisely *the feeling of being rejected and abused* that accounts for the borderline patient's depression—a mild depression. There have been many articles in the literature pointing to the devastating effects of depression in one member on the other family members. The depression of the borderline is not deep, but it is *chronic*—a reaction to life's stresses. This is reflected in the hopeless attitude the patient has toward doing anything that will change his situation. He feels encased in a sadomasochistic bind, and in interpersonal relationships he depends largely on "the other" for his cues for activity. He has been "programmed," by his parents, to look to them for his cues for behavior, and he carries this through, in transference, with others. He is most resentful at being in this position but has the feeling that it is his lot in life. His parents have made him understand that they need to use him as an instrument in the service of their own adjustment and that, therefore, he must inhibit some of his own normal impulses and give up certain of his normal needs, particularly certain activities that have a relation to peer groups. If he rejects this position, the borderline is made to feel guilty, and through punishment he learns to conform. His depression is associated with anger and low self-esteem.

In a study at Yale University it was found that children of depressed women, as compared to the children of "normals," had more problems in school, were more overactive, got into more fights, and had a larger number of accidents. It has been observed by several authors that the mothers of borderline patients are angry, combative, and depressed. Husbands who are in the unemployment category are prone to depression, and with unemployment for more than nine months, the individual often develops problems of self-esteem and sexual impotence. After two years of unemployment divorce is a distinct possibility. There are many divorces in the upper middle class and there are many borderline patients. In the lower economic classes desertion appears to be the rule. There is no data so far as I know on the kinds of separations that take place in these families, but I have found that there are many borderline patients who come from homes where the parents have detached relationships but remain under the same roof. The majority of my own borderline patients come from homes where mother and father have not separated though they often lead stormy (sadomasochistic) existences with periods of detachment.

Descriptive Designations

The borderline patient has been described as an addictive personality, due to his being an "oral character." It is a fact that alcoholics who seek treatment seem to have depressive symptoms and are often in the borderline category, but not all borderlines are alcoholics or have additions. Addiction, it is true, is a way of counteracting depression and detachment, and of avoiding the consequence of interpersonal experience where anxiety is overriding.

Gunderson and Kolb (1978) have suggested variables for diagnosing the borderline patient. Depression was one of the symptoms noted. These authors confirmed many of my own early impressions of borderlines stated in my first paper in 1952. For example, the idea that borderlines maintain relationships with others and are not loners; that these associations are most often with members of the opposite sex; that borderlines are very manipulative; that they tend toward low achievement[1]; that some of these patients have brief paranoidal experiences and certain occurrences that might be considered brief hallucinatory episodes (Wolberg, A., 1952, pp. 694-696); and that they have disturbed interpersonal experiences (1952, pp. 695-700). I find that these interpersonal disturbances are due to the sadomasochistic life pattern which is associated with denial of the good feelings for others, as well as repudiation of the importance of successes and the good outcome of activities or behavior. I also have noticed a kind

---

[1]However, many of my borderline patients have achieved great status in academic and social life, but their activities are not what they could be for their abilities.

of twelve-step cycle (Wolberg, A., pp. 694-696) associated with what might be called a mood swing in relationships, and I found that reality testing was present, albeit disturbed by anxiety and defenses.

Prior to the establishment of DSM-III, Spitzer, Endicott, and Gibbon (1979) did a reasearch study in an effort to see whether there was enough evidence from practicing psychiatrists for the borderline category to be included in the new psychiatric classification. The study revealed two types of "borderlines"—a "schizotypal personality" and a "borderline personality disorder." My impression is that the first category is probably a form of schizophrenia, while the second designation more nearly conforms to what I conceive of as a borderline. The DSM-III scheme now includes a borderline category.

In a study done at the Postgraduate Center for Mental Health Baumwoll (1979) found that psychoanalysts on the staff who responded to her request produced a list of 278 items related to "borderline patients." This list was returned to the respondents after being given a 5-point rating scale. Clusters were evident under the following headings: *anger, sadomasochism, guilt, fear of closeness* or intimacy, *traumatic childhood, poor self-concept.* The headings were organized around a global use of *projective identification* and a particular symptom picture related to anxiety. The defenses organized around projective identification were anger, masochism, projection, splitting (dissociation), denial (selective), "black-and-white" thinking, a shifting of defenses, problem-orientated rather than solution-oriented responses (paranoid trend?), idealization, gradiosity. The symptoms were fears, anxiety, complaints of empty feeling (depression; or apathy?), changeable moods, impulsivity, frustration, somatic complaints, intolerance of loss, feelings of danger, suspiciousness, and acting accusatory of others.

The "Defective" Ego

The idea that "the ego" can be defective due to a hereditary factor has been proposed by many authors other than Freud, and this thesis was elaborated by Dickes (1974) in making what he called an "alternate proposal" to the current concepts of "borderline states." He quotes Freud (1937): "We have no reason to dispute the existence and the importance of original innate distinguishing characteristics of the ego. This is made certain by the fact that each person makes a selection from the possible mechanisms of defense and he always uses a few only of them and always the same ones. This would seem to indicate that each ego is endowed from the first with individual dispositions and trends, though it is true that we cannot specify their nature or what determines them." Dickes (1974, pp. 13) then goes on to say, "It may be added that not only are the choices concerning defense mechanisms laid down at birth but so are the endowments concerning the id and the ego factors involving such matters as intelligence, perception, mobility, etc." (Usually when psychoanalysts refer to the "the id" they mean aggression and sexuality that must be held in check by defenses.) Differences in characteristics, Dickes says, have been found in men as contrasted with women. Citing many instances of individual differences, he then suggests that a return to the thesis is in order to the effect that drive endowments differ, as do ego capacities, due to genetic factors. There are some similarities in this idea to the Kernberg proposals that the borderline is "different" and "pathologically so" from birth (Kernberg, 1975, pp. 122-124). Dickes, however, uses many of Kohut's concepts in that he focuses on ego trends and the development of ego functions rather than on defenses per se. He sees this idea as completely different from the continuum idea advocated by many.

Dickes does not like the continuum concept since he believes that it means that one traverses from neuroses to the borderline area and then to the psychotic state, and he comments that, "there is no single road or continuum," apparently because borderlines are destined to become borderlines from the start. Others feel that if the borderline is a member of an actual category or group, then he cannot have symptoms similar to people in other categories. In order to be distinctive, there must be something unique to characterize the syndrome. The actual fact is that borderline patients do have mini psychotic episodes. But these are temporary and short-lived, and they seem to appear at periods of intense anxiety and stress. They do not have steady psychotic symptomatology as in the case with the chronic schizophrenic, for example. Freud sometimes called these patients "mixed types," but he also used the term "borderline" in the last sentence of the introduction to Aichorn's book (see Aichorn, 1945 [1925]).

The idea that people are foredoomed to be neurotic or psychotic from birth is not new. The impression that individual differences have an effect on whether the individual will become neurotic or psychotic is also not new. It seems to me that if we have a multifaceted concept of neuroses and psychoses, based initially on the influence of social factors, one need not see this as opposing the concept of individual differences nor the idea of a continuum. Some borderlines have had psychotic attacks and so have gone from neuroses to psychoses depending upon circumstances. It is my impression that these psychotic periods occur in the borderline when he senses that he has no control over a given situation. When he cannot have his way or the circumstances are too confronting for him, he becomes angry, frustrated, or fearful due to conflict. The fleeting period of psychoticlike activity is a kind of substitute rage reaction, or it may be a temporary escape from the situation tht is too anxiety provoking as in a mini amnesia or depersonalization episode—a kind of "I-am-not-here" feeling or a "this-is-not-really-me" experience, where he saves himself. The saying goes that, among other things, "we all have our breaking point"; that is, it is possible for anyone to have a psychotic episode if the circumstances are dire enough. It takes less for some people to "break" and more for others, and this is a sign that the traumas and deprivations of the past have created a greater or lesser degree of chronic anxiety in one individual than in another rather than that he is endowed by birth with the precarious condition. From my point of view these breaks mean that the conditions of trauma exist in the present situation and it is not that the individual is suffering only from traumas that accrued in the distant past (see Wolberg, L.R., 1966).

Among psychoanalysts it has become almost commonplace to reject the idea of a constitutional factor in neuroses and psychoses; nevertheless, this is the theory of many authors who have written about borderline conditions. We also find this kind of genetic theory reflected in certain papers concerning the IQ's of blacks as compared to whites. Aggression too is regarded not as a function of a social system, i.e., of relations with people, but of genetic origin. The implication is that we must leave the social system alone and blame destiny for the problem. In practice, however, the borderline patient seems to make a better adjustment when he can depart from his family and get into a more autonomous position. For hospitalized patients it may be that an outpatient therapeutic experience is necessary before such a move can be made.

As far as hospitalization is concerned, there is usually a point at which the anxiety factor is so destressing that the individual must leave the situation. The fact that individuals reorganize readily once they are removed from the environmental situation that creates the "breaking point" may account for the finding that brief hospitalizations are preferable to long hospitalizations. In general, the latter are said to promote "regression." There are exceptions to this rule, of course; for example, people who are dangerous to themselves and others and who have suffered chronically for years before hospitalization, such as certain paranoid persons who have become criminalistic and excessively destructive. In general, however, brief hospitalization is preferable to long-term confinement since a long hospitalization is demoralizing. There is an interesting statistic that seems to hold in the case of both hospitalization and brief therapy: one third of brief-treatment patients return to the hospital or clinic, thus two-thirds usually do not; and one third of the latter also return after their treatment has been ended. In my experience brief treatment for the borderline patient, if hospitalized, should last no more than three months with several months of outpatient followup. For nonhospitalized borderline patients brief therapy means at least 30 to 32 sessions. At the Postgraduate Center for Mental Health (an outpatient service) in New York City we found that about 75 percent of our patients can be helped with no need to return in 30 to 32 sessions on a once-a-week basis, and this group included a considerable number of borderline patients. Other patients were being treated in psychoanalysis on a long-term basis (3 to 4 times a week) while the remainder came twice a week.

The Social Factor in Emotional Problems

There is no doubt that people differ in intelligence, in capacities to do various tasks and so on, but both "geniuses" and "normals," rich and poor, Democrats and Republicans may have neurotic, borderline, or psychotic problems. Durkheim (1897) was one of the first to illustrate the connection between social factors and individual character in his study on suicide (aggression turned inward), and many modern investigators, notably Brenner (1973), have established a relation between *stress* as a function of dealing with the vagaries of the economic system (particularly unemployment) and increases in the rates of neuroses and psychoses, criminality, depression, and suicide. Environmental factors are, in turn, a function of the political climate, which creates such phenomena as crowding, poverty, unemployment, wealth, power, and aggression. It was Allport (1954) who said, "Aggression is not a primary tendency to hurt or destroy, but an intensified form of self-assertion and self-expression . . . a secondary result of thwarting and interference." He was only partly correct: aggression is definitely a reaction to thwarting and interference with some of the basic autonomous rights of the individual, but it is an expression of self-assertion only in the sense that aggression is a revenge act after continued frustration. The individual becomes angry at being frustrated and attempts to counteract the frustration or remove the obstacle through his rational efforts; but when this is impossible, he feels trapped. It is then, as the condition persists over time, that the individual becomes enraged, revengeful, and oppositional and develops neurotic symptoms. Aggression is a reaction after much frustration and defeat. The borderline patient, found in all of the economic classes of our society, has been frustrated mainly by his parents, over time, and he is *revengeful*. The concept of aggression is a topic that embraces innumerable theories and concepts—the two main ones being that aggression is an inherited trait and that aggression is a reaction to protracted frustration. This latter proposition will be discussed in more detail in the section on Harlow's experiments.

Individual differences are factors in human life due both to genetic and social ingredients, no two individuals being exactly alike. No two individuals have the same environment—even in the same family. Lack of opportunity has a great deal to do with certain kinds of individual differences, and this is true for individuals in families of both rich and poor—even in the same family.

The question is often asked, Should not professionals in the mental health field involve themselves in movements, political and otherwise, to alter the environmental stress factors? Obviously, the mental health professional in his or her practice is not a politician; one can influence political events only to the degree that one participates in political movements with others. There was a time when psychiatry, psychology, and social work were looked upon as the means of correcting the ills of society, but the fallacy of such an idea is now patently obvious. It is true that these fields have at their disposal some attenuated means of reducing the incidence of mental illness, but there are at present two considerations that must coexist if these fields are to make a real impact, neither of which are currently present: (1) the personnel in these fields must have the proper training so that they can utilize appropriate techniques, and (2) a more equitable distribution of income for the general population must be operative so that there is much less inflation and unemployment, the two social components that create havoc in the general society and evoke personal anxiety and stress. Were these two conditions to be corrected, however, it would still be many years before the results of the remedial measures would have an impact on large numbers of the population. Neuroses and psychoses have lingering and persistent effects upon family members and social institutions. There must be several generations of a family who live in "good" social conditions before the long-term benefits can be felt. Neurotic parents will raise neurotic children, but the latter may change somewhat if the parents can give these children a proper social climate. By the third generation there might be considerable difference in character patterns, all things being equal.

Perhaps it is because the idea of a continuum puts less weight on heredity and more on anxiety due to environmental factors as causes of the neuroses and psychoses that Dickes (1974) and others disagree. They credit Freud with having suggested the concept of a continuum. Freud wrote, *"Every normal person, in fact is only normal on the average and to a greater or lesser extent* and the degree of its remoteness from one end of the series and of its proximity to the other will furnish us with a provisional measure of what we have so indefinitely termed an alteration of the ego"* (present author's italics). I believe that if we wish to speak of "alterations in the ego" we should consider this concept in the light of the *defensive processes*, rather than in a developmental sense, particularly according to the degree and kind of the projective defenses: on one hand of the continuum are the less projective defenses and on the opposite end of the continuum the more projective. The problem is not developmental according to a theory of infantile sexuality or special "ego lacunae"; it is dependent upon the nature of the stresses and anxieties created in the individual by his experiences in this world with people and situations beginning in the family. Anxiety and life stress are functionally related to symptoms that have to do with both mental and physical problems (see *Science News*, 1977). The individual and society are interactive from the time of the individual's birth.

Psychoanalysis Should Be a Multidisciplinary Theory

As we have said, Freud considered constitutional factors more important than environmental in his final idea of "greater or lesser normality," and the problem of aggression loomed large in his evaluation of the constitutional element. I, on the other hand, would credit the environment with the greatest importance as a source of stress and anxiety and being more influential in the development of emotional problems than genetic factors. The concept of ego functions accruing or not accruing in the developmental sense has failed to give us understanding of the neurotic and psychotic processes since the concept "ego functions" is so all inclusive that it embraces, besides defenses, such processes as learning, development, perception, and thinking. The use of the term "ego" in this way exceeds the bounds of psychoanalytic theory if we wish to restrict the theory to a specific field. In addition, it is obvious that most people have all their "ego functions" operative as these functions are currently defined (see Wolberg, A., 1973, p. 68). But the defensive systems do organize in different ways, and there is a continuum in the sense that neurotics have less projective and paranoid trends than character problems, while borderlines and schizophrenics have more, apparently in that order.

Freud in his brilliant originality expounded on psychoanalysis as a theory of neuroses and psychoses and the psychological treatment thereof. Gradually, however, he diluted his concepts and, in a somewhat grandiose manner, insisted that psychoanalysis was the basis of all psychology—and indeed of social dynamics as well. The ego ideal, for example, was considered by Freud to be an important concept for group psychology (Freud, S.E., 1914, 14:61). One sees, however, that the "culture" or the social order, or what Durkheim called "collective representations," is what distinguishes the individual from animals.

In discussing the problem of the environment versus heredity, we encompass in the literature many misunderstandings that contaminate thinking in multidisciplinary circles. Usually this is due to the practice of taking a frame of reference from one discipline and applying it ill advisedly in another field. This was brought home to me by an article I once read concerning delinquency. The author considered delinquency as "normal behavior" because the child was complying with the "norms of his group." If we accept the concept of environment as a factor in the development of neuroses and psychoses, then we come up against the dynamics of society (the group or the social system). It is in relation to the theoretical concepts involving the individual and the group that we discover a plethora of conceptual confusion. The pot-pourri of biological and genetic ideas and the theory of intrapsychic processes immerse us in many misconceptions. While the field of psychoanalysis is a narrow field, some multidisciplinary and interdisciplinary training is essential. When the idea of prevention is added to the concept of diagnosis and treatment, multidisciplinary theory becomes even more essential. The notion that delinquency is "normal" due to the fact that the delinquent may be complying with the norms set up by his delinquent companions is an excellent example of confused thinking and the need for multidisciplinary training in the field of mental health. It is true that in sociology we find the concept "norm," but this concept has no relation to "normal" vs. "pathological" as applied in the psychiatric field. The problem of "higher" and "lower" ego organization, it seems, falls into this same confused form of thinking, based on the idea that the brain has an evolutionary history that is reflected in its structure.

The structural theory in psychoanalysis contains the concept of "higher" and "lower" brain layers in the developmental sense in applying this concept to the organization of the three agencies of the mind. Kernberg (1975, p. 7) uses this theory, saying that he has attempted to build on the work of Menninger a model that will "improve our understanding of the specific archaic levels of defensive organization in patients with borderline personality organizations." It is on this basis that Kernberg has suggested his "classification," placing borderline conditions on a "lower level" than the "narcissistic disorders." Lewis Wolberg (1977, pp. 412-414) also constructed a classification of defense. In his scheme the more destructive forms of acting out were assigned the areas where fantasy tended toward delusion. As I have often said, it appears that these defenses are related to the degree of trauma and stress within the family and experienced by a particular individual and to the kind of identifications he or she has been forced to develop.

Defense vs. Developmental Theory

The dynamics of identification and the defenses surrounding this major defense are much more important in understanding the various syndromes than any theory that uses the concept of a developmental system. I am reminded of Geleerd who wrote, "In order not to lose the parents' love, the child adopts their repressions, denials, reaction formations, etc. Thus only by taking over a considerable part of his parents' neurotic ways can he join the human community" (1965, p. 122).

Some defenses appear in the infant at birth, and so they do indeed have a genetic origin. It is the social situation, however, that creates anxiety in the child and stimulates mental elaborations and overlays in the use of the basic defenses. Perhaps the fear response that develops between 8 and 12 months is, in fact, a defense of genetic origin that has a self-preservative effect. Such a postulation does not discount the relation between the structure of the society and the rate of suicide. As we have said, many studies indicate a functional relationship between social dynamics and mental problems. Henle (1972) and Brenner (1973) have emphasized the relationship between symptoms, stress, and social situations.

The studies of Jackson, Weakland, Johnson and others have accented what has been known for some time—namely, *the family is the seat of the onset and stimulation of a great deal of neurotic and psychotic behavior*. A social system theory is important in understanding the derivation and dynamics of emotional disorders, particularly as social dynamics are related to identifications set up in the family. It is the conceptualization that we see reflected in the patient's repetitive dreams and fantasies. The history of the child is delineated by the associations and these may be connected with the phenomenon called the Zeigarnik effect (see page 153). *Identification* is a *group-determined phenomenon*; thus we must learn something of the dynamics of groups. For example, the kind of stimulation in life that the infant receives is thought to influence future behavior (Caplan, 1973, pp. 87-97); but whatever the stimulation, the factors of intelligence, learning, reality testing, memory, and so forth, are not affected in the sense that they can be eliminated or prevented from operation. They are genetically determined. The fact that learning may be disrupted by anxiety does not mean that the learning process has been destroyed or damaged. Those theorists who feel that there are lacunae in learning or that there are gaps in understanding in the borderline patient are, I believe, in error.

A reevaluation of the first years of life, in view of the various theories concerning the borderline patient is in order. In the light of modern knowledge we must take a second look at the concepts of narcissism, fixation, primary process, and other speculative concepts such as the ego and the id. The concept of heredity was a primary factor in Freud's evaluation of the early phases of life, and yet it is Freud's theory that has influenced many theorists to look at the family as the source of stress and neurosis. The environment can be a primary source of stress for parents and children alike, and this fact affects all classes of people in their relations with others. Parents of borderline patients who themselves have been traumatized by their own parents react with aggression, depression, withdrawal, and other defenses when they feel anxious. And they use their children in the interest of their own defenses (this is the basis of neurotic identification), but their learning capacities have not been destroyed.

It seems to me that the concept of the "cumulative trauma" due to frustrating experiences with parents is the basis for a more reasonable hypothesis of emotional disorder than defective instinct derivatives with the birth trauma as the prototype for anxiety leading to a weak ego with no boundaries. Stress is a factor in body response (and it may be that untoward chemical reactions in the body systems can be stimulated by various degrees of stress and can effect not only the physical systems but the neurophysiological systems as well). Spitz and Cobliner (1965, p. 139) have posited a "strain trauma" and "chronic traumata." Selye (1956) has given us data regarding stress. Freud (1926, 20:133, 138) assumed an automatic trauma at the beginning of each regular phase of development. Later he emphasized separation from the mother as a source of early anxiety. The cumulative effect of development itself, according to Freud, was a basis for anxiety, given a defective heredity. Eventually, he considered traumatic events and experiences with parents as a source of reviving the original anxiety.

Spitz wrote that he observed "identification with the aggressor" in a child of 16 months (Spitz and Cobliner, 1965, pp. 186-187). This would mean, I believe, that the 16-month-old child had already adapted to a sadomasochistic mode of life in the family. One would have to say, however, that this particular child does not have a neurosis at the age of 16 months, but if the child were to develop a neurosis in later life, we could assume that the symptoms of identification with the aggressor persisted and had a major effect in the life style of this particular individual. In other words, the child continued to be in a stressful situation up to the point where the neurosis (the defense) was organized and then found his own stressful situation in order to perpetuate the neurotic defenses. If we substitute the concept of "identification with the aggressor" for the idea of "fixation" (which is a nebulous concept at best that creates confusion and misunderstanding in psychoanalytic theory), then with the idea of "cumulative trauma," and the recognition that the traumas require the gradual development of a defensive system, we may be on the road to more clarity in our concepts. Freud's idea of the dynamics of development, however, was that identification takes place automatically as a function of the learning process and that identification is a prime dynamic in the organization of the ego and the secondary process beginning in the stage of "secondary narcissism." Identification, along with idealization of the parents and the formation out of these of an ego ideal, was the basis for the organization of a superego, which was an "internalization" of social experience related to the oedipal problem. The oedipal problem was the stimulus for the defense of repression. The concept of "internalization" is the psychoanalytic explanation of learning from social experience.

If we were to think in terms of "cumulative trauma" as the consequence of the parents' need to use the child in the service of the parents' projective defenses, as I suggested in 1960 and again in 1973, then we would have to consider identifications with parents (the aggressors) as a function of the parents' neurotic needs and their active use of the child in maintaining their neurotic (or psychotic) homoestasis. We would recognize that identifications develop slowly over time in the social milieu of the family as a resolution of the anxiety created in the relations with parents. The sexual line of development may proceed in somewhat the way that Freud described, but the whole social system cannot be explained on the basis of the oedipal problem. But early phases of infant development we understand today do not evolve quite as Freud conceived of them. Freud was often willing to say that he might be wrong, but when a colleague argued with him about his ideas, he was relentless in his defense. In discussing how phylogenesis might repeat itself in ontogeny, Freud made many questionable statements although he understood only too well that the environment, over the eons, had a role in influencing genetic or hereditary factors. The interplay between environment and the individual on the biological and psychological levels was recognized by Freud, but he still clung to the idea that heredity was more important in the everyday existence of each individual. Freud pointed up many bipolar phenomena that would automatically create friction or problems that had to be resolved; the individual and society, the ego and the id, the ego and the superego, male and female, ego libido and object libido, parents and children, and on and on.

Adelaide Johnson and her associates appear to have documented the environmental theory and the role of parents in creating the defense of identification with the aggressor as a fundamental dynamic in the neuroses and the psychoses. In my opinion, this is an important dynamic of borderline conditions. A brief statement of the application of her theory to antisocial behavior is found in a paper she wrote with Szurek (Szurek & Johnson, 1952):

> Our thesis is that the parents' unwitting sanction or indirect encouragement is a major cause of the specific stimulus for such anti-social behavior as fire-setting, stealing, truancy. By means of study and concomitant treatment of parents as well as of the child involved in anti-social behavior, it becomes unmistakably evident that one or occasionally both parents derive unconscious vicarious gratification of their own poorly integrated forbidden impulses in unwittingly sanctioning and fostering such behavior in the child. In every patient brought for treatment in whom simultaneous study of the parents was possible, the child's defect in conscience was traceable to a like defect in the parents.

This paper was written the same year as my first paper on the borderline patient in which I was coming to a conclusion that was similar concerning all kinds of acting out—antisocial, self-destructive, delinquent,
nondelinquent. It took me another eight years to realize that it was an
interlocking neurosis that was involved between the parents and that in
fact the parents were using their children as projective objects in the service
of their own defenses (Wolberg, A., 1960, pp. 179-180).[2]

Winnicott and followers of Sullivan use the concept "not me" or the
"false self" in relation to what the early analysts called the "pathological
introject" and the "imagoes," alluding to what I would see as "identification with the aggressor." It is in this sense that identification is the consequence of a group process, and is defensive, rather than that identification
is due to an innate factor that automatically makes itself known at a given
time in the genetically determined unfolding of development. It is this
identification defense that creates the bedrock for the sadomasochistic
system that is the dynamic responsible for projective identification in the
borderline patient (Wolberg, A., 1973; also 1977). To think of sadomasochism as deriving automatically from an early phase of infancy where
voyeurism, exhibitionism, and other such phenomena are present is to project onto infancy characteristics that can be but symptoms of certain
neurotic adults or adolescents. Identification is not a manifestation of the
"innate schedule." Neither is sadomasochism in my opinion. The two,
however, are related in the dynamics of the borderline patient. Now we
may say that identification is reflected in an "internalization," and becomes possible through learning, i.e., through a combination of learning,
memory, the ability to imitate, and so forth. But identification becomes
viable because of the capacity of the individual to focus on certain types of
behavior, to communicate with parents on verbal and nonverbal levels and
on a host of other variables, such as the ability to inhibit certain creative
or other normal forms of impulses. Identification depends upon relations
with objects, but *the capacity to identify* is a function of several factors
that are probably genetically determined. My concept of the borderline patient, unlike that of Kernberg, is that his *emotional disorder* is a *product
of identification.* Over a long period in face of much resistance on the part
of the child, the parent finally imposes the identification behavior (Wolberg, A., 1973).

---

[2]I might mention that the "quote" in this 1960 paper about interlocking defenses is from
my lecture notes and an unpublished paper delivered at the Postgraduate Center for Mental
Health in New York City in November 1953. Von Domarus made some comments to the effect that the ideation I was describing in the borderline was in fact paranoid; he did not mean
that the patient had an organized delusion that was daily motivating but that the patient
tended toward paranoid thoughts in times of stress or anxiety.

There are numerous manifestations of the "innate schedule," including such phenomena as the "excitement" (the emotion) evident in the infant that accompanies new learning. (Is this like Freud's concept of libidinalization of the object a pleasant feeling or energy that Freud called "sexual" in learning? or communication via sounds and gestures?) Probably learning itself and memory have a relationship to the genetic code since these seem to be present at birth (see *Science News*, 1977, for new information on "The Brain and Emotions"). We know now that the brain and the heart apparently are organs that function early in fetal life. The brain is obviously needed in the unfolding of neural and physical fetal development and has a relation to learning even in prenatal existence. What the psychoanalyst calls "internalization" apparently has its origin in prenatal life since the fetus begins to be responsive to external events perhaps during the eighth and ninth months and then learning in relation to objects, or at least reactions to the actions of objects begins. (The fetus will move if a light clapping goes on outside near the mother.)

Usually the definition of "internalization" corresponds to what is meant by *learning in communication with people and objects*. Why the psychoanalyst must create a special definition concerning learning is not clear. The psychoanalytic definition of "internalization" includes the concept that *incorporation, introjection,* and *identification* are object-related mechanisms. There are many authorities who believe that there are no such mechanisms as incorporation and introjection, these ideas being based on Freud's and Ferenczi's notions in relation to the concept of "introjected object." They dispute the idea that the oral phase of development has certain atavistic phenomena based on certain ancient tribal practices which can be recreated in regression. This, I would say, is one of the erroneous concepts that has crept into the consideration of borderline dynamics and is now posed by many theorists. Many faulty concepts regarding borderline pathology result as a consequence of the use of Freud's developmental theory, particularly his ideas of primary and secondary narcissism.

The concept of learning and memory in infancy has been confusing until comparatively recently. It is now rather clear that even the day-old infant has begun learning in earnest. Memory is present shortly after birth, and probably before, and seems definitely to have been established in depth by the age of 3 months.

The studies of Szurek and Johnson (1952, 1954) and others have shown that there is a direct relationship between identification with the aggressor, fantasy and internalization, i.e., identification and acting out. I would say that neurotic fantasy is a representation in the mind of the identification process and the conflicts associated with these identifications (disguised) rather than a reflection of some kind of developmental phenomenon, or some primal "fantasmagoria." Fantasy is a disguised way of representing the interpersonal implications of the identifications, and this kind of fantasy must be distinguished from the kind of thinking that is related to problem solving and creative thought. De Casper (1979) has reported an experiment that he did with a newborn several hours after birth. It appears that the infant could cooperate with him, or at least there was communication between the infant and the experimenter to the effect that the infant accomplished the task of discriminating between the mother's voice and the voice of another person. From what I have gleaned there appears to be an innate capacity for discrimination in the infant—i.e., the ability to distinguish "pleasant" and "unpleasant"—and, together with the innate capacity to "perceive" with two or more of the senses, the infant is capable of cross-modal integration, a necessary process in learning. Can we say, then, that the infant engages in creative thought as he learns in this early stage of his postnatal existence? It seems likely that this kind of performance is more complicated than reflex response and thus could be called cognitive activity based on interpersonal experience.

Green (1977) has written about what he calls "the creation of neo-reality" in the psychoses (and in borderline conditions), saying that it is analogous to the neurotic world of fantasy. One can certainly agree with this so long as we use Freud's early definition of fantasy (Wolberg, A., 1973, p. 15). One could say that "neo-reality" means "fantasy" and thus can mean fantasy expressed in hallucinations and delusions, all the result of a conflict concerning reality. Freud's formula seems to say that neurotic defenses are not due to conflicts over reality but to "intrapsychic conflict." I have proposed the primacy of identification fantasies in emotional problems. The "neo-reality" that Green speaks of is in fact an *identification fantasy*, a loosely defined delusional system in the borderline, paranoidlike but not systematized as in schizophrenia (Wolberg, A., 1952). Green uses a "higher" and "lower" concept in his theory, which means a distinction for those terms between secondary and primary thought processes.

Freud wrote (1924) that "neurosis does not disavow the reality, it only ignores it; psychosis disavows it and tries to replace it." In this essay, however, Freud concedes that in the neuroses, as in the psychoses, the fantasy serves as a respite from reality. Thus Freud never quite succeeds in making a difference in this respect between the neuroses and the psychoses. He did say that the real difference is that in the psychoses the ego is subject to modifications of a different quality. Disavowal and the remaking of reality in the psychoses are contrasted with repression and fantasy in the neuroses, although is it admitted at the end that in both neuroses and psychoses a denial of reality exists, and thus repression would have to be present.

If we understand that hallucination and delusion are forms of the identification fantasy expressed in the context of projective identification (a remaking of reality), then we can see that a certain kind of mental organization representing reality persists in the psychotic, even in the midst of what has been called an inability to perceive reality. Freud remarked that the individual can correct a delusion in a dream (see Freud, S.E., 1938, 23:201-202), a feat that may be possible because the delusion in any case represents reality in a disguised form. The "false self," "neo-reality," or simply the "bad self" together with the "remaking of reality" are phrases that represent what I would call identification fantasies in various forms. They are also defenses. Associations to these fantasies and their dynamics reveal the patterns of interaction in the family that were traumatic. They are, therefore, repetitive and representative of the conflict that has been resolved in an unsatisfactory way and therefore might be related to unfinished tasks (i.e., the Zeigarnick effect is operative).

Green (1969, 1977) has elaborated a more complicated definition of "splitting" to explain the "remaking of reality" and denial than that of Kernberg. Utilizing Freud's concepts of the developmental differences between hysterical and hypochondriacal symptoms (this is a "higher" and "lower" level concept according to Freud's theory of sexual development), he has an explanation of three types of symptoms seen in the borderline that he feels have a relationship to "splitting": (1) that of denying pleasurable experience, i.e., the sensations or feeling accompanying the particular experiences are denied, (2) hypochondriacal ideas; and (3) the symptom of acting out. It appears that all of these phenomena might be considered to be hysterical-like in nature and that there are *fantasies* connected with each type of symptom—those connected with hypochondriacal problems being fantasies that tend more toward delusion. There is undoubtedly a difference between hypochondriacal symptoms where physical illness does not exist and psychosomatic symptoms where there is real illness, such as stomach ulcer or forms of colitis. Green discusses psychosomatic symptoms and seems to find, dynamically speaking, a likeness between acting out and such symptoms.

Green writes that it would be erroneous to think that splitting occurs only or mainly during the separation of the "external" from the "internal." In fact, splitting, he insists, also occurs (perhaps even predominantly) between "psyche" and "soma," thus consequently between "bodily sensations" and "affects." This dissociation takes subtle forms as in the isolation process that disjoins "affect representations" and "thought" (see the discussion of the "isolating process" on pp. 230-231. Motor reactions (which include acting out) may also be split off from the "psychic world." Two frontiers established by splitting are "between the somatic and the libidinal body, on the one side, and between psychical reality and external reality involving the libidinal body and action, on the other." As a consequence, "we may assume that the split-off soma will intrude into the psychic sphere in the form of a psychosomatic symptom."Green sees differences in the defenses between psychosomatic symptoms and those found in conversion hysteria and the hypochondrias; thus whereas conversion symptoms are built in a "symbolic fashion" and are related to the libidinal body (a higher level operation), psychosomatic symptoms are not symbolic but are simply somatic manifestations "loaded with pure aggression." He then says that hypochondriacal symptoms, on the other hand, are "painful representations of somatic organs filled with narcissistic delibidinalized destructive libido." One may assume, contends Green, that there is also a lack of symbolization in acting out. Insofar as it is a symptom, acting out may have a symbolic meaning for the analyst but none from the patient's point of view, he being blind to its possible meaning. It is not "linked" to anything other than its manifest rationalized content. (We may ask ourselves these questions: Is not rationalization a defense? A lie? And is not rationalization a defense against a reality that the patient "knows" exists? Is not rationalization an expression of aggression? Are not rationalization and lying connected with fantasies?) According to Green, the difference between splitting and repression is that in repression the psychic energy is bound, links are intact and combined with other representatives of affects (id derivatives), the original items in the associative link are replace by others, but the "linking function" is only transformed—not altered; in splitting, the links are destroyed or so impaired that only by intensive effort can the analyst *guess* what they would have been. Thus, Green "strongly objects" to the notion that borderline patients engage in primary-process thinking. This idea of linkages and the lack of them is used also by Rey (1975) in relation to a theory of group therapy.

Green agrees with Kernberg, who contends that the borderline patient's acting out is based on a raw discharge of instinctual energy rather than on any form of identification. In my opinion identifications can be discovered in the borderline patient in many ways, not the least of which is to have an interview with the family. In therapy sessions one can discern these links in the patient's productions by "listening with the third ear." The fact that the links are denied or disavowed does not mean that the patient does not tell us of them. The projective techniques that I have recommended for use with the borderline patient are a means of relating to the denied aspects of the patient's problem by discussing the dynamics of the "others" with whom the patient is in contact and with whom he is identified. My patient Sonia in sessions with me began to recognize her identifications with the people in her dreams and the particular characteristics of her own that are identical to those of the people with whom she is associated socially (see pp. 258-261) and who appeared in these dreams.

Green states that splitting is a force by which something is excluded—in fact, is disallowed and becomes unworkable or unthinkable. He does point out (correctly, I believe, but inconsistently with his theory) that there is a "return of the repressed" in splitting, with the difference that it will have an "intrusive persecutory quality" by way of projective identification. One would have to disagree that in the process of disavowal associative links are not operative or present since they are conceptualized and retained in the delusions and the hallucinations (which, as I have said, are merely projected forms of the identification fantasies) by way of projective identification. The identification fantasies activate acting-out behavior when current situations stir up feelings that are similar to those that existed in traumatic situations with parents and others in the past with whom the patient was associated; thus there are important links between mind and body action in the here and now. In impotency or frigidity, for example, we find a tendency to disavowal of pleasurable sexual contact. The denial of pleasure from work success is a symptom of the borderline's disavowal mechanism. The fantasies can be elicited, and Rosner (1969) has suggested how the associative process works in these cases. For example, L.R. Wolberg (1945, 1st ed.; 1964, 2nd ed.) in the case of Johann R. demonstrated by hypnosis that the "links" are obviously there. Acting out is, indeed, a symptom and a return of the repressed.

Green cites as important to the understanding of the borderline Bouvet's (1967) description of the "pregenital structures," especially his "depersonalization neurosis." He writes that Freud assumed the basic function of the instinct in the psychic field in relation to objects to be the lowering of unpleasurable tension. The British school assumes that the function of the instinct is "growth" and Green assumes that the basic function is "representation."

Does this term "representation" refer to the process of "internalization"? And are these the processes by which the mind forms both an image and an idea of an object? If so, then this is related both to learning and the organization of defensive fantasies, which like lying can be considered a manifestation of the creative process used as a defense, but for hostile purposes. It seems to me that, properly defined, the function of the instinct, if one uses the word to mean genetic factors, can have a relation to the lowering of tension and to adaptation and growth.

"Representation" as I understand it is a mental process, an aspect of perception, learning, and the "processing of information." It relates to the effects of experience in the world. The concept is used in relation to the secondary process as opposed to the primary process when "representational reality" is distinguished from "psychic reality." The concepts primary process and psychic reality, however, if these refer to fantasy, cannot describe

a nonrepresentational or nonsymbolic substantiality, for fantasy is in essence symbolization. As our information stands today, there is no nonrepresentational phase of development in the mental or cognitive life, since
the infant sees patterns as wholes from the first few days of life. Piaget's
nonrepresentational stage does not seem to exist, but there may be a pre-
symbolization period. The infant in his perceptions outlines an integrated
picture of the object with his eyes, and he "conditions" and learns very
rapidly with experience, associating "good" and "bad" or "pleasant" and
"unpleasant" with situations and with objects. We know that perception is
part of the process of representation. The latter is actually an integrative
capacity, which, in turn, is one of the "givens" of the individual at birth.
It is my impression that Freud wrote that the basic function of mind is
adaptation and survival, a self-preservation motif. When Freud talked of
an "innate schedule," however, he referred to the periods of development
according to his developmental scheme, i.e., oral, anal, phallic, oedipal, . . .,
and to the appearance of the sadomasochistic instincts at these developmental
stages and their effects rather than to an unfolding of certain types of behaviors like smiling, gesturing, the 8-to-12-month fear reaction, imitation,
and the like that are obviously behaviors that help in self-preservation.

Winnicott (1953a, b; 1965) according to Green, in his explanations of
borderline conditions, has provided us with the greatest insight into emotional development in his concepts of "primary maternal concern" and
"holding," shifting the attention from the overall "internal object" (Klein)
to the role of the external object. (Fairbairn was the English psychoanalyst
who introduced this idea.) Adler, Sullivan, Fromm, Jackson, and Horney
had similar concepts. As I see it, a shift in emphasis to the object means a
shift to the importance of family dynamics in emotional problems, which I
stressed in my 1952 paper. It was not until 1953, however, that I began to
realize the significance of an interlocking defensive process between parents
as the possible stimulus for the development of the identification role and a
primary basis for the beginning of an emotional problem in children. Finally, in my 1960 paper I tried to discuss these dynamics. I felt that the important research by Szurek (1942) and Johnson (1949) leads to the conclusion
that parents play a major part in the organization of emotional disorders in
their children. I proposed that it was due to their need to utilize their children in the service of defense that this occurred. These authors interpreted
their findings in the context of the structural theory, emphasizing the impact on superego functions. Jackson's research, however, over a period of
several years emphasized the concept of "family homeostasis" and measures
taken by parents to control their anxieties so as to perpetuate their neurotic
adjustment, and it is this "systems concept" that has proved most useful in
understanding the family dynamics and the relation of neurotic and

psychotic defenses in family members to the organization of identification behavior. (For a complete bibliography of Jackson's work see *Group Therapy: An Overview*, 1977).

Green (1977) credits Winnicott (1958) with emphasizing the interplay of the "external" and "internal" and "of the intermediate" or the "failure to create it." In his view Winnicott is concerned with the "fate of symbolism," the functional value of the "transitional field," and particularly "transitional phenomena" in borderline cases. Green contends that Winnicott would say, "The setting and the analyst do not represent the mother; *they are the mother*" (present author's italics). It is not clear as to the role Winnicott means the therapist to play. As Kohut suggests, must the therapist act as a mother, a corrective person (the good mother that the patient did not have) so that the defects that occurred in the ego or "self" from poor mothering can be made up? Or must the therapist in playing the role of mother actually *be* the mother? Or, does he mean that the patient has the delusion that the therapist *is* the mother or that the therapist has the delusion that *he* is the mother?

Modell (1963, 1968, 1975) has discussed Winnicott's concept of the transitional object and has compared the borderline's transference response to the therapist as similar to the infant's response to a teddy bear or a blanket. As part of this reasoning, Modell speculated that the borderline has difficulty in asking for help because he cannot tolerate refusal without developing hostile fantasies and fears of abandonment. In order not to have such feelings and fantasies, he does not ask the therapist for anything. Modell has made an important point in discussing the patient's pattern of "not asking," a response that is transferential due, I believe, to the rejecting pattern of the parents toward the child. The patient asks and asks and asks. It is only when rejection is forthcoming that he stops asking, recognizing that it is futile. He does this also so that he can have a certain amount of security and not be entirely rejected or abandoned. He fears the retaliatory hostility if he persists in asking for his rights. The transference feeling is that he will be rejected by the therapist—or by anyone from whom he may ask. This is, of course, a masochistic pattern. On the other hand, this patient does have a way of asking even when the request is not verbalized and he resists help even when seeking it. He is the help-rejecting patient who seems to take pleasure in frustrating the people from whom he is asking help and making *them* feel impotent. He seems to be showing hostility and revenge patterns with this masochistic stance. Modell said that the patient does recognize the therapist as existing separately from himself, but, unlike the neurotic, the borderline does not have the capacity to recognize that the attributes assigned to the transitional object (the equivalent of the blanket) are projections (or, rather, "perceptions") emanating from within himself. (I believe that the patient may recognize this, but he does not always take the recognition into account, i.e., he denies what he knows.)

Winnicott thought of the blanket as a *protective shield* and an object used both lovingly and in a hostile manner (the child mutilates the blanket and loves it, two opposites—Eros and Thanatos), the expectation being that the blanket must survive both kinds of usage. (Is this another way of talking of sadomasochism?) The blanket, Winnicott avowed, was something that possessed characteristics of its own, such as warmth and texture. Winnicott's idea that the child needs warmth, acceptance, understanding, love, and other forms of stimulation is certainly valid. I think we must understand the patients' aggression, however, in the light of frustration and the cutting off of feeling as a manifestation of the identifications with parental figures. Winnicott's idea is that the blanket or the teddy bear takes the place of the mother, and like the mother (according to Melanie Klein) it must withstand love and hate.

Melanie Klein (1946) conceived of all mothers as being in a tenuous position with their infants—being the object of love in some instances and the object of hostility at other times. If the mother could survive the ambivalent usage, then the child had the opportunity to be healthy, but if she had difficulty, this did not bode well for the child. Fintzy (1971), Mahler, Pine, and Bergman (1975), and Volkan (1976) use the idea that the transitional object is related to a phase of development in the child's separation from the mother. Rey (1975) has suggested that in group therapy the members serve the function of transitional objects who provide the "missing links" (an idea similar to Green's) or the missing "representations" that did not occur in the mind at appropriate periods in the patient's development due to poor mothering. This is a lacunae theory.

Winnicott writes about the "false self" or a "not me" as an "overdemanding adaptation" to the "need-supplying object." (As I said before, I would also call the "false self" an "identification with the aggressor.") Winnicott's later concepts of "*noncommunication*," "*void*," "*emptiness*," "the *gap*," and the "impossibility of creating out of these another form of reunion with the object regardless of whether its energic aspect is wholly or only partly traceable to the instinctual drives once formed" are really important, in Green's estimation. Here we are unfortunately presented with the same controversy as that between Kernberg and Kohut. Does Winnicott think of "the void" and "emptiness" as defenses of the ego and the "gap" as a developmental defect? As a matter of act, "emptiness," "void," "blank," "apathy" are phrases that have a similar connotation to "life has no meaning." All are evidences of depression in borderline patients, as I view it, a depression that is often overlooked or missed by many therapists. However, as we have stated, in the context of "higher" and "lower" forms of development (preoedipal and oedipal phases) the borderline does not, according to Kernberg, have depression (a higher order of reaction associated with guilt and the oedipal problem), but experiences only apathy (a lower form of expression) and has *envy* rather than *guilt feelings*. Does the "gap" refer to "missing links" in the ego? To depression? Or to some other kind of phenomenon?

Green insists the return of the split-off elements (i.e., return of the repressed) is accompanied by signal anxiety and emotion, which is described by Freud (1926, 1927) as "helplessness" (*hilfosigkeit*), by Klein (1946) as "annihilation," by Winnicott (1958) as "disintegration" or "agonies," by Bion (1970) as "nameless dread," and by Green (1969) as "blankness." Apparently, these feelings are to be distinguished from depression, as Kernberg's theory implies. Kernberg speaks of the "dread of loneliness," which I take to be a depressive attitude related to fears of self destructive impulses. Summing up modern research, Caplan (1973, p. 92) tells us that at the age of 3 months the "higher brain" takes control. Does this mean that the "higher and "lower" postulations of psychoanalytic theory with respect to ego development and the concepts of primary and secondary process are in error? One can agree that the "return of the repressed" is accompanied by anxiety; in fact, in my opinion, it is anxiety that stimulates the return of the repressed—anxiety related to anger or fear or both. In Chapter 5 we shall see that many investigators feel that the infant of several hours of age engages in "higher brain activity."

Can we say that this "higher" and "lower" brain activity has something to do with ego development? Can we say that Klein's theory of early stages, i.e., the schizoid stage and the depressive stage, has something to do with the development of the ego? What has this to do with the adult state of depression? Does depression have a relation to the oedipal stage? Does the preoedipal stage mean that there is no true relation to objects and that, therefore, there is no guilt and thus there can be no depression? Could Klein have thought that depression was regression back to the earlier stages or was there a kind of in-limbo stage, one that vacillates between the schizoid stage and the depressive stage with no real footing in either? Freudian theory has been interpreted to mean that there is not guilt in the preoedipal stage and that, therefore, there could be no depression. These theories hinge upon the idea that idealization is a normal step in the advance to the oedipal period. Most theorists today say that the borderline has not reached that period in ego development where idealization of the object has solidified so that the individual can go on to the next stage where guilt and repression are present. However, Caplan tells us of a "self" in the seventh month of life and the ability of the infant to distinguish between family members. The mother becomes more important than others (Caplan, 1973, p. 93), yet the child shows preferences for other people too. Does this mean that by 3 months the supposed autism or the narcissism is broken and the object is valued for its own sake?

Incidentally, in the *Archives of General Psychiatry* relative to the drug treatment of borderline patients there is an article on depression, "Low-dose Neuroleptic Regimens" (Brinkley et al, 1979), one of the few double-blind studies done to indicate that antidepressant drugs, notably Tofranil and Nardil, were helpful in borderline cases. Brinkley found that low doses of such drugs as Thorazine and the like can be useful too. I have found that some borderline patients reject helpful drugs for the relief of depression and use the more harmful ones such as the amphetamine energizers, alcohol and others. To an extent, this is due to their masochism and their negativistic attitudes toward authority—and perhaps their hidden suicidal aims. There may be a relation between depression and masochism. A true idealization would mean that the depressive attitude (Klein) would have given way, and there would be no persecutory objects, as there are in depression.

It is the schizophrenic patient who so often has the "dead look"—"the void." This usually indicates that the individual has withdrawn into fantasy and is using the defense of detachment. But detachment and depression are not quite the same, although perhaps they are related. Detachment is a process of withdrawal into fantasy, a defense against feelings of aggression toward others. Depression is, in my opinion, related also to aggression, but the aggression is self-destructive in the face of feelings of misuse by others as well as rage at the latter. The schizophrenic is also self-destructive, but he has a defense of withdrawal that is somewhat different from that of the depressive in that he is likely to have persecutory hallucinations while the depressed person may have paranoid feelings but is less likely to have a hallucinatory defense. In any case, the depression in the borderline is not so severe as the endogenous depressive or the schizophrenic depression. The depression in the borderline is chronic—but it is of a less severe nature.

It is difficult to accept a theory that relates mental and emotional disorders to "fixations" at infantile levels developed as a result of distortion over limited periods of time during particular early developmental phases. I believe that it is much more realistic to accept that the kind of experience the child has in the family *over time* is the most important factor in the development of personality needs and defenses. Defenses can serve masochistic needs; thus they do not always safeguard the individual against self-destruction. Detachment is the distancing mechanism that accompanies not only depression but other defenses as well. Depression should probably be thought of as a defense since it is a mood or feeling, one associated with fantasies specifically of anger, revenge, and low self-esteem and with compensatory feelings of grandiosity, which are a function of the revenge feelings. Depression often derives from the original feeling of being abused, used, and rejected by parental figures. Both schizophrenics and borderlines have this experience with its accompanying feeling of abuse and misuse. I believe that it is this depressive mechanism (with a paranoid tinge, i.e., a projection to protect the patient's identifications with the rejecting parents) that is present in the pattern Modell has described.

Green considers Winnicott "the analyst of the borderline." He values the Winnicott concept of the "false self" built, as he says, "not on the patient's real experiences" but on the "compliance to the mother's image of her child." Since the mother's "image of her child" is a projection of the mother's identification with her own parents, which she wishes to deny, and the mother is *active* through her punishments and rewards in seeing that her child "complies," in my opinion this, indeed, is a real experience for the child. The eventual accepting of the identification, in spite of protests, is one of the bases of what Spitz (1965, p. 139) and others (Furst, 1967, p. 32; Kris, 1956, pp. 72-73) have called the "cumulative trauma," which promotes the neurosis and is the essence of the "false self" organization. The child does not automatically "comply" with the mother's image of her child. He resists. Thus the *identification* (for me the appropriate terminology for what Winnicott calls the "false self") develops over a long period of time. One needs to employ role theory to depict the dynamics of this identification process (Wolberg, A., 1960, 1977).

The "image" that Winnicott speaks of, to my way of thinking, is a certain fantasy that contains a specific kind of role that the parents project, the father being involved in such projections as well as the mother. There is punishment and reward in the parents' insistence on these roles, and *this is a continuous process—not simply in the child's infancy but over the years as the parents and the child live together*. The role is finally integrated by the child, and the process is an "identification with the aggressor." In turn, these identifications when acted out are aspects of the interlocking defensive system in the family. Rinsley (1976, 1978) speaks of this "image" as being one of the mother's own parents or a sibling, a projection she used to defend against her feelings of abandonment. I believe that Freud's "loss of object" as the "danger" in depression is similar to these "feelings of abandonment" (by the parent) that Rinsley and others mention. The basic problem, however, is not only a fear of abandonment. Rather, it is a realization by the child that he is *rejected as a person in his own right*, a realization that is the basis of his denial, detachment, depression, and rage and his consequent neurotic need for a sadomasochistic relationship. The picture is complicated by the fact that he must comply with the projected role, thus the two-edged function of depression as a defense against aggression toward others and toward the self. This defense does not prevent the expression of aggression, but it does inhibit the full expression of anger and revenge and helps contain the fear of the destructiveness of the parents, both of whom are involved in the projective use of the child. The child's deepest fear, I feel, is the fear of annihilation as a consequence of parental destructiveness.

It is the need to be related to a sadomasochistic object, (the object of identification) that creates the fear of "loss of the object" and what has been called the "fear of abandonment." ("If I don't do what my parents want they will abandon me, or send me away.") The identification, as Rank suggested, is an insurance against being destroyed, an insurance against death that does not always work in view of the numbers of infants and youngsters that come into the category of "battered children." On the parents' parts, the expectation of compliance is there, so long as the individual remains with his family. He perpetuates his compliance after he leaves home by finding someone with whom to relate who will interact in such a way as to provide the interlocking defensive relationship he had at home. If we must speak of a "punitive superego" (I prefer to use the concept "identification with the aggressor"), then we should define this as a compliance with the demands of the father's and mother's needs of identifications with them, which they have actively fostered due to their own anxieties. The "false self" is the internalization of the identification that motivates the individual to act against his best interest in favor of reducing the anxieties of his parents through particular behaviors. It is this compliance with the role demand of the parents for "particular behavior" that creates the further need for denial and stimulates the patient's self-contempt as he slowly "gives in" to the role. His self-contempt is compounded as he gradually, through identification, becomes in some respect like the parents, using patterns he both loathes and fears. He would rather give and receive love. It is this *giving in* and *becoming like the parent* and the wish that things were different—and the almost delusional thought that the parents will change at some time rather than accepting the fact that it is the child himself who must change—that are the basis of the borderline patient's denials and disavowals.

Freud (1931) mentioned the *fear of being killed by the mother* as a dynamic in females, while in males there is present *the desire to kill the father* (1921). "In Family Romances" (1909) Freud noted the child's wish to be in another situation—a member of a different family. In the essay "Female Sexuality" (1931) Freud spoke of love relations that are inhibited in their aims, the child's feeling that the mother did not "give" enough, castration fear. In "Civilization and Its Discontents" (1929-1930) he wrote of the dynamics of fear, guilt, and conscience, of aggression, but he did not put these all together in the context of sadomasochism. He pictured these in the light of the libido theory (sexuality) and the resolution or lack of resolution of the Oedipus complex, as well as the idea that in the end man will destroy himself and his civilization by his own aggression, which he will never learn to contain. Freud would never quite come to the conclusion that both the mother and the father were bound together in a neurotic contract, or defensive alliance, to maintain homeostasis or equilibrium and that the father too had excessive amounts of aggression, which the child feared.

In treatment the patient hesitates to step out of the sadomasochistic role in order to change because he has been made to feel responsible for the mental health of his parents by accepting the identification. On one level he would rather remain ill than to hurt them and experience the guilt he might feel by causing them to develop a psychosis or "go to pieces," but on another level he expresses his aggression and hatred. The ambivalent attitude is a hindrance and a defense. The conflict over the parental behavior is unresolved—or is resolved through submission, which is an unsatisfactory state. The patient denies and clings to the denial that he is sadomasochistic, particularly that he is sadistic and destructive and that he expresses his pattern of revenge as a consequence of the rejections by his parents. He projects his aggression and utilizes others outside the family upon whom to vent some of his rage. He does express anger toward the parents, who invite it to a certain extent in order to assuage their own guilts.

Actually, in the family as the parents deny their active role in the maintenance of their neurotic equilibrium using the children as projective objects in the service of their defense, the child (under pressure from the parents) has no choice but to distort his concept of reality in the presence of these rigid authorities and to become something he does not wish to be. In the group process that occurs as identifications leading to neurosis slowly develop, there is in the denials a dynamic that takes place that is similar to what Asch (1951) demonstrated in some of his experiments (Wolberg, A., 1968, p. 108). In his relations with parents the child eventually gets to the point where he will deny that the whole identification process has taken place at all. He will isolate, or deny out of fear, those feelings and thoughts he had about his parents when they forced him into the identification. He wishes to deny too his knowledge that the identifications are destructive to him and that they interfere with his safety and an adequate life adjustment. (It is my thought that phobias are defenses against the patient's fears of annihilation and the fear is two-pronged: fear of the rage of others and fear of one's own counterrage directed both to others and to the self.)

There are times in the analysis of the borderline when there are mini psychotic episodes (Wolberg, A., 1952, p. 694) and also suicidal ideas. These occur when the reality of the relations with the parents breaks through into consciousness and the recognition takes hold that he, the patient, must step out of the sadomasochistic role if he is to be cured. At these times it is evident that the patient is not ready to suffer the anxiety of the initial phases of such change and that he is still clinging to the defenses of idealization and indecision (ambivalence). In seeking treatment, however, he has taken a positive step, but his denial mechanisms are extended to defend against this step. He is full of anxiety about seeking treatment, and he denies that this is positive behavior. He belittles the step and the therapist at the same time that he has great hopes that something positive will happen.

Winnicott says that in treatment the "building of potential space" opens new horizons. Apparently, "potential space" refers to the idea that the therapist will be able to be less rigid than the parents; therefore, the patient will be encouraged to see more alternatives as his horizons expand under the impact of treatment. His "life space" will become greater, his movement more varied, his experience richer. (This may happen if the patient can overcome his guilt, fear, aggression, and ambivalence.) The social space widens, and the stimulation for the patient becomes greater from the point of view of new experience.

Countertransference

Winnicott points out the possibility of countertransference reactions in the therapist when working with the borderline patient. He says that the therapist is exposed to new ways of noticing his own reactions as a tool for comprehending the paradoxes of the borderline systems of thought. Much has been written of late of the therapist's reactions to the borderline patient and the idea that countertransference helps us to understand the psychodynamics and psychotherapy of borderline states. I do not agree that countertransference is helpful; much of it stems from the therapist's inability to comprehend the dynamics of the patient and the frustration that this evokes. If the therapist can correct his countertransference reaction, this is helpful. It may lead to insight about himself and the patient, but if he simply recognizes the countertransference feeling without being able to analyze it and to correct his position, then he will have gained nothing in the way of clarity concerning himself or the patient.

Grinberg, who writes extensively on countertransference and understanding the borderline elaborates his theory of countertransference by describing the concept of projective identification in operation in the group treatment of borderline patients, using a combination of Freudian and Kleinian theory. He especially refers to what he calls "projective counteridentification." He writes that normally (this is Kleinian theory) identification functions "practically from the very beginning of life, through what may be defined as the constant search for a balance between giving and receiving" (Grinberg, 1973). (Kernberg uses the concept of the patient's projection onto the therapist of "giving" and "ungiving" attitudes, which he says is a "mother transference" in borderline patients. One must realize, as has been repeatedly stressed in this volume, that this can also be a "father transference.")

Grinberg asserts that we should consider "the normal relations" that emerge from projective identification so as to take into account in therapy not only the subject's projective identifications conditioned by his diverse fantasies and impulses, but also his primitive object's projective identifications. In addition to this, he insists, one must appraise the projective identifications of each member of the group. In Kleinian terms projective identification is a "normal" developmental, defensive mechanism that leads to ego formation and the control of aggression.

Bion (1961) postulated a kind of psychotic bed (projective identification) upon which all individuals are originally grounded and which appears in the therapy group as a system of basic assumptions. These make up a combination of all of the psychotic beds of each of the group members. In a somewhat different view, Adler spoke of the patient's "private logic," meaning the fantasies, rationalization, distortions, and the like that the patient uses in his defenses. Bion has also a concept that is meant to describe the derivatives of the id or what Horney seems to have meant by certain patterns (tropisms?). Bion speaks of *dependency, fight-flight* and *pairing*. Horney, we will recall, spoke of moving toward, moving against, moving with, and so forth. Bion's basic assumptions are "givens," and upon these givens he projects basic fantasies somewhat as Freud considered the id as a source of basic irrational fantasy. In group treatment, according to Bion, the members work through their "basic assumptions," which are thought of a kind of "combined id" or "group id" leading to a more realistic outlook. The "basic assumptions," we have said, are evident in fantasies and in trends of thought. This idea is an offshoot of Freud's concept of the id and how it influences our lives in more important ways than reality dictates. Rangell (1955) quoted Glover as saying, "We are all larval psychotics and have been since the age of 2."

Grinberg points out that presumably the analyst has worked through some of his own fantasies (reflections of his basic assumptions), but he avows the borderline patient's projections are such that they tend to lead the analyst into "projective counteridentification." Grinberg distinguishes between this process and other forms of countertransference, a distinction that is difficult to understand. According to Kleinian theory, we all have projective identifications, starting at birth, and this dynamic is inextricably involved in learning throughout our lives. New experiences always stimulate projective identification in the individual since this is the basic mechanism through which all experience is integrated. Klein's theory does with projective identification what Freud's did with identification. The assumptions are that identifications (and projective identification) are normal aspects of mental development and the stuff out of which the ego is formed. As I see it, both identification and projective identification are two sides of the same coin: they are defenses, the first of the neuroses and character disorders, where projection has not been so systematically employed, and the second of the borderlines and the psychoses, each associated with fantasies, and the more persistently projective defenses.

Grinberg (1973) states that "projective identifications lay the foundation for human communication," a premise that is questionable to say the least. There is an assumption in sociology and social psychology that group dynamics emerge from the communications, i.e., the interactions of group members. However, communications related to projective identifications in group therapy would be considered, according to sociological theory, "self-oriented needs," and these would be impediments in (1) the problem-solving process and (2) the development of norms both of which are the basic goals of group life. Foulkes (1948) seems to have been the only psychoanalytically oriented group therapist who stressed the importance and the function of *norms* as they develop in the group therapy process, thus assuming a conscious group problem-solving process. Foulkes pointed out that norms are aspects of group dynamics (see Wolberg, A., 1977), particularly in relation to the standards that the group members expect to meet. He understood such standards to be an essential factor in the treatment process with respect to analyzing neurotic behavior, this being the aim of the problem-solving process in treatment. Bion does say that the group meets to do something, that is, *to work*, and that there are two levels of operation, the *work level* and the *resistance level*, the latter more or less unconscious. The work group and the leader interact in the therapeutic alliance to enhance the "observing ego's monitoring of archaic assumptions." These are "unconscious, underlying, primitive part-object fantasy remnants persisting from distorted perceptions of early life." This is a different concept of fantasy than the one I use. I believe that fantasies begin in early life as a means of overcoming fear or danger. The threat is real insofar as the welfare of the individual child is concerned, emanating from the neurotic activities of the parents as these affect the child's development, particularly his mental development. The mental reactions, in turn, influence the physical reactions. (Actually the effects of the environment are felt simultaneously on the physical as well as the mental level, for these are inextricably interrelated.) The accompanying fantasies are defenses to counteract the fears and other untoward reactions. Fantasies become more elaborate as the child develops physically and mentally and as he has continued experience with neurotic parents.

In Kleinian theory the introjective-projective reaction leading ultimately to individuation characteristic of early stages of life is never lost, and it may

be revived with special strength in any situation of stress that causes a feeling of helplessness. Freud felt that the prototype of helplessness was the
birth trauma. We have mentioned that Freud believed that nothing we
have once possessed (in the mind) is ever lost. Of course, if we thus mean
that the "fantasy remnants of archaic assumptions persisting from distorted perceptions of early life" are always present, then we assume two
things: (1) the basic life of every infant is a distortion and these distortions
persist throughout existence, and (2) in times of anxiety the individual regresses to this primitive level of mental operation. If we believe, however,
that the life of the infant is based in reality and that distortion is an aspect
of the defenses that accrue as the child meets various traumatic experiences day after day, then we have a different concept of the composition of
the mind and of fantasy as a defense. I support the latter idea.

Since communication provides the basis for group structure, Grinberg's
theory would mean that projective identifications are the basis of group
structure, an idea that would never be acceptable to the social theorist
(psychoanalysts often mistake the projective dimensions of the group members to be the main dynamic in groups). Moreno (1934) pointed out the
differences between the various types of communication in groups and their
meaning in relation to group structure. The communication system, he said,
is based on the choice-rejection motifs on the various members. Choices and
rejections are made for many reasons at various times. These are in general
the choices made for problem solving and for projective (defensive) reasons.

Bales (1950), Bales and Strodtbeck (1951), and others have amply demonstrated that projections and other "self-oriented needs" interfere with
the problem-solving aspects of the group process. Psychoanalysts often
forget that in the treatment process we must have an active conscious
problem-solving dynamic in operation for analysis to take place. The "observing ego" and reality perceptions must function in analysis—these are
essential in psychotherapy and psychoanalysis in order for the individual to
resolve his problems. And in the group it is important that the patient
understand the problems of each individual member as well as the group
process. Patients, however, present for our information in the group both
the reality picture of their lives and their distortions of reality as well. These
two levels of behavior interact in the dynamics of a therapy group (Wolberg,
A., 1977). The interplay of reality and distortion is evident in the one-to-
one situation as well. The analyst (therapist) must understand that the distortions are defenses and contain aspects of the distortions that represent
symbolically the reality picture of the patient's situations. Projective defenses are employed in the interlocking defensive systems that emerge as
one, two, or more group members identify with each other in respect to their
various neurotic behaviors and resist the implications of the interpretations

or statements of fact. These combinations in the group have been described by Moreno as "pairing," "triangles," "chains," and the like. It is on this basis that subgroups form. Subgroups related to problem solving emerge, however, as well as subgroups related to defense. At one time a member can be part of a defensive subgroup; another time the same member will belong to a problem-solving subgroup. This can occur in the same session, and the therapist must take note of these changes in order to understand the dynamics of each individual member (Wolberg, A., 1972).

Grinberg (1973) contends that with borderline patients the analyst is unconsciously and passively "led" to play the sort of roles that the patient hands over to him. (In my terms this would be a sadomasochistic role; thus the analyst would be forming an interlocking defensive relationship through identifying with the patient.) Grinberg calls this a partial but very specific aspect of the countertransference ("projective counteridentification"), but he believes that there is a difference between this kind of reaction on the part of the analyst and "countertransference reactions resulting from the analyst's own emotional attitudes or from his neurotic remnants, reactivated by the patient's conflicts." I find that borderline patients always attempt to involve the therapist in their sadomasochistic pattern, i.e., in their acting-out patterns, even when they know that if they are successful they will destroy the therapeutic process. They hope that the therapist will be able to resist this invitation (seduction). On some level they realize that they may eventually be rejected for their behavior if the therapist tires of coping with the pattern, which involves controlling and enmeshing the therapist as a mode of resistance to treatment, even when the patient wants treatment. I mentioned this pattern in my discussion of the case of the analyst who shifted his theoretical position so as to conduct treatment on the basis of Kohut's theory (case cited in Goldberg, 1978). It was my opinion (1978) that while the analyst was able to establish a working relationship with the patient, he let the patient know that he did not want to act out with him. It was clear, however, that the analyst did not reject the patient for trying to involve the analyst in his neurotic pattern. In this particular case the acting out had a perverse sexual connotation. According to Kohut's view, this acting out would indicate a lacuna in the "self," and the analyst would have to recognize that the exhibitionism was a residual of an unrequited early era of development; that is, it was an indication of an "unmirrored grandiose self." The analyst would then have to do "mirroring" as the mother should have done so that the deficit could be made up. In my view the patient was acting out a role he had been taught to play by the parents; he was acting out as a projective object of the parents in the interests of the parents' neurotic interlocking defensive system. Transferentially, he was attempting to involve the analyst the way that he and his parents had been involved, and still were involved, even though the patient was now away from the house and working. Identification (I) and projective identification (PI) are defenses that are learned roles (LR) projected from parents.

Grinberg describes two processes, *A* and *B*, that result when the patient leads the analyst on. In process *A* the analyst "selectively introjects the different aspects of the patient's verbal and nonverbal material, together with their corresponding emotional charges," and "works through and assimilates the identifications resulting from identification with the patient's inner world and then reprojects the results of this assimilation by means of interpretation." Here Grinberg assumes that learning about the patient and making an interpretation requires an identification with the patient. This is a use of Freud's developmental theory to explain the dynamics of learning. According to this theory, the individual "introjects an object" (a "form of identification) and then "works through by assimilating the identifications." He then "reprojects" when he interprets what he has learned. (This is a use of Kleinian theory in respect to the mechanism of projective identification as a function of learning, i.e., a necessary ingredient of the learning process.)

In process *B*, says Grinberg, one of two reactions on the part of the analyst may take place as he is the "passive object of the analysand's projections and introjections." The analyst's response may be due to his own conflicts, in which case he is indulging in a countertransference reaction; or, his responses may be quite independent of his "own emotions" and appear mainly as a reaction to the patient's projection upon him. The analyst may react in one of several ways: he may "properly interpret" and show the patient that "the violence of the mechanism has in no way shocked him"; or he may react in one of four ways if he finds that he is "unable to tolerate" the patient's actions toward him: (1) by a violent rejection of the projection, (2) by ignoring or denying his reaction, (3) by postponing and displacing his reaction to another patient, or (4) by "counteridentifying himself in turn." The response of the analyst will depend on his degree of tolerance.

Grinberg, conceding that Bion has a similar idea, believes that in "counteridentifying" the analyst may experience emotions aroused by the patient through the use of projective identification that to a certain extent are independent of the analyst's own basic problems. Thus, it is not the analyst's unanalyzed residuals that are responsible for his reaction to the patient, but the patient's revolting hostile or untoward behavior that creates the reaction in the analyst. Grinberg (1973, p. 148) describes one reaction that I would think is definitely a countertransference maneuver: He "will react as if he had acquired and assimilated the parts projected on him in a real and concrete way" and "in certain cases, the analyst may have the feeling of being no longer his own self." Accordingly, "the analyst will resort to all kinds of rationalization in order to justify his attitude or bewilderment."

Grinberg, as has been mentioned previously, assumes that projective identifications begin at birth or shortly after (when neither "ego boundaries" nor "ego relationships" with objects are differentiated) and that they continue throughout life being the means through which communication, empathy, and other such phenomena lead to "understanding" or assimilation. Grinberg's thoughts about the patient's revolting behavior reminds me of the reactions of W.A. Jones, who called his borderline patients "vampires," and said that they were ugly and disgusting.

Grinberg believes that in group treatment the emergence of roles takes place from the moment the group is formed. These roles automatically stem from the unconscious fantasies (the basic assumptions) projected by each participant onto the other in the course of their projective identifications. The roles and functions assumed by members of a group constitute the means through which the mechanisms of identification are conveyed. This is also the means through which communication takes place, according to Grinberg. As I see it, he makes no distinction here between *neurotic roles* and *problem-solving roles* in his conception of group dynamics. Grinberg says that the individual member's behavior or attitude toward playing the projected role (e.g., rebellious leader, submissive member, scapegoat) depends on the remaining members who will largely determine the emergence and the functioning of the role that they unconsciously view as necessary for the group's current situation. Actually, the members of a group come to the situation with roles that have been established by the family, but in the view of Grinberg the roles are derived from a mysterious "id" and are projections of this "id" based on a mysterious "inner core" in each member ("basic assumptions") that emerges at birth from the instincts and is expressed in fantasies representative of the instincts. The "unconscious," or what Bion calls the "basic assumptions," contains the activating motivation for all of the individual's behavior. There is no postulation of autonomous, "normal," "conscious" or goal-directed problem-solving behavior in the early stages of infancy.

Moreno clarified the concept of role (Wolberg, A., 1977) and understood the difference between *problem solving* and *projection*. He thought of transference behavior in the group as the projective aspects of the interactions and recognized problem-solving elements in the group members' interactions as they worked through their difficulties on a conscious level. Thus, he saw interaction as communication but noted the difference between projective goals and problem-solving goals in the interaction. Although Bion speaks of the "work" that the group does and he distinguishes the work level from the neurotic level in the group, it is not clear whether he conceives of work as problem solving on a conscious level. The exercises Moreno recommended for the group, i.e., role rehearsal and role reversal, were means of bringing insight to the individual through a process of conceptualizing the behavior of the "other" and then acting upon this conceptualization through such means as playing the role and expressing the attitudes and feelings of the "other." By depicting the person with whom the patient was (or is) in an interpersonal bind, the identification becomes clear and insight occurs.

Grinberg (1973) expresses his view this way: Identification is a process basically of "the transformation of a particular ego into another ego." As a result, the first ego behaves in certain respects in the same way as the other ego, imitating and "incorporating" the other ego. The individual identifies with certain reactions, attitudes, behavioral modalities or feelings of the different people with whom he comes in contact, and thus he forms an "empathic link" with the other. (This "empathic link" has been called by many names: bonds, identification, sympathy, libido, to cite just a few.) This link is a "normal" part of identification, according to Grinberg. Once the "empathic link" is established, "it becomes now possible to take the other's place and to understand his feelings. It also evokes a response in the object. . . ." The analyst's ability to "understand" the patient and establish empathy depends upon his ability to "identify" with the patient and put himself in the patient's place. (This interpretation follows Freudian develomental concepts.)

The orthodox analyst says that empathy, which is essential in analytic work, is based on identification (Moore & Fine, 1968, p. 43). Orthodox theory also contains the idea that identification is a "natural accompaniment of maturation and mental development and aids in the learning process" (Moore & Fine, 1968, p. 50). In my opinion identification interferes with the learning process and with understanding, for it is a neurotic process if "one ego behaves in some identical respect like another ego." We should not confuse identification with learning. In psychoanalysis one must work through the implications of identification (i.e., the "not me," the "false self," the "system") that relates to the parents' need for the identifications. This means recognizing certain patterns in oneself, patterns that one may abhor that are like those of the parents. But the analyst is *not* like the patient and has not had experiences similar to those of the patient. Each of us has had our own unique experience. We can only attempt to understand the patient. Identification with the patient would be a neurotic stance.

Grinberg says that projective identifications spring from diverse sources (and are "invariably functioning"), stimulating myriad affective responses in group members and in the analyst such as sympathy, anger, grief, hostility, and boredom. I can understand the analyst feeling sympathy for the patient, but if one is too sympathetic, one tends to treat the patient in a supportive and perhaps a somewhat derogatory manner. I can understand, too, getting bored at times with a patient, for most psychoanalytic endeavors have their boring moments due to the repetitiveness of some of the patients' productions. In general, however, the therapeutic experience is interesting. To feel anger, grief, and hostility, I believe, is to have countertransference reactions.

Following Freud's libido theory and his "higher" and "lower" developmental scheme, Grinberg alleges that "tendencies and fantasies" of patients "correspond to libidinal phases" and these "give rise to projective identification" with oral, anal, urethral, or genital contents, which add specific connotations to the attendant object relations. In this context Grinberg contends that we "mention those unconscious fantasies projected onto the object in order to eat, chew, bite, or devour at the oral level; to poison or destroy with excrement or flatulence at the anal level; to burn or destroy with urine or its equivalents at the urethral level, etc." In this way Grinberg accoutns for aggression.

To support his contention concerning projective identification and communication, Grinberg cites the instance of a monopolizer who was encouraged in this role by the group members in that they made no attempt to restrain him. Grinberg suggests that the group members "laid this member's role onto him," which he accepted. When this was interpreted to him, he stopped talking in the group. At this point the other members urged him to assume the role that was masochistic, but he remained silent, behaving the opposite of how he had been acting previously. The other members continued to urge him to go on with the masochistic role out of fear of having to "reintroject their own denied roles."

It is rather interesting that Grinberg assumes the monopolizer is engaging in a role that is projected onto him by the other members of the group. It is true that the group members do nothing to control the monopolizer; they let him continue to monopolize and urge him to continue to do so. It is not true, it seems to me, that he derives this role solely from the other group members. They encourage him to continue in this role as an aspect of their own defenses, but such a monopolizer will always initiate the role and *try to control any group* in which he participates. It is one of his defenses against the anxiety of interaction. When the monopolizer stopped talking in the group, after an interpretation, it seems to me that this is a transference reaction, i.e., another kind of defense that was created by Grinberg's interpretation.

The Dynamics of Groups

Jackson commented on the problem of taking into account the interactions of group members. Rey (1975), whose ideas are described later, states that the problem of understanding the interactions in a group is monumental. Jackson (1957) said that "the incredibly complex picture one obtains in studying family interrelations during family therapy sessions—the simultaneous consideration of more than three interaction instances, is at present, an insuperable task for the mind of man." We must accept our limitations and "make the most of certain aids available." One such aid is "collaborative therapy. The unfolding of the psychic drama as two or more therapists relate and correlate their findings embodies the dynamics of chess and the topological fascination of a jig saw puzzle." Jackson thought that unfortunately, collaborative psychotherapy is difficult because the therapists must deal with each other in addition to their patients." Today the practice of two therapists working in the same group as co-therapists has become standard in certain situations—sex therapy, for example, after the manner of Masters and Johnson, as well as marital therapy, couples therapy, and family therapy. A second aid in conceptualizing, Jackson avowed, was the adding of a "temporal concept" to our more or less "spatial image" of the family. This concept is facilitated by "constructing a picture of the probable family interaction at a period the patient is discussing or at that period where such and such a symptom seems most likely to have been engendered."

Jackson then said that we can utilize "information about the patient's siblings, about the age of one or other of the parents when significant events occurred, about the differential handling of the children by the parents, and so forth, to help obtain the proper setting for understanding what might have been momentous to the patient at that period of his life." The idea here is to select a kind of slice of life, in time and space, of some period of the patient's past. In my opinion, this "slice of life" should not be thought of purely in the developmental sense, focusing on psychosexual development, nor from the point of view of ego functions that are present or missing, but should be considered from the point of view of the *interferences* that the child has from parents that affect his emotional attitudes toward himself and others due to the parents' anxieties. The emotional development of the child in relation to objects has much to do with the anxieties of the parents and their inhibitory reactions. The actual physical development of the child in the biological sense may be fostered by anxious parents, but their attitudes toward his growing up as an independent being may be inhibiting. Physical development proceeds willy-nilly, and psychological processes such as learning, problem solving, reality testing, judging situations, are always operative as long as the patient is alive.

The effect that parents' attitudes have on the individual's emotional and physical condition and the consideration he has of himself counts most in the evolution of a neurosis (or psychosis). It is in this light that the term "ego development" becomes confusing and ambiguous, especially if we attempt to define "ego" in terms of functions. As defined at present, ego functions are intact and operative in individuals whether or not they are neurotic or psychotic (see Wolberg, A., 1973, p. 68; also Moore & Fine, 1968, pp. 40-42). It has been established beyond a doubt that, in general, neurotics and psychotics have operative ego functions but that at times these may not be used adequately or normally in specific situations. The "use" may be for adaptive purposes or at times for neurotic aims. Self-actualizing behavior per se is a "given" in human development. It is the reaction of parents to this self-actualizing behavior and the effects on the interpersonal relations between parents and children (the group process) that creates *inhibiting responses* and certain kinds of *defensive maneuvers* on the part of the child. It is true that during periods of development many questions arise in the child's mind and anxieties may develop, but whether these anxieties become the source of neurotic behavior will depend for the most part on the responses of the parents to these anxieties. The problem rests on the parent's own unresolved anxieties, which are superimposed upon the anxieties of the child. Kohut is correct in assuming that mothering—more precisely child-rearing practices—has a great deal to do with the child's concept of himself. The fact is, however, that the child does have a reality concept of his situation with the parents even as he responds to their projections and selectively denies his reality-testing capacities.

Jackson (1957) remarked that considering the difficulties of forming a concept of the emotional interactions of a family gorup, i.e., in the here and now, the obvious rejoinder might be, "What is the value of such brain-racking exercise on the part of the psychiatrist?" He felt that two main benefits may ensue: (1) facility in understanding the patient's present situation and (2) theoretical and research implications brought to light by this kind of orientation. One must take into account the "significant others" of the patient's life, said Jackson. This concept essentially agrees with Fairbairn—that in object relations theory it is the behavior of the other (the object) that is important rather than the instinctual drives of each individual. This also seems to be the position of Kohut and Masterson, even though they consider that both instincts and the environment are important.

I believe we shall have to think of "instinct" as meaning in psychoanalysis the genetic factors that promote self-actualizing and self-preservation behavior. We have already mentioned Green's comment (1977) that Freud assumed the basic function of the psychic field was the lowering of unpleasurable tension. (Freud meant tension from the instincts as the derivatives are expressed in the environment, i.e., with people.) Freud looked upon the lowering of tension as an important factor both in development and in adaptation. Today we know that tension reduction *is* important, even life saving. We find that tension is created by the environment and often is increased by the individual's reactions to the tensions of important family members. When the individual is frustrated, this often leads to destructive tension-relieving behavior, i.e., to displacement behavior.

In my opinion the research value of family therapy is very important. The therapeutic benefit derives from helping the parents change their behavior with the child as their tensions and anxieties are reduced through understanding. Family therapy gives us a great deal of information about how the family group functions, and it provides a most important living example of the dynamics of family life in a given family society at a particular period in time. In relation to neuroses and psychoses, the interlocking defensive system is evident in the family being observed, and the therapist becomes aware of the cumulative effect of family relations on the various children who must relate to neurotic parents. The need of the parents to have children act out is obvious. The different kinds of relationships the parents make with different children are also revealed. Whether we are doing group or individual treatment with borderline patients, all astute therapists, through relevant inquiry, should uncover the family picture to gain the kind of information that Jackson suggested of certain periods in the life of the patient, i.e., *those periods that seem crucial to the patient*. The therapist must learn, however, to distinguish between those periods that are important but are, nevertheless, in the telling being used in the session for defensive purposes rather than to work through a conflict.

Originally, Jackson studied psychosomatic and physical problems in patients. As he began to see the influence of emotions on these conditions, he sought psychoanalytic training. Later he was to work with schizophrenics in both individual and group sessions. He coined the term "conjoint therapy," recognizing the value of both individual and group treatment. He realized the importance of family dynamics in the perpetuation of a patient's neurotic and psychotic problems, and in 1957 he wrote the important paper: "The Question of Family Homeostasis." This paper suggested that, in the neuroses, and particularly in the psychoses, the effect of the parents' behavior was to keep the family system as "closed" a system as possible. (The family can never entirely be a "closed system," but the attempt is made by the controlling and anxious parents. A truly closed system tends to disintegrate.)

In sociological literature doubt is cast on the concept of homeostasis as a factor in the persistence of groups. The opposed concept states that *change is a constant variable in human life and that a theory of equilibrium should be substituted for the concept of homeostasis*. This concept recognizes that change creates temporary disequilibrium, and disequilibrium is probably just as constant and necessary as homeostasis for the phenomenon of change. The idea is that in a social group or social system, disparate opinions create the possibility of change and this is cause for disequilibrium. But as the members of the group accommodate and assimilate the implications of these various inevitable changes through discussion, a consenses occurs that provides the basis for a decision. A *norm* must be arrived at, which creates a standard (of opinions) related to what the members should do about a given matter, i.e., how they should behave in a given circumstance. The group therapist's role is to help the members create the atmosphere where adequate changes can take place. This means unlocking the cohesion in the defensive systems among the members and helping to create the kind of problem solving that will enhance the positive goals of each member. Jackson made lasting contributions to the field of family therapy and his colleague Weakland and others are carrying on and extending this work.

Among recent papers on group therapy that deal with the treatment of the borderline is one by Rey (1975). Superimposing the developmental concepts of Melanie Klein as well as utilizing some of Chomsky's ideas, Rey proposed that, due to lacunae in the ego, patterns of acting out, which are evident in the group, have been laid down in the "primitive stages" of the "paranoid-schizoid position," that is, in the first three or four months of life when the patient's "internalized objects" belong to the earliest or sensorimotor (prerepresentational) stage of development (Piaget). This includes the "part-object stage" (Freud's autoerotic stage). Rey postulates that in the case of borderline patients the "constructs" or "schemas" of the mind have remained "unlinked" with words, due to "splitting." Rey surmises that in the early "part-object stage" or even in the early "whole-object stage" of narcissism, the defense of "splitting" is usually used because of the infant's excessive amount of innate oral aggression, as Klein and Kernberg have emphasized. The infant who will become borderline *never* goes beyond this period.

Rey suggests that the use of "action therapy" in the group, i.e., "nonverbal types of communication" [psychodrama] will supply the linkages with word representations that have never taken place. Rey states that the "preverbal stages of internalized action schemas" have to be undone in treatment, and he suggests that encounter techniques be used, inferring that perhaps these may contain the "nonverbal meanings" that verbal communications would convey. The nonverbal communications may serve as a medium to buttress the verbal communications of the members of the group. To depend on purely verbal schemas, he says, would mean that we would be attempting to alter the "original action schemas" (those laid down in early infancy) at the level of "phonetic symbolizations"—or, in Freud's terms, at the level of "surface structures"—rather than at the sensorimotor level of the part-object stage. To make the appropriate connections with nonverbal aids would be to help the individual in making up the lacunae. Thus, we would assist the patient in the manner in which the infant proceeds from the sensorimotor stage to the next stage of development, i.e., from the part-object stage to the whole-object stage of narcissism.

Rey thinks that in group therapy with borderline patients, the group members can act as "transitional objects" (Winnicott's terminology); that is, they can provide the "linkages" for the patient who is acting out and who has not made these "word representation" connections in his own development. As the patient accepts the linkages from the group members, he gradually "internalizes" them. This, Rey believes, is a form of identification with the members of the group. For Rey acting out means that no true identifications have been formed and that there are "no linkages between action and verbal connotation." (A common practice of psychoanalysts in my opinion is to project into the group process developmental phenomena, thus displaying a misunderstanding of multidisciplinary thinking.)

While we may not agree with Rey's theory, we do understand that psychodrama can be an important vehicle to use when the patient denies, represses, or dissociates. Psychodrama is a way of emphasizing reality factors and is employed to help the patient gain insight with the hope that he will use the insight to change some of his neurotic behavior. The problem with Rey's idea is that the "linkages" do exist in the patient's mind, but he denies that they are there due to his great conflict. I believe that Green too has described a denial mechanism rather than "lack of linkages" in his concept of "splitting." How do we know that linkages exist? That there are no lacunae? One of the most useful methods of refuting the theory of lacunae and the lack of linkages is through the use of hypnosis. Lewis R. Wolberg presented a paper on hypnosis at a Macy Conference in 1952. One of the comments of Rapaport during that presentation was that psychodrama as well as hypnosis can sometimes break up repression to a point where the patient will respond to the analyst and express what he has been repressing. (Not only are memories repressed but current transference feelings can also be repressed and usually are denied.)

Another way to understand that the linkages exist is to utilize the projective therapeutic techniques that I have suggested in working with the borderline patient to deal with what is denied and repressed. The verbalizations that take place between analyst and patient as he describes the behavior of the "other" with whom he is identified, and whom he uses as a projective object, tell the story of what is being avoided or disavowed. What the patient says about the "other" applies to himself as well. My session with Maurice Belk (see Chapter 11) illustrates this technique. The verbalizations about the "other" that accompany the patient's projections show that the linkages have been made although they are projected. Repression is found to be an important factor in the denial, and this can readily be demonstrated by hypnosis.

The results of adequate psychodramatic technique *show the connections with repressed material* rather than *"providing linkages"* that never existed. In encounter groups psychodrama is one of the main techniques in the "games" that people play. The goals are cathartic, and an effort is made to have the individuals "talk out" as well as "act out." Often a great deal of emotion is elicited before talking is evoked. The aim of the individual who participates in an encounter group, I believe, is to break up his detachment and depression so that he can *feel*. There can be in the borderline patient a "split" between psyche and soma—or between mind and feeling. It is not a permanent split but a dissociative process used in periods of intense anxiety. Another way of looking at this "split" is to see it as a hysterical mechanism to control feelings and to maintain distance, using denial as a main defense. There seems to be in the infant a "given" that probably has a great deal to do with the ability to detach, to dissociate, and to concentrate or to withdraw. We mentioned that the infant can "tune in" and then "tune out" when stimuli become too irritating, or he can fall asleep to avoid certain stimuli. This, together with the neurophysiological mechanism discovered by McCarley and Hobson (1977) will account for the ability to develop hysterical defenses such as the dissociative phenomena and denial. But just as the ability to imitate may have some bearing on the capacity for identification, so "tuning in" and "tuning out" may have a relation to hysterical phenomena, but these phenomena are not the same. Imitation is not identification or learning, and the infant's ability to "tune in" and "tune out" is not the same as hysterical phenomena such as *denial*, dissociative processes, hypochondriacal attitudes, and the like.

Rey, (1975) as we have mentioned, considers the group a "transitional object" rather than a peer system. He does not in his 1975 paper say that the therapist is a mother, but he does tend to think of the group as a family. The fact is that neurotics and psychotics tend to project the family hierarchical structure into the peer group. It is this projective (defensive) phenomenon that encourages some therapists to think of the therapy group as a family.

Since both Rey and Grinberg have a Kleinian orientation, they look upon group life as determined by Klein's interpretation of the dynamics of projective identification. Rey, for example, says "an understanding of group dynamics" will depend on understanding how "intrapsychic groups" work. It would seem to me that an understanding of those dynamics that evoked the neurotic defenses in individual members. It will enable us to see that the patient's repetitive fantasies (his "intrapsychic groups" or his "not me," or his "false self," and so on) all have a relation to the traumas associated with accepting the identifications over time at the hands of his parents. The repetitiveness of the parents' neurotic behavior is a factor in the perpetuation of the "inner objects," or what I would call the *identification fantasies*. An understanding of group dynamics will give us insight into how the so-called "intrapsychic object relations" have evolved. But these "inner objects" represent not only "primitive" or early objects, they also represent the relations with parents throughout the time that the individual is interacting with the parents, which can extend into adulthood. I would consider that "intrapsychic groups" mean the internalization of external and traumatic relations with important persons in the patient's environment that are disguised in the form of fantasy. I believe that "inner objects" should connote only the mental representations of the object relations relative to the identifications with parents, which may be disguised. The repetitiveness (repetition compulsion) should be interpreted to mean "incompleted tasks" due to conflict, inhibitions, and defenses (the Zeigarnik effect.[3]). Unless we define "inner objects" in a restricted way, the term would imply all relations that the individual has throughout his life time with objects (both animate and inanimate). In that case the definition would be so broad that it would have no scientific value.

A final way to refute the idea of "lack of linkages" is to recognize that all acting out is related to fantasies that constitute the direct linkage between interaction with parental figures and identifications. The fantasy is a representation of the meaning of the identification. It is a repetitive phenomenon and is a factor in the defense acting out the identification. Freud alluded to the fact that fantasies were associated with acting out; the essay on hysterical fantasies and their connection with bisexuality indicated this relationship. In his earlier papers symptoms were considered to be hysterical in nature and bracketed to identifications with important people in the patient's life, but the activity in relation to symptoms was not thought of at the time as an acting out of a fantasy. The fantasy was considered by Freud to be a fantasy instinct (later the id) rather than a consequence of experience with important persons.

Rey (1975) wrote that the important thing is to be able to evaluate how "the existence of groups of inner objects and primitive intrapsychic object relations [what I have called the sadomasochistic identification fantasies] contribute to an understanding of group dynamics" as these operate when the patient is in a group therapy situation. As mentioned, these identifica-

---

[3]Zeigarnik postulated that memory for incompleted tasks is more vivid and persistent than for completed tasks. We may postulate that where frustration has caused inhibition of action, this may be felt as an incompleted task and may account for the patient's intrapsychic conflict and his repetitive fantasies. It may also be an impetus for seeking treatment.

tion fantasies (the inner objects) are not the stuff from which the total group dynamics are made. When the fantasies, however, are acted out in the group, or anywhere else, they constitute a special dynamic related to the transference. The self-actualizing behavior is an aspect of the group dynamics having to do with thinking and learning associated with the autonomous functions used in problem solving. If we define "inner objects" as identification fantasies, then we shall have to say that these fantasies are the essence of the patient's unconscious, at least that part of the unconscious that relates to repressed or denied and disguised memories. We can understand the connection of the fantasies to the historical relations with parental figures, disguised in their various forms. The interactions in the fantasies represent the meaning and significance of the interactive behavior that evoked the identifications. All acting out, therefore, is defensive and represents some form of transference behavior. It is based on identifications with persons who are influential in the life of the patient. The links to the identifications can be found in the associations and in the analysis of the fantasies and dreams.

In a group we can understand the way in which roles operate whether these be neurotic roles (Wolberg, A., 1960) or adaptive roles since we see these roles performed before our eyes. As therapsits, we can also *relate the neurotic roles to the patient's fantasies* if we understand that the patient's projections are stimulated by his fantasies. His verbalizations concerning his projections have meaning in relation to the situation he had with his parents when he learned the neurotic roles. As therapists, we must be able to distinguish between aberrant and rational roles as these operate in the therapy group. The patient brings a repertory of roles with him into the group, and as the members of the group interact (i.e., communicate), these roles are set into motion. Every person has certain "normal" role behaviors that he enacts at certain times, even neurotic and psychotic individuals; and these "normal" roles operate in the therapy group too as a function of the individual's reality system. The patient functions simultaneously in two ways: adaptive and neurotic—and in relation to these interacting ways he operates both consciously and unconsciously.

We know that the patient's emotional problem, as it is revealed in the group, interferes with the therapeutic group task of helping to eliminate the neurotic and/or psychotic problems of each individual in the group. As Moreno (1934) and Jennings (1950) pointed out and as I have reiterated (1972, 1976), there are at least three dimensions of the behavior of individuals in the group related to group dynamics that the therapist must consider: the *projective dimension*, the *problem-solving* dimension, and the choice-*rejection dimension*. When one thinks of interactions (communications) in the group in terms of these three categories, it helps to organize the data in borderline conditions that one perceives so that meaning emerges and interpretations can have greater effect.

It is important to remember that at any given time in psychotherapy we deal with only *small* aspect of the patient's "total mind," namely, that part of the mind that is concerned with the emotional problem, how it affects the patient's adjustment, and what can be done about this problem. The focus is on the "here-and-now" events that occur in the group. When we say the here-and-now events, we do not mean that the group does not talk about the past, but when the members do discuss the past, it is because the here-and-now interactions are reminders of past experiences. Or, to put it another way, the conditioned responses of a given patient may seem inconsistent with the present situation and the question arises, "Where did this response come from?" The current situation seemingly is not one that would normally evoke such a response. This means that the patient sees the other in a different light from how the remaining group members are seeing him and the discrepancy is so great as to require explanation. In this case the patient sees the "other" through his fantasy. As communications become less vague, group structure changes, and the group proceeds with its task. Resistances (defenses) do occur, and pauses in group work toward the task take place for a regrouping, which occurs as one phase of the task is accomplished and the group prepares to go to the next sector of its general goal. At one moment A will communicate with B for purposes of defense; at another point that same member A will communicate with B to work out a problem. Or A will communicate with B for defense and will communicate with a third member C for working out a problem. Communication at any given point will depend upon the member's need at the time. The task of therapy is not easily gained with borderline patients due to the interference that their neurotic patterns (i.e., their defenses) provide to counteract the problem-solving process.

As Rey pointed out, there are "subtasks" to be accomplished in the therapeutic group. One of these subtasks is to have the members understand the relation of each member's fantasies to his life pattern as these evolved in their families and are now reflected in the group. Actually, what we want in the therapy group for the borderline patient, and for others as well, is for *each member to understand the relation of his fantasies to his acting-out pattern as this operates with members of the group and then to relate this to the defenses that were operative when the parents began to insist upon the acting out of the identification roles.* We must arrive eventually at the hard fact that in identification our patients are in some manner *like the hated and denied aspects of the parents*; and we must uncover and reveal through the patient's associations what this means to the patient in his responses to the group. The feelings that are associated with neurotic (identification) roles have to do with self-contempt, with fears of acting out revenge patterns, with inhibitions in expressions of love, and expression of autonomous behaviors at certain points in life, in relations with others.

Rey suggested that "dissociated patients," whom he calls borderline, are, in the group, an assembly of subgroups of unrelated parts. They are "concrete projections of autonomous primitive groups" (inner objects). (The patient may have dissociative tendencies but is never so dissociated that he is a "concrete projection of a primitive group" unrelated to the current group.) The therapist is also "confronted with people about whom the patients talk, says Rey, i.e., "real external people, however fantasy distorted they are," and the "complication of human interpersonal relationships" for all these parts become "flabbergasting." (If we keep in mind the three dimensions of behavior in a group [see p. 154] for organizing our data, we shall not be so flabbergasted.)

Grinberg and Rey assume that the projective identifications of the patients are what determine the group dynamics—in the family, in life, and in the therapy group—but as Moreno (1934) pointed out, the dynamics of groups have dimensions other than the projections of the patients, dynamics that are far more important in the maintenance of group structures. Group life can go on without the projective identifications of the members of groups. The problem-solving capacities and the group norms are the essence of group structure and function, and no group can exist without these binding elements, neither a therapy group nor any other group. It is the problem-solving motif that Rosner (1969), for example, in his essay on "working through" refers to when he says that creativity is more important than the neurotic traits of the patient. When we emphasize the conscious activity of the patient as being of most importance we are not discarding the idea of the "unconscious." Repressions create the unconscious elements in human behavior that have to do with emotional problems, and while the unconscious is a strong motivating factor in neurotic behavior, in my opinion, during therapy reality factors, creativity, and problem-solving capacities are more important to consider from the point of view of working through the emotional conflicts.

Splitting, Denial and Lacunae

Dince (1977), like Green, has touched upon the subject of what I call *detachment and denial by hysterical means*. Dince speaks of "dissociation," which he considers to be a primary trait of borderlines related to a conscious desire to deny certain aspects of reality. In this sense the denial, I feel, might be said to be bracketed to a kind of self-hypnosis; *denying that which one does not want to know, but does in fact know*. I think that denial is always associated with acting out the identification role and that the acting-out process may be in the nature of a post-hypnoticlike suggestion as Jackson (1954) mentioned in an early paper. Stern (1938), as we have noted, referred to the "suggestibility trait" in the borderline patient, and Freud spoke of the "suggestibility" in all patients attendant upon the masochistic traits (Wolberg, A., 1973, p. 27). The masochism would be due, it seems to me, to the fact that the parents have forced the identification role on the child through their repetitive and obsessive demands and suggestions, conveyed both verbally and nonverbally. Finally, the child acts out the role even though originally he fought against it; but he denies the origins of his behavior.

Dince writes of a phenomenon similar to the one described by Green, but suggests this may be the result of certian self-hypnotic phenomena (hysterical?) that may be seen in cases such as the woman who has sex and denies any feelings although she lubricates freely. (This is what Green calls a "split" between psyche and soma.) In this kind of situation there are two "selves" that are dissociated, says Dince, or exist as partially dissociated states (Kernberg's "ego states"?), and he refers to Cornelia Wilbur's *Sybil*, and Laing's *Divided Self*. I find that the kind of symptom Dince is describing is often present in the borderline patient. The defense should perhaps be thought of as denial rather than a dissociation. I suggest that we might confine the term *dissociation* to a description of the denial and disavowal mechanism in multiple personalities, in persons with fetishistic symptoms, in homosexual characters, and in schizophrenics who display certain bizarre acting-out mechanisms, since the dissociative defenses of the borderline patient are much less severe. The borderline patient does have depersonalization episodes, but these are fleeting and momentary; at worst they occur minutes at a time so that they are not too extensive. Dince reported that one of his patients read the books of Wilbur and Laing and was affected by them: "What began as a consciously directed process on a fantasy level became more and more systematized and less controllable" (1977, p. 335). Dince believes this is not the same as detachment or denial as defined in psychoanalysis. (Could it be that particular patient might well be schizophrenic and the symptom might be of a continuous obsessive nature?) These mechanisms are based on denial of highly charged aggressive or sexual affects, contends Dince, and the consequent dissociative action account for much of the symptomology of the borderline, as well as for some of the typical patterns of behavior that the borderline acts out during the analytic session. I have found that in the borderline such symptoms are sexualized and associated with perverse feelings and fantasies of a disguised aggressive nature, related to the identifications.

It has been my experience that individuals who have "dissociated selves," such as those referred to by Dince and others, or persons with strange behavior who wish to be a different sex and go about trying to "convert" their gender, or people who act out with members of the opposite sex in grotesque ways, or people who have weird amnesias or bizarre multiple personalities are probably not borderline—rather they are schizophrenics. Some phobic personalities are actually schizophrenics, and in the course of analysis they show widespread dissociative tendencies. There is, for instance, one of my patients, Sonia, who is an extremely successful woman but who refuses to "feel anything" in relation to her success. Her success she says is of "no import," it gives "no pleasure," and the like. Her "agonies" are much more important to her than her success. This is similar to Dince's woman who has sex and lubricates but has no feeling and Green's concept of the dissociation of psyche and soma.

One of my patients, Elizabeth Osgood (Wolberg, A., 1973, pp. 242-251) had this kind of symptom in her sexual relations. There is no reason to think of these defenses, insofar as I can see, as other than hysterical. However, they are different from the hysterical defenses found in true conversion reactions, the amnesias, and so on, since the dissociations in these are more pervasive and thus have a different effect upon the patient's life style. Elizabeth usually, when discussing sex, spoke of her father (with whom she was highly identified) as having "no feelings," being "all intellect." She described him as a firmly detached person, however, highly esteemed, as a professor in a prestigious university working on research of a "classified" nature. His prestige was apparently emphasized in the home, so that it would seem like a kind of sacrilege if a mere child should differ with the socially established and sacrosanct opinion of a person of this nature. Idealization of the father was a family business. Idealization helped to keep Elizabeth's criticism and anger toward her father concealed and held in check. He liked to putter around his workshop, and Elizabeth always felt that the only time he paid attention to her was when she made it her business to go to his workshop and ask questions about what he was doing. This made her feel that her father wished she was a boy. He had two sons, Elizabeth's brothers, but they both had emotional problems. One brother startled her one day by telling her that he was homosexual.

It is confusing to try to follow Freud's developmental theory here attempting to put these symptoms on a "lower level" of development than the hysterias, accrediting them to a hypothesized hypochondriacal (semidelusional) stage of infant development, considering them remnants of a preoedipal period. In Elizabeth's case, upon probing, one discovered a fantasy of a taunting father, a masochistic feeling, and a sadistic pleasure in denying gratification to the man with whom she was having sex. The sadistic side of Elizabeth's fantasy eluded me for two years, but it became clear when she began to have dreams of men who could not "handle her" and who could not give her sexual pleasure. She acted out this fantasy by finding men who took on the challenge of giving her an orgasm, only to fail. (Is this an oedipal problem or is it s hypochondriacal mechanism of preoedipal type?)

Rosner's 1969 and 1973 papers have been referred to in our discussion. They tend to refute the "lacunae" or "defect" theory of ego functions and explain the dynamics of "free association," which Rosner assumes are operative in all patients. It seems to me that therapists who are not clear as to a patient's dynamics and so do not distinctly recognize what they see and hear in the session make up a theory to account for what they believe is going on. The theories of "lacunae" and "defect" and "lack of linkage" fall into this category. Besides being false, these theories require that something be done that has already been accomplished by the patient many years ago. The patient realizes the therapist's theories that are presented to him are wrong, but he hysterically blinds himself in faith (a masochistic maneuver). He hopes that the technique being used will do the trick in relieving his anxieties, yet doubting all the time that this will be the case, and he utilizes the situation to buttress his defenses. The therapist, it is avowed, can utilize his countertransference feelings therapeutically. The argument goes that if the therapist is truly cognizant of "how he feels" towards the patient, even if he is angry and hates the patient, this is all to the good because he can point out that not only the therapist but other people feel the same way toward the patient. The patient's actions are such that they inspire these feelings in all people. In other words, the patient's behavior tends to make him rejected and hated, and he deserves to be rejected and hated at times by the therapist as well because of untoward behavior. It is my opinion that the therapist who truly understands the dynamics of the borderline patient will never have to depend upon his countertransference feelings to bring him through a session, for very few such feelings will arise. The more clearly the dynamics are conceptualized, the better chance the therapist has of relating to the patient at any given moment and the less anxious both the therapist and the patient will be in the session.

The unresolved masochism of the patient is often the cause of the hysterical phenomena we see in the borderline patient. This was evident in Flora, who had to look for another therapist since I was not in town often enough to see her regularly. She decided to be treated cooperatively by two different therapists who worked independently, one a behavior therapist and the other a psychoanalytically oriented therapist—both concentrating on the phobia in different ways. After one year this procedure was of no help; yet she kept going to both therapists. When she had been in therapy with me, we had not worked out her transferences, positive or negative, toward me, and she insisted on seeing me when I was in town. I had mentioned another therapist for her to substitute for me, but she would not take my suggestion. Her masochism apparently kept her in a bind.

Over the years I have worked in depth with more than thirty borderline patients and have supervised patients of other therapists as well. The masochism of these patients is extensive and self-defeating. Many of my current ideas on the borderline personality are based on a survey of thirty-three borderline patients in my own practice. These patients are listed on page 263 with, of course, fictitious names to conceal their identity. In the course of treating this group I met and interviewed fourteen sets of parents and had indirect contact through letters with two more sets. There is no doubt in my mind concerning the denigrating sadistic attitudes of these parents toward their children, particularly toward those who became patients. Of the thirty-three patients, only Sonia Gerber, Flora O'Toole Levy, and Gertrude Belan came from poverty homes. As adults, all were very well off financially except Gertrude Belan and Sonia Gerber; the latter, however, is now comparatively affluent. For years while in therapy she struggles unnecessarily hard to support her parents, masochistically denying that the burdens she assumed created rage and revenge feelings. She used the situation as a defense while denying and excusing the sadism of her parents and of herself. Harriet Hamburger, too, had years of masochistic work activity and self-defeating social relations before she finally broke loose from her self-punitive bonds. When she did, her economic status rose rapidly. After she became financially solvent, she spent a few more years in successive masochistic relationships with psychotic men before she finally extricated herself and found a "normal" partner.

I cite this information to suggest that 91 percent of the thirty-three borderline patients came from financially secure homes, yet all were abused or denigrated emotionally by their parents and both directly and indirectly sexually used as projective objects. The sadomasochistic partner that the borderline patient needs neurotically is reflected in transference, often eventuating in a negative therapeutic reaction. The masochistic appeasing and idealizing attitude is expressed in what Freud called the "positive transference." When Flora was finally able to express regret over my leaving town so often and said, "Well, that is life, that is how it is," she then found a therapist whom she recognized as adequate and who could help her. She feels content with this man, and she no longer seeks me out, al-thought she does occasionally speak to me on the telephone. The denial in Flora's case related to the fact that it was obvious she could not resolve her problems with these particular therapists yet she persisted, idealizing them and refusing to go to the therapist I had suggested. This refusal and denial was associated with the negative transference which, in the beginning, she refused to consider.

I have learned over the years that these patients often conceal their most destructive masochistic behavior, which sometimes assumes a suicidal intensity. Flora hid from me the fact that she had a lump in her breast. It is advisable for therapists who have borderline patients to ask pointed questions in order to ascertain the physical and mental possibilities and potentialities of masochistic attitudes. Often the masochism is not as obvious as the sadism, and one tends to discount the masochism in such instances. Both homicidal and suicidal tendencies may coexist. The homicidal tendencies reside in the sadistic trend and the suicidal in the masochistic behavior. Flora had a "good" son and a "bad" son; both were exceedingly neurotic. The "bad" son she fought with continuously, driving him away from the family while professing a desire to be close. She helped both sons financially. She finally had a fight where the "bad" son hit her, and thereafter she said she was very much afraid that he would kill her. Even though she had been most provocative and certainly played a role in instigating the physical assault, she professed innocence. The "bad" son settled down with a homosexual partner who helped him find lucrative work and encouraged him to get off drugs. He has made a good work adjustment and has left the drug scene. His homosexual partner has had relations with women but has found it difficult to maintain such relationships. The "bad" son has been rejected by women because he cannot maintain an erection when having sex. He had used his homosexuality previously as a way of soliciting money to buy drugs, but he is no longer a "prostitute" nor is he using drugs. The "good" son is a failure. He masochistically seeks jobs that are below his capacities, and when in a position that is equal to his talents, he loses the job either by fighting with his boss or by not going to work. He was a dropout from college, where he mainly served as a pusher; he maintained himself and his drug habit by selling drugs. At present he is still on drugs. This young man cannot bring himself to get into any kind of a therapeutic regimen that might conceivably help him. .

The Observing Ego

Rosner (1969) has written an interesting paper containing many points that are not usually considered in working with the borderline patient. He says that psychoanalysts speak of the "contract between themselves and the patient," and in an examination of the concept "contract," Rosner writes, we find that what is meant is that the patient must be able, in spite of his resistances, to cooperate with the analyst in the therapeutic endeavor. This means that he must be able to conceptualize and recognize, at least in part, *some aspect of his problem* so that in this area the analyst and analysand are reality oriented in their joint work. It is expected that the analysand will be able to follow certain kinds of dynamically oriented instruction that make this particular relationship psychoanalytic rather than some other kind of an interpersonal relationship. In other words, there is a definite problem-solving capacity in relation to the goals of psychoanalysis and the roles of analyst and analysand. It is assumed that the patient can engage in certain kinds of problem-solving behavior, that he can reach defined goals, and that these goals are different from problem solving in some other types of process, such as learning how to play the piano, learning arithmetic, or solving a problem in chemistry. Through this particular psychoanalytic behavior the patient is presumed to gain insight.

Rosner says that *associations are important in the psychoanalytic process* even with the borderline patient, and can be influenced by: (a) the reality situation: with the analyst, with friends, and with others; (b) the day residues: how the patient has handled today's reality; (c) the emergence of warded-off drives from past experience, i.e., through memory and the "affects associated with the memories," e.g., feeling "good" and "bad" about certain events in the past; (d) by the interpretations of the analyst; (e) by the impact of leaving a task (analysis) and returning to it session by session (the Zeigarnik effect?); (f) by insights through self-inspection and the thoughts of the analysis when away from the analyst.

Insight is a complicated process "best described by learning theory," according to Rosner. It is a part of problem solving, and Rosner attempts to reconcile Gestalt theory and psychoanalytic theory to explain how associations can become stimulated by insight and vice versa. I believe that we might define the *psychoanalytic process* by saying that it is a way of learning about one's neurosis or one's psychosis and how this relates to experiences with parents and then doing what is necessary to eliminate or reduce neurotic or psychotic behavior by changing the defensive system or eliminating certain defenses and substituting for them assertive behavior without fear or guilt. Defenses are maneuvers, such as repressions, denials, and other mechanisms associated with both conscious and unconscious ideas and feelings. (In this kind of postulation we would say that the original anxiety began in the family in relationships with parental figures rather than during the birth process.)

Associations are, of course, one of the roads, if not *the* road, to the unconscious, that is, to the *repressed material* that one must uncover if one is to help the patient. Associations are the means through which repressions can be undone. They lead to an understanding of neurotic patterns. But, says Rosner, once there is this understanding, there must be a way of "working through" so that there is *changed behavior*. (Borderline patients—due to denial, the obsessive mechanisms, and the hysterical symptoms—have difficulty learning about the anxieties and the conflicts and accepting the idea of defensive behavior since the syndrome is organized in the overall context of a projective identification defense, a prominent part of which is an acting out of the transference rather than a talking about the transference. Like all patients who undergo any kind of psychoanalytically oriented psychotherapy, borderline patients do produce associations. Normally, these are concealed, in the beginning phase of treatment, by speaking of others and in the context of what is denied.)

Under *insight* Rosner lists several types of phenomena that he argues have a relation to learning, and he quotes from experimental work to support his hypothesis. He suggests the use of the concepts of *structuring, conceptualizing, psychophysical isomorphism*, and *problem solving* as contributions from the Gestalt field. He refers to Duncker's (1945) variety of dimensions in problem solving; Wertheimer's (1944) "similar operations" in productive thinking, and Kohler's (1929) classical experiments demonstrating insight operations. The very subject matter of analysis assumes causal relationships and an organization within the context of a total structure. Rosner brings to mind the Hoffding function (1910 [1968, 1977]), similarity of context for recall to occur and the fact that there is an interrelatedness in associations. Associations are not haphazard; they are a "pattern" a dynamic "whole," containing "contrasting" or "opposite" ideas. (Anyone who has lived to have experiences has a past, and this past is subject to certain laws of association in relation to the "present.") In interpretation the patient is faced with a high degree of ambiguity, "allowing greater play of central factors and thereby exposing distortion to a greater extent. This would also constitute a rationale for the couch." But, Rosner goes on to say, there is evidence to support the idea that the *creative impulse* is far more important in treatment than the neurotic impulses, and this evidence comes from a variety of sources. This important principle is one that is clearly forgotten by most therapists when they are engaging in the treatment process with borderlines, for it is assumed that these patients have no reasoning capacities and are totally dependent and focused on fantasy. Kohut seems to be an exception to this rule, and several psychoanalysts from the Horney School have emphasized working with the constructive side of the ego, i.e., the creative side. In my first paper on the borderline patient, I also stressed this principle, which derives from learning theory and which, at the time, I called "positive ego construction" (1952, pp. 705-707). At that time I also believed that the ego had "holes" (lacunae) and that in the treatment of these ego deficits they had to be "filled in." Today, I relate this problem of lack of "positive ego" to the sadomasochistic pattern and the various types of defense against anxiety rather than to "defects" or lacunae. It is my belief that the ego of the borderline has a special type of sadomasochistic organization which accrues in the family situation.

It is admitted by all psychoanalysts that the "observing ego" is essential in analysis, says Rosner, and he disagrees with those therapists who say that borderlines and schizophrenics have no "observing ego." In this I quite agree. (The "observing ego" is intimately connected with the creative impulses, and these are present and operative in the borderline patient, as we have just noted. In the first few days of life (i.e., after the fetus has changed its status through the process of birth to a relatively independent being) behaviors that are autonomous are displayed in addition to the so-called reflex behavior, which, incidentally, is much more meaningful for development than was originally supposed. These autonomous behaviors include the ability to "tune in" and "tune out" (Caplan, 1973, p. 28) capacities that aid in the various types of learning that occur as well as serve to defend against too much or unpleasant stimulation. "Tuning in" and "tuning out" also is a mechanism that relates to the "isolating process" involved in concentration and attention and makes possible the dynamics of the observing ego.)

Rosner's paper reminds me of the fact that Freud felt that associations and the "constructions" that one could assume from the associations were the road to the unconscious. Freud once pointed out that some dreams *tell the whole story of a neurosis (or psychosis)* but that in dealing with them we must proceed piece by piece, due to the problem of "resistance." I believe Freud's resistance means defense (this includes transference), and so we must gradually put pieces of the total together as the resistances are overcome. It is my impression that resistances (defenses) are overcome by outlining them, judging at what points they go into operation, *and understanding what the fantasies are that precede the patterns of behavior that constitute the resistances. To understand these fantasies, it is necessary to review situations in the here and now that set off the fantasies and neurotic patterns, then analyze these fantasies and neurotic patterns. The fantasies must be analyzed in relation to the present,* thereafter making connections with the past between the fantasies and the neurotic patterns. How to do this with borderline patients who act out their fantasies rather than consciously experience them is a problem, and this determines the type of psychoanalytic technique employed in the early phases of treatment. It is the coping with the acting out and relating this to the *identification fantasies* through the associations that require that the treatment of the borderline patient extend over several years. In the beginning and sometimes for a long period, for example, the fantasies related to idealization cannot be dissipated. (In the *short-term treatment* of the borderline patient, we focus on one small part of the problem, disregarding the major defenses, helping the patient to work through the focused aspect of the difficulty. We hope that the experience will enable the patient to generalize and recognize a similar situation in the future, working that through by himself.)

The borderline is said to be typically dissociative, and this interferes with the utilization of insight and the expression of association. It is true that the patient often has a negativistic attitude that he holds onto—a kind of attitude of "I will not let this son of a bitch influence me." This makes the utilization of insight difficult. It is an acting out of the transference, a resistance to the controlling parent, projected into the analytic situation.

My patient, Sonia, had this problem; she could not accept consciously the idea of any kind of "control" from another person, although she utilized her parents' control for years and would not budge from that position. Her masochism was intense and seemed almost inpenetrable. This struggle was very important to her sense of integrity and safety. She idealized her willingness to be trapped by her parents and to have to "take care of them." She was the "good" child, her sister the "bad" one. Kernberg might interpret this "good" and "bad" (as Sonia allocates the roles to her sister and herself) as not being willing to see the good and bad of the parents and of herself. In a sense, this is true. The projection of the "good" and "bad" of the parents is seen in the good and bad sisters. This was not a true dissociation, however, since Sonia did, on occasion, talk of the hostility of her parents. However, if one picked this up, she would deny it vociferously. It is this kind of mechanism that is called *dissociation* in the borderline. There is a consciousness of the facts while there is denial so that it is not a true "splitting."

Sonia also had a "bad object" (splitting and the projection of aggression) in her cousin as contrasted to herself, the cousin who came to stay with Sonia's family while her parents were settling themselves in America. It is not that Sonia did not see the good and bad of her parents: she did, *but she would not allow herself to act upon this knowledge*. In other words, she did with the good and bad of her parents what Elizabeth did in her sexual life—denying what she felt in view of her knowledge, dissociating, if you will. But it is the identification with her father that Sonia defended in this denial or dissociation. Later she began talking of this identification. It was the father who was house bound and who was "more neurotic than the mother," the father who was depressed, hostile, demeaning, arrogant, grandiose, and so forth. The mother was "more stable," worked hard, had friends, but she had the same contempt for people that the father had and always told Sonia that she was "above" the children in the street. Sonia's family was "good," other families not equal to them and were therefore "not as good," according to mother. Sonia was "better" and "luckier." Sonia could not play with other children. The truth was that Sonia was partially rejected by the children because of her personality, just as my patient, Elizabeth, was rejected by the "normal" group due to her peculiarities.

In the family there are "good" and "bad" children, but being the preferred child in a family does not preclude the possibility of that child becoming neurotic. On the contrary, the preferred child is usually extremely neurotic. Flora's "preferred son" (she has a "good" son and a "bad" son) is perhaps even more disturbed than the rejected one who became the homosexual; both, of course, have serious problems. Sonia would be called a help-rejecting patient due to her tenacity in hanging on to her defenses, particularly her masochism (and sadism) and her need to distribute her hostility so as to maintain an equilibrium. She could also be said to be "fused" with her mother. She fears annihilation rather than "abandonment" if she is not attached to a hostile figure; this was her original fear. She needs a figure to hate or to demean or else she will turn on herself in a much more hostile manner than she usually employs toward others. She holds herself together in this way. The "fusion" is thus a way of handling her aggression. Whether we call this phenomenon fusion or dependency or, as I like to think of it, sadomasochism in the context of projective identification, we must realize that we are speaking of behavior that bears no resemblance whatsoever to infantile behavior. Therefore, to call the behavior "regressive" is simply a misunderstanding of the dynamics. To call the aggression instinctive is simplistic and misleading since all behavior could be said to be instinctive. This type of behavior, like so much other behavior, may become possible through the neurophysiological mechanisms that are "givens," taking its shape and form from the kind of experiences the patient has in his relations with people and things over a long period of time. Each individual in this world has experiences that are similar to the experiences of others, but each individual experience has also its uniqueness.

The need for a hate object has often been mistaken for dependency and an unresolved "symbiosis." Kohut believes that the patient maintains himself against "shattering and disintegration" by clinging or "fusing" and Masterson speaks of "abandonment depression," a fear of losing the object, thus the need for clinging or "symbiotic" relationship. I believe that the depression one sees in borderlines is initiated by the patient's feeling of rejection due to the obvious need of his parents to use him as a projective object in the interests of their defense and equilibrium, a circumstance where he sees no exit and feels trapped. He develops anger but never feels that his anger is effective so far as getting himself free from the trap is concerned. His hate eventually turns to revenge feelings. And it is in the interest of revenge that he pits one person against another and is negativistic when it comes to utilizing insight. *The associations are the vehicles by which the personal experiences are revealed.* The symbols and situations in the dreams and fantasies are the means through which the implications of the patient's personal experiences are depicted.

Several family members are involved in most cases where neurosis and psychosis evolve, and they provide the experiences that are traumatic to the patient. As time goes on, the patient begins to fear the parent's aggression and thinks of it as life threatening. As he continues to assuage their guilts, he becomes attuned to the total sadomasochistic pattern. His revenge feeling beings to take form. As his own guilt mounts, the homicidal and suicidal impulses become more intense, and the patient fears annihilation if he is separated from a hostile object. This is not, however, similar to the clinging of an infant; it is rather the conditioned pattern of sadomasochism, which is quite a different matter from the early mother-child relationsip. It is certain that one must work with borderlines using projective techniques, and one must wait until the patient decides to pick up on a given aspect of the problem before the working through can be accomplished. The analyst may have pointed up a problem, using the projective technique, six months prior to the patient's mentioning it; yet the analyst cannot begin on the analysis of this particular aspect of the problem until the patient decides to give the go-ahead signal. This *waiting for the patient to pick up a trend for work* is different from how one would work with a neurotic patient, where the therapist might put together a construction and then *suggest* an area of work.

How are the patient's defenses and his acting out related to the family matrix? The parents' fantasies are "connected" to the acting out. For example, in my 1973 book (p. 46) I mentioned Freud's paper "The Psychogenesis of a Case of Homosexuality in a Woman" (1920). I pointed out that the "family system" was involved in this case. The father and mother had emotional investments in the daughter's homosexuality. The father loudly protested the "badness" of the problem (the girl's acting out was in part an aspect of her revenge), *but the mother was complacent*, almost showing approval of the girl's conduct. The picture of the flamboyant homosexual partner, the seductress, the exhibitionist, was a prominent aspect of the picture, a focus for much concern to the parents. The homosexuality was in truth a "family affair." I can say the same for the homosexuality in Flora's son. The instigation of homosexual behavior is definitely a process in the family that has meaning in the interlocking defensive system of Flora and her first and second husbands. The associations of Flora in her sessions and aspects of her dreams make this family pattern obvious. The present husband ignored one son's homosexual relationships early on and denied that they existed; just as he ignored the lump in Flora's breast, denying its existence. Two therapists noted that he also fostered both sons' drug habits and their failures. In one son's fantasies

VANDERBILT MEDICAL CENTER LIBRARY

there are references to these experiences with the parents and the resentments inflicted in the associations with respect to insight and/or learning. Here are some of the factors contributing to associative linking, which Rosner (1969) feels are present in all patients: (1) the need to complete an incompleted task (the Zeigarnik effect), (2) the factor of recency, (3) the Hoffding function, i.e., the selective effect of similarity,[4] (4) the law of contiguity. The latter refers particularly to "manifest content." The "latent content," Rosner believes, is more closely related to the laws of similarity, requiredness, etc. Since sheer contiguity is not a basis for memory the latent content must be coupled with "intrinsic similarity." Analysts could view the recalled contiguous event as covering over the important event by displacement, substitution, screen memories, etc. "Thus analysts would aim to remove the anxiety of a defense so that the event could be associatively related to the "main point of focus in terms of similarity requiredness and the like." Interpretation aids the recovery of "real memories" rather than "screen memories" and "paves the way for the patient to face the *affects* he has been avoiding through defense." (The borderline patient is loath to experience certain "affects" or "feelings" and defends against them strenuously. He is often willing to admit his knowledge on an intellectual level, but he denies feeling.)

In this chapter we have touched upon questions of theory and technique that confront all therapists in their treatment of the borderline. Thinking through these different viewpoints and focusing on a rational theory helps the therapist in his work with these difficult patients.

---

[4]In the interpretation of dreams or fantasies, for example, we use the "just as" formulation of Freud in understanding identifications with figures in the dream, i.e., the similarities with the patient's personality that are represented by the people in dreams. This principle is also important in the use of projective therapeutic techniques that necessitate the use of similarity in focusing on the problem of the "others."

VANDERBILT MEDICAL CENTER LIBRARY

PART III

Understanding the Borderline Personality

CHAPTER 5

Infant Development and
Antithetic Diameters

For many years certain psychoanalysts have been doubting the validity of some of the major tenets of psychoanalytic theory and suggesting that revision of the theory is necessary. For example, Freud's ideas of aggression were questioned by Rapaport (1967), and the instinct theory itself has been criticized by Lashley (1957) and Holt (1962), the latter having written a paper on "free and bound cathexis." In the last ten years those who have studied infant behavior have stated flatly that Freud's developmental theory is inaccurate.

In my 1952 and 1960 papers I suggested that the reality system is intact in all patients in spite of the symptoms and the distortions they may evince. This idea was based not only on my own observations but on certain of Freud's ideas expressed in the "Outline of Psychoanalysis" (1938, 23:201-202, 203-204) and on the work of some of the psychologists who were using psychological tests with patients. I felt that distortions were to be looked upon as *defenses* rather than as an indication of some mysterious kind of infantile mental functioning due to the infant's inability to perceive his environment as it really exists, and thus a function of a mystical id/ego undifferentiated state. Psychoanalytic concepts of development are applied currently by theorists who describe borderline patients both in the area of the genesis of the borderline's basic conflict and in the milieu of treatment. As matters stand today, it looks as if theorists are superimposing upon a social theory (object relations theory) a developmental scheme that does not in fact depict what actually happens in infant development. This confuses the picture and prevents an understanding of the dynamics of borderline conditions interfering with development of a rational therapeutic endeavor.

In this chapter, we shall review some of the literature in the field of infant development that appears to negate the current psychoanalytic concepts regarding the early phases of infant life. These recent studies have important implications for the understanding of the borderline patient. Some case shadows of doubt over traditionally accepted concepts such as the "narcissistic phase of development" and assumptions about the "objectless period," "undifferentiated state," and "self-object." Information that is available today leads to the conclusion that the infant is an organized entity, with perceptual and memory systems intact, with learning and communicating facilities available, and thus with interpersonal capabilities operative, shortly after birth. We previously mentioned Anthony J. De Casper's (1979) result that infants 24 to 36 hours after birth learned and could remember what they had learned to the extent that they could repeat a pattern associated with the sound of the mother's voice, which they could distinguish from the voices of other people. There have been many other studies demonstrating that infants can perceive stimuli quite effectively (for example, Caplan, 1973), and all investigators have come to the conclusion that perceptive systems are highly developed at birth and that perceptions and learning may even be operative before birth.

De Casper's thesis was that infants have well-organized perceptual systems, including auditory capabilities at birth, and that learning begins almost immediately. It has been postulated that these functions are activated around the seventh month of gestation. There is in all normal infants a *synchronization of systems*, such as perception, memory, discriminative capacities, and other neurophysiological mechanisms, which are all intact and functionally ready. There is no data to show that this is not true even of infants who when they become adults have emotional problems. In fact, the data show that in these adults such systems are still synchronous and operative.

The infant is not a "closed system" with the mother or with any other person, and what has been interpreted as normal "autism" is apparently the infant's preoccupation with learning about the environment. There seems to be no time that the infant is exclusively occupied with himself such as is hypothesized in some psychoanalytic theories. It is true that in the first three months the infant is asleep more than he is awake, but when he is awake, he is continuously interacting with the environment, right from birth. There is a great deal of evidence to indicate that normally the infant is an autonomous functioning individual who is *actively concerned with learning* about his environment. Under normal circumstances, the learning is *pleasurable*, but under the impact of neurotic and/or psychotic parents the learning in interpersonal relations with them is often painful or *unpleasurable*. The pleasure-unpleasure principle is a conditioning element in the infant's mental world. The vast amount of learning that the infant must accomplish in spite of existing circumstances is apparently taken into account by nature, or rather by the genes, since recent studies show that humans appear to have 50 percent more brain cell interconnections, or synapses, when they are infants than when they grow to adulthood, (*Science News*, 1979b, p. 89). In line with this fact, it is interesting to note that some of the activity of the infant concerns experimentation with space and time and with the alerting system, thus with learning about his place in the environment through interaction with people and things, particularly with how to manipulate objects and communicate with people.

Investigation of the Environment

The infant's investigation of the environment has often been seen through the screen of the experimenter's theoretical convictions. For example, the period of autism was considered a period of narcissism where there was no distinction between self and environment (Piaget, 1937, 1952). Schaffer (1958) wrote a paper to the effect that infants hospitalized do not "attach" to human beings (objects) before 7 months of age. At that age children do begin to be "attached" to the mother, and shortly after this they react untowardly to strangers. Schaffer noted that a child prior to 7 months who had been hospitalized after returning home showed an "extreme preoccupation with the environment . . . for hours on end the child would crane his neck, scanning his surroundings without apparently focusing on any particular feature." This behavior continued for the first day home. Other children under 7 months in similar circumstances reacted the same way (some of these children were 3 weeks of age). With a few the scanning period lasted only twenty or thirty minutes, but for some it lasted as long as four days. Schaffer interpreted this to mean that children of this age have a "global, undifferentiated, syncretic stage of development." Children who were older than 7 months (none of the children observed were more than 51 weeks of age) had a different kind of reaction. Schaffer noted that "the central feature was overdependence on the mother . . . of the same order as described by Prugh et al. (1953)." The overdependence was shown by such behavior as excessive crying when left alone, continual clinging, and a fear of strangers. Schaffer concluded that the first group demonstrated Piaget's theory of cognitive structure, i.e., the way in which perceptions are organized, and the second reaction was interpreted in terms of Mahler's theory of the "omnipotent symbiotic dual unity" (Mahler et al, 1959, p. 822).

The same data presented by Schaffer might be evaluated in a different way. One might argue that the described "scanning period" is a function of the infant's synchronizing ability to explore and size up the situation in which he finds himself in a short period of time. The second reaction might be accounted for by the phylogenetically determined fear reaction that makes its appearance between the ages of 4 to 12 months and is perhaps a self-preservative reaction.

The characteristics that make possible the "organized mind" are functions of the "innate schedule" that evokes the appearance of behaviors at certain age level in all infants regardless of culture or environment, such as the ability to focus (to isolate one object from another, i.e., to discriminate), to gesture and communicate (see Trevarthan, 1974), to emote with pleasure when learning (activating the pleasure center in the brain), to prefer *people* rather than objects when people are present in the environment (at 3 months), to "attach" to people at 7 months of age, to demonstrate a fear reaction that is activated between 7 and 12 months, and to imitate at 10 months (perhaps this begins at the 2-month period with the ability to imitate gestures), which may have a relation to the capacity to "identify" at later stages. Thus, we might have a different idea about the 7-month stage than what is described by Mahler as symbiosis. Signs of distress appear at 7 months. It is at this stage that the *fear reaction* occurs in all children; it may have been hastened in the children Schaffer was observing by the hospital experience.

It is at the 8-month period that a child can retrieve a toy that has been hidden; thus he has developed the capacity to "retrieve structures for events not in the immediate field" (Kagan, 1979a). In reference to this principle, the comments of Muller and Richardson (1979) concerning Freud's report of the "Fort! Da." game recorded in "Beyond the Pleasure Principle" (Freud, S.E., 1920) are of interest. The theory these authors expound has a relation to the development of language, which is an important factor in development. The theory, in brief, follows: The world of *meaning* concerning things and people becomes viable through the *presence* and *absence* of the same object—two opposites. (There would be other opposites as well, I suppose, e.g., *pleasure* and *unpleasure; yes* and *no; hard* and *soft*; and so on.) In this bipolar experience the child attains the rudiments of language, attaching sounds and later words, phrases, and sentences to the experiences connected with ideas that are integrated along the lines of either selection or combination—two principles that permeate the entire structure of language. Based on the presence and then the absence of something, selection would be represented by the nonpresence of a mutually complementary (opposite) effect, and combination would be represented by *two presences* even though they would be opposites. Muller and Richardson presented this concept in relation to their discussion of the ideas of Lecan, a French psychiatrist who believes, as do many of us, that Freud's greatest accomplishment was his work "The Interpretation of Dreams." The central message in this opus, according to Lecan, is that "the unconscious is structured like a language." This idea is not so unusual if one believes as fact that dreaming is a form of thinking and the unconscious is a reservoir of thoughts and feelings that were once conscious but are now repressed or temporarily forgotten. In our work with the emotional disorders we are interested in the repressed thoughts and feelings since we believe these to be related to the unconscious conflicts that are unsatisfactorily resolved by the neuroses and psychoses. The dream is a form of communication to tell us of these unsatisfactorily resolved conflicts. The acceptance of this interpretation of a dream leads us to presume with Breuer and Freud that to complete the reactions that were inhibited in the dream might produce relief or cure and resolve the conflicts. The impetus to complete incompleted tasks would thus be a motivation to resolve emotional conflicts (Wolberg, A., 1973, p. 4); in other words, the Zeigarnik effect would be the evoking principle, and the chronic condition of frustration in relations with parents would lay the groundwork for the development of the neurotic condition.

Freud's "game" that Muller and Richardson recalled was that of a little boy who had a wooden reel with a piece of string tied around it. Freud said of this boy that it did not occur to the child to pull the toy along the floor as a wagon or carriage; instead he held the reel by the string and threw it over his cot (bed) so that it *disappeared* at the same time that he uttered "o-o-o." He then pulled the reel out again, and when it reappeared, he said joyfully "da," demonstrating a "cultural achievement" (said Freud), i.e., the renunciation of "instinctual satisfaction" which the boy had made by allowing the object to disappear as his mother could leave without his protesting words—thus overcoming separation anxiety.

If I were to evaluate this particular game, I might think that the child was discovering some of the laws of physics or learning about space relations. Of course, this could apply to the mother's disappearing and appearing, just like the reel was appearing and disappearing, but I would not think of the process as related to "separation anxiety" or "object loss," for example. Since the child was enjoying himself, I might think that he was experimenting with space and time. From birth the child must get used to people appearing and disappearing, the mother and other people as well. When he is 7 or 8 months of age, he is anxious, he has a fear reaction when something unusual occurs. But it is at this same period that he can retrieve a toy, and it is at this same age that he begins to integrate his learning in a way that gives him a sense of peace or danger. He has "representations" in his mind of the realities of his experience; his meaning system has developed. When frustration or forced isolation prevents the child from receiving an adequate amount of stimulation from people, then he cries for the presence of people—perhaps not a particular person but a family member with whom he is familiar and who is not frightening to him. It is the quality of the interpersonal encounter that makes the difference between the experience of pleasure or unpleasure. The game that Freud described may have nothing at all to do with people per se; it may be an exercise of individual autonomy related to the principle of memorizing a situation and then remembering it long enough to reproduce it. The principle is applied in many different kinds of situations with people and with objects.

Learning in Interpersonal Relations

There are several studies that refer specifically to interpersonal relations and to what has been called in psychoanalytic parlance "the internalization of objects," a phrase that means, as far as I can fathom, learning in interpersonal relations. For example, based on some of the experiments and ideas of Harlow, James Prescott, a developmental neuropsychologist, postulated a relationship between violence and early infant care practices. He points out that "mother" does not mean purely the behavior of the mother —it means the behavior of *anyone* who performs the child-rearing practices, (this can mean mother and father, father, or anyone who serves the child-rearing role). The mothering process, as a matter of fact, is usually carried on by several people. The Harlows' experience (1962) was that monkeys that had been isolated in infancy and childhood as adults were withdrawn, self-mutilating, and aggressive toward other monkeys who might try to come close to them. When they themselves had young, the isolated females became unstable and brutal. Apparently bodily contact and immediate comfort are important in forming the early trusting interpersonal relationship, and these females had been deprived of this and were then, in turn, depriving of their own children. The borderline patient has some of these characteristics but not in as severe a form as the patterns of Harlow's monkeys. The borderline patient is hostile, withdrawn, and self-destructive. So are other types of patients. The difference between a borderline patient and a schizophrenic in relation to these traits may be a matter of degree. In my experience the aggression toward others is more intense in the schizophrenic, and the chances of the patient being homicidal are much greater in the schizophrenic than in the borderline.

Prescott felt that the idea of movement in the mothering activities is important. For example, the brain pleasure pathways are stimulated by rocking, caressing, and other forms of normal interpersonal stimulation; thus the role of environment is important in the development of normal brain activity. The "pleasure center" must have a "memory bank," so to speak, of pleasant stimulation in order for the individual to have a favorable outlook on other people and "self." In my opinion Kohut and Winnicott have a similar view. For example, "mother" and "holding," and the like, have a similar connotation except that Prescott is making a connection between interpersonal behavior and the neurological system, while Kohut and Winnicott are making a connection between early interpersonal relations and a later capacity to withstand anxiety or frustration, and the presence or absence of emotional problems.

Prescott theorized that *any* movement, including holding and sucking, results in a train of impulses that travel to a specific part of the brain, the cerebellum. When an infant is held or rocked, there are impulses in response that go to the pleasure center. The cerebellum is the area of the brain that coordinates movement. Prescott thought that in the case of disturbed children perhaps both touch and movement receptors and their connections with other brain structures have not received sufficient sensory stimulation for normal development and function to occur. Prescott reasoned that first it had to be demonstrated whether or not the cerebellum is connected with "emotional control centers of the limbic system," and he took some of Harlow's monkeys to Robert G. Heath at Tulane University to test his hypothesis. Heath (1972) found the connection. Prescott believes that when there has been insufficient experiences of pleasure, good feelings cannot be transmitted to the appropriate parts of the brain because there are fewer cell connections; thus the pleasure centers are blocked. Prescott concludes, therefore, that there must be a physiological condition of fewer cells involved in the pleasure tracts under certain circumstances.

It is likely, it seems to me, that the pleasure centers can be stimulated by the individual himself, i.e., by his own activity. The "need" or the "instinct" for pleasure will find expression. The pain centers are also stimulated when the child has untoward experiences with parents. When pain outweighs pleasure, the individual is thrown into conflict, and the pain centers are stimulated. The borderline eventually becomes sadomasochistic since he has been conditioned to pain through frustration; this kind of conditioning has occurred in the parent-child relations. The patterns of the parents tend to cut off many pleasures that the child begins to experience. The sadomasochistic behavior of the parents toward the child stimulates the "unpleasure center" more often or as often as the pleasure center. The child who later becomes borderline has been conditioned to have guilt if he himself does not cut off the pleasure as the parents do. He must internalize this pattern, so to speak, as an aspect of his identifications that his parents demand of him. This is the normal impulse of the child for new learning and new experience that is pleasurable but that is thwarted by parental control when the parent is neurotic, anxious, and defensive. In the case of neurosis or psychosis, after the experience of having been thwarted and frustrated by sadomasochistic parents, the child through "identification with the aggressor" turns off his pleasure himself and then admits only the pain of the frustration, *even though he may have felt the pleasure as well.* This was the case, for example, of my patient Harriet, who had sex, was aroused (pleasurably) and lubricated, but when she began to feel pleasure, she had to cut it off. Of course, pleasure was eventually cut off as well by the activity of her partner in addition to her own efforts, but this was after her partner had had many difficult experiences with her.

Evoking frustration and consequent pain that has values for the person that outweigh pleasure might then be the reason why we see the phenomenon of the "help-rejecting complainer," a characteristic or trait of many borderline patients. When guilt is evoked in the presence of receiving pleasure, the individual must put a stop to the pleasure—an "undoing" takes place to reduce the anxiety associated with guilt. This might account for the phenomenon described by Dince (1977) and Green (1977).

The theory of masochism and sadism was never satisfactorily elucidated in psychoanalytic theory. Could this have been due to Freud's hesitancy in implicating parents and therefore the family system as a "cause"? He ultimately turned to the instinct theory as the source of both masochism and sadism, and later he conceived of these in terms of his developmental theory, namely, that the aggressive instincts appear automatically at various stages (i.e., in the "oral" stage in biting and in the anal stage by "expelling," and the like). The concept of interpersonal relations was missing in these ideas since the behavior was considered separate from behavior based on the pleasure-pain principle. Freud (1921) invoked the concept of the repetition-compulsion to explain these phenomena, which he said seemed to be unregulated by the pleasure-pain principle. These he thought were mental operations that are more primitive in a biological evolutionary sense than those regulated by the pleasure-pain principle. Freud connected the "fate neurosis," the enactment of childhood conflicts (acting out), and self-defeating behavior in the character disorders to the repetition compulsion, and it was on this basis that he postulated the life and death instincts, two opposites. From the observations of such individuals as Szurek and Johnson (1942), Szurek (1952), Jackson (1957, Lidz et al (1965), and others we postulate the idea that masochism (the tendency to repeat painful behavior) is a consequence of training and learning in the family and is thus a result of the pleasure-pain principle in interpersonal relations with parents. It is very interesting that the experiments of Heath with the Harlow monkeys suggest a connection between experience with "objects," neurophysiological processes in the cerebellum, pleasure-pain centers, and emotional reactions.

While neurophysiological systems are not a part of psychoanalytic theory per se, it is, nevertheless, of interest that these systems are interconnected, and interpersonal behavior has a relation, as Freud suspected, to the brain and undoubtedly, as he suspected, to bodily chemical reactions as well. We shall probably learn more of the connections between chemical systems, anxiety, and interpersonal behavior and between biological systems and interpersonal behavior in the future. What current studies do indicate is the relation between anxiety, stress, pleasure, and unpleasure, and interpersonal behavior and brain function. It has been quipped that some behavior therapists do not accept the brain as an intervening variable. Of course, most behavior therapists do acknowledge the central role of the brain in learning, and I suspect that these investigators are well on the way to accepting some of the more rational findings of psychoanalysts.

Aggression

Some of the current theories about the borderline patient, and particularly regarding aggression and its vicissitudes, are refuted by many studies of infants, including some of animal young. The concept that automatically the infant must defend against his own aggression shortly after he is born, that defenses against this instinct must be put into operation early, that there is a period of autism when the infant is unrelated to objects, that there is a time when the perceptive apparatus is so primitive that the infant cannot integrate his images, and so on, and so on—all of these ideas are under challenge by modern investigators.

The Harlows (1962), as we already noted, found that female monkey infants "raised in total isolation exhibited a level of self-aggression that was nearly suicidal." When these isolates became mothers, they exhibited two different behaviors toward their newborn: (1) "they either totally ignored them or (2) they violently abused them." Sometimes the abuse was fatal. Harlow believes this finding can be applied to human mothers who engage in child abuse. He has not explained the father in child abuse, but one could assume that fathers too have been used in untoward ways by their own parents. In the human family the father's role is important, and his influence is felt even shortly after birth. We find that in actual child-abuse cases it is often the father who is abusive, but when the mothers separate from the fathers, they (the mothers) eventually carry on the abusing patterns. In the human family there is an interlocking defensive relationship between father and mother.

Harlow said that the "loyalty" of the battered infants to their mothers was intense. The little monkeys showed "clinging fearfulness" and "prominent displays of hostility." I think that "loyalty" is probably the wrong word. A few of the "motherless mothers" who were unsuccessful in either killing their children or ignoring them finally succumbed to their babies *persistent efforts to nuzzle and cuddle*—and they accepted their offspring.

I propose that the child is a "group person" right from the start. This is not to say that "individual development" is not a fact, but we must take another look at what is "innate." Innate patterns that appear at stated intervals in development, regardless of the culture of the child, appear to support self-preservative functions. It is the group that provides the stimulus for many of the individual's experiences, however, and it is on the basis of these experiences (good or bad) that conflicting thoughts, hopes, and fears are based. Each individual in the family group has a unique experience and thus a unique history. Communication is the medium through which the group survives. When the pleasure system is disturbed by the behavior of the parents in early life, the infants try to wrest what they need for their own growth and development, just as Harlow's monkeys did and as that child Roxanne Felumaro attempted to do (Wolberg, A., 1973, p. 12). The child will try and try to save himself from the hostility of the parent. Anna Freud found that children from concentration camps tried to get what they needed from adults. Sometimes children do succeed in changing the behavior of the parent. In the case of the borderline this has not been the case, and when self-assertion fails, aggression comes to the fore. I have noticed in the reports of criminals who have maimed or murdered people they did not know that prior to the incident of their murdering they have often had an altercation or an experience with a person whom they do know which they have taken to be self-demeaning. The aggression is in retaliation—but with an unknown object. A young couple have had a "blow up," the man has been rejected, for example, and he goes out and attacks some girl sexually, maiming or killing her. The same can be true of a woman. We have learned that women often instigate fights so that they will be attacked, and, as we have said, battered wives who leave their husbands and take their battered children with them usually begin battering the children themselves when the husbands are not around to do so. The rage reactions of those who will become borderline patients are seen in temper tantrums by the age of 2 or 3 (Geleered, 1945). Hate, revenge, and envy are later developments. There is a paranoidlike flavor to the transference in the borderline when he perceives the analyst as a sadistic person; thus a paranoid trend seems to serve as a defense against admitting the person's own sadistic impulses and wishes which are aspects of the revenge motif, and his identification with the aggressor. Severe frustration brings aggression to the fore.

Harlow (1976) indicated in a lecture at the New York Academy of Medicine describing the results of 40 years of research with primates that mother love and *peer love* are important in teaching a child control of those "innate learned emotions, hostility and aggression, *which are not apparent at birth* but mature late in the mother-infant system of love" (present author's italics). Harlow believes that *peer love*, or love of child for child, manifested in playful interactions is the major determinent of subsequent social and sexual development. While we cannot compare directly work with primates and work with humans, the dynamics of aggression in relation to frustration can be seen in both. It seems evident that the frustration-aggression hypothesis has more of a bearing on the kind of aggression we see in the neuroses and psychoses than a theory that purports that aggression emerges at birth and the infant must defend immediately through projections. In the human aggression is a defense against threat. It is not an imagined threat but a real threat, which is the aggression of the parent who is forcing the child to act out a role that he must accept through identification while at the same time he must deny that this is so. The individual's conflict rests upon several antithetical propositions: see—do not see; do—do not do; accept—do not accept. We may hypothesize several formulations from our work:

1. Children will try to obtain what they need from parents even though the parents are rejecting due to their own problems.

2. Children make an adjustment to parents when they cannot change them, if they are to survive.

3. When the parents are neurotic, the child is forced to play a sadomasochistic identification role, but first he fights against the identification and actually tries to change the parent. When he cannot do this, *he succumbs to identification as a means of survival.*

4. Peer relationships are essential in the development of the child and at a certain point are more important than parental relationships.

In this discussion of infant development we are obviously touching upon the need for multidisciplinary thinking in the field of psychoanalysis, recognizing that the psychoanalyst needs to have information from several disciplines and must be able to utilize the knowledge to understand his own role better, to adapt knowledge from other sources when this is relevant, and to know when the other discipline has only peripheral relevance to the psychoanalyst's work. In this present illustration pertaining to infant development we can learn, for example, what to discard in our psychoanalytic theory. The work of McCarley and Hobson (1977) tells us how the neurophysiological mechanisms aid in the operation of certain mental capacities. In discovering the mechanisms that set off dreaming, they have also told us something about thinking, for dreaming and thinking are related processes. Their work tends to explain how the human individual is able to concentrate, i.e., how we "tune out" and "tune in." Also, it tells us how the defenses of repression, denial, and dissociation can be evoked as well as some of the abilities of the individual to engage in hypnosis and to have the capacity to observe one's own behavior, thus to engage in psychotherapy through self observation.

Rehabilitation

The relabilitation efforts in Harlow's experiments are geared at helping the isolates who exhibited "abnormal" levels of withdrawal, depression, and/or aggression *to join with a group* of younger, "normal monkeys, who acted as corrective peers." The influence of *the group*, even in animals, is, therefore, an "experimentally demonstrated fact." We have in human society, however, groups in organized crime and certain political groups whose goal is to be destructive or to undo forward moves that have been made to safeguard the welfare of all the people in society. There are also economic groups whose purpose is to control and maintain power at whatever cost, devastation of the environment and hostility to people being techniques that are used. To paraphase the thinking of such individuals, "I have to have money in order to maintain a certain standard, a position. How the money is obtained is my affair and any means is permissible, as long as I am not caught." There are thus antithetical subgroups in the society. Harlow, however, was speaking of a *constructive group* as a rehabilitative vehicle, one where the security of the members is maintained. In psychoanalytic terms this would be a psychoanalytically oriented therapy group. Group therapy for the borderline is important. There are, as we have said, subgroups also in the therapy group that have antithetical goals at times.

Irenaus Eibl-Eibesfeldt, then director of the famous Max Planck Institute for Behavioral Physiology in Bavaria, at a conference held by the Kittay Foundation in March 1974, disagreed with the theories of Konrad Lorenz, the former director of the Max Plack Institute, who held that aggression is an inherited trait of the human race from its animal ancestors—the aggression being related to the animal characteristic of fighting for space and territory. Since aggression is so rampant in our society and creates such distress and havoc among people, and is a factor in all emotional disorders, it is interesting that Eibl-Eibesfeldt (1974) in refuting Lorenz's idea referred to phenomena among animals and birds that are similar to the signaling systems used by children isolated from ordinary forms of learning by being both blind and deaf. He spoke of the ritualistic behavior of cormorants, for example, in the Galapogos Islands. Lorenz said that "peaceful man" is yet to be born, and that modern man is a "link" between his animal ancestors and an ideal creature that has shed his inherited instinct of aggression. Eibl-Eibesfeldt reminds us that man is equipped with all of the restraints on violent behavior that prevent animals of a particular species from killing one another. Chimpanzees have signals for displaying friendships, for example, that are much like those of human beings. They press their lips together in what seems like a kiss, and they extend hands: One chimpanzee will offer his hand to another, and the other will cover the hand. The first hand, according to Eibl-Eibesfeldt, is extended palm upward while the other covers the first. Many examples from animal and bird life were presented to support the thesis, and George Serban, the medical director of the Kittay Scientific Foundation, at the time, said that this information may help toward reconciliation of the two views that have long divided psychologists into camps represented by the "nature" and "nurture" concepts relevant to the roots of human behavior. Eibl-Eibesfeldt remarked that it is the culture (society) and society's development of weapons that permits killing and destruction. There are inborn signals of peace and friendships, such as smiling, crying, and there are many kinds of acts that are conciliatory in effect. In the modern world there are treaties of friendships, agreements, and concords. In essence these agreements and concords represent norms that the participants are expected to respect. Human survival depends on our cultural development rather than on the technology that we develop. We are beginning to understand that techniques can be used for the good of society or for its destruction.

We mentioned that in the human group there is the important dynamic—the development of norms—that is essential if the group is to survive. This dynamic is based on a consensus of opinion, on agreements after several solutions to a problem have been discussed and one solution is agreed upon. A norm is a description of the kind of behavior that the group deems appropriate for individuals in a given circumstance. The "norm" is a guide to the roles of individuals in groups, and the "role" is the connecting link between the group and the individual. In emotional problems the neurotic role is indicated by the parent who trains the child in the identification process, the vehicle for accepting the neurotic role.

The fact is, as Winnicott (1965) has pointed out, all children need adequate mothering in order to grow up with a minimum of neurotic traits. I would add that they cannot have "good enough mothering" without good enough "fathering." Right from birth the father enters as an instrument in the rearing techniques as early as the mother, and the reciprocal relationship of the father and mother has an influence on their attitudes toward the child. There is a great deal of self-assertion in the infant at birth that helps the child to be involved in a kind of self-feedback system in relation to objects. When the objects are human, responses are received that give him pleasure and unpleasure, thus lending impetus to the development of defenses.

Communication

The structure of the group is attained through communication. In fact, communication along with memory are fundamental elements not only in the survival of the species but of the individual as well. Learning involves the synchronization of the individual's various systems and is an important element in the survival chain.

As communication operates, the family structure emerges, and it is partly the stuff out of which individual personality develops. There are those theorists who propose that communication in the form of language is the binding force in group life and that there are natural laws that apply to all communications in the group, regardless of the culture. Communication means any kind of language: sign language, guttural sounds and words, phrases, sentences, any form of signaling that indicates meaning. Possibility for communication is inherent in the child at birth. Cooing, sucking, spitting, looking, the startle response, the manifestations associated with the alerting tendencies and other activities of the limbic system all play a role in the infant's ability to communicate. The genetic base for communication is embedded in various behaviors. Trevarthen (1974) has suggested that the child's ability to communicate with gestures is already developed at birth. The child is prepared genetically for group life. The world of meaning is established through communication. It is the communication system on both its conscious and unconscious or repressed levels that we meet in dreams and fantasies with their associations. We need several types of communication to understand the language (the preconscious material as well as the unconscious or repressed material) that is directed to us in distorted form in dreams. The distortions are a disguised kind of communication that we learn to decipher through the associations. We have learned a great deal about this communication system from "The Interpretation of Dreams" (Freud, S.E., 1900). Dreams reveal aspects of the memory system and the meaning of a particular memory in relation to events in the here-and-now. This point has been discussed by Lewis R. Wolberg (1962) in his book *Psychotherapy and the Behaviorial Sciences*.

Apparently the principle of polarity or contrasts is important in language and communication. It is indeed a principle in interpretation in psychoanalysis and psychotherapy. The polarity of pleasant and unpleasant begins in infancy and is a primary factor in learning and in interpersonal relations. Interpretations to the borderline contain many polarities. There are the polarities of sadism and masochism, anger and love, good and bad, aggression and appeasement, self and object, distortion and reality perception, self and environment, and on and on.

The psychoanalytic therapeutic relationship is in itself a form of various types of communication. There has been much in the psychoanalytic and psychotherapeutic literature as well as in sociological writing concerning communication. Many therapists feel that nonverbal communication is important in the treatment of borderline patients. There comes a time in the treatment when it is necessary to work through the detachment and the patient's pattern of cutting off pleasure. This is related to the struggle that the patient had in trying to communicate with a detached parent and the ambivalence and hostility of the parent and finally the identification with the parent. This working through is a most delicate and arduous task, requiring the therapist to make use of polarities or opposite attitudes on the part of the parent. The detached parent usually makes feeble attempts to be friendly, but the patient cannot appreciate these attempts and will either withdraw from the parent or attack—whichever way the sadomasochistic pattern has evolved between them. The communications from the therapist must point to the opposites in the parents' behavior as well as in the patient's.

In the treatment of any patient, including the borderline patient, the help seeker and the therapist are opposites in a sense, the therapist being the more healthy of the two. Nevertheless, areas of cooperation must be found. Inevitably the patient's parents and the therapist are opposites in the sense that the parents had a definite role in promoting the patient's illness, while the therapist (hopefully) has no such role—quite the opposite —the therapist promotes the nonneurotic side of the patient's personality. The defensive structures are opposed to the interpretations of the therapist. The interpretations upset the equilibrium of the patient—they throw him out of balance and so forth. If we think of Harlow's work, we may understand why love, compassion, and closeness are important as opposed to isolation, hate, greed, or unreasonable "control" of one person over another or one group over another. There are some opposites that create not only dissension but also aggression and war if no compromises or agreements exist. As a matter of fact the child's neurosis or psychosis is a compromise that went against the well-being of the child. The child makes the compromise by becoming either neurotic or psychotic, the basic defense being identification with the aggressor.

CHAPTER 6

The Problem of Identification

The importance of identification as an aspect of the neurosis was one of Freud's great discoveries, but the concept was largely neglected by him, it seems to me, due to the difficulty he had of accepting the idea of the active role of the parents in the development of the child's neurosis and their influence on the shape and form of the child's emotional condition. He solved the dilemma, not by evolving a logical social-psychological theory relating to identification (an interpersonal process), but by organizing the mysterious libido theory and the developmental scheme (infantile sexuality) which had its roots in ancient ideas, folklore, fable, tribal procedures, beliefs, and teachings.

The theory of identification as both an interpersonal concept and an "internalization" would have been a logical outcome of Freud's theory in the "Interpretation of Dreams," where he postulated that people in the dreams had significance for the dreamer in terms of his identification with them. It is the environment that forces identification on the individual rather than the innate schedule. The ability to imitate, which apparently has genetic roots, makes it possible to defend through identification, although the latter is a different process from imitation. It is possible that this capacity to imitate has a relation to the ability to "give in to the other" and to identify with and appease another, an enduring characteristic defense of the borderline patient.

In the family, as has been repeatedly stressed in this volume, *displacement began with the parents' projections onto the child of that aspect of their own identifications with their own parents that they* hated and wished to deny (see Wolberg, A., 1960; also 1973, p. 26, footnote 5). The child fights against the identification, but he finally accepts it and the sadomasochistic pattern it involves. The basis for his acceptance is the punishment and reward system (a conditioning factor) set up by the parents as a means of forcing the child to submit to the identification role and the child's fear of danger that is inherent in the parents' aggressions in the form of punishment. Punishments include devaluation, derision, the instigation of guilt feelings, the fear of annihilation, and occasionally physical battering. As a consequence, a sadomasochistic pattern is finally established.

Parental Fantasy, Identification, Borderline Fantasy, and Acting Out

Szurek and Johnson found a relation between *the fantasies of the parents and the acting-out patterns of their children.* Reasoning that the parental fantasies are functions of the acting out of the child, we may then propose the dynamics of this kind of connection to be through the process of identification, which is an interpersonal phenomenon, registered in the mind in the form of fantasy, a repetitive fantasy (defense) representing the memories of experience with parents that led to the identification. The repetitiveness of the identification fantasies is an indication not only of a conflict, but also of an incompleted task: an inability to relate to the parent so that the child could reach a reasonable autonomy. There are two opposites: (1) the child's need for autonomy and (2) the parents' efforts to force the child to identify with the parental neurosis.

Identification creates aggression since it is a frustrating experience resulting from the inhibitions instituted by parents over time as they demand the identification role and deny their actions in doing so. The child's aggression is a counteraction to the aggression of the parents as they inhibit certain aspects of the child's normal behavior due to their neurotic anxieties. The aggression is also a parentally determined factor because of the need of the parent to have the child act out aggressive patterns so that the parents can gain vicarious sadistic satisfaction denying this and forcing the child to deny.

The children of these families around the age of 3 and 4 begin to organize sadomasochistic fantasies associated with their fear of annihilation due to the parental aggression as the adults enforce conditions propitious to the acceptance of the identification role. The mental representations of this struggle are sadomasochistic fantasies tht are depictions of various experiences with parents, disguised. The fantasies are defensive in that they are products of fear stimulated by the social situations in which parental demands were forced upon the child. Part of the "self-image" is gained through the identifications that are thrust upon the child. These images are embedded in certain self-representations and together with corresponding object representations they are reflected in the child's fantasies. These take the form of what have been called "basic fantasies," i.e., "beating fantasies," "family romance fantasies," and the like. The romance fantasies appear around the ages of 7 to 10 years, while the beating fantasies may begin as early as 4 or 5 years of age. Prior to the beating fantasies the dread of annihilation is expressed in fears of shadows on the walls, fears of falling asleep, and the like.

The "Self" vs. the "Self"

There is another side of the self-concept or the self in the picture of the individual's condition. This aspect contains the opposite of the images based on the projections of the parents (these communications that contained the neurotic demands of the parents to act out the identification role). They represent the opposing forces in the self that have to do with the child's understanding of his *differences from his parents*, the self *he is* and *would like to be* were it not for the necessity of acting out the identification role. There is a polarity in what the child wants to be in his uniqueness as opposed to the role his parents need from him to quiet the parents' neurotic anxieties. The fantasies are the internalizations or representations in the mind of the several polarities that make up the total conflict of the child's dilemma. The fantasies, like the child's dreams, tell the historical story of these opposites. The exaggerations in the borderline patient's dreams and fantasies are residual of the early fears the patient had as a growing child when he was overwhelmed by the aggression and punishments inherent in the controlling mechanisms of the parent. To counteract these fears, the child *remade reality* in the form of idealizations and "cover" memories, such as one sees depicted in the "family romance."

In the early stages of life, when identifications are reluctantly being incorporated into the behavioral pattern of the individual, the child can react with temper tantrums (Geleered 1945), fears, depressive phenomena, and eventually symptoms, inhibitions and behavior patterns that are organized around a passive-aggressive sadomasochistic character with a periodic acting out of the identification roles in times of unusual stress. The neurosis (or psychosis), based on these sadomasochistic interpersonal relationships within the family, is important in the family but an impediment to adequate adjustment in the larger society. The patterns of interaction that the individual develops are meant to reduce stress, but they cause the individual a different kind of stress. "Identification" means that the child has adopted actual behavior patterns that correspond to the communications that he has received from his parents to act out certain roles that will relieve the parents' anxieties (Wolberg, A., 1960). The roles are destructive not only to the patient but also to the others with whom he interacts. The fantasies that the individual organizes are sadomasochistic in character, for this is the nature of his experience with caretaking persons as expressed in their anxieties for control.

The Defense of the Identification Defense

The identifications in the borderline patient are defended against by a process of projection; thus we say that the basic defense is one of *projective identification*. These projective defense phenomena are associated with denial of certain aspects of the identification roles and the acting out of these roles. The parents demand the denial of what is going on in the family, and a condition (distortion of judgment) such as Asch (1951) demonstrated in his research with groups seems to exist. (Group pressure if sufficient will cause a person to deny reality.) This dynamic in the acting out of an identification role is typical of the patterns of interactions of borderline patients (Wolberg, A., 1968).

At the same time that there are the denials of reality, the patient "knows" the reality but represses his knowledge, usually refusing to act upon it. Thus a duality exists in his mind: "He knows but he does not know," as Freud put it, and this is another source of conflict for the patient. The patient has two systems at work counteracting each other: his *reality system* and his *denial system*, reflected in the mind in his sadomasochistic fantasies (identification fantasies).

The pull toward neurotic behavior is great since it has been used as a means of compromise in his conflict, and in the family it was life saving in that it was in obedience to the parents who needed his behavior. The individual has been made to feel responsible in a sense for the equilibrium of the parents, to his own detriment (Jackson, 1957). He builds resentment, anger, and finally revenge feelings (Searles, 1963), defenses against which he must develop counterdefenses. He becomes susceptible to the demands of others in view of his acquiescence to his parents. He has acquired the trait of susceptibility in that he is prone to "identify with the aggressor." He defends with all of his strength against acknowledging this fact, for in such acknowledgment he would have to face his sadomasochistic traits. He is particularly defensive insofar as his sadism and sexual perversion are concerned. The patient can use idealization, distancing, denial and other mechanisms to control the therapeutic situation.

In one session Sonia said to me, "I have three different reactions to three different people—you, Dr. Wolberg, and Dr. X. With you I cry a lot; with Dr. Wolberg I feel I can't get through—there is an impenetrable barrier. I try humor; I try many other approaches and *there is nothing*. With Dr. X I have a good time. I can feel free to express myself. I can be active. He is crazy, of course." Dr. X appears to me to have a Reichian approach in that he utilizes techniques like touching and has a theory that there is an interruption of the life-energy flow due to repression and that this effects seven rings of "muscle-armoring." By manipulating these rings progressively from head to feet conscious awareness of painful vegetative sensations occur and energy flow is encouraged. Dr. X uses Gestalt methods too, and he does do interpreting of a psychodynamic nature. For example, he told Sonia that she was very defensive when talking of her parents, something I had ponted out as well. It seemed that when Dr. X told her the same thing she was more inclined to talk about it than when I spoke to her—not once but many times—of this defense. A defense of the parent is one of the reasons for the negative therapeutic reaction. This is a passive aggressive maneuver but a defense with sadistic overtures. In the case of the borderline it relates to an oedipal reaction to people about which the patient has tremendous guilt. The oedipus complex usually means that the child has been used as a sexual object as well as an object of scorn and derision, a stance that is often a sexualized power feeling of the parent. Free association is the method by which the individual catches conscious glimpses of his repressed ideas and feelings, those ideas that are related to the meaning of his fantasies and his oedipal behavior. He begins to see the connection between his fantasies and his neurotic reactions to the present and his past life. The borderline patient does use free association but it is a denied aspect of his productions as long as he defends against the reality picture of his parents and utilizes the idealization of them that was so important to him as a child. In the borderline patient the defense of the parents is a defense of the patient's sadomasochism and an idealization of it. The defense is strong because it helps to contain the patient's rage and anger, but it also enables the patient to deny that he was rejected and abused by his parents, and that he now is like them in certain respects. This denial is particularly strong with regard to the sadistic perverse traits.

Depression is bound up with the sadomasochism in the sense that the patient feels he cannot or *should not* be glad, happy, have a good life. As Sonia, my patient, explained to me, "I had a very enlightening experience with Dr. X. He told me to stand on one foot, as long as I could possibly do so. He put a pillow down for me when I would need to fall. When I got so tired I could not stand any longer, I fell to the floor, but I did not use the pillow. When Dr. X asked: 'Why did you not use the pillow?' I responded, 'Because I'm not supposed to. Can't see it! I'm not supposed to be comfortable or happy." "Yes," I said to Sonia, "I think we have understood this for some years, but now you *know* this is one of your neurotic feelings. It has been demonstrated to you." "Yes," said Sonia and was about to end the conversation about the incident, but I would not let her do so. "I have always thought it was because you had to protect your father. He had aspiration that were never fulfilled and you have succeeded where he failed. You feel guilty about that and every time I mention this you defend your father in some ways as if I were casting aspersions on his character." "Yes," said Sonia. "The other day I was cleaning my apartment. I do this every so often because you know I always have in mind that in the end I may commit suicide and I don't want the apartment to be a mess. Well, as I was cleaning I was looking at some old photographs, one of my father. I realized as I looked at the photograph that he was a weak man." I said, "I have never heard you say anything like that about your father." "No," she said, "In our house my father was a god. To me he was a god, to my mother he was a god, to my grandmother he was a god." Sonia's father had very high ideals; he was strict in his ideals. Actually, Sonia has these same rigid ideals and systems by which she lives. She will have to work this out before she can be free of her problems.

The perverse habits of the patient derive from the ways in which he had been surreptitiously used as a projective sexual object by the parents in the expression of their own sexually perverse impulses. The parents have had unfortunate experiences in their own families since their parents' problems included fears concerning normal sexuality and a conflict regarding sexual role. Moreover, there is often a projection of sexual guilt onto other biological functions. A mechanism that is involved here was suggested by Levy (1932). He connected parental "gazing," for example, with hypo-chondriacal ideas. It is my opinion that this use of the child's body parts is a sexual preoccupation of the parent (a perversion) and that this parental practice is a source of the child's hypochondriacal ideas. Such activities as parental anxieties concerning the child's stools, the giving of frequent enemas or obsessive or compulsive talking *against* certain practices (see Wolberg, A., 1968) are also disguised ways of perverse parental practice. Sexual identifications occur on the basis of the parental perversions.

We find in the borderline patient a "rapid shifting of defenses" (Wolberg, A., 1952, p. 695). Some analysts have thought of this characteristic as a failure of defense, as I used to think of it, but I now regard it as *a particular kind of defense against change that might disrupt the patient's equilibrium and force him to admit his identifications*. Perhaps this idea is similar to Chessick's (1977) "phobia of penetration," meaning that there is a poignant need to maintain the defenses and control situations in which the individual finds himself. In the therapeutic relationship, for example, the patient acts out the role he played with his parents and attempts to engage the therapist in the kind of sadomasochistic pattern he had with them. This is a transference reaction—a partially nonverbal performance—which is a resistance to treatment, to penetration, as it were, and it is a *pantomimic activity* with no apparent consciousness of the meaning to the patient. These pantomimic activities are the core of the defense of projective identification. Other defenses can be used in rapid succession—masochism, appeasement, idealization, repression, undoing, withdrawal, and so on.

The reluctance in giving up the sadomasochistic pattern that is related to the identification was evident in the remark of one analyst's patient who said, "Perhaps I do not want to get well. I have been wearing a hair shirt for so long that I would feel naked without it. You may be right in what you are saying—in fact you are right, but I am afraid to take off the shirt." One of my patients, Gretchen Schwarb, said, "Will the real Gretchen Schwarb please stand up!" The opposite of the sadomasochism is the normal wish to shed the pattern and to realize what one wishes to be. The patient's reality picture includes the neurotic picture, but the realistic picture also embraces the realization that he, the patient, is not precisely like the parent and that his potentials may be quite another matter if he were not burdened with the neurosis. The denigration in the identification is reflected in such remarks as "I can never be first, only second." One father said in relation to his two sons, "James is different from John. James never really pulls his punches—he hurts when he hits me. But John's punches are feints—he never really hurts. John said that he is afraid of James, and he does what James wants because James could actually kill."

A very frustrating experience for a therapist is that the patient will behave in a constructive manner and then act out to destroy or disrupt these moves. What does this kind of activity mean? This is what my patient George Frank Quinn says happens when he wants to make some forward moves or when he would like to follow through on some successful endeavor. It has been my experience to find that in their relations parents have cut off the child's pleasure in performance in those areas that give the parents anxiety and the child eventually "internalizes" (identifies with) this pattern. In other words, the child is conditioned to do to himself what the parents did when the parent is not around, or he marries someone who will play the inhibiting destructive parental role to which he can be obedient.

While internalization and learning are similar, we should specify by "internalization" that we mean the *acquiring of a role through the specific instructions of the parents*, when we speak of the neuroses and psychoses.

In the context of my definition of identification we would consider the "internalization" the learning of a *neurotic role* specified by the parents in the interest of their maintaining their neurotic defenses. We can use the concept of the superego in this context by adopting (Richman's idea that the superego is a form of maintaining object relations (Wolberg, A., 1973, pp. 49, 166, 252, 257). We can signify this total concept by the designation S(IA) meaning the destructive aspect of the superego based on identification with the aggressor. This must be what Freud referred to when he said that there is some connection of the superego with the id "that is at present unknown to us." One can also conceive of an SC, i.e., a superego part related to constructive behavior. These S behaviors would be distinguished from autonomous behavior (AB). Patterns associated with S(IA) are related to a parental prohibition but a prohibition that is definitely destructive to the child.

My case histories are filled with examples of these behavior patterns, Flora O'Toole Levy's husband (a physician) told her it was "nothing" when for two years she talked of a lump in her breast, asking him what he thought about it. His response meant "Don't go to a doctor with that complaint; it's nothing!" or "I hope you drop dead!" This was a very destructive attitude on his part and a "susceptibility" on her part to obey the authority even if the authority is irrational—this is a result of S(IA). When she finally did go to the doctor, it was cancer. Flora always said that her mother was irrational and destructive. She was an "ignorant uneducated Irish maid," basically a "stupid woman." Her father had run away from the mother when Flora was 5 years old and was never heard from again. The mother was inconsiderate, and she would "take no nonsense" from Flora, who had to do exactly as the mother wished. When Flora was 14 years of age, she did challenge, screaming at her mother and calling her stupid and irrational. She was locked in a room. The police were called, and she was taken to Bellevue Hospital (in New York City) on her mother's complaint that she was dangerous. After hearing her story and talking to the mother, the doctor in Bellevue advised Flora to leave home as soon as she could find a job. Flora's younger brother did leave home at an early age. He became an alcoholic, however, and died in an automobile crash with his wife "while driving under the influence of intoxicating beverages."

George Frank Quinn's father had no patience to show him how to do anything and would always take on the task himself. He would never help Frank build with his blocks, and later Frank was criticized by his parents for being inept; "You do not known how to handle money; you cannot learn to drive a car; you will fail at physical games; it is funny the way you act," and so on. The father suggested ineptness in his child by his attitudes. Kurt Blair's mother said, "You are sick with asthma, you can't play football, you can't engage in sports, you can't go with the other boys," and so on. Kenneth Wolcott's and Doris Berman's parents had a "yes, but" syndrome. "Are you sure this is what you want?" This will be like the other thing you did, you'll lose interest and never finish it." "It's *a good* idea *but* I don't think it will be good for you." "You say you want to do it *but* it will interfere with your summer work." "It's nice to do *but* we can't afford it." "It's good food *but* too much is dangerous." Flora Levy, when she had children, usually managed to create a ruckus in the house whenever her sons had to pass an examination at school; as a consequence they often failed.

James Weber failed three times in three tries at medical school. Each time his father had great misgivings about his son's motivations for going to school. He was always admitted on the basis of his tests and his marks, *but* he could not stay due to study problems. These difficulties did not present themselves in the graduate schools of psychology. His father, a doctor, was proud of being a physician and often talked of the stiff competition in getting through medical school, "a stiff competition that many people cannot stand up to."

The "I do not want to get well" syndrome that we find in borderline patients has to do with these "yes but" experiences or the "you can't do this" type of attitude or the "oh it's nothing" denial of importance on the part of the parents. Some consequences of this problem are the acting out of a help-rejecting transference, trying to gain punishment from the therapist, exercising aggression, being masochistic, being sadistic, and being teasing; having self-contempt due to the pattern of not winning or being second best in social situations.

Many of the acting-out patterns have to do with sexual equivalents and perversions such as exhibitionism, voyeurism, and other symptoms that have sadomasochistic implications. Voyeurism and exhibitionism have a secretive aspect that has meaning to the observer and the exhibitionist. They are forms of acting out by secret body language, accompanied by word language meant to disguise the meaning of the body language. Projection is a factor in this operation—more precisely, projective identification. The parent has been secretive in his communications as he set about to inculcate the neurotic role in the child. If he is actually confronted with his behavior, in a direct way, he will punish the child and make him feel guilty.

In both voyeurism and exhibitionism roles are interchanged and reversed in the mind's eye, so to say, and the sadomasochistic acting out is in fact a masturbatory equivalent, a picture of a fantasy, if you will, of the object of the masturbatory satisfaction. Both the voyeur and the exhibitionist convey the response they need from the other, be it sexuality with scorn or some other form of devaluation. This is a sadomasochistic love, the only kind of love the individual is used to—a transferential object in the context of denying the reality of the sexual interchange.

James Fuchs (Wolberg, A., 1973, pp. 252-253) acted out a Peeping Tom masturbatory experience when he was in the army that was a continuation of a practice he had at home. At home he excited himself by looking into the neighbor's windows. He acted out also on the subway by rubbing his elbow against the place where he could feel women's breasts particularly their nipples. This was an especially dangerous perversion since he ran the risk of being picked up by the police. James said that it was amazing how many women tolerated this rubbing experience without moving away. In the sessions he finally verbalized the wish to rub the therapist's breasts with a kind of "Tea and Sympathy" fantasy. His mother, of course, had used him as a sexual object in that it was her habit to accompany him into the bathroom, "watching" him as he performed his various duties. Later she added the practice of going into his bedroom after he came home from a date to receive blow-by-blow descriptions of his relations with girls. His behavior would be an identification with the aggressor (mother) to form a section of the superego that would be reflected in the identification fantasy as an impulse to act out by putting one's self in danger in order to appease the object. The perversion is a secret communication with the object. James felt that in sexual relations with his wife he experienced no sexual thrill, and after sex he usually retired to the bathroom to masturbate using a sadomasochistic fantasy. We might depict these various perverse acts as MTP (SIA), i.e., a pattern based on a mother transference that results in the sadomasochistic acting out of a perversion using another as an object.

Parents can use each other in these perverse ways. The father transference would be a perverse pattern based on identification with the father. The acronym translated is MTP or FTP = mother or father projected transference, acted out on a pantomimic level = sadomasochistic fantasy that is related to SIA, i.e., that part of the superego that is a function of the identification with the aggressor. There are many forms of acting out these transferences.

Projective identification consists of utilization of the projections of the parents (onto each other or diverse objects)—projections that are in fact denied identifications (unwanted) with their own parents. There is a self-hatred involved, both in the parent as he projects the roles and in the child as his acceptance of the neurotic identifications becomes a reality. The child is disgusted with himself, and this lowers his self-esteem. This is augmented by the fact that the interlocking defensive system is binding, and the patient's neurosis has kept him from seeking the peers whom he needs in his development. At school and in social groups he is usually rejected by the more "normal" children. Consequently, he has to join groups of peers who have neurotic traits for example, ("odd-ball" groups, delinquent groups). This prevents him from developing the kinds of social skills that are necessary in normal emotional living so that he perpetuates his neurotic behavior and seeks out those who help him perpetuate it, to his detriment. There is a rejection of certain aspects of the child's autonomous behavior due to the parents' anxieties.

The rejection of the child by the parents creates a sadness in him and guilt, along with defenses to deny the condition. The patient will be rejected by healthy members of the opposite sex due to his perverse habits, not the least of which may be frequent spells of impotence. Thus the oedipal problem should be reinterpreted to mean that the parents, in their disturbed sexuality, stimulate the child in perverse ways due to their own anxieties. There is hostility in closeness, since transference feelings are readily aroused in intimate relations. Detachment, undoing, and other destructive actions are used to break up intimacy at certain periods. Closeness evokes intense hostility, which the patient wishes to avoid, for he does not want to break up the relationship entirely. He needs the sadomasochistic experience with a member of the opposite sex. Normal reciprocity has never been experienced by these patients, thus the frustrating image that accompanies all relationships both sexual and nonsexual. When the participants have attempted sex, they have usually been disappointed—he could not have or maintain an erection at times, she could not have an orgasm, she could not *feel* or rather *denied her feeling and excitement*. There are then two images superimposed upon the efforts to have sex: (1) the image of the parents and their rejection of their parental sexuality, the opposite parent pushing the child toward the parent of the same sex, and (2) the frustration that the individual has "internalized" with which he is now "identified" (more precisely conditioned) so that he cuts off the pleasure himself. This is an internalization of a neurotic pattern, an internalization of the identification roles as depicted in a theme related to associations to a dream or in the flow of the session that relates to a particular theme. The "internalization" is in fact a fantasy, or, to be more precise, a cluster of fantasies.

The representations of the roles associated with the identification fantasies, which were in the beginning distortions of reality, actually became associated with reality in the sense that the problem is symbolized in relations with people. The conflict is: $R:D::UT:T$ (R = reality; D = distortion; UT = unfinished tasks; T = transference). The resolution is through analysis of T (transference). Neuroses and psychoses are realities. The conflicts are realities, complicated because they involve (1) the parents' insistence on the distortion of reality, (2) the acting out of guilt when the child resists the roles, (4) the child's anger over the situation, (5) the disillusionment with the parents, (6) the fear of the parents' punishment when the child challenges and how this generalizes to create inhibitions, (7) the fear of the person's own (child's) counteraggression and hate, (8) the problems when the school or other reality gets in the way of the parents' neurotic needs, (9) the inhibitions against certain rational impulses that must be held in check in order to act out the identification roles, (10) the defenses that must go into operations so as to pursue the neurotic cause, (11) the anxiety and the physical distress of conflict, (12) the idealization of the parents, a denial of the way they actually are, and (13) the depressive mood that develops as the child feels rejected and demeaned.

Harriet Hamburger when she was working through the last phase of her treatment with me was not sure that I was not a homosexual. This problem lasted for three years during which she called herself a homosexual although she had never had homosexual experiences. She had slept with her grandmother during the period when she was 4 to 9 or 10 years old, and she felt demeaned by this experience. In all of her life experiences she felt second best, not good enough. She said she acted like a "jerk" in relations with others. She kept herself from success and worked at jobs far below her capacities for many years. Freud (1916) wrote a paper that touched on the fear of success.

Kurt Blau—Case Illustration

The following session with Kurt Blau contains several themes that are operating when the patient is about to embark on the last lap of analysis. The themes are (1) he wants success but fears it, (2) he feels he can do it, but is not sure, (3) he feels closer to the therapist but not tied, (4) he feels he can size up the therapist—see him as he really is with all his faults and all his good points, (5) he can begin to work through his identifications and defenses—particularly those that are most like the father (cruelty, aggression, detachment, perverse habits, and the like). There is a review of problems, an assessment of what has been accomplished, and what remains to be done. There is *a wondering whether* one can succeed in *"straightening out"* in view of the background, the family problems, and the stresses to which one was subject while living in the family.

Pt.   How do you do!
Th.   How do you do!
Pt.   I was thinking about this girl—this was in my youth. She was a neighbor, planting in her garden, in the yard of her house—in the city—in Brooklyn. We went to look and to laugh at her—my mother and her brother; and I guess I did too.

Both my mother and father had rich relatives, but they never took my parents into their businesses—I told you this before—they never helped him in any way. But my father was always visiting his relatives—his mother—his brothers.
Th.   Your mother and father were both big masochists when it came to dealing with their relatives. That's what you always told me.
Pt.   You're right—they were always "doing good"!
Th.   They didn't get any reward for it.
Pt.   No—I told you about the time I lent my archery set—and I wanted it back—I only lent to my aunt's son. When I went to pick it up, my aunt said, "How do you do. What do you want?" The set was ripped, and I was disgusted. I don't know how wealthy they are, but they have everything! She never bought me a new archery set.

I want to get a car—a Lincoln Continental or a Jaguar. [*He then tells a story about work where he was trying to be helpful to someone—"trying to please"—and the whole thing backfired. He "didn't get any place."*]

Th.   Trying to please—being helpful—that's part of your neurosis that you inherited from your parents.

Pt.   You said it.

[He talks of a girl he saw at work—a patient in a hospital. He thinks he will have sex with her. Another patient he talks of is an employee in a hospital; he sees her in a clinic in the city where he works. He says he gets very angry at her. She talks on and on; he wants to blow a gut. He says that when he talked to his supervisor about the case, the supervisor told him he feels impotent in the situation. He says he does not feel impotent.]

Th.   If the situation is impossible, then why should you feel impotent?

Pt.   This girl Clo [*the girl he saw at work*] everybody in the class [*at the hospital*] thinks there's something wrong with her. I think she really wants it—needs it—I wondered whether I wanted it too. She can't be "genital"—no object constancy—no depth of feeling, no real life pattern. Perhaps I should say "You and I can really make it together—genitally. I'll help you and you'll help me." My wife and I are having a hard time these days. I think she fends me off. She says, "Can't we have a conversation sometime? Does it always have to be sex!" Does that mean something? Is she saying something to me? Am I a sex maniac? And—I still feel close to you—I still have a feeling of wanting to touch you.

Th.   In what way?

Pt.   My hand

Th.   Where? How?

Pt.   Easiest place is to touch you on the leg—I was thinking of touching you on the breasts—just to stand and hug you. Expand with you.

Th.   Hugging—embracing—being close—that sounds nice.

Pt.   It's like if you can put the two doors together—they can slide—they expand. It's like the closeness, the warmth will come out, if I can expand, if I can spread out, if I can . . .

Th.   Um hum. Warmth—uh huh.

Pt.   I don't know if its euphoric. I don't know if its *fusion* . . . It's sort of like you should know me all the way—all of me.

Th.   Uh ha!

Pt.   Then I would know all of you.

Th.   Yes? Well, would you?

Pt.   Actually, I think I would—this is fantasy—somehow I will know you well enough to be a social friend, and my wife and I will know you well enough too. There's some kind of "other relationship" than therapy. Are you a substitute mother? People who really feel and think the way we do—There are very few people we can do this with. I'd say I can with B [*his wife*]. We share most things together—we like each other.

Th.   You said *euphoric* before.

Pt.   It's a kind of oceanic feeling—fusion—that's what Freud [*an instructor*] talks about. (*pause*)
      I feel very tired now. It's like I think I know my ego boundaries—I don't think I'm afraid of fusion—the loss of ego boundaries. I think I can be with you *without worrying*; I used to worry about what I'd tell you.

Th   You don't worry any more?

Pt.   I don't think so.

Th.   You're not so afraid to come closer?

Pt.   I don't think I am any more—like last week, I said we never talk about closeness.

Th.   Well, you were afraid of closeness.

Pt.   I never knew it, but I was.

Th.   Uh huh.

Pt.   I was never close, I guess, to people—there was always a distance. I never felt close without guilt. The only person I ever felt close to was my aunt, and there was a lot of guilt.

Th.   Guilt?

Pt.   Guilt and anxiety. I don't know what you want to call it . . . It was like I enjoyed being with her when I was a little kid. She attempted to be close. I was afraid of her husband. He was a very strict guy, a typical German Luftwaffe. In her way she's reserved . . . She mixes me up with my father—she calls me Hymie many times, that's my father's name. I remembered when I was 5 years old. She was in her nightgown. I saw her breasts. I don't know whether a 5-year-old boy wants to see breasts . . . I always have that image of her in her nightgown with her breasts and my wanting to see her breasts.

I remember her taking a shower while I was in the coffee room—the vacuum was standing there—at 5 or 6—and I had the handle of the vacuum against my penis and when the shower stopped, I started moving the vacuum around the room.

Th.   You were 5 or 6?

Pt.   Yeah! At the most, 7. I once wanted her to buy me a machine gun because I saw a kid with a machine gun—but her husband thought I should have a xylophone—and I had a temper tantrum and he beat me—and gave me a xylophone—and I used the xylophone. I learned to play the xylophone. I used to be there—in their house—on the weekends. My parents would leave me there. And when my parents would come to get me—I'd put my face in the water—I'd try to look at ships—I'd get goose pimples.

Th.   You mean you didn't want to go home—you'd get goose pimples when you got home?

Pt.   Yeah, I'd like it there . . . I remember my father—he'd go work at his mother's house on the weekend.

Th.   You mean every weekend?

Pt.   Every Sunday that he wasn't working—he'd go over to his mother's. It was very rare that he'd go anywhere else on a Sunday—to his mother's or to his brother's. She'd be waiting to give him some . . .

Th.   What?

Pt.   He'd fix things—go do it—fixing locks—working for nothing. My mother used to scream at him for doing this. He was always running out—to his mother's. She'd want to go some place—relax—he'd go to his mother's or brother's every time.

Th.   Maybe he felt himself isolated from people that way.

Pt.   I don't know how he developed it. He used to work with his father. His father he tried to please, I guess . . . All the others moved out—went on their own. He had to please his father. The other brothers got free. My father always had a lot of resentment toward his father. He resented going to religious school Saturday afternoons. I'm sure he had a lot of resentment.

Th.   Resentment for what reason?

Pt.   For what reason! His father never let him be—never let him get away—he was always on him in a sense—demanding from him. His father gave him a bike, but heavy duty, for delivering ash cans. I never got a bike . . . He always promised me one, but I never got one. My father could never do anything for sheer pleasure—bike work—for work—but no object for just pleasure. I think he was tied to his mother besides—I think he would wish to be tied. He was the youngest in the family.

Th.   The youngest?

Pt.   The youngest—at least four or five—brothers—two sisters that I know of.

My mother is the youngest also; she too has four or five brothers and two or three sisters. She was never close to her father—he lived in the basement—he was an iron worker—I've never seen any affection between them. My uncle used to say that when my grandfather would shake hands blood would come out of the hands . . . He would say he tried to match strength shaking hands, but he couldn't win.

TH.   Which uncle was that?

Pt.   My aunt's husband—the aunt I liked. I never saw any affection between my grandfather and any other human being—mother's mother died when she was young. My mother's sister had multiple sclerosis—she married an alcoholic—she must have been a schizophrenic . . . When I'd see her, she always looked out the window. She starved herself—to death—she sat there—a living death—nothing—some welfare worker would come there and sit with her—once a week. Fucked-up household! One of my uncles lived on the top floor . . . Another uncle was quite old—then he just left them—after the first uncle's wedding he just walked out and left—they don't know why—all his rage. He was the one that got the most gifts—he was the "good" one—he never came back. I even tried to be close to him once . . . He tried to help me—he said "Why don't you get out?" When I got older, "Why don't you get out?" I really did not know what he was talking about at the time. The cousin who lived underneath me—he left too (the other side of the family); they went away. The wealthy relatives I never knew. Everybody was so really estranged—no closeness. The other woman who was close was a blind woman, my Aunt Alicia. Her husband had a heart attack—on the street—they think he was drunk—died at 28. He was under a strain too, always broke—he dropped dead running for a bus—no one gave a shit. His wife was left with four kids. Everybody said "Fuck you." They got a lot of gifts—I went to the wedding—It's bizzare. I'm exhausted.

Th.   I'm a little confused about the relationships, but do you mean all these people were living in the house—the same house you were brought up in? Had they all lived at one time or another in either the upstairs apartment, or the downstairs apartment, or the basement?

Pt.   That's right.

Th.   Your sister and her husband now live in the upstairs apartment? Or they're going to live there, and you are going to move, perhaps to Manhattan. But you don't live in the house now.

Pt.   I guess I'd like to have a cigarette. You said you gave up cigarettes—you don't smoke.

Th.   I did at one time, but I gave it up—heart palpitations—the symptoms went away when I stopped smoking. Anyway you've had a difficult time talking about your family—these families—and you are exhausted . . . You want to get some relief or relaxation from smoking. It was a difficult household . . . But things seem to be straightening out for you anyway. Do you feel guilty about that? I guess so.

Pt.   Yes, in a way. Not so much anymore.

The *guilts* of these borderline patients are very strong and often so unrecognized, just as the mild depression that attends the guilts. Guilt, like masochisms, is evident in almost every session and must always be recognized. Guilt about aggression, about sexuality, about normal impulses, about stepping out of the identification role, about forward moves in therapy, about leaving therapy, etc. Unlike Sonia and Harriet, Kurt worked through his problems in eight years. At this point Kurt is entering the third stage of treatment described in Chapter 9.

CHAPTER 7

The Problem of Feeling Demeaned

In psychoanalysis with the borderline patient the problem of feeling demeaned as a child arises constantly and has to be dealt with repeatedly. The feeling of being demeaned is functionally related to the problem of having created an identification with the neurotic patterns of the parents. The "giving in" to the identification is a demeaning experience, and self-contempt and masochistic fantasies accompany these feelings. The repetitiveness of failing to gain the respect of the parents creates both depression and a self-contempt. The guilt and fear accompanying the feelings of wanting to be different from the parents, of knowing that one *is different* yet the fear of acknowledging this is evident.

Anger is an accompaniment of the feelings of being demeaned, and often the patient invites an attack. The paranoid attitude is a function of feeling demeaned, and the projections in the defense of projective identification are associated with the repressions and denials and with the isolating techniques that defend against two opposing feelings—that of feeling demeaned associated with masochism and the feeling of grandiosity, a function of the patient's sadism. The inhibitions (the "expression of a restriction of certain ego functions [Freud, S. E., 1926, 20:89] and other autonomous behaviors) of the patient infuriate him; yet he must put them into operation due to his identifications. The anger is reactive rather than a raw expression of aggression. The rage begins when the child at last allows himself the consciousness of being demeaned and inhibited in his functions by the parent. Later when he inhibits himself (after the internalization of the identification), he is angry both at himself and his parents. He must contend with his anger and with his feelings of demoralization through the means of defenses such as undoing, denial, grandiosity, which like repression are processes of derealization and depersonalization, which like repression are forms of flight from reality. The stimulus for these defenses are anxieties associated with feelings of danger originally evoked in repetitive traumatic relations with parental figures and later derived from projections (transference mechanisms, i.e., projections of identifications) onto others.

In the case history that follows we can see how George Frank Quinn used his problem of feeling demeaned as a defense against interpretation.

George Frank Quinn—A Case Illustration

The patient is a physician of 32, married. He engages in occasional homosexual episodes as one aspect of his acting out. He does not, however, have a true homosexual adaptation. Often, when he would be ending a session, he would say he feels like acting out homosexually; he wants to have some "excitement." We often tried to discover what it was in the session that made him feel like acting out. We knew that it had to have something to do with what went on between us. Lately, he has been able to "zero in" on some of his feelings. He has stopped acting out, and he can thus begin to think and to verbalize, to "unloose some of his repressions" and to "talk out," as Freud used to say, instead of "acting out" his sadomasochistic fantasy. In one session we had gone through an interpretation of a transference feeling, and he then said he was beginning to feel he wanted to act out. This was strange because he felt that the session had been useful. He had told me of an episode with some of his colleagues in the hospital where it was found that the wrong summary had been attached to the X-ray plate of a certain patient; this was discovered by one of the technicians. His name (Quinn's) was signed to the summary. He was being made to feel guilty for the mistake, and he was angry about this. He felt "put upon."

He was in individual treatment twice a week and in group therapy once a week. This was his seventh year of treatment and his 529th session. What had upset him also was what went on the night before in the group.

Th.   What was it that I did that was demeaning?
Pt.   You were mocking me.
Th.   When?
Pt.   When you were talking about me being a little boy. My "little-boy act."
Th.   I didn't say you *are* a little boy, only that you were *acting like one* in the group, and I also mentioned that you acted the same way at work.
Pt.   You were mocking me, acting toward me as if I don't know anything, as if I'm a silly child.
Th.   I think you are mixing me up with someone else I've heard about. I do not think you are a child, neither do I feel that you are helpless nor that you are silly.
Pt.   All right, all right, but you were mocking me just like my parents did.
Th.   Your parents told you that you couldn't do anything right. I don't remember saying that; and the group members, although they agreed that you were acting like a little boy, certainly were telling you that you are a good doctor, one they would have confidence in. That was the whole point of Ralph's talking to you. You couldn't accept his idea that you are a competent doctor with high ethical standards.
Pt.   The point is that *you* had that attitude.
Th.   Well, I won't argue with you.

Pt.   You were angry at me.

Th.   For what?

Pt.   For making a mess of my job.

Th.   Well, I can't say it made me happy to hear about it; I'm not sure I was angry.

Pt.   Yes, you were. And you think I'm a mess!

Th.   I don't think I'm angry, but I'm not happy either.

Pt.   You are angry; you acted angry in the group; that's why you were mocking me, imitating me—the little boy.

Th.   Perhaps I sounded sarcastic. Do you think I was being sarcastic to Harriet when we were telling her how she was acting? You were telling her, and I agreed with you.

Pt.   No, I don't think you were being mocking with her.

Th.   Well, what was the difference? I think she was annoyed; she didn't exactly like what we were saying.

Pt.   Well it was different.

Th.   I still don't think she thought so.

Pt.   We were right about her.

Th.   Yes. And about you too?

Pt.   Well, you were right, but not entirely. You were mocking to me.

Th.   In other words, I want to humiliate you, not Harriet. I want you to suffer, but I feel more kindly toward her.

Pt.   That may be.

Th.   I think you really know what I think about you and your capacities and talents. I think I feel a great deal different toward you than your parents did—or do—at least according to that letter from them that you let me read.

Pt.   Of course, you don't have their attitude.

Th.   Indeed I don't!

Pt.   Well, what were you saying anyway? . . . It's not too clear.

Th.   Well, I was saying that when you talk about recent incidents, you do so with the idea of *evoking sympathy* rather than talking about *the problems that got you into the mess*—and the group was agreeing with me. Sympathy isn't going to help work out the problem, and if we don't work it out, it will happen again. It's happened already twice, and it's time we took the matter seriously. Oh, yes! There was another thing we were saying. About being serious. Are you serious in wanting to work it out or are you still only trying to get sympathy or a pat on the back. *You know you have sympathy*, but that hasn't seemed to help work out the problem. What keeps your neurotic feelings and actings recurring? We were wondering whether you are serious now in wanting to work it out.

Pt.   Well I am, but I don't know how to do it—how do you go about it—what can I do—what can I say? [*This is a passive-aggressive gesture.*]

Th.   Well, can you think of anything?

Pt.   Yes, the problem is not that I am so particular, that I'm such a good doctor, but it is that *I don't want to make a mistake*. And I confer a lot. I want to talk it over with others.

Th.   And that makes people annoyed at you—they feel you are bugging them and wasting theirs and your own time.

Pt.   Yes. So much conferring doesn't work out in private practice for every minute counts moneywise. They say I'm too slow. But I know I also don't like to work; that is a fact. [*He is in a group practice, having left a university setting.*]

Th.   I've heard you say that *you do like work* and that you think there are some interesting problems you come across. You must have both feelings—opposite feelings.

Pt.   Yes, but there is no time to do anything about the interesting problems. Only in academia is there time—but there's no money—so it's a conflict. I still have to work out this conflict. I think I'll have to give up a lot and go back to the university—I'll have to give up my boat, my vacations, my trips to Europe, my way of life.

Th.   You'll have to give up everything. How do you figure that?

Pt.   Well, if I'm earning a lot less, then I can't live like I do now.

Th.   Are you sure it is necessary to give up so much?

Pt.   Oh, yes.

Th.   I think that all you have to do is give up some of your neurotic habits, and that's what you don't want to give up.

Pt.   Why do you say that after such a long time? I would think that you would know that if someone spends seven years working at something they are serious. Now you are mocking me again!

Th.   That's what you think—I'm mocking you?

Pt.   Yes, that's it.

Th.   After seven years that's what you think.

Pt.   Don't try to turn the tables on me! You now you are discouraged and angry at me.

Th.   Well, angry is perhaps not the word—it's frustrating to you and perhaps to me—I don't know—perhaps it's frustrating.

Pt.   Well, if you're frustrated, you're angry.

Th.   Perhaps. But are you going to get down to business, or are we going to play games?

Pt.   Let's get down to business but how? [*Again the masochistic stance.*]

Th.   Now you are acting like the helpless little boy again.

Pt.   Oh you make me so mad—you are infuriating.

Th.   What do you want to say to me?

Pt.   That you are infuriating, like my parents.

Th.   I refuse to be thought of as just like your parents.

Pt.   Now, we really are wasting time.

Th.   Yes, let's stop that.

Pt.   Yes, well let's talk more about the job and how I act.

Th.   Fine.

Pt.   Well, I don't want to make a mistake—I guess I want to be perfect.

Th.   The old orthodox analysts used to say that this is a narcissistic need—to be perfect. But, I think it's more complicated than that.

Pt.   What do you mean?

Th.   Well, we've mentioned wanting to control and being obsessional due to anxiety.

Pt.   I can see that with the technicians—I don't want them to do anything different—*I* want the routines the way *I* want them—it makes me anxious if the routines are changed.

Th.   Well, why would they be changed?

Pt.   Well, for example—I was working in the hospital and was acting pretty much like the boss—then they appointed this fellow who came in and changed the routines . . . He was the new director.

Th.   That made you angry?

Pt.   For many reasons. I was displaced.

Th.   Well, actually you knew you were not going to be appointed chief. You weren't going to have the chief appointment in that hospital at all.

Pt.   Yes, but—well, I didn't like it—but changing the routines upset me most of all. It was unnerving to me—it was a reflection on me too—putting me down.

Th.   That's one way to look at it.

Pt.   Well, how else?

Th.   Perhaps that need to control—to have it your way—the way your parents acted with you and you had to act with your parents. But at work you act more like your parents did with you—at least with the technicians—like a taskmaster. Kill the unruly people! How dare they! Not having your own way makes you angry. You think of it as a defeat—as a put down.

Pt.   Yes, that's true—but not quite anymore.

Th.   I guess that feeling has been broken up a bit. I was thinking that you need to control out of some kind of anxiety. But when you deal with the "bosses," you become the helpless little boy, and they control you.

Pt.   Yes? I don't want to make a mistake—that's all I can think of.

Th.   Well, once in a while everybody can make a mistake. I know that plenty of mistakes are made in hospitals.

Pt.   Yes, but I don't want to make one.

Th.   I wonder—was your mother like that?

Pt.   Not at all—but my father was! [*Identified with the aggressor and the controlling male.*]

Th.   Yes. I know he was a "put-down" artist too—but so was your mother a "put-down" person, I mean. Was your father a perfectionist too?

Pt.   Yes, Yes—I said so already. Well, somehow I don't get so angry at my father as at my mother.

Th.   That's kind of strange. They both participated in that terrible letter they wrote to you. Calling you impotent—not capable of managing your financial affairs, and all that! Perhaps it was because they were angry at you for demanding the money. They said you'd lose it all within one year through incompetent managing.

      [*His parents had set aside $40,000 in a way that they were able to avoid some taxes. The money was in his name. He was still a youngster when it happened, but last year, after he finished his residency, he decided to take the money. The parents had never anticipated that he would do that. They had no choice but to give it to him since it was in his name.*]

Pt.   Yes, they must have been angry. I don't know what we're talking about this for anyway. We're at the end of the session and we haven't accomplished anything . . . Sometimes I wonder why I keep coming here! Oh well! I'll see you next week. [*He has great anxiety about making decisions or being assertive.*]

The Following Session - 530th

Pt.   [*The patient lies down on the couch although he has not been made to feel that he has to use the couch.*] I feel the same way I did last night. [*He refers to the individual session he had the evening before and the group session in which he participated after the individual session.*]

Th. Well, let's talk about it.

Pt. I feel like I did when I was a teenager. How am I going to do all these things? My mother would fret: "I don't know how you're going to get all this done." I'd be having school, confirmation sessions, dancing school, piano lessons, and she'd keep saying, "How are you going to do all this?"

Th. In an anxious way?

Pt. Yes, yes!

Th. And your father was anxious and "nervous" when he did things.

Pt. Oh yes—he didn't help matters any. They were both anxious.

Th. Did *they* want you to do all that—or did *you* want . . .

Pt. No, *they* . . . last night at the group I had all I could do to prevent myself from breaking down and crying.

Th. I could see that.

Pt. It really—one thing that really got me angry was Ralph. "You seem nicer now," he said. A fucking sadist, he is. When somebody's really down, he likes them better. I don't like to say this but . . . What did you mean? I was confused—you said: "We're not really going to help you; you'll have to help yourself."

Th. Did I really say we're not going to help you?

Pt. Yes! But I'm not really sure what area you were talking about.

Th. Well, what comes to your mind?

Pt. Well, just working out this whole business and not having anything happen again. I know wherever I go, it'll be the same thing all over again.

[*He is referring to the fact that he has been asked to leave two different medical groups because he does not work fast enough, because he "bugs" people and has authoritative attitudes that upset technicians with whom he has to work. And the group—they're sadistic. He does not say this openly about me, or about himself, although in the group he did accuse me of being sadistic when I pointed out his little-boy stance, actually his masochistic attitude. He had an association in the group of going to his mother when he had a "hard problem" with schoolwork and asking her to help him—a "What shall I do?" attitude. It was this kind of problem that he was referring to when he said that instead of helping him the therapist was pointing to his little-boy behavior.*]

Th. Well, I thought that the implication was that we, the group, and I the therapist, am not going to give you the kind of help your mother gave you because you are a man and can focus on working out the problem rather than acting out [*in transference*] with us. And we're not going to help you like your father did. He took over and did it himself in a flustered angry way instead of helping you do whatever it was.

Pt. Well, isn't that sadistic? Yes? I felt the group was sadistic too. Incidentally, the Supreme Court was unanimous in telling Nixon he must give up the tapes—that's one piece of good news. [*Patient has hardly ever mentioned current events. In his therapy he has been too preoccupied with himself. This is one of the first times he ever spontaneously referred to what is going on in the world.*]

Th. That really is good news. Maybe it's good news that you have made some changes—you say you have. Do you feel guilty if you don't act like your parents?

Pt.   What the hell are you writing? [*I was writing this session as the patient talked because I wanted to use the material. Usually I do not take notes in the session. The patient was always supersensitive to my behavior whether sitting or on the couch. If I moved around in my chair, wrote, or answered the telephone, which rarely happened, or if I tapped my foot or moved my fingers on the arm of the chair, he would get very annoyed—he'd be distracted.*]

Th.   I'll show it to you some time.

Pt.   That Ralph [*a member of the group*] I really got mad at him. He's a real sadist.

Th.   You mean he gets some pleasure out of taunting you? [*He means that I am a sadist too.*]

Pt.   Oh yes, he's pretty fucked up. That really was terrible; he's really perverted. I was thinking about my perfectionism. I don't know why; I guess some authority figure is going to laugh at me to say I'm wrong. Burke [*his boss in the hospital*] always enters my mind. I don't like to have him say I'm wrong. I like to have him agree with me and say I've done it right. Another side of it—so many times I'll look at a film. I'll feel lazy; I'll feel blocked. It's too much for me. I don't want to work it out. I'll really have to work too hard. There are three things to work on—to work out—(1) the half-assed report that I do and put in the folder, (2) going for help—if I'm really not sure and I go for help, I may hedge a little, be vague—(3) feeling like giving up. No straight answers.

Th.   What does that mean—no straight answers?

Pt.   Oh, probably this: better be vague than wrong. [*This, I believe is a transference reaction that occurs when he is with any person that he takes as an authority. I think that such reactions, i.e., not wanting to make a firm statement about a given matter, come from experiences with parents where the parents always had to have the last word and the child's opinion was never accepted.*]

Th.   But when you work it out, it's not so bad. Are you saying you don't want to spend the energy? It's impossible?

Pt.   I realize what the reality is—but I really feel like a poor little thing—not helpless, but hopeless—too much to do. The only way out of it is that I'll latch onto something that seems okay, repress some things, and then do something neurotic that seems to cover it up.

Th.   Like act out?

Pt.   Oh I don't know—perhaps—I know I get mad.

Th.   Feeling hopeless isn't such a good feeling. Latching onto something! . . . There are not other alternatives?

Pt.   I feel that what I've been doing is too much and I've been sliding through. I get trapped in my own perfectionistic ways. Something gets out of context. I feel anxious—the whole thing isn't right. *I'll say it's pretty good, and then I'll want to act out and I won't be able to figure out why I want to act out.* Pretty easy to feel muddled in the mind in the whole business. [*He feels guilty when he feels he does a sloppy job. But he also feels guilty when he does a good job.*]

Th.   Tell me about the feelings regarding Burke.

Pt.   I have a fantasy. I had the same with the group—that they're making fun of me.

Th.   If they don't agree with you? Or if they criticize anything in your be . . .

Pt.   I want him to agree with me. The person who was laughing the most was my mother. [*To Ralph he had a mother transference.*]

Th.   Mother—not father.

Pt.   I remember at camp, she disagreed with me and argued and humiliated me in front of the others. I wanted to go home. I felt out of place. The others didn't accept me. I felt weak, unable to compete in games.

Th.   Did she often disagree with you?

Pt.   Did she! Often! [*He could never be "right" with his parents, and this made him furious but he would have to take it without remonstrating. The only way he could feel like a person would be to feel angry and oppositional. But then he would feel guilty. And then to get out of the situation, he would do things sloppily and feel guilty about that.*]

Th.   You say you want Ralph to agree with you.

Pt.   Yes, *she disagreed with me a lot.* This makes a situation where one is never satisfied. [*He disregards my remark about Ralph and continues to talk about his mother. She was never satisfied; therefore, he could never feel satisfied.*]

Th.   Never satisfied . . . You felt these feelings in the group, and you feel that way with Burke and also when you go through your perfectionistic routine? [*The mother transference.*]

Pt.   Yes. I'd like to hear that I've done one good thing. I'd like to hear that from her.

Th.   Do you think that you are afraid to be right, or to make a decision? In spite of what she may think or feel?

Pt.   About success? *I want to talk about that.* I can handle success pretty well now. There was the time when I felt I didn't function well; now when I'm reading something for knowledge and I'm beginning to enjoy it, *I begin to feel anxious.* Then I want to get up and talk to somebody, tell somebody something, or I'll start to block. It's only in the context of when I want to do something *I feel I have to do* that it's much harder.

Th.   You're fighting authority. When you have to do it—is that it?

Pt.   Sometimes the authority is myself.

Th.   Yes. Or the situation—people sometimes just make the situation seem as if authority was telling them to do something.

Pt.   (*Silence.*)

Th.   Then you become a bad kind of authority to yourself? I wonder what makes you think that way?

Pt.   Usually it's something I'm doing with somebody else—or I can . . . or with others around. I get a fantasy of success, a good feeling. Then boom! I'm blocking and the feeling of wanting to act out comes on. [*This is similar to Dince's and Green's observation about a patient dissociating his good feelings from his experience or, more precisely, his psyche from his physical reaction to the experience, i.e. his soma. I am also reminded of Freud's paper, "Those Wrecked by Success."*] For a while I thought it was a problem about succeeding, but I don't know whether that's the whole answer.

Th.   What else could it be?

Pt.   Well, I don't know . . . when I'm succeeding I get upset, and I sometimes feel I want to kill somebody. I feel like I have to *do* something . . .

Th.   What do you mean killing somebody? There's a fantasy?

Pt.   Well, I'm accomplishing . . . It's like I want to kill somebody who has had me in jail. Like when I was sailing—I have been very passive in the sailing—but last weekend I handled the crew fairly well. Then when I've done something well on the boat—then I want to act out. I'll drive home, and I'll feel I want to act out. I sometimes dream when I'm driving—I do it *without thinking.* The other drivers will yell at me.

Th. You sort of sink into a withdrawal fantasy and not pay attention to what you're doing? And then you do something you shouldn't to demean yourself, acting out the thought in the fantasy and then they yell?

Pt. Yes—especially if I'm working on the boat with a crew. And another thing, this business of "blobbing out" so often at the university. I'd have an afternoon, I'd be free, I wouldn't know what to do with myself. I'd be afraid to tackle anything. The minute I do something that I want to do, I stop it and start "flitting around." Then I'll remember something I hadn't done; then I wouldn't know what to do.

Th. That sounds like guilt. It's as if you make yourself feel guilty. Who criticizes you? Who makes you feel so *guilty*? Who spoils what gives you pleasure?

Pt. Guys at the office. I'd have five or six things to do, and I'd flit from one to the other and get nothing done.

Th. You do make yourself feel guilty?

Pt. Yes.

Th. Guilty because . . .

Pt. *Why do I need the masochistic fantasy?*

Th. That's one of the problems.

Pt. Why so masochistic?

Th. It involves what we call a mother transference, doesn't it?

Pt. Yes, it is.

Th. I started to ask you, do you think your mother *enjoyed* laughing at you?

Pt. Well, I remember this particular instance; it was such a loud type laugh— she must have. It's hard for me to think. She must have—it must have been some kind of *relief* for her.

Th. Some kind of relief.

Pt. Yes, just projecting. I'm projecting. I laugh when people make stupid mistakes. There's something very funny about it, the very stupidity of it. Somehow I feel my mother was laughing, sort of enjoying my mistakes. And I do it too. [*Identification.*]

Th. Mmmmm . . .

Pt. No, I get scared to death. I'm afraid I'll get blurred up; no—there are just sometimes when I feel this other way.

Th. Like what?

Pt. Like distilling something out of a situation.

Th. The cork blows off, and then you laugh.

Pt. The whole thing seems so funny.

Th. You mean people . . .

Pt. An instructor tells you not to do something—I can remember being around a haggard person—I was afraid. When the person gets a suffering look, then it seems funny. I want to laugh. The instructor was very serious, and the whole thing seemed so funny. My mother seemed to have the idea that everything serious was so funny.

Th. It sounds like she too had a problem of accepting certain feelings, and then she cuts off the feeling part. You do something to stop the enjoyment. She stops her feeling by laughing—she cuts it off. I don't know exactly what she was feeling about you . . . Was it anger, embarrassment, good feeling, what?

Pt. Yes! I guess so—I don't know. I guess so.

Th.   If she laughs, it's a *relief*. It's also a way of laughing at the *person*—kind of
        sadistic?
Pt.   I think so. I don't know.
Th.   Is there anything we can say here in recognition of something you have ac-
        complished? Without making you feel guilty, I mean.
Pt.   Oh yap! I guess so.
Th.   What would it be?
Pt.   I have broken that pattern to some extent. I told you that!
Th.   Yes, you have broken it somewhat. That is all to the good. I really don't
        think you need praise from me to reinforce your own knowledge of what
        you have recently accomplished. You feel reassured, I guess, if someone
        praises you.
Pt.   It's silly. Yes, I want Burke to say a kind word to me.
Th.   He's like a father, I guess. But you say your mother too was never satisfied
        with what you did or accomplished. It does seem strange for parents whose
        son has gotten through medical school to tell him he is inept and inadequate
        and a poor manager. You seem to have managed.
Pt.   They don't count that.
Th.   They seem to consider you about 11 years old; they act like you are—it
        seems. I suppose it's hard for most parents to believe that their children
        are grown up.
Pt.   I guess so—I wouldn't know.

The Integrative Links

The concept is presented by most of the writers on the borderline that a
patient who acts confused as Quinn does in the session above is a person
who in early life could not integrate the contents of his mind, and his
perception of objects is either a misperception or a dissembling of the object. This dissociation theory, which stems from some of the early psychoanalytic ideas, overlooks the fact *that there are actually in the patient's
mind links and connections that indicate an integrative function at work
even when dissociation and denial are used as defense.* Freud and Breuer
disagreed on this point: Breuer felt the patient could not integrate the contents of his mind, and Freud saw *associations* and from these he deduced
"motives at work." There is a *fantasy*, a masochistic feeling, devaluation
of self in this particular dissociation process that we are describing in
Quinn. *The fantasy contains the elements of the links*, as in a dream.
When my patient Elizabeth Osgood had this kind of feeling while having
sex, she had the fantasy of her father taunting her. "You can't make it;
you can't make it; you can't make it." She felt her father wanted her to be
a boy. Most of the theories now conceive the borderline patient as so low
on the totem pole, developmentally speaking, and so defective that he has
not made the appropriate connections between words and feelings, or if he

has, these are so tenuous as to be nonexistent for all practical purposes. This idea is quite different from the concept of hysteria or hysterical mechanisms where the "hysterical blind do see" or where the feelings are there, though denied. There are connections between words, thoughts, and feelings that the borderline patient denies. An isolating factor is at work in the denial process. To think of this defense as the consequence of deficits in the psychic structure (the ego) is a hindrance to an understanding of the dynamics of the patient's behvior.

One of the papers that I cite by Rosner (1969) is a step in helping the therapist understand that *integrative links are operative*, and in a paper given at a Macy Conference L. R. Wolberg (1951) described a hypnotic session where the patient brought out the links in a dramatic fashion. There was a trend throughout Freud's writing from comments on the hysterias (the hysterical blind do see) to the "Outline of Psychoanalysis" (Freud, S. E., 1938) that emphasizes the fact that patients have a reality sense. Penfield (see Wolberg, A., 1973, p. 21) has probably demonstrated a tenet that Freud espoused to the effect that "nothing which we have once mentally possessed can be entirely lost," a quotation Freud used (1900, 4: 20) from Scholz (1893) and a reference from Delboeuf (1889). Free association was recommended by Freud as a means for discovering the appropriate links in the patient's mind.

The projective therapeutic technique is also a method of approaching the problem of these links. In acting out the patient "forgets" the conflict, but it is reactivated when something in the present reminds him of it and stimulates the memories of the conflict. What is remembered, however, is a fantasy that is a *defense against the actual memories*, which are disguised in the fantasy. This is not a replica of the fantasy of childhood—but rather a more complicated fantasy depicting the internalization of the identifications with parental figures. The relief of the tension is the goal of the fantasy that creates the so-called "pleasure" the individual feels in the expresison of acting out either masochistic or sadistic acts. The tension is most often associated with *guilt* and consequent feelings of devaluation (masochistic fantasies). The individual is not supposed to feel glad or to have pleasure sustained. He has been "programmed" in his family to feel guilty for normal feelings of pleasure that are associated with actual accomplishment. When he feels pleasure, he feels guilty and cuts off the pleasure. Then he feels resentful and angry—he "feels like killing someone who has kept him in a trap." But instead of doing that, he turns the aggression on himself or acts in a sadomasochistic way, finding someone he does not know and who will spoil his pleasure by endangering his existence. He does not feel like being alone in such circumstances because he will do something foolish or perhaps dangerous to himself. Quinn, for example, several times has put himself in jeopardy by cruising and picking up a homosexual, then acting in a way to frustrate or infuriate the person.

When the person is deprived in some way of objects upon whom he may vent his aggression, he becomes depressed and lonely—and often suicidal. (Schizophrenics often become homicidal under such circumstances.) The patient is afraid to be alone, must seek constant company. Elizabeth did not feel or think of her "loneliness" or her fear of what might happen, but she sought out company at the apartments of others, often staying beyond the time when she was welcome. Then, eventually, she would feel rejected. Finally, she went to live with a man who liked her but who was essentially rejecting. She felt "safer," however, and protected in his home even though she saw little of him.

One can see in my second session with James Weber (Chapter 11) that the sadistic transference is expressed in teasing, but there is a fear that the analyst will change and "be like the father." Being like the mother is a more acceptable feeling and undercuts the fear of the father transference, which would necessitate the working through of his homosexual excitement and his identification with his father—the most rejecting parent (MRP). The use that the mother has made of the child in the sexual realm and his identification with her is much less threatening to the patient than the use of him by his father. Yet the idea of giving up the masochistic role with the woman is threatening too. James makes the mother "give" and can thus express his aggresion through the relationship. In his relations with patients, however, he would feel guilty if he taunted and bedeviled them. So he says in one session that he will always need a supervisor as long as he treats patients. Does this mean that James never reached the stage of "object constancy"? It means that he has not worked out his fear of *a woman*, nor his hostility. And he has not worked out his homosexual fears. He says he thinks he will find a rich girl and marry her and hope for the best. James feels guilt often. He cannot love his girlfriend, but he "idealizes" her by saying that she would make a better therapist than he, she is more sensitive, she is talented and more intelligent than he. But then he becomes critical of her: she is not rich; she is not ravishingly beautiful; she is lazy; she is a sloppy housekeeper; and on and on. He has these ambivalent feelings in transference too, but for the most part he hesitates to verbalize them. Occasionally they break through, and he expresses them in teasing.

In the patient's fantasies one recognizes the aggression of the parents depicted, and due to his identifications the patient is more or less like the parents in his neurotic ways. In analysis *this identification is one of the final problems to be worked out after the patient recognizes his feelings of rejection.* The guilt about being different from the parents and giving up some of their values, particularly those associated with their neurotic feelings, must be worked through. Once the patient begins to act differently from the parents, he is on the verge of breaking up his identification with them. This is like killing them off, and he frequently has dreams that he is harming them or causing them distress or that he is going away from them, finding a new life, and so forth. The anxiety associated with his guilt feelings often is expressed in somatic complaints. In my experience the prevailing depression is a defense against the recognition of the parental rejection and is associated with the need to deny and repress the knowledge of these feelings.

I have noticed that there is a poignant attempt or hope that one can get along with a rejecting parent. The individual tries and tries to do this, but often without success. The borderline patient, son or daughter, has been brought up in the sadomasochistic relationship and has failed to change the relationship; he reconciles himself to the relationship that he feels he cannot change no matter how he tries. The patient's revenge feelings aroused by the parental rejection and aggression tie him to the parents due to his superego guilt and these cannot be worked through in the beginning of analysis. The revenge feelings and the denigration (the sadistic trend) are expressed in teasing, in hostile acts, in sadistic maneuvers, in frustrating the object, in sexual degradation (perverse habits), in exploitation, and in a nagging to get what one can from other people. In the case of Quinn, as demonstrated in the two sessions presented, I would be more inclined to think of *guilt in the face of success and change in working through his identifications* as being the important factor at this particular point rather than the patient's wish that someone would call him "great" for having success.

PART IV

Treatment

...retical Orientation

Psycho..... ....as been under attack on many fronts. Aside from Szasz, who feels that .... ..ntal illness is in the eye of the beholder, and E. Fuller Torrey, who believes that the services of psychiatrists are expendable except for some brain diseases such as schizophrenia, which eventually can be cured or controlled by a handful of drugs that will be administered by general practitioners, there are many professionals who challenge psychotherapists to prove the effectiveness of their craft. In the face of this, it is astonishing that so many different forms of treatment flourish in the field. Recognizing the dilemmas that present-day psychotherapy poses, the cover story on psychiatry of *Time* magazine, April 2, 1979, stated, humorously, in the first sentence: "Each day millions of Americans talk, scream, confront, jump, paint, dance, strip, tickle, and grope their way toward emotional fulfillment." The outcome studies on psychotherapy appear to me to reveal that lack of training on the part of most therapists is a cause for many failures.

It is obvious that millions of Americans need psychotherapy and are seeking ways to relieve their anxieties and their emotional problems. Because of the many contradictions confronting psychotherapy, substitute alternatives are constantly being promoted—and the borderline is very prone to welcome these. Prominent among these are mind-altering drugs, such as alcohol, marijuana and the "hard stuff," all of which are used to deaden tension, take the individual "out of it," and give him surcease from his worries.

The borderline is not to be blamed entirely for his escape attempts, for one of the reasons that psychotherapy and psychiatry has been so "bad mouthed" is that within the so-called "helping professions" themselves there are relatively few individuals who have taken the trouble to receive the kind of training that is required to work successfully with individual emotional problems. The therapist who wishes to use short cuts is not anxious to undergo training that requires at least four years of study under supervision. Psychotherapy means *therapy of the psyche,* and this involves an understanding of the manifestations of the psyche from which we obtain the data with which to work—dreams, fantasies, thoughts, fears, conflicts, etc.

216

It takes considerable time to learn intricacies of the psychotherapeutic method. Even if there were enough properly trained people, the borderline would undoubtedly seek short cuts, for he has the habit of seeming to seek help, when in fact he is loath to undergo the necessary travail for true corrective therapy. He has been conditioned in a sadomasochistic mode of life that he stubbornly holds to even as he seeks help.

Many borderlines share with many physicians the hope that good drugs may be found to "cure," or "alleviate most emotional disorders." The discovery that there are many types of neurotransmitters, i.e., chemicals that provide the communication in the human neurophysiological system that help to establish certain behavior patterns, has heightened this hope. The elongated fingerlike cells in the brain and neurophysiological apparatus are connected by the messages they receive across the synapses through the release of the chemical neurotransmitters. Jumping across the synapses, the chemicals seek only those sites or receptors on the nerves that are specially designed for this task. Experimenters have speculated that when the body produces too many or too few of such chemicals, behavioral problems ensue. Depression, for example, may be associated with altered activity of neurotransmitters like monoamines (serotonin, adrenalin, and dopamine), while schizophrenia is characterized by dopamine defects. The borderline patient is considered by most drug-treatment-oriented therapists to be a form of schizophrenia, although this is still a moot point. As we have mentioned, experimental data puts the borderline in the 8 to 35 percent bracket with respect to constitutional factors. Since some neurophysiologists believe that drugs alone will change neurotic to normal behavior; they see no reason for training in psychotherapy.

It is evident, however, that the environment has something to do with body chemicals and thus with the composition of neurotransmitters. The intake of foods, as well as other types of events, i.e., *pleasant* and *unpleasant* interpersonal experiences, have an effect on the neurophysiological pathways to the brain. Today the pleasure-pain centers and their pathways are the focus of much research. Freud put a great emphasis on the pleasure-pain mechanisms in his theory of psychoanalysis. The pleasure-pain principle is an important factor in the development of the borderline personality. It is the means through which the environment has an impact upon individual development as opposed to what Freud called the "innate schedule" or the instincts that he presumed made themselves felt at stated periods. The instincts pressed for discharge regardless of the environment.

It is, of course, in the family that the habits, customs, foods, manners, and behaviors of individuals have a direct relation to brain activity and to the kinds of neurophysiological pathways that are established leading to individual adjustment. Whether external pressures and events have a relation to the manner in which the chemicals increase or decrease or whether less or more of a given chemical is constitutionally determined is not known at this point. It is obvious that the individual, while he may be composed of innumerable systems, genetically determined, is himself an open system dependent upon the varying environmental forces that bombard him from all sides. The interactions between the individual and his environment contain variables of which we still have no knowledge.

In this chapter I shall try to summarize my ideas regarding the dynamics of the borderline condition in the context of the theory that environment plays a decisive role in the etiology of the neuroses and the psychoses. In doing so, I shall repeat what I believe are the important dynamic themes as they appear in different forms in order to accent their importance. I shall try to explain what I think is important in the treatment regime so that the patient can modify his behavior sufficiently to relieve his tension and resolve his main conflict. This, in my opinion, revolves around his having acquired identifications with parental figures that are detrimental to self-preservative impulses. The latter are what we should think of as determined by the genetic schedule and therefore the "id." But the id, I believe, should be thought of as the *genetically determined survival equipment* rather than as some mysterious chaotic, unorganized mental miasma. The id contains the wherewithal for ego organization; in fact, the ego, as currently defined, begins to function (as Fairbairn suggested) at birth since the self-preservation instincts have prepared the way for the survival of the species.

In the first section of this discussion of theory, I shall sketch some of my ideas in broad outline regarding identification, the relation of identification to dreams and fantasies, the attempts of psychoanalysis to depict interpersonal relations intrapsychically, the transitions in Freud's thinking with respect to theory, and the turning to a developmental scheme away from the influence of the environment with the evolvement of the instinct theory, which looms so importantly in the minds of most theorists today with regard to the borderline patient. In the minds of many theorists, ways of looking at data concerning the borderline are grouped around the concept of narcissism, the early aspects of the developmental theory such as "oral" and "anal" aggression, and the "sadomasochistic instincts" that are attached to these early phases. Fixation accounts for much of the behavior of borderline patients according to most current theories. My ideas are different, and I have tried to explain some of the differences, recognizing that on the clinical level we all see the same manifestations. In order to clarify some of the ideas concerning fixation, sadomasochism, identification, I have found it necessary to go into some of the historical developments in psychoanalytic theory. We must use sociological or interpersonal theory to explain the interpersonal dynamics that create the borderline condition. We must also use some of Freud's ideas, particularly some of his early concepts of defense and his thoughts about identification and internal representations of experience. In treatment the interpretations of therapists revolve a great deal around their theories; yet in our actual practice many of us do the same thing *regardless* of our theories.

In psychotherapy we should be concerned with the family conflicts and the immediate environment where the individual resides. We are interested thus in the intimate human group or groups to which the person belongs and the effect that these social systems have had on the emotional life of the child as reflected in his dreams, fantasies, and symptoms. In other words, we are interested in the way his experiences have influenced his thinking and physical reactions. It is in the dreams, fantasies, and symptoms that we find the ways in which the individual has survived by developing defenses against anxiety socially derived. The defenses hopefully counteract the anxieties that are evoked as traumatic experiences (cumulative traumas) become *dangers*. It is also in the dreams and fantasies that we learn about the conflicts that the individual has developed in relations with family members; we learn about the individual's wishes, angers, and fears.

There is little doubt that a stress-illness factor in the human body prevails (*Science News*, 1977). It is apparent also that various brain-body links are mediated by a person's endocrine and autonomic nervous systems. The conclusion of many is that "it may be that the most important factors in the stress-illness link are the chronic, daily hassles rather than major life events" (*Science News*, 1977). This is certainly true. The daily necessity to cope with work and family situations is the main problem for most individuals. An inopportune family environment results in neurotic development and thus, over time, handicaps the individual in his ability to cope with the travail of everyday life. The stresses and the defenses against the stresses take so much energy that the individual has no strength to resolve his problems in an adequate way. His vicissitudes then cause conditions that lead to more stress. Research, for example, reveals that people who are married have lower death rates than those who are single, widowed, or divorced. Persons undergoing bereavement, separation, and other situations involving loss of a loved one or "dashed hopes of being cared for" are identified as high-risk gastrointestinal patients. Members of groups experiencing social and cultural mobility have higher rates of coronary heart disease, lung cancer, difficulties of pregnancy, sarcoidosis, depression, and other neurotic symptoms than members of more stable groups. Behavior and cardiovascular processes are intimately linked. Hypertension and job loss, economic deprivation, and crowding are linked. Men who work in supervisory roles get ulcers at a significantly greater rate than those in other work roles.

The borderline patient is a tense person. He has been "programmed" in a conflict-laden environment, and his relationship with his environment is thus full of everyday "hassles." It is the nature of the borderline to find adjustment extremely difficult since in his family the customs or the mores (the normative behavior) are at odds with what the larger social group expects of the individual in the way of interpersonal relations (Wolberg, A., 1952). The borderline's mode of behavior is sadomasochistic, and he cannot make an adequate adjustment to authority. He resists the demands of authority; yet he has been taught in his family that he must knuckle down to authority whenever authority demands this. His fantasies, dreams, fears, anxieties tell the story of a person whose developmental years were linked with parents who were bound together in a sadomasochistic interpersonal defensive system and who utilized their children in the service of their neurotic struggle. The child is a member of a social system (the family) that attempts to shut out some of the influences of the other social systems of which the family members must inevitably become a part. Within the family system the children are cogs in one sense (projective objects); on another level they are expected to conceal the dehumanizing aspects of the family system from the members of the school system and the broader social systems such as clubs, leisure time activities, sports groups, religious affiliations, work groups, and such.

In the family we often find that in addition to being sadomasochistic the parents of borderlines have a depressive attitude. Myrna Weissman (1976) found that depressed women lack energy and are apathetic and are not interested in their children. We see this condition often in mothers of children who later become borderline. The depressed woman, says Weissman, cannot communicate with her children; she exhibits hostility toward them and loses her feeling of affection for them. Borderline patients usually have mild chronic depression related to feelings of having been rejected and abused by their parents. They feel uncared for. They are suffering from what Freud called the feeling of having "lost their objects." While they *have* "lost their objects" in one way, i.e., they have felt the brunt of rejection and abuse, on another level they have retained their original objects through their identifications, which are the ways in which they are like the neurotic aspects of the parents. They are separate, but they are also tied by their identifications, and they are filled with self-disgust, anger, rage, and depression. It has been my observation that the depression of borderline patients is not a severe kind of depression, but the parents of borderlines when they are depressed, usually are more than slightly depressed and manifest hostility rather than extreme withdrawal as in the severely depressed person.

The treatment of a neurosis and even a psychosis is best advanced, it seems to me, under the aegis of a dynamic psychoanalytically oriented theory. But traditional theories it must be recognized have some defects that will need correction. In the field of psychoanalysis little was done for the borderline patient until comparatively recently due to Freud's idea that these cases were untreatable. One of the great handicaps has also been the rigidity of some psychoanalysts in their belief that if one is not seeing the patient five times a week and if the patient is not on the couch, then one is not doing psychoanalysis. Dynamically oriented psychotherapy, which seems to be the treatment of choice for borderline patients, is not psychoanalysis according to the rigid definition. Analysts who insist on being purists refuse to treat borderline patients, for when they do so, they believe they are not being true to their standards. Common misconceptions are that if the patient sits up, it is not psychoanalysis; and if discussions and activity on the part of the therapist take place, this is not psychoanalysis; if the patient does not have a transference neurosis, the procedure is not psychoanalysis, and so forth and so forth. The criticism is leveled at the psychoanalyst by many nonanalysts that psychoanalysis is a "cold" procedure, a one-sided discussion, with the analyst limited to saying "Oh hmm!" All of these criticisms are obviously naive, but many psychoanalysts *do* have a rigid view of psychoanalytic procedure so in fact they are not able to treat borderline patients.

Projective Identification—A Main Defense in Borderline Personality

Throughout this volume it has been stressed that one of the major defenses of the borderline patient (actually, this is a system of defenses) is *projective identification*. We must reinterpret this concept, however, in a way that differs considerably from the ideas of Melanie Klein who introduced the term in the 1930s and from those who more recently utilized Klein's concept of the mechanism in infancy as a defense against "oral" aggression. While I use the concept of projective identification as a defense, I consider that the infant who will become the future borderline patient is born with the same psychological and neurophysiological equipment as the individual who will have a more "normal" development. Klein's concepts of oral aggression, of the schizoid and depressive positions in infancy, must give way to more rational explanations. *The experience with the parents is what determines the way in which the defenses will be organized.* Neuroses and psychoses are systems of defense. The borderline has a particular kind of ego defensive system.

We have seen that projective identification can be interpreted to be a defense unrelated to developmental phenomena, a defense that is organized gradually over time and is solidified later than in infancy through relations with parental figures. The developmental theories of Freud, Klein, or

Mahler as these apply to the dynamics of the borderline deal with the so-called preoedipal phase of development and are inadequate to explain development as revealed in current infant studies. The new information regarding infant development will change our ideas about infant life, emotional and mental. Therefore, they will require that orthodox psychoanalytic theory, particularly as related to the first three years of life, modify its preoedipal concepts. Such concepts as "developmental arrest," "fixation," "innate oral aggression," "sadomasochistic instincts" that appear in the "oral" and "anal" stages connected with biting, breathing, "taking in," or "expelling" are useless in the understanding of borderline conditions. Current ideas regarding an objectless stage in infancy and concepts of narcissism will have to be discarded.

To reiterate once more, projective identification is a defense developed over time in view of the particular experiences the child has from birth onward with parental figures, both father and mother. The aggression that is an aspect of projective identification is a primary symptom in borderline conditions, but it is evoked by repetitive traumatic experiences with parents, who excessively control and inhibit the child's behavior. Later on, aggression is tinged with ideas of hate and revenge, which provide the basis for the necessity for developing the projective identification defense. The frustration-aggression hypothesis explains the dynamics and the foundation of ideas concerning aggression. In general, the concept of "ego defect" should be replaced by a new concept of "defense," one that posits that the borderline individual denies the true nature of the reality situation in the parental home. The situation is too anxiety provoking for the child to accept as is, and he relieves his anxieties through symptoms, defenses, and other means, often through the use of alcohol and various drugs. A sadomasochistic role is assigned to a child by his parents, who have an interlocking defensive interpersonal relationship and who use the child as a transferential object in the service of their own requirements. The sadomasochistic role is based on the parents' urgencies to employ the child as a projective object in their own defense, and their punitive and controlling modes require the child to inhibit certain of his "normal" impulses or "needs." These normal needs find expression periodically based on the fact that they are instinctually or genetically organized and form part of the self-preservation aspects of the child's behavior. The ensuing neurotic and psychotic processes evoked in the child are defenses against a harsh reality with which the individual tries to cope, and the crucial defense mechanism is identification with the parents who are aggressors in that they use inflexible controlling mechanisms and punitive measures to keep the child in line with their neurotic needs. Sadomasochism is a *learned* pattern in this relationship with parents. In projective identification there is passive and masochistic behavior with sadism as its goal; the parents insist on a sadomasochistic position as a defense against their own intense aggression. The patients deny certain aspects of their autonomy and, out of rage and revenge, force others to do for them what they should do for themselves.[1]

Identification in this situation is not a form of development or ego growth but rather a sadomasochistic type of object relations, and in psychotherapy this projective identification has to be unraveled and broken up. For example, in transference the borderline may think of the therapist as a sadistic parent image (father or mother—or both), while the patient experiences himself as the frightened attacked child; then, even moments later, the roles may be reversed. The initial goal of the therapy (which may take three years) is to show the patient that in his projections, his dreams, and his fantasies he sees in others what is also in himself. This serves to explain to the patient his "internalization of the identifications" and his defenses against the implications of this internalization, which include repression and denial. In treatment the dreams connected with repression and denial make it possible to discuss the unconscious motivations, the fantasies, and the defenses of "the other" as a first step in the analysis of the patient's identification system. These goals are accomplished essentially by confrontation at appropriate times (when the patient indicates the points of least resistance). Projective identification in a woman patient was evident, for example, in her denial of the sadistic side of her controlling mechanisms when she said that she is really "good." She would never have acted that way with her sick neurotic mother (a hostile way) if her father had not made her do so. She denied that she acted this way with her husband, although in previous sessions she had alluded to this.

Projective interpretation is a first step in outlining an interlocking defensive pattern between two people. The purpose of projective identification is to defend the patient both against his own powerful aggression (his reactive aggression) and his fear of destructive retaliation from others as a response to this aggression. As a defense, he projects his aggression onto others, while at the same time he gives direct expression of it in his interpersonal

---

[1]See A. Wolberg (1973, pp. 211-213) for the origin of this dynamic in the parent-child relationship. In the example cited it is the mother who is involved in the development of the pattern, but it can easily be the father too who evokes this behavior as in the instance of Frank (p. 214) and Lisa (p. 208). As one will see from the material these patients produce in the sessions, it is the *identification with these controlling and sadistic parents* that the patients act out that interferes with making an adequate adjustment, and it is just this problem that is so poignantly denied while asking and pleading for help. This can be a frustrating experience for the therapist who is treating the borderline if he has no adequate therapeutic technique to deal with this defense.

relations. The mechanism also helps the patient perpetuate the inhibitions and other defenses that help him continue his sadomasochistic bind.

In the beginning the child fights against expressing the identification but finally he succumbs due to the punishments and the encouragements he receives—the verbal and nonverbal communications that indicate the parents' wishes that he act out the identification roles.

In my 1973 book I have schematized this model, which, in fact, describes the milieu in which the oedipal situation develops (Wolberg, A., 1973, pp. 159-161). The result for the borderline is a "confusion of sexual role" that is associated with what others have called a "lack of identity," but in reality it is a function of a latent homosexual trend. The kind of interaction in the family depicted in the oedipal model is what I have termed an *interlocking neurosis* between mother and father (1960, pp. 179-180). Later, equating neuroses and psychoses with *defensive systems*, I spoke of this parental relationship as being *an interlocking defensive system* (1973, pp. 2, 147-149). The borderline patient has a compulsion to express aggression. This obviously is not limited to borderline cases. Freud reported such a need in himself. He said he always needed "an enemy," and we saw this acted out in his relations with Breuer, Fleiss, and Adler. He needed a friend and an enemy simultaneously. His hostility toward the opposite sex is evident in his writings. Sadistic patterns showed in his scorn, his tirades against those who disagreed with him, and the like. Yet he had great compassion too. The projective orientation of the borderline patient makes projective therapeutic techniques a necessity.

Chessick has called the projective technique an "externalizing of the introject," a phrase coined by M. Coleman, referring to the patient's mental projection. In my terms "externalizing the introject" would refer to the identification role and to projecting or displacing one's own characteristics onto others, i.e., one's unwanted patterns (denial patterns) that have to do with identifications with parents, *the characteristics of which one feels ashamed.* This is a basic mechanism in projective identification. Thus, "introject" would mean identification, and identification refers to an acting-out role related to parental insistence.

In discussing identification we should recognize that while in some instances the patient has the exact kind of behavior as that of the parent, in other ways the same patient "acts out" according to various patterns that are dissimilar to the parents but are, nevertheless, within the boundaries of the type of sadomasochistic behavior that would titillate the parents or appease them. I am aware, of course, that many theoreticians feel that the borderline has no identifications, and, developmentally speaking, he has not reached a point where these can be formed. Obviously, I disagree with this point of view. I know also that some theorists contend that the borderline's acting out has no relation to his identifications or his relations with his parents—but again I disagree. The studies of Szurek and Johnson (1952, 1954) with respect to the delinquent acting out would seem to confirm my viewpoint.

The patient must eventually see the relation between his acting out and his interlocking defensive relationship with parents, i.e., his identifications with them. The patient must see this or, rather, *admit* this (he sees it in any case and knows it on a cognitive level). That is, he must verbalize what his "observing ego" sees, and he must then talk of the necessity of ridding himself of the patterns and of dealing with his resistances to change. *It is in the resistances and in the attempts that are made to change the neurotic behavior that one sees the emotional difficulties that are associated with the patient's conflict.*

The Families of Borderline Patients

It is possible to make several generalizations about the families of borderline cases. Borderline patients come from a family in which the parents were unable to provide a functioning social unit adequate for healthy development. Mothers are found to be very disturbed in a variety of ways and can be classified as (1) obsessive-compulsive, (2) self-oriented, competitive, and masculine, (3) paranoid, or (4) passive, schizoid. In many cases the mother is "there," but she really is not. That is, she may profess avid interest while ignoring many of the child's needs; she goes through the role of homemaker and mother, performing all the "duties" of the role yet not giving thought to herself or the child as persons; and she is preoccupied with her own fantasy world; she is withdrawn and neglectful.

Fathers of borderline patients can also be classified under four categories: (1) passive-aggressive, (2) hostile, aggressive, attacking, and controlling, (3) paranoid, and (4) mildly psychopathic, promoting antisocial behavior.

I have proposed a model of triadic relations in the family of the borderline, based on Freud's continuum of acceptance/rejection in the severity of emotional disorders. The interaction between mother and father posits different patterns for male and female offspring. For males, the father is rejecting of the son, *pushing him toward the mother*. The mother expresses hostility toward men by pitting son against father. Yet, because the son needs the father, the son identifies with his hostile patterns, with ambivalence, guilt, and hatred. He also identifies with the mother. In the case of the female patient, the mother is seen as rejecting the daughter, *pushing her toward the father*. The father expresses hostility toward women by pitting daughter against mother. Thus the child develops identification fantasies serving as defense mechanisms against a traumatic family situation. These fantasies indicate the sadomasochistic role assigned the child by the parents when the child becomes enmeshed as a projective object in the services of the parents' defenses.

On a cognitive level, to use a current phrase, the patient must relate his fantasy to his current behavior and change his behavior, even though in the beginning anticipating change will give him anxiety. The family dynamics (interactions) are most important in understanding the origins and types of identifications that the patient must act out. The "observing ego" is the cognitive aspect of the patient's role in treatment. Here again I disagree with those colleagues who say that the borderline has no observing ego.

Jackson (1951 a-c) and his associates (1964, 1965) studied the communication system in the families of schizophrenic patients, which to my way of thinking is similar in many ways to that in families of borderlines where the patient's parents make known their neurotic wishes and their needs for the patient to act out the neurotic identification role. Jackson spoke of *acting out* as being *in the nature of the dynamics of a post-hypnotic suggestion.* The parents communicate their neurotic wishes but, nevertheless, deny what they are doing and demand that the patient deny this as well. Nevertheless, through punishment and reward they see that the child acts out the identification roles. This dynamic helps the parents perpetuate their neurotic homeostasis, thus enabling them to avoid self-confrontation. The masochistic trait in the patient's personality comes from the experience of being controlled and punished by the parents whenever he steps out of his identification role. He is finally conditioned to act out the role whenever one of his normal impulses that is threatening or anxiety provoking to the parent begins to express itself. He inhibits the impulse himself when his normal desire is about to influence his behavior. This conditioning is a result of the "Yes-No" attitudes of the parents, *but then he acts out after the inhibition of the normal impulse.* The patient has a reality concept of his situation even as he defends, denies, and distorts reality. The patient's rage and his *feelings of humiliation* are aroused in his relations with his parents, and gradually over time he develops the borderline condition. He has undoing mechanisms that he applies to normal impulses and to some of his more dangerous aggressive impulses as well. These patterns are observed in the relationship with the therapist, and they constitute aspects of the transference. The patient's reality system is in operation simultaneously with his defensive system, which contains his distortions, repressions, and denials.

I have described the mothers and fathers of borderline patients elsewhere (Wolberg, A., 1952; 1968, pp. 109-111). One must point out that there are great variations in the combinations of fathers and mothers. In general, one is "sicker" or more mentally disturbed than the other. It may be the father who dominates the scene in one family, while it is the mother in another domestic milieu. There are some common conditions, however. One parent must be "protected" and appeased more than the other. In the family of my patient James Weber the father controlled the family. He is obsessive, domineering, and hostile. The mother is more passive, and she appeals to James "to be good" so that the father will not "take it out on me." The mother gives the impression of being a passive but hostile schizophrenic. In the original home of another patient, James Fuchs, the father also dominated the scene. He, however, was the more unstable of the parents and was finally hospitalized as a manic-depressive psychotic. The mother was passive and in my opinion was probably schizophrenic in view of her bizarre behavior with James (see Wolberg, A., pp. 252-253). She was never hospitalized, for she lived in a protected atmosphere. The father was action oriented, a liar and a cheat in business, and an acting-out person. The mother "lived through" James's acting out and must have experienced sadomasochistic pleasure from the father's antics as well. James's main fantasy was a "Tea and Sympathy" fantasy in various forms at various times. His acting out was based on identifications with both father and mother, which is the usual case in borderlines. For example, the father was teaching James to cheat and bribe his way through life while the mother was relating to him in a "Peeping Tom" way. He was acting out and endangering his existence by operating on the edge of the law (or over the edge) and he was also acting as a Peeping Tom.

Acting out is based upon the activations of the patient's identification fantasy that originated as a defense as the parents projected a role upon the child and demanded his acting out of the role. The projected role was dependent upon the sadomasochistic relationship the parents had with their parents. The identification fantasy of the borderline serves as a defense against the anxiety he (the borderline) feels in the interpersonal dilemma of being forced to identify with his parents or their substitutes ("the aggressors"). The fantasy aids in the denial of reality and gives the individual "distance" from the traumatizing objects (the parents or their substitutes) with whom he must deal daily. The patient in his relations with others projects traumatizing roles upon others as an aspect of his defense of projective identification. Harriet Hamburger's mother ruled through hysteria. She was a "Queen." When Harriet was born, the father said, "Another Queen has been born!" The father and mother both shared this "Queen" fantasy with regard to women. The father was afraid of women and had a suspicious nature. In dress he was somewhat of a dandy. The mother had fantasies of the father being unfaithful. The father was a "masochist in business," letting his partners "cheat him and walk all over him." He told Harriet to appease the mother in every way, but he had a "secret" with her, telling her of the difficulties in living with a hysterical woman. Harriet slept in the same bed with her grandmother for several years. The father would say, when Harriet wanted to "get close to him," "Go to your mother! go to your mother!" She resented having to stay with women, but she too finally developed the Queen fantasy with contempt for men. Harriet's Queen fantasy is an identification fantasy.

The fantasy is not a true memory; it is stimulated by memories or experiences that were traumatic and have created conflicts that have never been adequately resolved. The conflicts provide the basis for the anxiety that motivates the patient to seek treatment. These conflicts relate to inhibitions that were demanded by the parents but that have interfered with the autonomous behavior of the patient and his normal impulses. Even though he inhibits them, they, nevertheless, seek expression.

The identification is a function of the patient's superego organization. Originally, Freud connected what he called the "criticizing faculty of the ego" with a dynamic he described as "the ego as altered by identification," (Wolberg, A., 1973, p. 102). He seemed to imply, correctly I believe, that in an identification there is associated a form of aggression. Freud talked of the superego having some mysterious connection with the id that "is not yet understood." Rickman (1926) spoke of the superego as the way that the individual had of "maintaining object relations." The superego is a concept that can only emerge as a consequence of human relations, and at least in Freud's writings we find that this concept was associated with "good" and "bad"—with our ideals and with our aggressions. The mysterious connection of the superego with the id was never clarified, but there was in his work a trend describing the child's idea of the parent as "good" and as "bad" due, I presume, to the parents' punishments and rewards.

Punishment and reward is a dynamic in the pleasure-pain reactions of the child. It is my thesis that the punishment-reward system is operative in the parents' neurotic relations with the child, and this influences the superego, which has, through the process of identification, encompassed some of the neurotic fantasies of the parents. These fantasies, in turn, stimulate, in transference, hostilities, aggressions, and perverse habits. Freud's idea that in identification the ego is remodeled is a way of saying that identification changes the ego, meaning the behavior of an individual, so that it is in some ways like that of another person—a person "loved" or "feared." Object relations are implied in the concept of superego—i.e., the superego is a concept that embraces the influence of particular people in the environment on the development of the patient's personality. It is in the concept of the superego and in family dynamics that we must recognize that psychoanalysis must derive from multidisciplinary concepts and be a systems theory rather than a developmental theory.

The Borderline Personality, A Gradual Acquisition

The borderline syndrome develops gradually. The problem, as I stress again, is related to the use of the child *over time* by the parents as a projective object in the face of the parents' anxieties. The identification is a life-saving mechanism, albeit a defense. The child feels rejected because of the activity of the parents in pursuing their neurotic aims. One can say that the superego is in part a self-destructive mechanism due to the parents' needs to utilize the child to maintain their neurotic homeostasis. The child has been made to believe that he must act out the identification role in order for the parents to survive. He is a cog in the balance or organization of the family. If the child attempts to break out of the neurotic role, he is made to feel guilty. His action is looked upon as aggression toward the parents. The guilt is now an aspect of his superego. The destructiveness of the parent in forcing the child to identify is a danger that the child fears, and he *idealizes the parent*, in defense, at the same time that he "gives in" or "knuckles under" at the insistence of the parent. *The child develops self-hatred for his "giving in," or his "weakness"—to be more precise, for his masochistic behavior.* He feels rejected by the parent and is depressed as a result. As he becomes depressed, however, he develops anger toward the parent and resentment for the way that he is used. He must find ways of controlling his anger to some degree. Therefore, he develops repressive defenses, denial, hypochondriacal symptoms that represent symbolically the injuries the parent heaps upon him and are often indicative of the sexual usage the parent makes utilizing the child as projective (transferential) object. Over time the anger becomes associated with sadistic sexual feelings aroused by the parents as they invite the behavior to assuage their own guilt in the face of their use of the child on the sexual level.

There is, however, an "innate schedule" that unfolds for each individual, and I dare say that this schedule changes over time as the culture and environmental circumstances of the society change. A given individual is but a small iota in the history of the species, but each individual has an innate schedule that is the basis for his self-preservation techniques. Such phenomena as defenses that appear shortly after birth, gestures that are evident by the age of 2 months, eye contact that is present shortly after birth, smiling, cooing and other verbal utterances, communication techniques, and many other neurophysiological phenomena are evidences of these self-preservation mechanisms. There is an interesting neurophysiological phenomenon that has recently been brought to our attention by McCarley and Hobson (1977) that may be called the "isolation process." This may well be the neurophysiological system that Freud guessed must exist in view of the individual's tendency to concentrate, his capacity for self-observation (the observing ego), and the ability to create defensive patterns, particularly hysterical mechanisms and obsessive symptoms (splitting or dissociative processes). McCarley and Hobson believe that they have disproved Freud's theory of dreams. Actually, they have shown us the neurophysiological process that makes dreaming and remembering the dream possible. They have not explained the content of dreams, but they have disclosed the mechanisms that make possible our dreaming, our concentration, and other forms of thinking. There is a tendency toward growth, toward health, toward adaptation to the environment. It is the *self-actualizing tendency*. It is a factor in human life that will correct what the environment did not allow if a more propitious environment can be enjoyed. Research has confirmed that trauma in early years can be overcome if the environment is changed for the better (Dennis, 1938; MacFarlane, 1963, 1964).

The neurophysiological mechanism that is associated with the process of thinking is what McCarley and Hobson have studied. Thinking includes, however, several kinds of mental exercises such as fantasying, dreaming, problem solving, creative thinking, speculating. The process is made possible by the same neurophysiological mechanism that allows for the development of the "observing ego," the delusion (a fantasy), and concentration.

McCarley and Hobson report that the crucial mechanism setting off dreaming (and I would say, therefore, thinking) is in the positive stem in the back portion of the brain. This "mechanism" acts like a "generator" that evokes "outbursts," automatically, and through the midbrain this periodically activates the forebrain, which stores sensorimotor information. In dreaming (and therefore in thinking) certain "input" is inhibited so that the dreamer deals only with "sleeping pictures" without interruption. Thus this neurophysiological mechanism makes possible an "isolating factor," which is an "automatic process," being an aspect of the autonomous behavior program of every individual.

In the sexual area, notably Masters believes that sexual impulses automatically occur in both males and females at intervals during the night, and in men these cause erections every ninety minutes or so. Charles Fisher has told me that he has found this to be true in men, but he has yet to discover a repetitive sexual mechanism in women. These automatic arousals and neurophysiological systems are only now being studied and revealed so that we may have to revise many of our ideas concerning what goes on in the human body and the effects these mechanisms have on the mind. It is my impression that these discoveries will disprove Freud's developmental concepts and affirm other ideas that he proposed. It is obvious that this isolating factor would be necessary in the contents (conscious and unconscious) that relate to the defenses. It may well be that the instincts seek expression and that when they are inhibited in life, a conflict is created that makes the individual feel he has many "incompleted tasks." This is the cause of the repetitiveness in dreams that we take as a manifestation of neuroses and psychoses. One must, however, revise the current ideas concerning the instincts and associate these with "good" impulses, i.e., self actualizing, self-preservative, and creative behaviors that are stifled in the course of relating to neurotic parents.

The repetitive trait as well as the isolating factor are characteristics of hysterical and obsessive mechanisms, and I count *denial* that is so prominent in the borderline patient as one of the hysterical phenomena. Freud noticed that hysterical blindness was a form of denial, and he made references to certain forms of frigidity as types of denial and as forms of hysteria. Frigidity and impotence were symptoms that Freud observed in his early patients many of whom we now recognize as having schizophrenic and borderline characteristics.

At the present time we become more and more mindful of memory as a dynamic concept, not a static concept such as the "memory bank." The "unconscious" or *the repressed aspects of the thinking process comprise a dynamic constellation affecting the present.* Not all of our patients' memories are associated with neurotic patterns. It is the bed of normal and creative thoughts in operation that enables the patient to find security in treatment that requires change.[2]

---

[2]Freud had a concept of an *unconscious unconscious* i.e., a bed of drives and impulses. The id was the mental representation of this *Ucs-Ucs*. The defenses went into operation due to the anxiety that these raw impulses stimulated. Society would not allow these raw impulses to be discharged. There were ideas associated with the id, which were what Freud called *innate ideas* (a racial heritage as it were). Later Freud felt that the ego too had an unconscious level. But the ego was based on experience in this world, a part of the id split off to form the ego, which was, in fact, a mental reservoir of the effects of the experience with objects. The superego was a split-off part of the ego. Actually, both the ego and the superego were derived from part of the id that underwent a metamorphosis, i.e., that part of the id that dealt with the outside world. Freud was trying to conceptualize the genetic process in mental terms in his concept of the id since he noticed that there were not only repetitive impulses coming from the individual organism such as sexual impulses, but also there were repetitive defensive patterns. He conceived of the repetition compulsion as a factor in the constitutional equipment. We know that there is this innate schedule in development and in life itself, but we also know now that the two systems—conscious and unconscious—so far as mental life is concerned do not run parallel to physical development. However, it is true that physical development has an effect upon how the person conceives of himself and how he reacts to people. From what we know today from modern studies, it seems more reasonable to conceive of several systems operating

Freud suggested that in all emotional problems there were "mnemonic fragments"; i.e., there were memories due to conflict over traumas. Although his time periods for defenses such as "repression" or "fixation" may be off, there is merit in the idea that the neurosis (or psychosis) begins with repression. A corrollary is that traumatic memories bifurcate, i.e., part of them are put aside (repressed) and replaced by fantasies ("projective" and thus "protective" fictions) and symptoms. What we are not accustomed to do is to connect these mechanisms to part of the thinking process in current situations. We now know that traumatic memories are associated with "protective fictions" or fantasies; thus they are components of memories but the current situation stimulates memories and memories interfere with the interpersonal process in the current situation. Memories are components of the thinking system. *Thus identifications that are functions of acting out are associated with fantasies that activate acting out that is related to memories and to current situations.* Identification, to emphasize what I have said before, is a form of adaptation, a necessary kind of accommodation in view of the original family dynamics and the interlocking defensive system of the parents that arises as the parents use each other as transferential objects (objects of displacement), i.e., objects of projection. Identification is related to both conscious and unconscious thoughts. In our current theory regarding borderline patients (in fact, in any patient) we discard Freud's use of the idea of an unconscious unconscious and recognize that it is conflict-laden thoughts and feelings that are frightening and unacceptable to the individual that he represses.

---

simultaneously in the human body but not necessarily in a "parallel" sense as Freud thought and postulated in his developmental scheme. The concept of *memory*, however, is primary in any theory of mental life. It has a prime place in Freud's scheme of the unconscious and of the conscious as well. Freud confused this concept with his idea of psychophysical parallelism in the various stages of development so that such concepts as "oral," "anal," and with mental equivalents is not a valid theory. These concepts, however, are applied in the case of the borderline patient by most theorists today. The intricacies of the body and mind are beyond my comprehension and beyond that of the scientists who are working in these areas. In other words, scientists still have much to learn and are marveling at what they are learning. Two concepts are relevant to our needs in relation to understanding the "systems" and their operations in regard to specific types of emotional syndromes: *memory* and *the integration of experience* or what the psychoanalyst has called internalization (of objects). We shall have to look upon these phenomena in a somewhat different way than Freud suggested. In this realm of multidisciplinary thinking it has been very easy for psychoanalysts to misapply concepts from one field into another. The important point is that while man is a group animal, he is, nevertheless, an individual—and this has presented a dilemma to many theorists. We must understand both individual and group phenomena in the treatment of all patients. Whatever the experience in the environment has been it is nevertheless *the individual who must cope with the correction of his behavior.* The individual with his fears, dilemmas and conflicts is the ultimate focus of psychotherapy.

The Human Group and Communication

Various forms of thinking are the meat of our therapeutic focus. Individual therapy in my opinion is the treatment of choice for the borderline patient with the addition of group therapy. Family therapy is a revealing medium, but it is not a substitute for group therapy or therapy with peers, which is also important for the borderline. A few basic remarks about human groups and group and individual therapy are relevant here.

The human group is a group of members who communicate over time for the purpose of solving problems. Communication (a function of thinking) is attained by the exchange of information. Information is transmitted in any given situation where the member of a group may choose to interact by signals, symbols, words, or patterns that are transmitted, i.e., sent to another or to others. The *set* is the milieu where these categories of signals are transmitted, and the categories are called the ensemble or repertoire of the group. Mathematicians say that the amount of information is measured as the logarithm to the base of the number of alternate patterns. When $MX - Y$, then X is referred to as the logarithm of a system that processes it. Communication in the group acts geometrically: as one person in the group puts in information, it stimulates others, and their responses increase the number of probability of response for the others because the more the possibilities for solutions to problems are suggested as each member adds to the information pool, the better the solution may be. This is not always true, of course. Groups can make harmful decisions, and these can be made by the majority of the members. In these cases however, the decisions are made on the basis of the neurotic communications of members in the group rather than on their rational reasoning. In the therapy group one of the duties of the leader is to help towards the goal of rational reasoning.

In living systems the observers, i.e., the group members, select variables from the infinite number of information units and relationships that exist. The unit of communication is the amount of information that relieves the uncertainty of members when the outcome of a situation with two equally likely alternatives is known. In group therapy, and in the individual treatment process for that matter, by way of information, several alternatives for a solution to a problem are offered. In order to act or to change the individual must choose one of those alternatives.

Information is the opposite of uncertainty. Thus to a social system (for that matter a community or a nation) information is the unifying factor creating the network which is defined as the *structure of the group*. The giving and getting of information and the method whereby the members receive the information to set up further communication channels are the foundation of structure. The word "marker" has been used by cybernetics specialists to refer to those bundles, units, or changes of matter-energy whose patterning conveys informational symbols. Cybernetics as a systems theory refers to many different kinds of communication, however. For example, Indian signals, cuneiform writing, magnetic tape, arrangement of nucleotides in a DNA molecule, the pulses on a telegraph wire, or the verbal and nonverbal expressions of the members of a therapy group that convey information to the members for that particular small group. It is this latter that concerns us in the treatment process. In communication the marker moves in space, and this movement follows the same physical laws as the movement of any other sort of matter-energy.

The mass of matter-energy that makes up a systems marker significantly affects its information processing. It has been estimated that no system, living or nonliving, can process information at a rate greater than 2×10^{47} bits per second per gram of its mass. The random state or disorder of a system is known as its "entropy." Order is the opposite and is known as "negative entropy."

Communication is the change of information or its movement from one point to another over space. Communication is of fundamental importance in that informational patterns are processed over space and the local matter-energy at the receiving point can be organized to conform to or comply with the messages. Matter-energy and information always flow together. Information is always borne on a marker. There is no regular movement in a system unless there is a difference in potential between two points, which is negative entropy or information. The word "system" means that there is a set of units with relationships among them by way of the communication that provides these relationships. The word "set" implies that the units have common properties, or interests. The state of each unit in a system is constrained by conditioning by or a dependence upon the state of the other units. A set of elements stands in action for the purpose of a goal.

In a therapy group interest and action between two or more members can be for one of two goals, problem solving or defense (resistance). Function is a correspondence between two variables such that a value of one depends upon a value of the other. This is called "conditionality" by group dynamics experts, and it is the basis of what Moreno (1934) spoke of as "pairing," "triads," "chains," and the like. Function means that there is a relationship between a number of variables in the system. In the human group this means the functional relationship between two or more people. A "state" in the system is a set of values on some scale (a measurement) that its variables have at a given moment. In sociology these are called "norms" and "values." Moreno suggested that it is just such a scale that the individual uses in his judgment to band with one or two other members for some particular reason to form a subgroup. He called this the "choice-rejection scale" in his system of sociometry. To him, this is the way in which one individual decides at any given point to join another (either for problem solving or for defense) to make a "dyad," a "triad," or a "chain."

We have noted that the random units or the disorder of a system is "entropy." In a closed system entropy increases, but actually there is no such thing as a closed system (unless the universe is one). It is true, though, that some systems are more closed than others. The family in which neurotic parents control is a system that is partly closed. The parents are the subsystem that keep the system together and see that it is organized in a particular way (this is the "housekeeping energy" according to some systems theorists). Negative entropy is organization. Negative entropy means functions or relationships between units. In the small group, which is what we deal with in psychotherapy, "relationships" refer to "who interacts with whom?" as Moreno pointed out. The structure of a system is the arrangement of its subsystems and components in three-dimensional space at a given moment in time. In group psychotherapy there are several types of subsystems. For example, the individual is a subsystem; two or more persons interacting over a period of time are a subsystem. Moreno (1934) has explored the dynamics of the small group in his presentation of sociometry. Simmel in 1908 wrote the first definitive treatise on small-group dynamics. Simmel's work has been translated by Wolff (1950). Other important studies on various aspects of the small group have been done by Homans (1950), Bales (1950), Bales and Strodtbeck (1950), Asch (1952), Bales and Borgatta (1953), Cartwright and Zander (1953).

The communications of the borderline patient will at times be cryptic, and one must learn to translate the information at points where it is likely that the communication will be received by the other with the least resistance. For example, Kurt Blau told me of his own depressive moods by first talking of one of his clients (when he was practicing social case work before he received psychoanalytic training). Since the message was not about himself but about a client, I talked of the client's depressive problem. It was four years later that I was able to speak to him of his own depression and relate it to some of his mood swings. When in a depressive mood, nothing that Kurt did would please him. It was a direct expression of an "identification with the aggressor." This was not a deep depression that immobilized Kurt—not at all. He was still doing a massive amount of work, carrying many family responsibilities; yet he had the desire to "get away from it all." He felt trapped, and although he was now very successful in what he was doing, he, nevertheless, did not know whether his work was really what he wanted. He might like another field, but he is not now free to pursue what he would like, even if he knew what that would be, because he is so burdened with family responsibilities. This kind of reaction is multidetermined and very complicated. Part of the problem is that the patient cannot stand success. His guilt is still active and must be analyzed further. Self-reproach is a hostile gesture toward the successful self, a need to "tear down." We see this kind of dynamic in schizophrenic patients as well, but the borderline's reactions are not as severe as those of the schizophrenic.

I was interested in a paper by Schwartz (1978) reporting on the communications of an institutionalized schizophrenic woman who was rambling on "like a word salad" mumbling, "teddy bear," "bed," etc. When the head doctor came near her on his rounds, he shouted, "Young lady you ought to find out who you are!" The patient "became normal" and said smiling, "Yes—I do often confuse my identity with my bed, my table, my teddy bear." (This can be a depersonalization in the face of an interpersonal encounter.) We very often see schizophrenics who "clear up" from such episodes and have periods of clarity for many hours and some clear up for many years. It is the *meaning system* in the communication that is important.

The borderline patient too "clears up," but he also has depressive feelings, panics, schizoid states, paranoid attitudes, explosive episodes, antisocial episodes, and sadomasochistic and "infantile" behavior. I see similarities in traits such as explosiveness, "infantile and narcissistic behavior," and antisocial behavior. There are similarities, too, in passive-aggressive, sadomasochistic, depressive, manic, and explosive episodes. What we call "narcissism" and "infantile behavior," however, is often *withdrawal behavior* and self-preoccupation in response to great anxiety in interpersonal situations or in anticipation of anxiety-provoking interpersonal encounters. In a protected environment or when the situation is at a minimum of "to-do," the patient seems quite "normal."

The patient indulges in a "word-salad," and when the therapist says, "Young lady, you need to find out who you are," she breaks into rational talk and says that she confuses herself with her bed, her teddy bear, the clouds, and so forth. One must wonder why she can clear up so readily and speak normally and tell us what she does. This is a manifestation of ego integration. The "word salad" is actually a part of her fantasy, her masochistic, depersonalization fantasy into which she lapses after emerging temporarily.

Another patient says to her therapist, "You are unreal—you don't exist. I can't stand your dead feel, your fishy eyes, your calculating mind. How can it be that I chose you instead of the others who want to be friends, who want to work with me." The therapist says that not long ago she felt that way about herself. The patient then talks of birth, relating a "beautiful" fantasy of a sea horse having millions of babies but only a few survived. The therapist thinks of "the self" and a "shattering" or a fear of attack or disintegration. If I were the therapist, I might think of masochism, the "beauty of her fantasy being an idealization of a traumatic experience and her masochistic response to other people. Then it would be an acting out with idealization of the fantasy as a representation of her identification experience.

The catatonic young woman responds to the therapist after many days of silence saying that he should abandon her, send her away, destroy her, put her to death. (Is this a masochistic response to his plea, "I want to help you! I want to talk to you. I want to be with you"?) The woman then looks away in despair. Weeks pass, and finally she makes "cutting" gestures in front of her abdomen. He thinks she is trying to cut the umbilical cord. I, though, might think that she is telling him of her fears of sex, her sadistic fantasies about sex, and her masochistic feelings, which are her only avenue to sexual feelings. The therapist probably realizes that she is using him as she may have been used—she is acting like the parents. The patient then finally makes a "date" with the therapist. Her tear-filled eyes and her plea for the date is a masochistic maneuver. I believe this is an acting out of a "beating fantasy." I do not say he should not have made the date. She says that his "hello" on the wards is "phoney." Why does she say phoney? Is this a trap for the therapist? It may be. This may have little to do with "self" in a developmental sense. It is an exposure of a masochistic role on the masochistic self; she is herself; it is a manifestation of *low self esteem*. The girl must beg for a date, must evoke the guilt of the other. The patient is acting out masochistically as she did with her parents instead of being a person who is recognizing her ego capacities within the confines of the therapy situation.

As we have mentioned, schizophrenics and borderlines do act out with the therapist in the beginning phases of therapy in an attempt to involve him in a sadomasochistic pattern, thus knocking him out of his therapeutic role. In the second phase we outline this pattern and emphasize the transferential significance. By the third phase this acting out of the transference has ceased, and more direct transference manifestations are evident. Has the analysis made up for ego defects? Or has the analysis been such that the anxieties of the patient have lessened considerably and he can now address the therapist directly without acting out as he did with his parents? I believe it is the latter. Has the patient finally adjusted to the non-acting-out atmosphere of the therapeutic situation so that his acting-out pattern is reduced through lack of stimulation—a deconditioning process? I think so.

The "good side" of this acting-out maneuver in the first phase of treatment is that the patient's behavior is an indication that he is developing a relationship with the therapist. In the case of the borderline and schizophrenic it is a sadomasochistic relationship, and he will try to trap the therapist with acting out—the pantomimic transference (PT)—but he must accept this relationship. In the case of the catatonic young woman in the hospital the therapist realizes the hazards, but he must take the chance that he will be able to tell her eventually that while he wants to be of help, he cannot conceive of having a relationship where he would injure her, have contempt for her, throw her out, and so on. He will have to let this message come across to her in some kind of acceptable words at an appropriate time so that she cannot possibly feel rejected. Or if she does, she will recognize with him that she knows she cannot have sexual feelings without having these sadomasochistic fantasies and acting them out in some way.

This pattern is the result of the group interaction in the family with the neurotic parents as the controlling agents in the family group. In my opinion, the patient who acts out in this way is not a suitable member for a group at this point. She should be introduced to a group after she has worked through the pantomimic transference (PT). Freud (1916) wrote in his paper "Those Wrecked by Success" of the problem of guilt and the self-destructive dread, or obsessional worry, "signal anxiety." "You are not good enough; you are not going to succeed" is the internalization of the destructive identifications, the extensive kind of PT that is manifest in the schizophrenic patient. But each in his own way acts out the transference in the beginning. My patient Harold Hemple, for example, was nearer to the neurotic side of the spectrum or continuum than another patient, Sonia. He came into therapy with a very restricted mien. He was so precise, so orderly, so withdrawn, so "proper" as to look almost manneristic when he walked. His man/woman drawings are reproduced in Figure 1.

Harold looked like the man in this drawing when he first came to therapy. He was restricted in his walk and his talk but very precise in all that he said. He had a fantasy of himself creeping into the session like a cringing animal. Interpreting the drawing he said: "The woman is angry. The man is just defending himself. He can see other things in the world, but the woman is so obsessed with anger that she cannot think of much else. The man would like to have sex with someone; she is too upset and hostile. That's like me—I would like to get married, have a girlfriend, but I seem too afraid, too particular, I'm not easy in the presence of women. I have to have a girl who is refined, and I haven't met too many of that type."

Harold was very masochistic and would become so in the presence of women, but then he would have grandiose fantasies as a defense, and he was scornful of most people. He did not want a male therapist, however, because that would be too threatening for him—he could not compete with men. The woman was the dominant figure in his family (the man was dominant in Sonia's family). The father was passive in my patient Harriet's family (in Sonia's family the woman was passive). In the family was the in-

FIG. 1. Drawings by Harold Hemple, January 7, 1962. (See text.)

terlocking neurotic relationship between the parents, i.e., the interlocking defensive pattern. Harold crept into the analytic presence. In that sense he acted out his fantasy of being a beaten animal.

Theoretically speaking, I believe that masochism and self-castigation are an acting out of the "beating fantasy." I do not know whether all children have beating fantasies, but I do know that when the family situation is such that, over a long period of time, the individual feels constantly demeaned, he persists with his beating fantasy, and we see it enacted in a great variety of ways. The persistence of the fantasy is an indication that the communication system has had a demeaning effect upon the child over a long period of time.

If the Family Is the Seat of the Problem, What of Family Therapy?

The study of the family has been a focus for psychoanalytic theory and practice in the treatment of neuroses, psychoses, and borderline cases for almost half a century, and out of the old child-guidance clinic has emerged the "family-therapy" concept. The child-guidance and child-therapy fields were the source of the ideas that parents have a much greater influence on the neurotic behavior of the child than Freud was willing to admit. It was in the social agencies and the child-guidance clinics that the concept of family dynamics was developed. This concept requires a knowledge of social theory as well as a theory of dynamic psychology if we are to understand our patients, including borderline and schizophrenic patients. Family therapy is a form of group therapy. All people, with few exceptions, are members in life of several groups, and often these groups are at odds from the point of view of goals. Family therapy has been suggested as a therapy of choice for the "sicker" patients, which group includes the borderline patient.

There has been a controversy in the past twenty years between those family therapists who follow Freud's developmental scheme and those who use dynamic concepts but are "group" or sociologically (systems) oriented rather than psychoanalytically inclined. Haley, an example of the sociological group, espouses a number of concepts that I shall mention. Some of these concepts seem valid, while others show the tendency to try to merge the individual into the group so that the individual's autonomous behavior is ignored. Haley (1971, 1976) writes, for instance, that a person exhibiting psychiatric symptoms is a person who has adapted to a unique family situation. This is certainly true. He then continues that this orientation raises the question of the unit to be studied in therapy, and he suggests that *the family* should be considered the patient rather than the individuals in the family. To my way of thinking, the latter proposition is an anthropomorphizing of the group. Haley argues that we must study the social context of the individual since he is adapting to the social situation, and one could certainly agree with such a statement. But then he states that if one changes the context of the group, one changes the individual. It was assumed by Freud and others that psychiatric problems represent maladaptive behavior, but in Haley's view the behavior is adaptive. I can agree that the behavior is adaptive, albeit defensive. When Haley infers, however, that a change in the group will ergo make a change in the individual, then he is using a simplistic concept and ignoring the dynamics of individual change. Change from neurotic to normal comes about slowly. Resistance to change is strong even when the individual wishes the change to take place. This is particularly true for the borderline patient. Change occurs over time, but it will occur.

Haley suggests that the dynamics of families who have a psychiatric patient are different from those who have no such member, and in this we can agree. But he then asserts that if families containing a psychiatric patient are different from other families, the social context must be different, and the social context must change for the individual to change. The entire orientation of therapeutic intervention hinges upon these factors. I would suggest that the patient can change by *leaving the family*, and he can change *before* other members change even when he remains in the family. Other members may then change in behavior if they wish to maintain their relationship with the person who is receiving treatment. But the therapist must be ever alert to the *nuances* in the dynamics of change. It is a fact of life that certain family members will bring great pressure to bear on the individual who is in therapy to give up therapy and to go back to old neurotic habits. Family therapy does not eliminate this pressure automatically.

Haley raises several significant questions:

1. Are families that contain a member who is "abnormal" different from families where all members are "normal"?

2. Is a family that has a member having one type of psychiatric disorder different from a family that has a member with a different type?

3. Is one part of a family different from another part? That is, is the parental relationship with an "identified patient" different from relationships with his siblings?

4. Are parental relations with extended kin different in different families?

5. Does a family change to a different system after an individual in the family has had treatment or after family therapy?

There are some answers to these questions in results of family studies that are of importance to our understanding of the borderline patient—for example, the following:

1. "Normal" families have members who are less hostile, aggressive, dependent, immature than other families. (Borderline patients, as Grinker's research has shown [Grinker & Werble, 1977; Grinker, Werble, & Drye, 1968], live in families where hostility and aggression are ever present.)

2. In studying family structure the emphasis is on whether family members fulfill their roles properly: the father role, the mother role, the role of child, and so on. (In any psychotherapy we try to ascertain in what way these roles are fulfilled, whether in neurotic or normal ways. It is understood that when we use the word "normal," we mean families contain-

ing all members who are comparatively mentally healthy. Perhaps there is no truly "normal" person.)

3. Normal families communicate more clearly, exhibit less conflict and discord, have fewer disagreements, have more stable coalition patterns, and shift to different patterns of behavior if the setting requires this more easily than families that contain emotionally disturbed members. The latter families are rigid and resist outside influence to change. (It is interesting, too, to realize that when disturbed family members do seek company in other groups, they turn to groups that have similar destructive members as their own families.)

4. Normal families solve problems more quickly than abnormal families and with less "noise."

Psychoanalytic Concepts To Be Discarded in Treating the Borderline Patient

In studying the borderline patient and in reviewing some of the material related to the early stages of development, which is the period that most analysts say is the "fixation" stage for the development of borderline conditions, it occurs to me that the following is a partial list of the psychoanalytic concepts that we shall have to discard:

1. The early interpersonal state of the infant is "objectless." An autism exists where there is no distinction between self and objects.

2. At birth the psychic apparatus is in an "undifferentiated state."

3. Psychic representations of other people are at first partial, i.e., breast, face, and so forth.

4. The mother is the only emotionally charged object for the infant in the first two years of life.

5. The primary process is the bedrock of the intruding fantasies of the patient.

6. In response to the smile of the mother the infant smiles in return, and this imitation is the precursor of the later psychic process of identification, the basis of much ego development.

7. Toward the end of the first year, the child has "separation anxiety" in the mother's absence and this is associated with a "fear of strangers" ("stranger anxiety"), which is the beginning of recognizing objects as such. Defenses against painful stimulation begin to develop.

8. In its primitive functioning the ego follows the model of bodily functions, i.e., the mind introjects, "takes in," as in nursing, what is pleasurable and seeks to ward off what is unpleasant, or to eject, evacuate, (externalize) the impressions of unpleasantness.

9. During the second year the infant develops the capacity to be alone.

10. In the early stages of development the infant cannot know how helpless he is because his needs are satisfied as if by magic, as if he were omnipotent. Later when he realizes that he is helpless he attributes the omnipotence to his parents and he thus begins to idealize them.

11. Due to their influence on superego development, social institutions can be considered elements in a biological frame of reference.

12. In everybody's mind there is a bed of unconscious, underlying, primitive, part-object fantasy remnants persisting from the distorted perceptions of early life.

13. In treatment there is a temporary "splitting of the ego" into an "experiencing ego" and an "observing ego." This is normal, but there is a more permanent and pathological form of "splitting of the ego" in the process of dissociation, seen in such conditions as fugue states, multiple personality, fetishes, and many other types of perversion. There is a similar "splitting" in the borderline patient's psyche.

14. Identification is an automatic, unconscious process whereby an individual becomes like another person in one or several respects. It is related not only to maturation but also to learning, mental development, the acquisition of language and speech, the adoption of interests, ideals, mannerisms, and so forth. The individual's adaptive and defensive patterns are a function of identification with either loved, admired, or feared persons. In order for identification to occur, there must have been enough psychic development so that the individual can distinguish himself from others, i.e., self-representation must be distinguished from object representation. This does not occur before the age of 10 months and rarely until 16 months; the final separation process occurs at age 3.

15. The mother must act as an "executive ego" for the infant.

The fifteen premises that I have presented here are all used in present speculations concerning the borderline patient. If they are all erroneous, one can imagine that our ideas of the development of borderline personality will have to change considerably.

I would like to suggest that there is no primary process in the sense that Freud thought of it. The thinking of the borderline patient that has been called chaotic, disconnected, in various degrees has a relation to the patient's sadomasochistic identification fantasy. In fact, these bits and pieces are part of the fantasy that is evoked by *intense anxiety* either in interpersonal relations or due to certain types of thoughts that are fearful, dreadful, or both. In disguise, the ideas are symbolized, broken up, distorted, and the fantasy parts are dissociated, a masochistic act.

Freud felt that the patient was finding atonement in the masochistic illness when he would not allow himself to enjoy success. The "need for punishment," he felt, was one of the worst obstacles to treatment, Freud finally, in "Analysis Terminable and Interminable" (1937), located the roots of this problem in Thanatos (the id). It has been suggested that this discouraging aspect of treatment in these cases (the borderline is a case in point) was one of the factors in Freud's formulation of the death instinct. The concept of Thanatos made masochism a derivative of a constitutionally intensified aggressive drive. Another major reason for Freud's solution concerning that aspect of the superego "as yet unclear to us" (i.e., the connection of the superego with the id) was that Freud chose to avoid any implication that the parent had a major role in the organization of the patient's emotional problem. The interpersonal theory would suggest a conditioning factor over time in view of the repetitiveness of the parent's neurotic pattern and the need of the parent for the child to play a neurotic role. This possibility was vehemently denied by Freud. Would the patient's masochism be less if we could assure the parent that the child is "whole" rather than "defective"? I doubt it. The masochism and the related sadism do not derive from the instinct; they are man-made.

Chemotherapy and the Borderline Patient

There are those analysts and therapists today who believe that chemotherapy should be administered to the borderline because the chief seat of his problem is a chemically defective neurophysiological system. Chemotherapy does seem to enable the patient to tolerate the anxiety that he must feel when he finds it necessary to dissociate the parts of his fantasy. Or is it that the patient does have a chemical imbalance? I would opt for the answer that the dissociative process is part of the defensive system and has nothing to do with the neurophysiological system. Perhaps if parents thought that chemicals would cure, they would have a different attitude toward the patient, but I doubt it. Some theorists insist that if the patient were not defective, the parents would not have anxiety and would not "beat at" the child. Why then do the 40 percent of schizophrenics who do not show chemical defects and perhaps 100 percent of the borderlines who do not, nevertheless have emotional problems? It is the psychotherapeutic process that is essential and important for the borderline, whatever the cause of his problem. There are times, however, when chemotherapy can be useful, particularly for depression and intense anxiety states.

CHAPTER 9

The Treatment Process

Although there is a general pattern that applies to all borderline patients, the uniqueness of each individual is what makes the treatment process so interesting. Recently one of my former patients who had been in treatment with several therapists before me and whom I had seen for five years and then referred to another therapist when I went to Mexico for six months returned to me. It was interesting to see that in the four years that I had not seen her she was considerably better than when she had been with me. When she came to me, she had many self-reference ideas and many other paranoid types of reactions. For example, she would tell no one where she lived and would not even let my secretary know her address. She had many locks on her doors. Now she had changed. She had moved to a new address, and when I told her that my secretary would need her address and telephone number, she gave it to me readily. She was angry with her last therapist, saying the therapist had not helped her in any way. She had worked on her own but recently had made a suicidal gesture and had been hospitalized for a few days. She did not want to destroy herself, but she felt she might if she could not break her pattern of idealizing some man at work and then thinking that he was communicating with her in relation to a possible affair, only to be rejected later on by the man who would complain that she was molesting or pestering him. This obsessive clinging to the feeling that the man was sending her love messages was a masochistic fantasy where she was tortured by the possibility that she would be doing something that was driving the man away from her.

Perhaps one can say that the patient who has an obsessive idealization defense that is accompanied by paranoid projections (particularly self-reference stimulated by current events upon which the patient projects) is one indication that the treatment process will last for twenty years or more. This is not to say that the patient will be immobilized, for the patient can work, enter marriage, have children, and so on. There will, however, be difficulties in interpersonal relations, and in some instances the individual will have to leave work situations every year or so until the core problem has been worked through to a point where direct and verbalized transference can be tolerated in the interpersonal relationship with the therapist. This process can take anywhere from seven to twenty or twenty five years. Such a patient are my patients Sonia, Harriet, and Flora, whom I refer to often in this volume. It is my thought that the dynamics of borderline cases may be more evident if I discuss in this chapter the more resistive types of cases, those that are closer to psychosis, and who may be in treatment for as many as twenty years or more.

Working Through

We know that in "working through," understanding the problem is not enough. The patient must be willing to tolerate the anxiety of changing his behavior. If we have resolved small parts of the problem and he has worked them through in relation to the anxiety, this helps in the working through of the next part. During problem solving if we deal with pieces of problems, aspects of the whole, then finally we can put the puzzle together much more easily. But it is almost impossible at any given time to make a statement about the "complete whole." As Rosner (1973) points out, the "psychological field" is ever changing, the configured structure of the field is fluid, and new ideas (or old ones, for that matter) can be aroused when they are related to a preceding thought in the process of association. The whole process, as we have suggested, advances in a geometric pattern. Once the new ideas, which may merely be a combination of old ideas put together in a new way, are in effect (i.e., are integrated), then the mental constellation changes into something new, and behavior changes at the same time that this process takes place in the mind so that the person is never quite the same again. (We must remember that this "law" applies to the infant's learning, experimenting, and integrating as well as to the learning of adults.) With the patient who has an emotional problem it is his anxiety that impedes his learning. With each new experience the mental "schemas" change, and the individual is different from what he was before.

We must not forget that the patient changes his behavior in relation to other people. Thus he is in a group process as he "works through." He learns about his transference reactions in the analytic situation, not only his reactions with the analyst but with others as well. He learns how the behavior of others sets off certain reactions in himself. The analyst is working in relation to the transference in a group process, and his knowledge of the patient comes from two sources—(1) what he observes in the individual and group sessions and (2) what the patient tells him about his relationships at home, at work (or at school), and in his leisure-time activities.

When the borderline patient changes as we work through the pieces and parts of a problem, these changes can be so subtle that they do not show externally until a considerable time has elapsed. The borderline patient is resistant to the stimulation of new learning, because of the *guilt* that it evokes in him, the *fear* that he experiences in stepping out of his neurotic role, and the negativism or anger that he employs in relation to the transference figure, the therapist, and to others with whom he has transference reactions. The pleasure of autonomous behavior in areas that have been prohibited is at first a frightening experience, and he must learn to give up his masochism piece by piece as he goes along. The sadism (his revenge feelings and his vindictive behavior) is the last aspect of the problem to be worked through, for they are the most hated and most denied parts of his personality even when they are obvious.

The Initial Phase

The borderline patient, in spite of what many investigators think, has a concept that "something is wrong." With an active questioning in the initial interview the therapist can begin to be in touch with the patient's "observing ego." One must then try to ascertain what aspect of the total problem the patient is willing to tackle with his observing ego and where he is willing to make a change in his behavior in the immediate future. This is the part of the total problem where one must focus initially and work through to a successful conclusion. Having had this minor success, the patient goes on to another minor success and another until a more global working through finally takes place. In the beginning the patient's ideas concerning his dreams and fantasies are elicited and used as his associations. The borderline patient does feel symptoms to be "ego alien," and the "Zeigarnik effect" motivates him to go on to more satisfactory solutions than what the borderline state affords. We might note in our record for the first session what aspect of the problem is available for a cooperative focus. Joint work between the therapist and the patient can begin in the accomplishment of a "small gain." In the initial session with one patient I recorded for example, that the young man in question, Jerry McDonald, had obsessive symptoms that bothered him, but he also had a fear of what damage his early life experiences might have done to him. He verbalized wanting to work out his perfectionistic ways and why he felt a person is all good (idealization) or all bad (hostile); or, in other words, why if he sees that a person has a flaw, does he reject the person after having idealized him (Wolberg, A., 1973, pp. 195, 199). This, however, is a major problem that can be talked about but cannot be taken as a small focus to begin with. Jerry feels immobilized, but he feels he is not really inadequate even though he acts inadequate at times. On some

VANDERBILT MEDICAL CENTER LIBRARY

days, he said, he gets no more than one hour's work done in the whole day. This might be a specific area upon which to explore what actually happens on such occasions. What are the steps that lead up to such a day? He is not immobilized every day but only on certain days. Think of this problem as if one were going to do short-term therapy. The important point is for the patient to have success working in a circumscribed area. We might say that the focus (F) is to understand the circumstances that lead up to a "bad day." What happens? What are the incidents that precede a bad day? What interactions does he have with people and who are the people that create in him the kind of anxiety that is immobilizing?

Harriet Hamburger, too, had the feeling of being immobilized. She came into therapy at the insistence of a social worker, Mrs. S, who was employed in an agency where the Hamburgers had gone to inquire about adopting a child. Harriet and her husband were refused a child based on what Harriet inferred were psychological reasons. They had seen a psychiatrist who referred them to me. When the Hamburgers came to me in November 1950, Nelson (the husband) was working and attending college at night to acquire an engineering degree. He felt that he had no problem and was not interested in therapy despite the rejection for a child and Harriet's inferences. He let me know that he had no desire to go further. However, he was willing to take a "quick" look at the Rorschach cards. He noted that he had had a Rorschach test in 1941 but was vague as to why, just stating that it had something to do with school.

In the remainder of this section I shall present abbreviated illustrations from Harriet's case history, plus very brief comments about Jerry McDonald where applicable, to point up our discussion at the outset of the section.

11/14/50—Nelson Hamburger's Response to Rorschach Cards

1. A grotesque butterfly.
2. A bat.
   A torso.
3. Two comedians on the stage—
   Dancing.
   Holding a muffler.
   Slapstick comedy.
4. Vulva on top.
   A grotesque dancer.
   A bear or gorilla.
5. Bat feelers and everything.
6. Leaves me cold.
   A bear rug.
   A penis.

7. Two girls picking at each other; making tongues
   at each other.
8. Two mice monsters—
   Climbing
   Hard job.
   On the rocks.
9. A nice design—testicular.
   Clouds—I like this.
10. A something with an arm coming to a divide (blue crabs).

11/14/50—Harriet's Responses to Rorschach Cards

1. Two elephants and two something else—some animals.
2. Bears kissing; paws dripping blood.
   Two elves.
3. Two men in full-dress suits dancing around a pot.
   A headless person or animal.
4. A man with tremendous boots—apelike face, hands small.
5. A bat.
6. A vulva and a penis.
7. Figures and persons in airplanes.
   Also plumes and tails.
8. Two rodents holding on to the top of a tree on a mountainlike cliff.
9. Two people back to back.
   A fierce storm.
   People on the bottom of something.
10. Faces in the pink part.
    Spiders holding on to green birds.

At the same session Harriet, at my request, made a drawing of a man and woman (see Figure 2). After she completed the drawing we discussed it.

FIG. 2. Man and woman drawing. Harriet Hamburger, November 14, 1950.
(See text.)

Pt.   The man has short hands.
Th.   What are your associations?
Pt.   Maybe I'm castrating him.
Th.   What is your next association?
Pt.   I feel like him. He was passive—dominated by wife—castrated. I feel
       castrated. The woman is dominant. The absense of a relationship with my
       father and the possessiveness of my mother make me oppositional to
       her—and secretive fighting rather than an open anger. I was full of anger but
       a conforming child.

11/16/50

Harriet says that she must please and be liked; she feels uneasy if she is not needed;
she verbalizes with friends and husband to allay anxiety; she cannot refuse the
demands of others; she must help others to figure things out if they ask her. She cannot say "no" to people even if what they ask of her is inconvenient. She often has a
fantasy that she has a kind mother; she talks of feelings of hostility with guilt. She
says she plans what she will say in the sessions. She asks permission to talk the sessions over with her husband. In the previous session she spoke of a girl who was angry
at her husband; in a social setting this girl made a terrible spectacle by expressing her
anger at her husband.

Patient says that she is frightened of men and mentions a man in the apartment
house. He just returned from a mental hospital; he is a paranoid and she is frightened
of him. He never does anything to her, but she is frightened to meet him.

Patient describes her relationship with women. She is passive, dependent, she is
drawn to aggressive women, women who express their aggression through talking and
acting efficiently—she does not see these women as overtly hostile. (This is like her
mother.)

Patient says she has feelings of frustration and hostility when she tries to do
things—feels inadequate. She really does not want to do anything.

She asks therapist to teach her to say "no" so she can use her time the way she
wants to.

Both Jerry McDonald and Harriet Hamburger asked for help in a direct
way about a certain problem. One can assume that these pleas have a defensive quality but even so, one can nevertheless explore them, for while they
cover deeper problems, they are areas that the patients are willing to explore. Harriet talks of phobic and paranoid traits, hysterical qualities, and
intense hostility, while Jerry talked of a "tearing at" characteristic of an
obsessive nature. Both spoke of negativism, and of dependency. Harriet is
drawn to aggressive women. Jerry is seeking a father who is controlling, and
he wants the therapist to be someone he can depend on. He wants to un-
burden himself on someone who is wiser and helpful. Harriet wants help in
saying "no" to people who make demands upon her and whom she feels she
must obey compulsively. Each say that they have negativistic feelings. In
Jerry's case there was a vague reference to needing a man—too much—or
wanting to be attached to a man.

A few sessions after the first week Harriet revealed her depression by having a dream of two caskets with one child (or teenager?) in each casket. The atmosphere was bleak, barren. Two parents were somewhere near in the dream. She also had a sexual dream, and her associations were to someone who was a pervert. She asks the therapist what she would think if she discovered that Harriet was a pervert?

12/1/50

Harriet reports a dream about her grandmother, but she cannot remember the dream. She thinks her grandmother was dead, and she felt terribly, but not sure. Her associations were that when she was 5 years old, she visited a neighbor who told her of her son who was negativistic and if you want him to do something "just tell him the opposite." Patient was playing with the little boy and wanted him to do something, so told him the opposite. He did. His behavior was some misdemeanor (not so but thought of as so). Reminded her of her grandmother. Her grandmother blamed her and humiliated her before the family. She could not answer back and defend herself. She felt hurt, maligned and helpless.

Patient uses these memories as masochistic fantasies and sometimes looks for slights. The grandmother was the mother's mother. Patient feels in a masochistic position in the session. Takes comments of therapist and uses them masochistically.

12/5/50

Harriet talks of her previous dream—an anxiety dream about her grandmother. She says she never could stand up to her grandmother; she must have been afraid of her. [*Transference fears.*] She reported three dreams:
Dream: She was working in a large office. She had ability and had come to the attention of the executives. But she was supposed to be let go. She was standing before a girl at a desk, humble; she was being let go because there was no more work to do. [*Fear and wish and transference problem, rejection fear.*]
Dream or fantasy: Something about her needing something, perhaps from therapist and she was told, "I can't help you now; you'll have to wait." [*Rejection.*]
[*Therapist asks about the office where the patient works. There is a new woman in the office; apparently this causes her anxiety. She does not know how to deal with this new woman.*]
Dream: A certain area in Brooklyn. An unknown man in the office. She thinks of her cousin. (Her cousin has three children; she adopted a boy. Cousin and husband complain about the behavior of their children. [*Patient doesn't like to hear of these complaints*]) In the dream there is complete desolation, no human sound, a musty odor—some pestilence must have been here. How did the people move out so quickly? Then it was like a Catholic funeral parlor, but there was a man and a woman, a Jewish couple. A priest had said something about children; the man and woman rushed around the corner. There was a coffin—a man and woman were close. Were they husband and wife?
[*Fighting and arguing and rejection and depression—these are the mood feelings.*]
She denies having *any feeling*—she is like her mother-in-law. She detaches [*dissociates?*] from her feelings but she is hostile. She feels guilty about her hostility

but she cannot help feeling that way. She acts with her husband the way the mother-in-law acts with him. There is conflict between them.

12/8/50

Patient says she belongs to that group of intelligent individuals who can express neither grief nor anger; her mother-in-law is one of those people too. One woman told her mother-in-law to leave and not come back again. Patient says her mother would be very angry at the mother-in-law; husband was the peacemaker. Most children had gained their independence, but not her husband. Patient tells about how she blew up at one of the tradesmen [*safe*]—"I wanted to attack my mother-in-law. I was very nasty "[*guilty*].

Dream: My brother bought a dress that cost $60 for his wife (in reality this was for a wedding). My brother and I were in bed; he had his head against my breast. I said "He's very reticent about hurting me"; something about sexual relations hurt [*sadomasochism*]. Her associations were that her mother and father were always fighting, they are always going to separate; once they had a big row and he went to live with his mother.

"I was ashamed; almost everybody knew about the affair; I was more sympathetic with father; mother had been abusing him; she would go out to play cards and neglect him. My father was the appeaser; she would tell everybody what a beast he was; she wanted people to agree with her that she was abused. He would come back and then shower her with gifts; she said that he was with another woman." This was a pure fantasy with her [*the mother*], but she kept insisting that this was so. He said to her that she had wronged him so that he could go ahead and wrong her by having an affair. He gives her the money; she holds the purse strings; father asks mother for money. She is stingy. Father would say he wishes he could have a good steak; mother would not give them any extras to make them happy—only necessities. She would always say that she served a nice table and she is a good cook—this is true. Father feels deprived; he always would indulge himself when he could.

The patient feels in the session that she is deprived; she has transference feelings that I do not give her enough. Actually, we have not focused on anything other than that she cannot say "no," and she is angry about that. I asked if she felt her relationship with her husband is similar to her mother-in-law's relationship with her son (patient's husband). She replied perhaps, but she hopes not.

1/4/50

Harriet reports having a dream: Her boss and his wife are adopting a child: I don't think he wants the child; he's doing it to please her; she adores him; he tolerates her; calls her "Baby"—father and daughter attitude. The wife appeals to patient for help. She doesn't just ask me to do something." She talks of the problem of giving presents to in-laws. She wants to give but not too expensive; her husband does not want to give.

Dream: A box of Kotex is being exposed in a room, and I'm trying to hide it because people would be coming around.

Dream: I have a desire for an ice-cream cone.

She has associations about entertaining company in her home—three couples. Estelle and husband; ditto Edith and Marion. Marion cried on patient's shoulder when she had her second child; she has angry feelings toward Estelle and Edith. Estelle asked patient once why she did not discourage Marion's confidences and use her to tell of troubles. Marion is very emotional, sometimes like a child; she shows her emotions. Edith denies emotions; secretly she'd like to express emotions as Marion does but she can't. That evening the patient was the referee. Estelle and Edith were particularly argumentative. Edith has money but she does her own work in the home. Estelle always takes the easy way out of everything; she has professional aspirations.

Edith and patient have been very friendly; patient helped her and thus put her on the spot. She feels uncomfortable and guilty—she's jealous. Edith will talk about Estelle to patient; Edith is caustic, hostile—then does things to regain love. People's confidences mean very little to her; she has a sharp tongue and will reveal confidences to others. Patient has used has as a confidante. (Will the therapist act the same? She may have this fear.)

People tease the patient and her husband because they go everywhere together. One day the four girls were visiting and patient's husband went out. Edith said, "Oh, my God! don't tell me you let him go out!"

Edith and her husband are on the verge of divorce. Edith is pregnant and uneasy about it—thought she was going to die or that the baby would be born dead. Patient said, "I'm sure I'd never get involved in any such relationships."

When patient left the last session she was uneasy, what is this woman [*the therapist*] like? How will she react [*she was thinking this about therapist*]? Asked how she thought that therapist would act, she said she was afraid. She thought the therapist might pity her; also thought that she would think patient very special [*these were grandiose feelings*].

She mentioned that when she was born her father said "A Queen was born." Queens are special.

The first focus was on her inability to say "no." The second (briefly) was on transference feelings: How would the therapist think of her? How would she size up the patient? Would she be giving—helpful? What was the therapist doing that was not helpful? There was some discussion of her oppositionalism and the idea that it might mean that she has fear of letting someone be too forceful or too submissive as with her mother. The focus then changed to her work situation and how she manages with women bosses and with men who are "in charge." Along with the feelings about bosses, the discussion included the way she acted in the marital situation and how she and her husband get along. Harriet was vague about what went on between herself and her husband but was much clearer about how she performed at work so the focus was primarily on what she could do to improve her professional chances and how she could change her attitudes at work. Throughout there were vague references to transference feelings and how she and Nelson (her husband) were getting along. There was much hostility toward her husband but, "We are glued together." Then all of a sudden she decided that she had to get separated and try for a divorce. *Why* was hard to ascertain and she never gave any reason except to say that her husband is paranoid and a schizophrenic. They were finally divorced, and her work situation improved. She went back to school and began a career as opposed to being a secretary. She was afraid of men. Over a period of ten years she continued to see the therapist.

12/15/60

It's not funny; I was very backward. I had guilt about departing from my family when I got married—I felt guilty about wanting to go. When I went to work, I felt this way too. And I was unsuccessful. It frightens me; I seem to have a purposeful desire to frustrate my own ambitions. My work history is a complete flop. I am horror struck when I think of it.

My mother has three children; my father is one of them and then there are my brother and me. My father was crazy about my brother; he had to have a sweater like my brother's. My brother was a famous basketball player on the college team.

My mother was central in the house, then grandmother; my father was controlled by my mother. Nelson was not a husband to me but a competitor—and he was in competition with my father and brother; I controlled Nelson. He's a strong man, but his mother tells him when he's right and when he's wrong. He says, "She's killing me; I'm dying." My father always pushed me toward my mother; he forced me to get from her what a child would want from both a father and a mother. She represented a haven to me. I hated her, but I could depend on her. It seems to me that this is important in my relationship with men; my role with men is some kind of a caricature. I've felt threatened by the idea that I could be hostile to my mother. I've been very much like my mother in my behavior with men. And my mother taught me "Thou shalt not compete with me successfully." I'm in a state of semihysteria while I'm talking. My father was not a father. I felt that he forced my brother and me into a hostility with my mother, pitting her against us. He showed his hatred for my brother by forcing him into an altercation with mother—mother was extremely hostile to my brother.

I felt very threatened when I thought of my mother being hostile—I mean now—not as a child. I must have been threatened, but then I did not even think of such a thing—she was so hostile, so competitive with me. It still is hard for me to say that my mother did not want me to be happy. I feel detached from that idea. My mother had a terrible fight with my grandmother. One of the things that my grandmother said was that she was going to rip the mask off my mother's face—to reveal her as the mean person that she is. That was my father's mother.

It must be that other people get threatened when they have to realize certain things about their parents. It's a woman-centered world, emotionally—what does that mean exactly? The universe centers around the strong mother figure. If you look back at the drawings I made when I first came into therapy you'd probably find that the woman figure is bigger than the man figure. I can't help but feel that this thing has a lot to do with my not remarrying yet—my father's role in the family.

I asked her to do another drawing. She said she would. She has had three disastrous relationships with men—each man being "very odd" (neurotic) and the last man was definitely psychotic. She feels hopeless about finding someone and says she would like to go to a match-making organization. I tell her that I think she should be able to find a man on her own. She says she would rather go to a dating bureau where they serve people who are serious about marriage and where they do tests to determine who would be good for whom. She says that she heard me talk about such a service. I give her the information. She goes to the service and within three months she tells me she has found a man, a worthy man and one she can respect, one with whom she hopes to establish a good relationship. It is at this point that her analysis takes on a form of dealing with her problems in a direct fashion. It was not until seven years later (1967) that we saw changes in the patient's behavior. During that period she had "gone with" the man she met at the dating bureau for about three years. They had some difficulties making an adjustment, but both were determined to "make a go of it"—they did marry about four years after they met. Three years after the marriage, Harriet was still in treatment, but her man and woman drawings had changed (see Figure 3).

FIG. 3. Man and woman drawing. Harriet Hamburger, 1967. (See text.)

Breakup of an Idealization Fantasy

We cannot tell how long it will take a given patient to work through the idealizing and denigrating transferences, which in my opinion are related to the patient's deepest neurotic feelings. Sonia Gerber is only recently beginning to do so after thirty-two years of dealing with several therapists, twenty-two years with me. Her first treatment began in 1948. She is one of those patients who tended toward the psychotic edge of the continuum. She is one of the few patients I ever had who never married after a divorce in early life, although she has had many "affairs." She has had an ever present "hate figure" in her sister. This problem of hating some people and idealizing others that we find in the borderline patient has great significance in treatment. It is the essence of the sadomasochistic transference, and it takes many years to work through. This is the phenomenon that has been attributed to "splitting" or to the "breaking up of the object," or the inability to see "good" and "bad" in the same person, or "the inability to perceive the object as he really is," and so forth. I see this as transference, as an aspect of the patient's defensive system and as a hysterical mechanism with obsessional overlays. The aim of these hysterical or denial mechanisms, and the obsessional elements, has to do with a *denial of the identifications* and what these mean to the patient (Wolberg, A., 1973 pp. 165-166, 173-174), a denial of the destructiveness (of both the patient and the parent) and the rejecting attitudes of the parents; and the patient's fear of annihilation as a consequence of parental destructiveness. More importantly, it is a denial that the patient now, as a consequence of the identifications, is like the parents in certain ways. Such patterns must be outlined, delineated, and eliminated in treatment.

As we have said, the patient's aggression is actually a counteraggression, a defense aroused by the frustration at the hands of the parents. It is frightening to the patient, and he defends by distributing his aggression among several objects, i.e., by projecting on to these objects and being hostile to these objects, sometimes in subtle ways. These objects are substitutes for the parents. If the patient has relations with the parents the interpersonal encounters are always sadomasochistic. Actually, these dynamics are aspects of the global defense of projective identification, which is partly a defense against aggression and partly a defense against the impulses toward autonomous constructive behavior that the patient has been taught to inhibit.

We have noted that the patient experiences feelings of disgust with himself for succumbing to the identifications and fears that the therapist and others will feel the same; and often others do have this attitude toward the patient. As these feelings of the patient are given expression in various forms, the therapist should recognize them and interpret their meaning. With the therapist's help the patient gradually works through his identification conflict while simultaneously strengthening his autonomy. This allows him to shed his sadomasochistic self-demeaning pattern, which takes many forms and has to be pointed out and worked through step by step, or piece by piece, over and over again until the whole pattern is clear. If one is attempting to help the patient toward any kind of personality change, this process can take many years in view of the denials and the projective aspects of the defensive system. Projective identification is a most complicated defense, and to work it through is a difficult task.

In working through the transference where projective identification is present, one finds that the most highly defended area is the identification with the most rejecting parent (IMRP). After Sonia had had a straightforward transference reaction to me that she could verbalize (this occurred, to be exact, on August 20, 1979, when she declared that I am "cold, ungiving, detached"), she talked of her father for the first time in a different way. She told of holding her father's penis—and she spoke of this as if it were unusual but in ordinary tones rather than with shame or excitement. She described a series of sexual incidents with her father. It was only after this that she was able to break up her idealization defense. She began to tell me the story of her sojourn with her parents when she was 9 years old to the southern part of Russia where her father had gone to work. She spoke casually and mentioned that she told it to me many times before, which was not true.

In the therapeutic process we are confronted with the transference that is opposed to a realistic image of the therapist. In working through the transference we are dealing with the conflict of opposites; the neuroses or psychoses of the parents versus the well-being or the autonomy and creativeness of the child. In the neurosis (or the psychoses) we have the bipolar "identification with the aggressor," i.e., the internalization of the identification roles versus the self-preservation impulses of the individual, the need for "safe" neurotic adjustment versus the autonomous behavior. The defense of projective identification has supportive defenses of denial, repression, and idealization. The opposite—anger, rage, revenge, and grandiosity—are the elements that create the conflict that intrapsychically then is presented in the dual object representations, i.e., the fantasies. The projections and denials and the idealizations (the remaking of reality) account for the paranoid trend or the delusional material. We may symbolize the dual self- and object representations in the fantasies by the following—DSRs and DORs. We must remember, however, that the fantasies are not actual memories; rather they are "psychical outworks constructed in order to bar the way to memories," and "symptoms and fantasies like dreams have a similar mental construction" (Freud, S.E., 1887-1902 [1954], p. 197). D = denial; S = self; O = object.

All of my borderline patients, when they began to work through the last phase of analysis, ushered in the period with talks of (1) *some kind of perversion*, often several kinds, (2) *paranoid reactions* (in the last stages of working through transference the patient mentions his own identifications with the paranoid attitudes of another person and then of his parents), (3) *lifelessness*, (4) *guilt*, (5) *masochism*, and finally (6) *sadism* and *hostility*. The latter are the last matters to discuss from the point of view of losing such feelings and working them through. When Harriet Hamburger came into treatment, for example, she alluded in the first two sessions (in guarded and defended tones) to a possible kind of sexual perversion. What if we were to discover that she was some kind of pervert? What would I think of her? She would be terribly ashamed. There were vague allusions to people like Catherine the Great who used animals for sexual stimulation. Harriet's depression was depicted in the dream of two caskets, and her "ineptness" and "dependency" were evident in dreams of needing support due to an inability to stand on her legs without help. She also had dreams of being attached to women and wanting to be rid of her husband. She acted out by calling me after sessions to see if I were all right. When she began to work this through twenty years later, she spoke of her peculiarities at work, her suspiciousness of her fellow workers, her paranoid traits, her anger, and her envy. She likened this to her father's activities with his partners at work.

Sonia who is now working through the last stages of analysis, after having had a direct transference relation to me, says she feels she has been "sick since she was 9—really all my life." She describes herself as being depressed.

Th.   You weren't born "sick."
Pt.   I guess not—no—I wasn't but I got that way very early in life. I seemed to be happy until my cousin came to live with us—she ruined my life.
Th.   Not your parents!
Pt.   Well—no—*she* did! She squelched me; she prevented the other children from playing with me. She said she was ashamed to walk with me on the street.

Sonia mentions that she recently met her cousin, and the cousin recalled how hostile she was to Sonia when they were children. She does not know how Sonia could have stood it. [*The direct transference reaction, which was a father transference, makes me think that the father was the most rejecting parent and that the memories of the cousin, although the experiences with the cousin were real, are being used as cover memories, defenses, to protect her from her feelings about her father.*]

Pt.   She said I was jumping around too much.
Th.   How so?
Pt.   I was full of life and excitement. I'd go along the street jumping and skipping—happy—she didn't like that. I was interested in things; I'd stop to look at flowers—I'd sing. I was very good in school too. My cousin was no intellectual—I was.

She talks of a dream she had. She dreamt of a married couple she knew, emigrees from Russia. They are very paranoid, cannot get along with anybody. She speaks of their hostilities, their odd ways—their detachment. She [*identifying with them*] says she has been like that—no trust in anyone. She talks of her father who was sick and isolated. He had an attack, his first, one year after he came here. People had helped him get a job, but he couldn't work—he was too sick—physically—she and her mother had to work. [*She identified with her father*] "I have reproduced his symptoms, his attitudes. I have stopped working, given up, became depressed, especially since mother died. But before, when my original symptoms occurred, the phobia I did the same." She talks of her refusal of life. She speaks of the refugee girl who is getting married [*the refugee from Russia*], the one for whom the engagement party was given. The girl will marry, but she does not love the man. She wants security and money. She [*the girl*] acts a role. Her life is a role or several roles; she is an actress, a doll. She lives through her fantasy life—the beautiful doll, ethereal—an idyllic fantasy. The girl will be very unhappy. She [*Harriet*] says that she realizes she is talking about herself—not the same kind of fantasies but someone who lived in a dream world, a fantasy world.

[*I say that her realities were most difficult.*] She did have the feeling that her father was jealous of her; he was a frustrated and disappointed man and although he was proud of her, he resented that she was successful so that she had to feel guilty about her own success. [*This is a theme that I introduced several years ago and one that the patient rejected for a long time. She accepted this idea only reluctantly but finally gave it some credence. I had pieced together this concept from some of the dreams and associations.*] She notes that she can be very jealous, but she always has insight into her reactions. Her father was going to write his autobiography, she said, and he worked on it for several months. Then when she went to work for the WPA, her father "gave up his writing due to his great humiliation of his daughter being on relief." [*Sonia insists that her father told her that his humiliation over her work was the cause of his giving up writing.*] She estimates that her father was ill from the time they were in Latvia until he died. She was 13 years old when he became ill (1922) and he died in 1946; she is now 70 years of age (1979). She began with her phobia when she was working on WPA and her father had his first "stroke" one year later.

Sonia often said that her symptoms are similar to her father's. She has no physical symptoms as he was supposed to have had but has hypochondriacal ideas, and whenever she does have a physical problem, a cold, a virus infection, or something else, she becomes extremely preoccupied with herself, fearing death, and so on. Often I find that hypochondriacal symptoms are associated with perverse feelings that derive from physical contacts with parents or from parents using parts of the child's body as an object for *gazing* in the interest of using that part as a sexual object. The gazing is associated with a sexual fantasy. If this were acted out in a different way, it might be in the nature of a fetish.

About five months before Sonia had her first direct transference reaction with me (August 1979), she had told me that although she feels suicidal each day she does not really want to commit suicide. I told her that I realize she does not want to, and that my feeling was that she is so guilty about her success that she cannot yet allow herself to enjoy it. I felt it had something to do with her unresolved feelings about her father. Apparently on a subconscious level she took this interpretation seriously and spent the last part of the year talking about her father. It was on September 4, 1979, that she told me of the dreams about the paranoid couple (Russian refugees). In that same session she spoke of her father and mother and herself being in the southern part of Russia:

"Where father had gone to work—there was no work for him at home." It was there that she had her "sexual experiences with her father." Saturday night was "my night with father"; it was then that she slept with father, and mother went to another bed. She would lie awake waiting for him to come to bed. She would scream: "Come to bed father!" When he would finally get into bed, she would hold his penis.

It was apparent that she was telling me of her denigration by her father. He did not look up on her as a child but something to be used. When she was much older, he blamed her for his unfinished opus—just as she blamed her sister and her cousin for her problems rather than her parents. It is true that the sister and her cousin did the things of which she accused them—the cousin told me so.

Whether Sonia's story of sleeping with her father is true, I do not know. When she told me the story, she asserted that she had mentioned the episodes many   times before. Her "affect" was detached and "amused." After she finished telling of the experiences, which lasted over a period of nine months, she then came back to the "emigrees," discussing their problems and particularly their various neuroticisms, including the paranoia of the couple in her dream. No one would ever be able to satisfy them, she said, and she realized they had inordinate amounts of hostility. She then said she felt less hostile herself toward the bourgeois attitudes of the people who were at the engagement reception she attended. Toward the end of this session, she said she felt like crying; it was like "burying them." I said a few words about how people often feel sad when "working through" their problems.

The next week Sonia came to the session full of rage concerning the matter of an artist who had lost some material belonging to Sonia. As she finished talking of the artist she said, for the first time, "My anger was all out of proportion to what the matter required. I realize I've had these kinds of reactions a good part of my life. I don't know why I'm so hostile." She had mentioned her anger previously in the sessions when she had told me about her lessened feelings of anger toward the bourgoisie and their petty competitiveness, their grasping ways, their use of others, their manipulations, and so on. She said she was indeed describing the emigrees as well as the bourgoisie in America. I had suspected for some time that her attachment to these people had more to do with her identification with her father than for any love of the emigrees as a group. She has been very angry at the Russian government. Now she admits that there are emigrees that she does not like—some rather famous, but others she is very fond of. She admires their abilities, their brains, their guts, and so forth. It occured to me as she talked that she has "identified" with several psychotic persons: paranoid people, schizophrenic people, and manic-depressives who cannot seem to get better no matter what kind of treatment they receive—people who have no motivation to be "well" or to be rid of their symptoms. Does this mean that her parents were very ill emotionally and did not wish to be well? Or does this mean that she has no motivation? I feel she does have motivation since she was able to have the direct transference feeling toward me and since she has admitted her identification with the persons in her dreams. She can now say "I am like that," and "I was like that," and she can say, "I am hostile but I do not know why." "People don't like me," she said, and then she says that people do like her. She is working through her feelings. One might say, however, in relation to her emotional problems, that she is working through her "identifications." We would mean by this, identification with the aggressors.

Acting Out

A basic defense in emotional problems, as has been noted, is the identification with the neurotic aspects of the parental figures, an identification that is forced on the child by the parents' use of the child over time as a projective object and the parents' denials of this defense stance. An interlocking defensive pattern gradually evolves, and then the child, as adult, begins to look for a similar social situation as that in his family so that he can perpetuate his defenses, these being felt as life saving. The defenses are accompanied by mental representation of the situations and of the conflicts that have arisen due to the anxiety created by the situations. The mental representations are subject to the kind of modification that Freud found in his analysis of dreams and his discovery that dreams and fantasies have similar dynamics, i.e., dissociation, distortions, repressions, denials, and so on.

A recent paper by MacHovec (1980) is of particular interest in respect to symptoms which can be seen to be social or family situations: "Hypnotic Recall in Psychogenic Fugue States: Two Cases." The dynamics have some similarity to borderline states. The paper illustrates, to me, the difference between the manifest and latent content of fantasies and dreams and the importance of getting the patient's associations to his dreams so as to understand what it is in the present that is similar to what was in the past. The paper also underlines the dynamics of *acting out* in relation to *guilt and the inhibitions* that were set up in the past, with respect to criticism of an authority figure, and the consequent "splitting" or dissociation (I prefer to think of this dissociation as a form of *denial*) as a consequence of guilt with the need to act out the aggression that was held in check by *repression*. The experience of expressing the aggression by acting out had to take place in order for the individual to survive mentally. The borderline patient's acting out patterns, however, are not as dangerous as these patients described by MacHovec.

The pioneering work of L.R. Wolberg (1952, 1980) in hypnosis demonstrated beyond any doubt that repression is a factor in acting out and in symptomatology and that inhibition had to be present before acting out would take place. This is contrary to the ideas of theorists whom I have mentioned who describe the dynamics of borderline patients.

In the borderline patient inhibitions precede acting out. The inhibitions are definitely a function of the repressions that are related to the thoughts and feelings directed at authority figures who are feared and hated and to whom the child over time has been of necessity attached for survival and thus with whom he is identified. There are many varied forms of acting out, some of which are less horrendous than others. Acting out can be a husband's impotency with his wife, or it can be a child setting fire to the family's apartment. It can be lying, or misleading, or an act of murder or suicidal behavior. In all cases it is an expression of aggression in the face of inhibitions related to direct confrontation of the figure who, for one reason or another, represents authority. Thus acting out is transferential behavior in a particular form. Acting out is also related to fantasies, which are disguises and depictions of the relation with parents transposed into the current situation. This does not mean that the current situation is being misunderstood. In MacHovec's illustration, one woman who could not get along with her husband set the house on fire and then went into a fugue state. Later when she discovered her inhibitions and began to understand her symbolic behavior, she decided to get a divorce because her husband is, in fact, impossible to live with. Her neurosis was such that she could not handle the matter directly so had to show her aggression in this nonverbal acting-out way in order to bring matters to a head. In the meantime she could have destroyed herself since she remained in the burning building in a fugue state. L.R. Wolberg (1952) did the pioneer work that demonstrated the relation of current symptoms and inhibitions to current situations and the past, although the patients he worked with did not resort to such violent behavior as the woman cited in MacHovec's paper. Borderline patients do not have fetishes, nor do they develop fugue states, but they can utilize dissociative mechanisms, and denial is ever present. Acting out usually follows a feeling of having been demeaned.

An Outline of the Treatment Process

In the following scheme I have attemped to outline the treatment process in the borderline patient. I conceive of the process as having four main stages, in line with the general treatment scheme of psychotherapy outlined by L.R. Wolberg (1977). An adaptation of Wolberg's treatment scheme to the dynamics of the borderline patient includes what I have called "projective treatment" techniques for handling the projective references of the patient in the first phase of treatment, remembering that in utilizing the "other"one is at the same time outlining the patient's dynamics and the dynamics of the patient's parents with whom the patient is identified. In speaking of the projections of the "other," one would be outlining the "introjected and projected" objects (the identifications).

My ideas of borderline patients and their treatment are based on intensive study of thirty-three individuals. I have observed in them similarities and dissimilarities in the defenses in their dynamics. These patients are given fictitious names in the list below for purposes of identification in the text.

33 Borderline Patients and Their Time in Treatment

1.	Charles Bander,	6 yrs.	18.	Harold Hemple,	6 yrs.
2.	Gertrude Belan,	25 yrs.	19.	Harriet Hamburger,	22 yrs.
3.	Maurice Belk,	4 yrs.	20.	Flora O'Toole Levy,	5 yrs.
4.	Jack Bennett,	3 yrs.	21.	Seibert O. Lachstein,	3 yrs.
5.	Doris Berman,	6 yrs.	22.	Abby Newbold,	3 yrs.
6.	Kurt Blau,	10 yrs.	23.	Elizabeth Osgood,	5 yrs.
7.	Thelma Blocker,	1 yr.	24.	Gladys Bernstein Populus,	2 mos.
8.	Mabel Claire,	7 yrs.	25.	George Frank Quinn,	7 yrs.
9.	Authur Cohen,	6 yrs.	26.	Steven Roberts,	3 mos.
10.	Seymour Daird,	7 yrs.	27.	Henry Roberts,	2 mos.
11.	Polly Freiberg,	6 yrs.	28.	Marcia Salopolas,	10 yrs.
12.	James Fuchs,	7 yrs.	29.	Gloria Steinblatt,	7 yrs.
13.	Sonia Gerber,	22 yrs.	30.	James Weber,	7 yrs.
14.	Geraldine Girard,	6 yrs.	31.	Louise Woll,	7 yrs.
15.	Ellen Fitzgerald Gloss,	4 yrs.	32.	Kenneth Wolcott,	8 yrs.
16.	Cora Schultz Jonathan,	3 mos.	33.	Lisa Zane,	6 yrs.
17.	Frances Krasmire,	4 yrs.			

Brief Therapy (up to 6 or 7 sessions)

Gladys Bernstein Populus   Henry Roberts
Steven Roberts   Cora Schultz Jonathan

Brief Therapy (1 time weekly for 2 years-42 sessions a year)

Ellen Fitzgerald Gloss   Frances Krasmire

Combined Group and Individual Therapy

Charles Bander	Thelma Blocker	Seibert O. Lachstein
Maurice Belk	Mabel Claire	Elizabeth Osgood
Jack Bennett	James Fuchs	George Frank Quinn
Kurt Blau	Sonia Gerber	Marcia Salopolas
Arthur Cohen	Geraldine Girard	James Weber
Seymour Daird	Ellen Fitzgerald Gloss	Louise Woll
Polly Freiberg	Harriet Hamburger	Kenneth Wolcott
Doris Berman	Harold Hemple	Lisa Zane

Individual Therapy

Gertrude Belan	Flora O'Toole Levy	Abby Newbold

Steven and Henry Roberts were seen for only a few sessions, and were then referred to another therapist. Henry did well, but Steven dropped out of treatment.

Twenty of the thirty-three patients I have seen through to an adequate adjustment although they still have some problems:

Charles Bander	Elizabeth Osgood	George Frank Quinn
Polly Freiberg	Gloria Steinblatt	Louise Woll
Harold Hemple	Seymour Daird	Mabel Claire
James Fuchs	Kurt Blau*	Kenneth Wolcott
Sonia Gerber*	Lisa Zane	Frances Krasmire
Marcia Salopolas	James Weber	Arthur Cohen
		Thelma Blocker

*Still in treatment with the author

Some of the problems that these patients have are related to unresolved transference manifestations. In my opinion these transferences concern the relations with the most rejecting parent, and that this phenomenon has a relationship on the sexual level with those patients' perverse traits. For example, the sexual difficulties of Elizabeth Osgood, Harriet Hamburger, and James Fuchs all are related to fears of the opposite sex and their hostility and disgust in intimacies with them.

James Fuchs after seven years of treatment asked to be referred to his wife's therapist for family treatment. He did this at the request of this therapist. Elizabeth Osgood at the end of five years married and left New York with her husband, a member of the psychological profession. He found her a therapist in the state where they went to live. She made an excellent vocational adjustment but has not worked through her problem with men. Her sexual problem persisted in her marriage. A year after her wedding she "visited" with me and told me, in a somewhat gleeful tone, in a kind of competitive hostile way, that her husband was having trouble with erections. Happily, she stated that she is not the only one with a sexual problem.

Kenneth Wolcott improved in his work adjustment and in his family life with wife and children. He felt, however, that his *feelings* were stuck, *deadened* and he tried going to marathons and EST. I did not discourage these moves, and he did report some help in respect to his detachment which I felt was associated with an underlying depression from which he was never quite relieved while with me. Arthur Cohen was addicted to amphetamines and food. He was a brilliant man who used to spoil his chances by always being late with reports thus frustrating those who were waiting. He reduced this pattern considerably and began to tackle the food problem, then when his depression began to lessen, he was able to lower the intake of his pills.

It is interesting that the most detached of the borderlines received no real help from being in the group. The group members made no impact upon the detachment and deep withdrawal mechanisms. All of these patients had a social facade and were polite, never revealing their deep hostility although this was evident in their reports of dreams. Arthur Cohen, Jack Bennett, Geraldine Girard, Seibert O. Lachstein, Kenneth Wolcott were all such highly defended patients.

Marcia Salopolas is still in treatment with another therapist and doing well. She has an excellent work record but is functioning in jobs below her capacity. She looks for adequate work but has not found it yet.

Frances Krasmire was an addictive personality (food) who did not finish analysis and left owing me $1,000. Her husband, a dentist, did not want her in treatment and refused to pay her bill. She said he would not "yield an inch." She gained a great deal of insight into the dynamics of her food addiction, realized she had married a rigid paranoidlike person whom she felt had many of the traits of her father and mother (both of whom I had seen in treatment). The father was excessively controlling and "paranoid," using both his wife and his children as projective objects to hold himself together. He isolated himself from his wife by excessive working, but had a tight relationship with her. When he relaxed, he always remained with her for social life, and at home he would stay in her presence, harping at her as she was working around the house. His wife acquiesced in all that he wanted but fought and argued with him over every issue. She was addicted to overeating as was Frances. In therapy Frances worked on her family relationship with her son and to a degree with her husband. She finally paid part of her bill.

Geraldine Girard, a singer, of whom I wrote in my 1973 book (p. 237), never resolved her problems. She always went to the best doctors and

managed to pay them nothing. It is true that she had very little income and
was in no position to go to private practitioners. She "wanted the best,"
however, and I was one of her psychiatric helpers who saw her for no fee.
She left treatment highly insulted when I began to tackle her habit of going
to doctors and never paying. I suggested that she should attend a clinic or go
to the welfare department and make an application for funds. She was a
refugee from Germany, and finally when she received some recompense
money from that country, she gave me a token amount. Eventually she got a
job in her field (with a show) and was earning about $150.00 a week. She had
to leave town with the show; I heard from her indirectly on two occassions,
and after that—silence. She sent messages through group members indicating that she left with a "bad taste in her mouth" and great disappointment in me. I had been the "grand perfect" person until I asked her to consider why she would not go to a free clinic for her medical services if she
could not afford the specialists whom she sought out.

Cora Schultz Jonathan was in treatment a few months only. She thought
she felt better and said she was getting along well. Therefore, she left. I have
heard about her only indirectly from another patient who had referred her.

These patients have been loosely grouped according to Grinker's four
classifications, but since they are "mixed" rather than pure types, it is difficult to place them in either III or IV. Categories I and II seem much more
definitive. Thus I have classified the twenty in only categories I, II, and III.

Category I

*Inappropriate and nonadaptive behavior; deficient sense of self-identity and sense of reality;
negative behavior and anger toward other human beings*

Kurt Blau	Ellen Fitzgerald Gloss	Jerold Howe
James Fuchs	Gertrude Belan	Lydia Ransom
Mabel Claire	Doris H. Berman	Seibert O. Lachstein
Geraldine Girard	Steven Roberts	Flora O'Toole Levy
George Frank Quinn	Henry Roberts	Jack Bennett
Abby Newbold	Marcia Salopolas	

Category II

*Vascillating involvement with others; overt or acted-out expressions of anger; depression;
observing of indications of commitment of self-identity.*

Charles Bander	Arthur Cohen	Lisa Zane
Harold Hemple	Seymour Daird	Louise Woll
Gloria Steinblatt	Maurice Belk	Kenneth Wolcott
Polly Freiberg	Gladys Bernstein Populus	Cora Schultz Jonathan

Category III

Defenses of withdrawal; little affect or spontaneity in response to social situations; intellectualization; adaptive and appropriate behavior and complimentary relationships.

Francis Krasmire   Sonia Gerber
Elizabeth Osgood   Harriet Hamburger

In other chapters a number of sessions with some of these patients have been referred to. They illustrated certain kinds of problems and resistances that occur in the treatment process. The session with Maurice Belk exemplifies projective techniques. The sessions with James Weber in Chapter 11 are related to acting out and transference attitudes. These sessions also demonstrate other kinds of resistances, such as the use of idealization and both secretive and open hostility. The hostility includes pitting past and present therapists against each other and attempting to stimulate the competitiveness of the therapist by suggesting that one therapist believes the other to be inadequate; in this particular case the group therapist, James said, was casting aspersions on my adequacy. James was trying to get me to be angry with the other therapist rather than concentrating on his problems. Some interviews are examples of working through and other aspects of the therapeutic process.

Working through the transference with a borderline patient is a long and tedious journey. It begins, as we have said, by interpreting the interactions between the patient and others in the interpersonal relationship—the patient's interlocking projective defense. Later it focuses on the patient's attempt to involve the therapist in a sadomasochistic pattern. This usually begins in an acting-out pattern right at the start, such as Harriet's calling me twenty minutes after the session to see if I were all right. After the interlocking defensive relationship is understood, we then move to the patient's reactions to me. One is impatient with me. Another feels that I am slipshod; I don't notice things. These are projections of some of the patients' own traits that are identical with the traits of their parents. It was apparent that the patients had to tolerate these traits in the parent and to act as if they did not notice them. These are undesired traits related to each patient's identification system that have to be analyzed and eradicated. The beginning of this process is illustrated in Chapter 11 in my interview with Seymour Daird and in the interview with Louise Woll.

The final phase of working through the transference is a direct projection on the part of the patient toward me similar to what went on between Sonia and myself when she accused me of being cold and detached—two traits that she knew very well and later admitted that I do not possess. From this direct encounter, Sonia had dreams. In her associations to the dream she recognized her identifications, first with the individuals in the dreams and then with her father—the parent who had rejected her most but whom she was zealously defending, projecting his (and her own) coldness onto me (see p. 257). While it took many more months to work through her thoughts and feelings, this was the final step in her analysis. It is true that borderline patients are difficult to treat and that countertransference problems often make it necessary to transfer the patient to another therapist, but if we persist with those who stay with us, we can work through the transference and resolve the basic problem.

The following outline indicates a schematized way of looking at the four phases of treatment with the borderline patient.

The Four-Part Treatment Process

Phase I

Objectives (Establish a Working Therapeutic Relationship)

1. Let the patient know under what circumstances he can be helped.
2. Show him that he is understood (reference to his positive values and some of his inhibiting patterns).
3. Show him he will not be ridiculed—not by talking about it, but by having a respectful attitude toward the patient as a human being who deserves consideration.
4. Decide with him where to begin. What area of the problem can be dealt with first?
5. Define a tentative goal. This must be done in the context of the particular patient's defensive system. The goal must relate to the total problem, but one selects a partial goal having relevance to the total problem, that can be attained within several months period.
6. Clarify misconceptions about treatment.
7. Orient the patient to an understanding of the treatment process.
8. Create an understanding on the part of the patient that neurotic mechanisms can be "set off" by anxiety and that they are not "in operation" all of the time, only in certain kinds of situations.

Therapeutic Tasks

1. Draw attention to mechanisms of defense—detachment, withdrawal, the dynamics of masochism, "acting out," hysterical mechanisms—by using the frame of reference of the "other" in the interpersonal relationship so as not to create anxiety-provoking confrontations that increase anxiety and help to perpetuate the patient's patterns.
2. Help the patient to understand that defensive behavior operates in the interpersonal relationship.
3. Help the patient to identify the destructive (sadomasochistic) aspects of "acting-out" behavior, particularly masochism (self-destructive behavior). Leave interpretation of sadistic behavior until later phases but not denying this if patient

brings it up—merely accepting it as a possibility. (Do not use words like "destructive"; merely outline the behavior.)

4. Emphasize that "acting-out" behavior occurs in relation to *anxiety stimulated by repressed feelings, thoughts, or fantasies* that arise in interpersonal encounters.

5. Emphasize that neurotic symptoms such as somatizations (conversions), headaches, bodily sensations, numbness, or feelings of extreme tension occur as a consequence of thoughts, feelings and fantasies that have been stimulated in interpersonal relationships but which have been denied and repressed. (Use the "other" at first in this kind of interpretation.) It is assumed that thorough physical examinations have established the fact that there is no real physical reason for the symptoms.

6. Show that there is a relationship between "acting-out" behavior and behavior of the parents who stimulated the behavior originally. (Use the "other" for this kind of interpretation at first. The "other" being the parent. Point out the behavior of both parents and others who are in parental roles.)

7. *Point out denial mechanisms* of parents and others with whom the patient has been in a relationship; also, their angers, their hostilities, and their "good" points, if they have them.

8. Delineate the frustration-aggression motif. (This is a sadomasochistic mechanism based upon an adaptation stimulated by the parents' use of the children as "scapegoats." To relieve their own neurotic anxiety, the parents force the children to act out certain "roles" that complement the neurotic needs of the parent. Inhibition of certain normal impulses in the child must be put into operation in order for the child to act out the neurotic roles. Stress the fact of inhibition of normal impulses first and wonder about this, finally exploring the dynamics. The sexual side of this problem reveals itself in thinly disguised perverse activities of the parent with the child. Sometimes these blended with rearing techniques and were rationalized as important for the child.)

9. Explore the development of neurotic and/or psychotic behavior patterns and discuss the inhibition-guilt-aggression constellation. Take as much history as possible in the first two sessions and then wait for the rest to unfold.

10. Handle the anxiety and the defenses of the patient when the therapist does not accommodate himself to the sadomasochistic scheme of relationship. (Use "others" as illustration first so that the patient will see that not conforming to the "other" creates anxiety in the patient and in the "other" as well. Delineate the anxiety behavior of the "other.")

11. Take notice of the normally assertive creative behavior of the patient even when it is expressed in the minutest form.

12. Take notice of the patient's efforts to involve the therapist in his sadomasochistic pattern and point out that this would be defeating the therapeutic process.

Technical Processes

1. Encourage the verbalization of anxieties about feelings, fears, hopes, rages, jealousies, and revenge feelings in order to undermine acting out, somatization, and other hysterical symptoms.

2. Encourage verbalization of feelings about therapy and talking of "fears" or "hopes" or "feelings of disappointment" insofar as they are related to fantasied ends.

3. Interpret all information not by confrontation but by *accenting certain aspects of the patient's verbalizations* and through the use of *projective therapeutic techniques:*
    (a) Explore by *accenting certain verbalizations* after asking questions aimed at

pointing out patterns in the interpersonal relationship; exploring the feelings and motivations of the "other" person in the relationship in order to point out the neurotic patterns or the character patterns of the defenses of the "other" person.

(b) Let the patient draw inferences: "I do this too." The therapist should not confront the patient with defensive behavior that he is vehemently denying—merely emphasize by repeating the words of the patient. The patient can then deny or accept the ideas as he identifies with the "other."

(c) Explore fears of acting out. Show the behavior to be complementary to the "other" person in the relationship.

(d) Accept the projection of feelings onto the therapist, and explore the nature of the projected feelings by asking what the patient thinks, what the therapist feels and why (usually these projections are related to guilt and anger). What will the therapist do? (Transference projection.)

(e) Use dreams to underline, accept, and explore *interpersonal encounters* and to delineate incidents of the day that caused anxiety; also to explore neurotic patterns in interpersonal relationships, first the "other" person or persons in the relationship and later the patient—if he can tolerate this.

(f) Use "attitude therapy" to make the connection between *feelings* and *defenses* (attitude therapy is worked in the context of the interpersonal relationship). This can be used first as a projective therapeutic technique; i.e., using the "other," then transferring to the patient when he accepts the basic propositions inherent in the dynamic interpretation. Explore attitudes and feelings of "others" and how these affect their behavior.

4. Provide for the administration of drugs when anxiety is too intense. (The drugs help repress the paranoid mechanisms and the elation and depressive mechanisms that interfere with the interpersonal relationship.)

5. Push certain therapeutic goals into the future, recognizing that, at present, they would cause too much anxiety.

6. Consider using hypnotherapy as a technique in the first and second phases of treatment when resistance is great and passivity and "identification" are so pervasive that it is difficult to handle the interpersonal relationship another way. Hypnotherapy employs basically projective techniques.

7. Consider using behavior therapy techniques, either by the therapist or by referring the patient to a behavior therapist who works concurrently with the psychotherapy. Behavior therapy is helpful for phobias, ruminating, inhibitions, etc.

8. Use imagery-evoking and forced fantasy techniques when indicated.

9. Do role rehearsal through verbalization.

Resistances (Defenses)

1. Controlling tendencies, obsessive rumination, compulsive mechanisms, concealing and denying, fabricating, compulsive talking, rapid shifting of defenses.

2. Masochism (guilt, fear, and appeasement).

3. Detachment.

4. Sadism (hostility and aggression).

5. Deluding or "trapping" the therapist into untenable positions. Making the therapist feel guilty.

6. Repressing by "tuning out" the therapist—selective inattention (withdrawal).

7. Secretiveness about neurotic mechanisms.

8. Attempting to throw the therapist into a nontherapeutic role.
9. "Ego shattering" (dissociative and repressive hysterical mechanisms related to guilt, fear, and anger).
10. Acting out.
11. Paranoid feelings or mechanisms.
12. Fantasies that are repressed but activating.
13. Depression.
14. Overactivity.
15. Derealization.
16. Depersonalization.

Phase II

Objectives (Establish a Working Therapeutic Relationship)
1. Identify the neurotic and/or psychotic behavior patterns.
2. Show that (neurotic and/or psychotic) patterns are repetitive and defensive.

Therapeutic Tasks
1. Recognize that anxiety stimulates the neurotic and/or psychotic patterns.
2. Discover what kinds of situations arouse anxiety and discuss the similarities in the various situations.
3. Recognize that fantasies are defensive and are organized by the patient in times of stress and anxiety.
4. Attempt to identify neurotic and/or psychotic behavior as "odd," "inappropriate," "self-defeating."
5. Analyze masochistic behavior: beginning with interpersonal encounters and leading to fantasies.
6. In the beginning emphasize *pieces* and *parts* of defensive behavior by repeating the phrases of the patient that refer to defenses.
7. Do not ask *why* questions—only *what, when, how.*

Technical Processes
1. Use projective therapeutic techniques when anxiety becomes too intense or when the patient has setbacks.
2. Analyze dreams.
3. Point out transference operations by repeating certain phrases of the patient and by asking questions about feelings toward others. Begin transference interpretations in the interpersonal relationship with others; refer to feelings *with others* and the feelings *of others* in interpersonal encounters that relate to transference. Delineate the fantasy associated with the transference feeling. Analyze feelings.

Resistances (Defenses)
1. Attempts to fend off therapist by detachment, attack, or making him feel guilty; i.e., sadomasochistic maneuvers.
2. Depression.
3. Anger.
4. Repressions and other defensive operations, such as dissociation, denial, undoing, appeasement, projection.
   (a) Unwillingness to give up repressive countercharge.

(b) Reluctance to renounce symptoms.

(c) Transference resistance—an effort to evade recollection and a reenactment of sadomasochistic experiences.

(d) The need for punishment arising out of the demands of the transference.

(e) The repetition compulsion: the need to repeat transference behavior.

Phase III

Objectives

1. Pointing to the neurotic responses and analyzing the situations where anxiety sets off neurotic behavior.
2. Pointing up the patient's incentive for change.
3. Supporting the patient's efforts to tolerate the anxiety that drives him back to projective modes of operating.
4. Analysis of the defenses that inhibit the patient's creative and autonomous behavior and tracing the roots of such patterns.

Therapeutic Tasks

1. Dream and fantasy interpretation through free association.
2. In the instance of projection, asking for associations to the behavior of the "others."
3. Moving from projection to the direct behavior of the patient when the material of the session seems to indicate this.
4. Helping the patient to adjust to the peculiarities of others with whom he wishes to live without reacting transferentially to their behavior.
5. Promoting self-esteem, self-actualizing, and guilt-free behavior.
6. Analyzing the transference and indicating its relevance to social adjustment.
7. Handling what has been called the "mourning process," the "separation anxiety," "the loss of object."
8. Begin the analysis of aggression.

Resistances in Patient

1. Resistance to abandoning sadomasochistic objects.
2. Resistance to normality.
3. Resistance to activity through own resources.
4. Resistances to giving up defenses: inhibitions, identifications, denials, guilt, anger, revenge feelings.
5. The dread of loneliness and isolation that occurs before the aggression is analyzed.
6. Continue the analysis of aggression and delineate the relation of aggression to inhibition, sadistic and revenge feelings, depression, apathy, etc.

Phase IV

Objectives

1. Terminating therapy.
2. Promoting patient's autonomous and self-actualizing behavior.

Therapeutic Tasks

1. Leaving decisions up to the patient with no analysis of anxiety but in the expectation that the patient will do this analysis by himself or in the session.
2. Analyzing sadomasochistic behavior when necessary, i.e., when the patient is blocked in self-analysis.

3. Analyzing transference.
4. Analyzing defensive resistance when patient is blocked from doing so.

Resistances in Patient
1. Continuing mourning and depression.
2. Difficulty in working out identification with the most rejecting parent.
3. Anxiety over confronting hostility and sadistic behavior.
4. Hanging onto shreds of guilt.
5. Anxiety over forward moves—fears of assertiveness.
6. Fusion of sadism and assertiveness.

The last two phases of treatment with the borderline patient deal with the transition from the projective defense (the projections and the displacements) to a major emphasis on the *direct transference*. The *depth of the hostility*, the problem of *fear of the transition*, and *the degree of the hurt* the patient feels at having been used and abused and rejected by the parent (parental rejection has a devastating effect upon the individual), these are the last aspects of the treatment that the borderline deals with from the point of view of working through. The patient has gotten to the point (1) where he can tolerate the anxiety of separation from the sadomasochistic object, (2) where he knows he has felt devastated by hurt, (3) where he understands that in the competitive world people injure other people, and (4) where he knows that in his relations with peers and with authority figures he can easily reexperience the hurt and angry and fearful feelings he had with his parents. In the transition period he can talk directly about these matters, but he still reacts in an emotional way to situations that arouse his anxiety. When we reach this point with many patients, the analysis is never finished because the patient feels better and leaves.

From the metapsychological point of view, depending upon one's theory, one could say that the patient has separated himself from the "pathological introjects," or from his "identifications with the aggressors." Or perhaps we might say that the patient's "observing ego" has taken into account the operations of the "pathological internalized object relations" (what I have called the "identification systems"). Some might say that the patient has made up certain "ego deficits" or that the analytic process has created the milieu in which the ego deficits can be made up (the appropriate ego functions have been instituted). Others might say certain developmental defects have been corrected. The patient has overcome his "developmental arrests." He has analyzed and seen how his "pristine or archaic psychic structures" have interfered in his personality structure and have impeded the development of various "ego functions." He has undone the "fixations" that have kept him tied to "early objects." Or one might say that the aspect of his superego that is tied to his id has been separated out, and he is now in control of his impulses. His ego has been formed and strengthened and has developed boundaries so that he has control over his id impulses. The split superego has been repaired. The ego functions have been restored. The splits in ego states have been cured so that he can now see the "good" and "bad" of objects.

Actually, the patient's problem is not entirely worked out before he has dealt with his deepest hurt—that of the rejection by his parents and his feelings about their manipulation of him and their disregard for him as a person in his own right. The patient at this point is "better," however, so that he can live in some kind of semicomfort. He avoids the last piece of therapy that has to do with the analysis of deep fears of annihilation that he has had from early childhood. He has understood (1) his identification with parental figures and (2) the relation of identification to his patterns of acting out; (3) he has been able to control his impulses for acting out in large part; (4) he has readjusted his sexual life to a certain degree, but he still may have the residuals of his sadomasochistic sexual feeling. He cannot rid himself of the lack of feeling during certain periods—the cutting off of feeling at a certain point. *He* may still be afraid of the vagina, or *she* may be able to have orgasm only by manual manipulation, but defense against the ability to feel enjoyment has been broken. The patient is aware of sexual stimulation from some minor perverse activity or thought, and there is no longer the need to hold back the feeling of pleasure. But the patient has made more normal relationships. He wants to be with more normal people; he has given up most of his sadomasochistic peers. Certain depressive elements persist. The inferiority feelings have not been completely dispersed, but the patient finally says in an open way something to the effect that he recognizes himself as a person, a separate person if you will—but more significantly a person different from his parents. He accepts his own identity, but he will still be excitable and easily hurt in intimate relationships.

The man and woman drawings done by Harriet Hamburger show among other things that it took her seventeen years to reach the third phase of treatment (see Figure 3, p. 255). It is in the third phase of treatment that the working through of the transference and its relation to the patient's most rejecting parent begins. For example, Sonia recently said that when she was a child she had three fears: fear of being smothered, fear of leprosy (rotting away of her body), fear of the end of the world. She related this to her subway fear, her phobia that began in her twenties when she was confronted with being feminine. She said that although she had fears of sex, she needed to be married in order to feel like a woman (actually in order to feel like a person). If she were to be a "separate" person she would feel like nobody, like nothing, and she had a dread of loneliness. Sonia tells me she has one face for the world and another face for herself and for me. With herself she is depressed, desperate, nothing, nobody. With me she cries and cries and cries. She expects me to help her with her depression. If I do not, she will have to commit suicide.

Gretchen S reports having similar feelings of nothingness. Gretchen is 35 years of age, and Sonia is now 70. In a session with me in the fall of 1980 Gretchen reported the following:

She must rid herself of her obsession of imagining that there is something between herself and a man when in fact it is "all in her head." She suffers the "tortures of the damned," imagining that she sees the man with other women, that she has done something that drives him away from her, that he will perhaps not look at her "as if she is a woman, as if she were worth something." *[She talks of a feeling similar to Sonia's.]* She must have that image otherwise she is nothing. She remembers a scene with her mother when she was 20 years old when Johnny *[the man to whom she is now married]* wanted her to go to California with him where he had a job. She knew she should get away from her mother, from her family, but she felt that she did not have the strength to do so. However, she forced herself to get ready to go. She was at home in the city, and her family had gone to their cottage in the country for the weekend. It was Sunday, and she was ready to leave. Her family returned, and she told her mother of her decision. Her mother said: "If you go, I will move to Florida and I will never return." She could not leave after her mother said that. She could not conceive of life without her mother. Without her she would be "nothing."

Shortly after that she said the same of Will, the latest man, who she imagined was in love with her. She utilizes this image to keep herself as a person; otherwise she is nothing. All she wants from Will is to recognize that she exists. She does not exist unless he will tell her that he cares for her, values her, thinks she has some sexual charm. She realizes she must have a woman in the picture, a competitor, someone who is preferred over her. She thinks this is a triangle—herself, her father, and her mother. Her mother is preferred; she has sexual charm. Gretchen thinks that the thing that gives her mother preference is that her mother has *feelings*. Gretchen is "dead"—she has no feelings (depression, depersonalization).

She describes her "state" as a person who is numb, no life, no spunk, no feelings except as she can respond to a great figure like Will; this gives her life, but her life in this way is torture. She has had this problem for many years. She experiences this pattern *[idealizing a male figure, imagining he is in love with her, and then watching every move he makes and thinking that his behavior refers to her]*. She cannot live this way. If she cannot resolve this problem, she will have to commit suicide. She thinks of her marriage, but it means nothing to her. *[She has been married for several years to a man who cannot support her.]* Johnny *[her husband]* "has all he can do to keep his own body and soul together." He has nothing to give her. She is the one who has to give to him. If her mother did not give her money, she could not exist. She can work, but when she gets a job, she always begins to focus on some man at work. In the end she is so tortured that she has to leave or she is asked to leave because she is so disturbed. She cannot live this way.

Both Sonia and Gretchen have feelings of being nothing, feelings of being detached, lifeless. When they put on a face, they are merely play acting—it is not real. I tell them that this is real, but so is the other feeling. They are split—Dr. Jeykll and Mr. Hyde. Their feelings of being nothing are what some people refer to as "depersonalization." Without another person who gives them cues so they can live and feel, they are nothing. Others think of this as "separation anxiety" and account for it as if the individual could not separate from the mother. (What Margaret Mahler calls the symbiotic stage; they have no individuation.) It is a denial of their own value and existence and a blotting out of feeling. Probing will reveal that these people have had such feelings since childhood. I have learned that these masochistic fantasies, tortured feelings, have been present in the life of these patients since the age of 4 or 5 and are really various repetitions in a variety of forms of the "beating fantasy." In adulthood these fantasies defend an identification with the most detached and most hostile parent, often the father for girls and the mother for boys. The mothers are hysterical and need the children for protection; they are the foils for the parents' projections.

I have learned also that these patterns are associated with *perverse fantasies*. Gretchen reported having a telephone experience that she insisted was a call by Will but appeared to me to be the call of a pervert, which so many people experience in a big city like New York.

"He called me. You see, he wanted to be in touch with me—but he said nothing. When I said, Hello, he said nothing but I could hear background noises that I recognized. He was playing games." Then she describes one day when Will really talked. "He called and I answered. He said, "Do you love me?" I said, "Yes." He said, "Do you need me?" I said, "Yes." She then spoke of her most recent suicidal attempt when she felt she could not stand the tension of needing him and not having him.[1] She told me that her brother had come to be with her when she made the suicidal attempt [swallowing pills—50 Valium tablets]. He had told her that some men do play games. They are teasers. He said they are "head fuckers." I had not heard this term. She said it was in popular use in the 1960s with the younger generation. "Head fucking" was sexual fantasy and secret communication among men and women but never coming across physically. Will was a man who played games—a "head fucker." She thought of her father [but did not elaborate. Her father was, so far as I can make out, a peculiar fellow]. She describes him as detached and zombielike. She tells of sitting on his lap even when she was in her twenties and of her mother saying she is too old for that. The father liked it, she said.

---

[1]She was seeing another therapist at the time, a man, but was disillusioned with him and had sought me out to renew our relationship. I suggested that I could see her until she could apply at the clinic, and if she wanted to see me when I was in town, even if she were seeing someone else, she could call me.

She had told me earlier that her father could not verbalize well. She often became irritated with him. She could not imagine that her father and mother could have sex and enjoy it because of the way her father acted, but her mother said they had a good sex life. Gretchen herself was always sexually "mixed up." She was very disturbed in adolescence—wore old clothes, unfeminine clothes. Her mother shopped for her and bought her unfeminine clothes. When she would shop for herself and get feminine clothes, her mother would protest and say the clothes were too frivolous. When her father bought her something, it was usually a boy's shirt. She related how she used to sit on her father's lap with her boy's clothes. She was always overweight—as much as fifty pounds at times. She would lose weight but then would gain it all back. Gretchen is a very tall girl (six feet), and when she was overweight, she did look awkward and huge. During the past year, she had lost over seventy-five pounds.

She did it for Will. She wanted him to see her as feminine. She had such loving feelings for Will. She never experienced such loving feelings. She could never have lost all that weight if she had not found the strength in her love for Will, it kept her alive. She needed him just to survive.

I mentioned that she has used these words about her mother, and I talked about transference. She was confused, stating, "I thought of my father because Will is a man, not my mother." I told her that both kinds of transference could be operating. I talked of the secret communications between herself and Will and his shying away from real sexual contact. She replied, "But I sat on my father's lap." (Gretchen had, many years before, told me of some sexual experiences she had with a married man whom she idealized, who wanted only to have her expose her bare back and backsides to him while he gazed at her. He was an artist. She gave me the impression that he used her as a masturbatory object and she let herself be used because she "wanted to be close to a man.")

Gretchen was very interested in transference and said that this is probably the key to her problem. She spoke of the problem in realistic terms whereas minutes before she had been speaking as if her fantasies were real and actual interpersonal experiences. It is my thought that she did have "secret communications" with her father and that there was a "nonverbal sexual equivalent going on between them." She would say that her father could be in a room with her for hours and never speak. It is a fact that her mother did squelch her expressions of femininity and that in adolescence she dressed like a boy rather than like a girl. She has always been frigid sexually and in fact has had very little real sexual experience even in her marriage. She thinks very little of her marriage. She needs somebody in the house, somebody to be there. It is also true that her husband has never supported himself until comparatively recently, and he has never supported her. They have often talked of separation but still remain married. He has been in therapy for years and recently has told her he might like to have a divorce. She has criticized him and has been hostile to him for years, saying they should divorce. When he recently thought it might be a good idea, she, however, began to be afraid to be alone.

My concept that sadistic feelings lie behind the masochistic fantasies comes from the many dreams of my patients that have revealed these dynamics, particularly when associations to the dreams are obtained. When Gretchen evinced interest in transference feelings, she asked how one goes about resolving a problem like hers by way of understanding the transference. I told her that one talks about one's feelings toward people, including the therapist, whatever those feelings may be and one discusses dreams and fantasies. I then asked if she has had dreams recently. She said that she had, but they did not seem relevant to what we were discussing. I asked her to tell me the dreams in any case. She hesitated but finally complied with my wish even though she obviously thought it a silly exercise. She reported that she dreamed of her current obsessive object, John, a man she met in an exercise gym who has said that he likes her. He works at the gym on Saturdays, a second job, in order to earn extra money. (She has decided that he likes her and she loves him and often she would go to sit with him to talk with him. On one occasion, she waited for him while he had business for one hour away from his desk. A woman who works at the place wondered what she wanted, "Why are you sitting here?" This experience embarrassed her somewhat, and she stopped lingering at his desk. She does not go to the gym on Saturdays in an attempt to stop her impulse to be with him [her acting out] even though she wants to. She does call him frequently on the telephone, and he answers. She realizes he has no time to see her, but she is sure he likes her and that is enough for her at present.) In response to my prompting, Gretchen reported the following dream:

John was dressed in a uniform, the same kind of a uniform that she saw in a scene in M-A-S-H where one of the men who was "very good looking," and whom she could love, was being accused unjustly by some other person and was to be brought before a magistrate. They were all dressed up in their fine uniforms rather than the "shit clothes" that they ordinarily wear. *[She sees no relation to our subject of transference.]* I said, "An innocent person is being accused and his life is in danger." She said, "I am endangering John's life." Then she lapsed into obsessive talk to drown out what she had said.

I have the impression that she could mean that when she "loves" a person it is really that she bedevils them. She pesters them and gains some hostile pleasure. Such patients resist deepening of the transference by such behavior as deflecting the conversation to unimportant details of current events, or by humor, or by utilizing the trappings of the external effects of analysis in a defensive way. There are innumerable ways that the patient can do this: the patients conceal information from the therapist, or lie about situations, or present the material in such a dissociated or distorted way that it is difficult to follow. They use denial and many other distractions from the analytic transference. Of course, all of these maneuvers are defenses. The therapist at the third phase of treatment must learn to confront the patient with certain transferential material. For example, I spoke with Sonia about her reactions to me and to Dr. Wolberg. Her first direct transference to me was similar to what she said about Dr. Wolberg—that we were cold and unresponsive. This is a transference reaction. Whom do we represent? It sounds to me like her father. I know however that she is talking about herself, the ways in which she is like her father, particularly his sadistic side. But I wait to interpret this until later. I will at another time say that her father was always expecting death or holding his death over others. When Sonia talks incessantly of committing suicide, she is acting like her father did when he was threatening the family with his death. This is Sonia's "identification with the aggressor." But she has other manifestations of this identification as well, for example, her rigid standards of conduct. Resistance of this kind has been called a negative therapeutic reaction. We are told by "orthodox" theorists that negative therapeutic reactions stemming from unconscious guilt and excessive superego pressures are prognostically more favorable in contrast to negative therapeutic reactions derived from primitive preoedipal envy and negative therapeutic reactions corresponding to a "psychotic identification" (in Jacobson's terms) with a primary sadistic object representation. I see these as reactions that refer to relations with parents in both oedipal and preoedipal periods, certainly corresponding to what Jacobson (1954) has called "identification with a primary sadistic object representation." In order for the identification to persist, this pattern with the parent must last over a long period of time.

In the last part of the third phase of treatment the patient stresses his feelings of regret that he could not have had a better relationship with his parents. He is still angry about this, but he is able to talk about his anger more directly and pinpoint his past with his parents as the source of his depressive attitude. He can now speak of his parents' patterns and those of his own that are like the parents. Certain defenses still remain. The patient may say, for example: "You see, I didn't know that I was capable, had brains, could operate as well as the next person. I know now that I can do anything I want! I can lead, I can plan, I can think"—this can be presented in the form of a maniclike outburst. "I'm not going to take any more crap from anybody—not anybody. You [the therapist] knew I had these skills, but I didn't *know*." The speaker of these words did not mean that he didn't *know*. He was a man with a Ph.D. in psychology. What he meant is that his masochism was such that he would not allow himself to accept what he *knows*. The patient knows that he can think, that he can perform, *but now he accepts the fact emotionally speaking*. He accepts himself without conjuring up the punitive superego, the identification with the aggressors, the internalized pathological object relations and the guilt that has been interfering with his behavior. He might say, "I felt it but I didn't know it." The therapist says, "I think you denied it." The patient now begins to act at times in an obnoxious way. He says he will not take any derogatory or sarcastic remarks without retaliating, and this occasionally becomes ridiculous. He feels he must retaliate even when the other person is obviously being neurotic. Such a point is sometimes unbearable for the person with whom the patient may be living. It is at such a point that the person who has had no training in manners or decorum who has not been taught the basic amenities of life can be truly inept and obnoxious at times. It is at this point that the patient may have difficulty in his relations with peers. If the patient has been in a group-therapy situation, he often wishes to leave the group since he cannot tolerate the anxiety of his acting out with authorities or peers. He is learning that the group is not like his family. The group, the individual, and the society are the triad of connected elements. His family supported his neurotic ways, the group and the therapist do not.

Although the patient had difficulties with authorities and with peers previously, his behavior is now different: he is assertive where before he was hostile and withdrawn, but his assertiveness is fused with hostility and with neurotic reactions in response to the neurotic behavior of others. He understands the neurotic behavior of others, but he still reacts punitively.

The therapist realizes that a therapy group is an important vehicle for the patient. His suggestion for the patient to go to a group must be much more carefully made at this time, however, and the suggestion more precisely explained, for the peer experience will be much more complicated than it would have been if the patient were just beginning treatment. Now the patient will be in the position of having to make an unneurotic adjustment to peers while initially he acted in a defensive way and was not required to give up his defenses, only notice them and see where they were most forcefully used. The task is different now. Therefore, he cannot be placed in a group of people who are novices and who are just beginning treatment. His fears and resistances to working through his anxieties are different from what they were in the initial stages of treatment. He can react both punitively and masochistically.

Group Therapy

When and how to introduce the borderline patient to a group is a matter for some discussion. There seem to be no general rules that apply to all patients. Some borderlines feel the need of a group at the beginning; others do not and will not be convinced that a group is useful in the early stage of treatment. Some will enter in the middle stage, while others will do so only when they feel they are in the last stages. Some borderlines have difficulty transferring to open relationships, and others are very familiar with peers but with neurotic peers whose goals are acting out. When such patients find that the therapy group does not encourage acting out, they want to leave. Some borderlines will reduce their acting out, but they must cling to some shred of an acting-out pattern, one that is less harmful than the major pattern has been.

At some point, however, the patient should join a group that will help in his working through in the third and fourth stages of treatment, for it is at this time that he will complete his analysis concerning authorities and peers. He will learn some cooperative ways of working with peers and with authority figures. He will learn that an individual is a member of a group by virtue of his activities in the group.

The individual represents genetic, biological, neurophysiological, and social action. The individual is a member of the group through the communication roles he performs to give and take information. Each group is a new experience, even if some members have been in groups before, for as Moreno (1934) pointed out many years ago, each group is different from every other group due to the subsystems, i.e., the various combinations of communication chains that arise. The individual is connected to the group by his *role* and his role as well as the roles of the other members change as they are either cooperative or defensive as the case may be. Dealing with the dynamics of groups means that one must have, in addition to psychoanalytic concepts, some group concepts as well for psychoanalytic concepts cannot explain the total group process. The group is not an individual. The group is a group of individuals, but the group has no "ego," no "superego," no "id" nor does the group translate into "father," "mother," or "family." It is true that in transference individual members may feel that the group is a family. The group is supportive.

The borderline patient needs a group therapeutic experience. Sometimes the patient attends several kinds of groups before he can join a psychoanalytically oriented group, e.g., a discussion group, a social group, a work group. Active work, learning work roles, and accomplishing work tasks are most important in the therapeutic goals of borderline patients.

For the borderline patient group therapy is a necessity, but it can be a process that may be interrupted several times. It is the patients who have a very social facade and who hate being alone that sometimes go into group therapy at the start of treatment. They are often afraid of a one-to-one situation because of the intense rage that such a relationship evokes. They are able to focus transferences on several group members (Lipschutz, 1957) and feel safer in the group. Later these same patients may become afraid of the group, but they are not in a position to analyze this fear so they leave and cling to the one-to-one situation. Usually in the one-to-one situation—soon after they have seen the sadomasochistic patterns that bind them to the "other"—these patients will then begin to work through the core of their problem. That problem is to recognize the strength of their aggression and the core of defense (detachment, denial, projection, displacement, etc.) that holds them and keeps them from having decent relations with other people. As they work through this problem and its implications, they then begin to think of joining a group again. The kinds of sessions that can lead to the patient's planning to join a group a second time are illustrated in the following with Gretchen. After she heard me talk about her strong feelings for Will (the reader will recall that Will is one of the men whom she focused on at work and whom she imagined as her lover and in secret communication with her), her feelings were aroused by the fantasy of the man. She spent several sessions during which she would alternate between talking as if the fantasy were real life and accepting it as fantasy. She did feel good about having sexual feelings and knowing that she could have them, and I agreed with her that she can have sexual feelings. In the past she had misgivings about ever having real feelings. In session she spoke of her need to have another woman in competition and related this to the triangle father-mother-herself. She stated that she would try to get Will away from his wife. That would give her satisfaction. It did not matter if he never had sex with her; she would be satisfied with just his voice indicating that he considered her worthwhile.

In several sessions she spoke about her despair over her body: she was hopeless; her body was grotesque; if a man saw her body, or if I did, it would be obvious to any observer that she does not have a good body. "I am a piece of shit!" " "No man would even accept me." Gretchen is married but unhappily. Gretchen is six feet tall, thirty-five years old. She has been married for seven years but has "been with" this man for fifteen years. She begins to describe their relationship:

Johnny is short, about five feet, he is becoming fat. She is disgusted when she looks at him. They have clung together in neurosis [this is true]. He is a baby. His family was disgusting. He was brought up like a pig. He always acts helpless, and she has had to play the role of a mother who is bringing up a child. She describes how her husband fails, fumbles, gets fired, says he can't learn. She is always tending him. She teaches him. He reports to her what he had done that is "bad," that makes him fail. She goes over each episode with him telling him what he should have done. She has to watch him like a hawk; otherwise he'll do something that will put them both in jeopardy. One time he told her he was late for work because he slept on the subway and went past his station. She screamed at him and said he doesn't care. She then thought of their house keys in his pocket. Anyone could have taken them and broken into the house. She recounts how she and her mother thought he should have a chance and they financed him in business. He failed, but they kept the shop because every so often he could sell something in his spare time. *[I have heard all this before, but I do not stop her.]*

Pt.	He is like a baby.
Th.	No. He is a man who is always failing and putting his foot in it.
Pt.	Maybe he does it to hurt me.
Th.	To bedevil you.
Pt.	He is hostile.
Th.	He acts toward you as if you were a keeper—or a harsh mother rather than a wife. [She has this kind of relationship with her mother.]
Pt.	But you know that I am hostile to him.
Th.	Yes, I know. *[She then describes how she rejects him, criticizes him all the time, beats at him.]*
Pt.	Lately I have felt that I could really kill him. He makes me so mad. I tell him that I'm tired of being his mother. I want a different relationship. Then he'll do something that is so frustrating that I can't stand it and I go berserk. I scream and yell and curse him.
Th.	You go hysterical?
Pt.	Yes, I go off in a hysterical attack—a regular mania.
Th.	You seem to use each other as transference figures. He is not a husband to you but a frustrating child, and you are not a wife to him but a hostile, complaining, castrating mother. You have what we call an interlocking defensive relationship.
Pt.	Exactly. *[But then she says]* I want to sift out what's my problem and what's his. I know that I am much more hostile to him than he is to me.
Th.	He is more sneaky about his hostility. You are more open and attacking.
Pt.	Yes, yes.

She then begins to talk about her problem. She says that she senses that she drives people and him away from her. When he is nice, she cannot stand it, and she always manages to spoil the relationship. She thinks she did this with Will and with many men. She is left with only a fantasy. But with Henry it may be different.

Pt.	Do you see? I need it *[the fantasy]*.
Th.	Yes, I see you need it now, but you don't need it forever. You are afraid of men. You want a man who will love you and satisfy you, but you are afraid. You drive them away. I think it is because of the relationship you had with your father.

She has told me many times about her relationship with her father, but this is the first time I have confronted her with the relationship. I do so now because of the way she is presenting the repetition story. She is much less defensive than she has been previously. Her father was detached, hard to reach, and he used to "linger in her presence." She repeats what she told me about her father, two episodes:

One day father was in the kitchen reading. He came in and did not speak "but just stood there." She spoke to him, but he did not speak. She then began to scream at him, "What do you want? What are you standing there looking at me for? Go away." We discuss this problem. She was always trying to get her father to notice her, to love her, to recognize her. She then tells again how she sat on his lap and hugged him even when she was 27 years old.

She then says that she is afraid of men. She was deathly afraid of Will, and she is afraid of Henry. She was madly in love with Will, but she is angry at Henry for he does not respond. He could pick up the phone and call her. But he never does. She always has to call him.

Th.   You felt you had to make the first move with your father?
Pt.   Yes, I always had to make the advances. I think he wanted to love me, but maybe he was afraid of mother.
Th.   I think he had emotional problems that did not allow him to think of you as a girl, as an attractive daughter.
       [After what to many therapists might seem extraneous talk, she said:]
Pt.   I think I must begin to talk about my problem. I am afraid of men, and I treat my husband rotten. I drive him away from me even when he tries to be nice.
Th.   This seems to be true.
Pt.   Your group told me that I was afraid of men—but at the time [four years previously] I didn't know what they were talking about. It meant nothing to me.
Th.   You know now what they were talking about?
Pt.   Yes...but I don't know how to overcome this problem. How can I overcome it? If I don't get over this—if I can't remove this block, then I might as well give up and take more pills. I can't go through another episode like I did with Will—I just can't take it....How do I get over this hardness, this block, this resistance, and this pattern of turning men away?
Th.   You are beginning the process right now—by recognizing the problem. It is your need to express your hostility that prevents you from getting close to a man. Of course, you never would let yourself realize how angry you were at your parents—your father.
Pt.   No, I never felt angry at daddy.
Th.   But, you can see that you must have felt angry and very, very frustrated by him. I had someone also tell me just the other day almost the same thing that you are telling me, and I told her about Harlow's monkeys. Do you know about Harlow's monkeys?
Pt.   No.
Th.   This woman [the reference is to Sonia who is 70 years old but talks about her

father the same way as Gretchen does] told me of an episode that keeps coming to her when she was 6 years old. She was in the washroom when two older girls came in and they congratulated her on something good she had done at the school. Instead of thanking them for the compliment, she turned on them and spat at them. I told her about Harlow's monkeys. Some baby monkeys were deprived of the love they needed from a parent, and when they grew up, they were hostile to their children and to others who came near them. *[I elaborated on the situation and concluded by saying]* Some mothers were so angry that they killed their children. A few children tried and tried to make the parent get close, and a few finally succeeded, and the mothers became loving.

> *[The session was over. As Gretchen walked out the door, she saw a group waiting to come in for a session.]*

Th. Well, maybe you'll join a group again after you work through this problem, maybe in three months.

Pt. I was thinking about that.

Th. I think it's a good idea.

There are many other kinds of situations that indicate to the therapist when the patient has a readiness for group and peer relationships are more important. Gretchen had left the group before when she felt that her anger had risen to a dangerous extent, but she had not recognized this problem at the time. She now added as she left, "Yes, I think I would not be so hostile in the group, and I'd get more out of it now." The patient must express a readiness or a need to enter a group before the patient can actually become a member.

CHAPTER 10

Brief Psychotherapy

Short-term therapy can be effective with the borderline patient even though certain borderlines benefit only from long-term treatment; but the borderline patient, for many reasons, does not get into a long-term treatment regimen readily. In the first place, it is difficult for him to establish a relationship of trust; in the second place, he is so anxious that unless he is treated in a special way during the first phase of the relationship, he will surely leave before he can appreciate some of the psychodynamics and psychopathology of the problem in a way that he can benefit from such knowledge. If he goes to a clinic because of limited financial circumstances, he must be encouraged on a practical level to take steps to change aspects of his reality situation so that he can improve his economic conditions and thus have a better standard of living as well as then be able to afford a modest fee.[1]

Short-term treatment to be effective for the borderline patient should occur on a once-a-week basis and be in the range of twenty-five to thirty-two sessions, with perhaps two weeks of vacation after fifteen sessions. This time basis is for outpatient treatment. This does not mean that crisis intervention will not be helpful to the borderline patient as it is to others. However, the patient seldom comes in to the outpatient setting in a crisis; rather, he comes with vague complaints such as "I don't know where I'm going," "I feel empty," or "I fear that I may hurt myself or someone else," and the like. It is the schizophrenic patient who actually does hurt someone else and then is caught. The borderline patient can get into trouble with the law if he is using drugs or alcohol, but he seldom injures others in a homicidal way. He is destructive in a sadomasochistic way but is inclined to fear his own and the

---

[1]Bernard Riess, then Director of Research, at the Postgraduate Center for Mental Health in New York City, in 1976, conducted a study which indicated that patients treated at the Center's clinic were able to advance themselves economically after 32 or so sessions of treatment. This advance was considerably higher than the average economic advance of individuals in the general society. In the clinic's caseload there were many borderline patients.

destructions of others and to set up some kind of controls, often asking friends to help him.

Some borderline patients when they are in a state of emergency go to the outpatient department of a general hospital; others go to a mental hospital for help. Their stay in the hospital is temporary, and the treatment is generally confined to the administration of a drug. As a rule the borderline does not seek hospitalization on his own; he is usually accompanied by a friend or relative who has been coping with the patient for a number of days and who cannot do so longer. Most borderline patients, however, are not hospitalized; they seek out friends or relatives when they are in anxiety states and manage to overcome the anxiety by either talking out their fears or managing to quiet themselves, using the friend or relative in their fantasy as a protective figure. Most borderlines who actually seek treatment are managed on an outpatient basis, either in private offices or in a clinic. I have seen cases where one session on an outpatient basis has been of great help to the borderline.

A book edited by Lewis R. Wolberg (1965), *Short-Term Psychotherapy*, contains many helpful articles on principles and practice in short-term treatment. His more recent volume, *A Handbook of Short-Term Psychotherapy* (1980), reviews current practices and delineates an original technique by Wolberg of one, two, or three sessions using hypnosis and tapes with suggestions for relaxation. In the 1965 volume, the patient I described was a borderline patient. The report by Helen Avnet in the same volume (pp. 7-22) details a research project financed by the Group Health Insurance organization in New York City indicating how short-term treatment was effective with the more disturbed patients—schizophrenics, borderlines, character disorders, and others. Nine sessions was the time period for this study. The work was done by psychoanalysts who were dubious about a favorable outcome; thus the effort was "dynamically" oriented. The results were rather startling in that the patients, on follow-up, had gained a great deal and the benefits were lasting. Lewis Wolberg's chapter in that book describes in succinct terms the theory and methods of short-term treatment from the psychoanalytic point of view.

When we use the phrase *short-term*, we have several kinds of treatment in mind: crisis intervention, behavior therapy, brief supportive therapy, and dynamically oriented psychotherapy. One example is the short-term therapy that Sifneos (1972) describes,—an analytically oriented, anxiety-provoking type of therapy of six to nine sessions based on the idea that tension is necessary for the working-through process. In this type of therapy the aim is to work through some aspect of the oedipal problem. Sifneos selects patients who have certain characteristics, such as (1) the capacity to develop a relationship quickly, (2) a past experience of a meaningful relationship, (3) good intelligence, (4) a ready acceptance of interpretations. Usually when brief therapy is done with borderline patients, it is not possible to select individuals with the characteristics that Sifneos suggests. The therapist can, though, relate to what is called in psychoanalytic parlance, the "oedipal problem." This problem, however, must be defined as "trouble with both parents," relating the family dynamics not only as these refer to sexual feelings and fears, but, also to aspects of the "superego," such as guilt, depression, certain value systems, and role behaviors, particularly acting out and its significance.

The Selection of a Small "Area" That Can Be Worked Through

In every brief treatment of one or two to six or seven sessions, which is the kind of brief therapy that Sifneos does, it matters little what the diagnosis actually is. Sifneos is obviously an astute clinician who can put his finger on a problem area that can be worked through, and *that* is the important point in brief therapy with any type of patient. The first step is to interview the patient and decide *what aspect of the larger problem can be worked with in a brief period.* In my opinion, one must be a very experienced therapist to be able to select such an area. Intuition will often help the inexperienced person find a focus for the work to be done. This was apparently the case in the Betz (1962) and Whitehorn and Betz (1960) studies, the *A* doctors having more intuition and "therapy sense" than the *B* doctors in treating schizophrenics. It was obvious that in neither of these groups did the doctors have a great deal of training in managing the therapeutic process. We can learn from these studies, however, about the way to establish a working relationship with a patient (any patient). We remember that the *A* doctors, i.e., the more successful treatment personnel, more frequently grasped the "personal meaning of the patient's behavior beyond mere clinical description" and they "more frequently aimed at modification of adjustment patterns and constructive use of assets rather than merely symptom relief or correction of 'faulty mechanisms'"; they "participated more actively in discussions, expressing honest disagreements"; they set realistic limits and "avoided passive permissiveness or interpretations of behavior in an instructional manner." Theirs was a dynamic orientation. In brief therapy with the borderline patient, I believe, this is the theory of choice. The approach to the patient should be the same for the borderline patient as the *A* doctors used with their schizophrenics.

In any treatment endeavor it is important to have a diagnostic understanding of the person one is related to in the therapeutic process. Therefore, I put very little confidence in behavior therapy for borderlines—except as it may be used as an adjunct to a psychoanalytically oriented dynamic process. The psychoanalytic postulations should be consonant with current modern knowledge of human behavior and not based on outmoded aspects of orthodox developmental theory.

Communicating with the Patient

In establishing a relationship with the patient it is important for the patient to know that he is understood. This is accomplished by speaking to him in dynamic terms, using everyday language. The therapist must convey to the patient in adequate and appropriate communicative style that he senses the meaning of some of the patient's behavior (conscious and unconscious) and his reasons for seeking treatment. The therapist must then select from the preconscious material a theme that most closely represents what bothers the patient, and using material easily available for discussion, he makes a definitive statement presenting the theme. This means that one communicates to the patient some of his possible repressed feelings and thoughts, applying these to an appropriate sector of the patient's current circumstance. Repression and other defenses are operating to reduce the anxiety that the patient might feel if he faced certain aspects of his reality situation. One might say to the patient who came in because he was afraid that he might choke his girlfriend something like the following:

Th.   The feeling stirred you up and made you fear you might really hurt her. I wonder if you were angry at her. It probably wasn't an impulse out of nowhere.

Pt.   No, I wasn't angry, although I wished she had been more pleasant that evening.

Th.   Well, you don't like to be critical, I can see that. Is it because you may feel that you shouldn't?

Pt.   Yes, I've been taught that one shouldn't be critical of others, but I often do feel critical.

Th.   Well, many of us often stray from what we've been taught. But I can see that it shook you to feel you have the potential for hurting someone. Perhaps we can look into the excessive guilt you have when you feel critical of another person.

The patient's defenses are against the very goals he seeks in psychotherapeutic treatment. Basically, the borderline is an angry person, often presenting himself, as we have mentioned, as "help-needing," yet utilizing all sorts of resistances against receiving help. This way of relating, as has been emphasized throughout this volume, is sadomasochistic and oppositional—the mode of a passive-aggressive character that is the typical pattern of the borderline. We have noted, too, that the borderline patient always has an acting-out problem. Our patient who may have felt like choking his girlfriend undoubtedly acts out with her in some kind of hostile way, and obviously she participates in the sadomasochistic exchange. As we know, the borderline patient makes use of denial, repressive mechanisms, and projective defenses to a much greater degree than the neurotic. This is a function of his use of projective identification, i.e., identifications with parental figures that are denied and acted out in a compulsive way.

General Dynamics Found in All Borderline Patients

In our initial statements to the patient, as a possible focus for short-term treatment, there usually emerge two or three themes, even though each patient is unique—like each thumb print is unique, or each snowflake is unique. Despite the many individual differences, there are some general dynamics that are operative in all borderline patients. I outlined some of the differences between the neuroses and psychoses and the borderlines in my first paper on the borderline patient (1952), suggesting the following: (1) Reality testing is intact. (2) The patient is sadomasochistic. (3) He has minor mood swings. (4) His sadomasochistic behavior occurs in a kind of cyclic manner, acted out within interpersonal relationships. The latter is done somewhat as follows: He submits, or demeans himself in his relationships, and he idealizes the other (Kohut has called this as an aspect of the developmental process in infancy, but I consider it an aspect of the sadomasochistic defense). In addition, he has grandiose fantasies. The idealization lasts until the therapist or the other person makes a move that the patient does not like, and then he devalues the person, perhaps not verbalizing this in the beginning but nevertheless acting it out and using his disappointment as a defense and an excuse for his feelings of anger. At the same time he feels exploited, demeaned, drained, and depressed. He acts out in whatever way is customary for him to revenge himself on the other, for he is not simply angry, he is revengeful. He may break off a relationship; he may get drunk and have a fight; he may become sarcastic with a friend; he may engage in a homosexual episode, humiliating and degrading the partner and then himself; *he* may assume a Don Juan pattern with a member of the opposite sex or *she* may play a "Dona Juana" role. If married, he will fight with his spouse, beating at the spouse verbally. Occasionally one spouse may strike the other, but usually this does not occur: most often, they express rage in words and in a punitive or retaliative way. There is then a hiatus or what might be called a "resting period," and later the whole pattern is repeated.

When this process occurs in the analytic situation, as it inevitably does, the patient tries to throw the therapist out of his analytic position and assign him, in transference, to the role either of parent or child, for he is acting out with the therapist a pattern that he had with his parents. In this acting out of the transference, the patient usually lays bare his problem—albeit in the context of denial. His acting out with the therapist, or his "acting in," if one prefers the phrase, is a replica of the behavior he learned in his relationship with his parents. Often he teases, he is angry, he tries to make the therapist feel guilty, and *inevitably he maneuvers to have the therapist become a participant in the acting-out pattern.* I see this as a need to use the therapist as the patient was used by his parents, i.e., as a projective object, creating an interlocking defensive system, a form of projective identification (Wolberg, A., 1973, 1977), an "acceptable" way of expressing aggression.

With respect to the patient's problem and how this is reflected in his behavior with the therapist and with others, one must understand, as I have often mentioned, that *projective identification* is a basic defense predicated on childhood experiences with parental figures and the "identification fantasy" relates to the acting out.

It is especially important in doing short-term therapy with the borderline to recognize that the patient (and perhaps all patients) is suffering from identifications that are formed *over a period of years* and not merely derived from some infantile trauma that occurred in a "narcissistic" period. The "childhood experiences" with neurotic parents, thus, are not confined to one particular developmental period but to events that are repeated with the parents during the entire relationship. It is not wise, therefore, to follow Melanie Klein's theoretical reasoning with regard to projective identification. I see this problem in the context that Freud indicated in his essay on "The Uncanny" when he described what I called an interlocking defensive relationship (Wolberg, A., 1960, 1966, 1968, 1973, 1977) between a man and a woman. Freud touched upon the acting out of a particular wife (she was flirting with another man including touching his thigh while talking). This was, it seems, an "unconscious" means of making the husband jealous. The husband, in turn, then felt "justified" in condemning the wife. In his essay Freud seems to have ignored the role of the wife, considering her behavior harmless and dubbing the husband "sick" because he interpreted her behavior through his own projection. I see this behavior on the part of husband and wife *as an interlocking defensive system*—each one in the marital pair using the other to project upon and thus to deny certain neurotic impulses and behavior in themselves and to justify their particular behavior. It is this type of interlocking defense that is the dynamic in projective identification, but the problem, in my opinion, did not start when the baby was born with excessive oral aggression, as Melanie Klein thought.

I agree with those English and American authors who feel that the mother must be neurotic for the child to be neurotic, but I also believe, as I have repeatedly pointed out, that the father is involved, too, *right from the start* and that he is an active part in the interlocking defensive relationship with the mother. He too involves the children in his defenses. As the children come along, they are gradually used in the family system as projective objects. This family dynamic described by Szurek and Johnson (1952) should be understood in this way, i.e., in the sense that interlocking defensive relationships are set up as the patients promote acting-out behavior in their children in order to use the children as objects of projection. The communication system of such families has been described by the Jackson group and their associates (for example, see Jackson, 1957). One must accept the idea, in my view, that all *acting out* is based on identifications with parental figures and that the parents promote the acting-out pattern; in fact they demand it, so as to maintain their own neurotic homeostasis. The parents, in denying certain aspects of their neurotic identifications with their own parents, project their hated or rejected parts or roles onto their children. By means of both verbal and nonverbal communications, and the use of punishment and reward, they enforce roles onto the child so that he acts out for them. It is not that they themselves do not act out as well; they do (Wolberg, A., 1960). The acting out is a patterned role that is not evoked in infancy due to the child's inability to control destructive impulses; it is developed over time due to the anxiety-laden insistence of the parents who beat away at the child in an obsessive manner until he gives in so that, against his will and better judgment, he begins to play a destructive sadomasochistic role. At that point he is sucked into the interlocking defensive system that pervades the family and as he uses others as projective objects in his defense, the "other" becomes involved (if he is prone to do so) in the dynamics of projective identification.

To reiterate my thesis, parents provoke identification behavior in the child in the interests of their own defenses. They each project roles onto the child that are associated with an aspect of their own identifications with their parents, roles they wish to deny (Wolberg, A., 1960). The child fights against the identification (Wolberg, A., 1977), but in the end he must succumb. Freud called this "giving in to the other," and he noted that this trait is related to a homosexual trend. One can find in the sadomasochism of the borderline patient a latent homosexual component related to the parents' tensions concerning their own sexual roles and the anxieties they experience when their children act in a sex-appropriate way with others. The parents then exercise aggression and guilt-provoking behavior as a way of controlling this normal behavior and then deflect the child into perverse channels. I would say that the trend Freud spoke of "giving into the other" is a masochistic defense and part of the perverse trend, the masochism and the projection in the fantasy being the defense against recognizing the patient's sadism.

The punitiveness and the guilt-provoking behavior of the parents create sadomasochistic responses in the child, for in this process the parents use their children in perverse sexual ways evoking neurotic sexual patterns. As they project their perverse feelings onto the child, they enmesh him in perverse sexual interchanges. In the borderline patient aggression becomes tinged over time with sexual and revenge feelings due to the child's frustration. These feelings, in turn, are related to depression and the individual's basic feeling of having been rejected and devalued as a person in his own right. It is the revenge aspect of the anger that needs to be analyzed in long-term treatment and that makes the problem more complicated than the simple expression of angry feelings. It is various forms of revenge that have been mistaken for dependency of a childish nature. The individual is attached to the object of his revenge. Many view this as an early dependency that has been unresolved and thus has persisted throughout the years.

There comes a time when the child sees through the parents' defensive maneuvers and mentions this, but he is punished and told in so many words or ways that he too must deny. When he protests, which he does in the beginning, the parents say in essence, "What you say you see, you do not really see," thus decrying the child's reality-testing capacities and making him feel guilty for noticing the parents' neurotic behavior and commenting on it. Due to the parents' problems, aspects of the child's nonsexual self-assertion and his normal sexual behavior are threats. In their efforts to protect themselves, parents often lie (deny) to their children, as a defense. The children see through this but cannot accuse their parents for fear of punishment. Kolberg (1963, 1964, 1966, 1976) has done research indicating that children understand the false morality of their parents.

I have suggested (1973) that the borderline patient must give in to the parent as his identifications are impressed on him over time. I, therefore, believe we cannot look upon the borderline condition as belonging to a particular period in development since the parent has this sadomasochistic relationship with the child as long as they live together, that is, from infancy through childhood up through adolescense. As the parent and child have relationships, the parent denies his role in the interlocking defensive neurotic relationship and forces the child to deny. The interlocking interpersonal process is defended by the sadomasochistic fantasy that depicts the relationship that the patient was forced to have with his parents. The fantasy, as I have said, is an *identification fantasy* and a defense against memories of the untoward experiences with the parents, who forced the identification through punishment and reward. Szurek and Johnson (1952) at the Mayo Clinic and also Szurek (1942) wrote that the *mother and the father unconsciously encourage acting-out behavior, which the child senses, and with which he necessarily complies.* Johnson (1949, 1959) noted that "identification with a parent consists of more than incorporation of manifest behavior of the parent; it necessarily involves inclusion of the subtleties of the parents' conscious and unconscious image of the child. Unstated alternatives exist in the mother's or father's behavior in relation to specific behaviors of the child." This is an indication that Johnson was aware of the "double bind." Johnson with her colleagues Litin and Giffin (1956) delineated some of the sexual acting out that parents promote in their children. We see all of these dynamics in the short-term treatment process.

Twelve Basic Tenets of Short-Term Therapy

Obviously, in short-term therapy we cannot deal with the borderline patients' total problem and must confine ourselves to an area of immediate concern, even though the patient gives us much relevant material. It is this *parsimony in focus* that is our first concern and is of such great import in short-term treatment. The need to understand the borderline's dynamics, however, lies in the fact that the therapist is prepared for many of the manifestations of the patient's emotional disturbance and does not then respond in an untoward manner (countertransferentially) but can attend to the problem before him in a therapeutic way. The therapist must recognize the behavior but know that he *cannot handle all* material the patient presents.

In short-term treatment the fantasies and/or dreams should be used to understand *the meaning* of the patient's acting-out pattern and to determine what is the area of least resistence. We find this focus not only by listening to the patient's productions, but also by eliciting some of the patient's dreams and fantasies. The least defended area is the area of least resistence. The patient attempts to involve the therapist in a sadomasochistic pattern, and the therapist must be aware of this and recognize that it is most important to avoid such participation. In short-term therapy, one cannot analyze this aspect of the problem; one might, however, in one sentence, in passing, refer to the problem. We have mentioned that Geleerd (1965, p. 122), remarked that "in order not to lose his parents' love, the child adopts their repressions, denials, reaction formations, etc. Thus only by taking over a considerable part of his parents' neurotic ways can he join the human community. It is a paradox that the human being, in order to communicate with others, has to learn their faulty ways of dealing with conflicts." This is one factor in the total problem that cannot be worked through in short-term therapy.

A second concern is the suggestibility trait in borderlines, which I believe to be a function of the instructions received from the authoritarian (controlling) parents to play the identification role so necessary to the parents' neurotic needs (Wolberg, A., 1960). Thus, *suggestibility* is one of the elements in the organization of the interlocking defensive system evoked in the family. Jackson's thesis in "An Episode of Sleep-Walking" (1954) regarding suggestibility (a trait also noted by Freud in relation to masochism that Freud thought was a characteristic in the positive transference) was that acting out has the quality of a *posthypnotic suggestion*, an important idea relative to the parents' obsessive insistence that the child act out a particular identification role. The parents' repetitiveness and their controlling and punitive behavior produces a conditioning effect similar to a posthypnotic suggestion, and acting out is a manifestation of this suggestive effect in view of the parents' sadomasochistic ways. One is especially mindful in this relation of what Lewis Wolberg (1978, pp. 13-33) has called the nonspecific effects in the therapeutic process since these are valuable aids in the therapeutic endeavor. The suggestibility trait can be helpful. However, this trait can be a stimulus for countertransference difficulties in the therapeutic process, particularly in short-term treatment. Suggestions for action that are necessary in the short-term process must be given in a way that will not represent a demand on the part of the therapist but will correspond with a rational wish on the part of the patient, a constructive wish for a particular kind of behavior. The particular focus in short-term treatment, then, must relate to a normal desire on the part of the patient. This desire provides the motivation for carrying out the task even though past experiences with parents may have produced inhibitory responses and guilt movement. Past experience may have caused the child to inhibit and substitute an acting-out pattern, a manifestation of identification behavior, that I call the PT (pantomimic transference).

A third tenet in short-term treatment is that while the identification role is a way of maintaining a neurotic role, and is evident in the patient's productions and in his relations, we, however, *cannot* work it through in short-term treatment. We can only be aware that in transference suggestibility and idealization of the therapist and appeasement are operative and that devaluation may occur too. One can give attention to this pattern only in passing. It is not a theme for real focus, for it cannot be worked through in a short period. An aspect of the pattern may be considered however, in relation to a practical problem, one that can be resolved.

A fourth corollary is that the destructiveness of the parent is evident in the interlocking defensive relationship. In this relationship there is a rejection of the child, as child, and the child is used as a projective object, and as an identification with the parents' parents; thus there is a need and a sadistic pleasure in controlling the child and having him act out. The patient is a person who has felt rejected most of his life and cannot take "love" or kindly feelings from another without feeling great anxiety. Therefore, it is imperative that the therapist does not try to sympathize or give undue praise—even while recognizing forward moves.

Fifth, the denial mechanisms of the parents and their demand for the child to deny their behavior creates inhibitions in the self-actualizing behavior of the child; consequently, over time, revenge feelings arise in the child. These revenge feelings are the basis of the patient's sadism, and his fears of his destructiveness. The guilt factor must be dealt with—not necessarily in regard to original figures but in relation to forward moves with respect to that small aspect of the total problem that is considered for the focus of the treatment.

A sixth factor is that the borderline patient's anger and rage is partially controlled by "undoing" and depression. Anger, guilt, and undoing are functionally related. This fact is the reason for the many attempts made by the patient to overcome his inhibitions. The patient makes many false starts, so to speak, before he can carry through on certain forward moves.

Seventh, the child has been made to feel guilty in his efforts to extricate himself from the role that the parents need from him. He has been made to feel that his protests are an act of aggression against his parents. If he wishes to step out of the role and act' in a more rational and constructive or autonomous way, he is punished. There is no punishment for behavior that gives no anxiety to the parents so that there are areas where the patient is free to act. When the patient comes into therapy he is a guilt-ridden person, for he is asking for help to release him from his neurotic role, an act that was seen by parental objects and his superego (the S(IA)D* aspect of the superego) as an aggression against them. They did all they could to counteract forward moves, and now the superego acts as the parental prohibition. If the patient is married, the spouse usually plays this prohibitory role too. One or two sentences regarding guilt are usually necessary in any given session. Anger can be explained as self-hatred in certain types of situations. Anger is mentioned as a response to guilt.

Eighth, in his family situation the patient has learned to deny certain aspects of reality, i.e., to ignore stimuli that provoke certain normal

---

*S = superego; IA = identification with the aggressor; D = feeling of denigration and depression.

'responses and to inhibit certain of his normal impulses. This mechanism is apparent in treatment and can be commented on with benefit. This must be done in common-sense terms using everyday language.

Ninth, the individual begins to fear his revenge feelings, he wishes to deny them. If interpretation of this mechanism is indicated, one uses a projective technique employing either the other or the therapist himself as the projective object for the deflection. Now he operates on two levels; he denies certain portions of reality, and at the same time he has an accurate perception of reality. These two levels are aspects of the "splitting" that has been noted and attributed to the ego. There is a repressed section of the patient's mind and a conscious section operating simultaneously and effecting each other according to the degree of the patient's anxieties. In short-term treatment we ignore many of the statements regarding the psychopathology and take note of the normal statements made by the patient, i.e., the reality or rational statements. We focus more on the reality constructs than on the productions that have to do with pathology. While we recognize the pathology, we interpret it only in relation to that aspect of the problem that we chose as a focus. Thus we must interpret only in the context of this focus.

Tenth, in the sadomasochistic situation at home the child learned not to trust the parent, realizing that he was unreliable and destructive. Thus he learned to fear authority as well as to distrust authority. This attitude can easily be transferred to the therapist, and for that reason in short-term therapy we speak only in clear everyday language making no ambiguous statements. We do not avoid the anger, but we do not try to analyze it— we only *show* how it can be a defense.

Eleventh, in view of the projective defenses, a projective technique is of importance in treatment (Wolberg, A., 1973, 1977). One must also have a concept of the kind of generalized treatment scheme to be followed with all patients and an understanding of how this scheme may be applied on a practical level within the confines of a segment of the problem. Thus, hopefully, the patient can work through his problems in the future when the therapist is not present, by applying what he has learned.

Twelfth, the principles of short-term therapy are the *first steps* in the long-term treatment process. We take a small aspect of the total problem and work it through with the patient hoping that the insights will help the patient when his next anxiety occurs so that he will see the similarity in his current situation with the one that he worked through in his first experience. This first success is what helps the patient trust the therapist.

Case Illustration—Mrs. C

I have no better example of a short-term case with a borderline patient than that of Mrs. C, about whom I wrote in the book edited by L. R. Wolberg (1965). Actually, in this case these were two trends that were followed, both having to do with the patient's fears of aggression. The "common-sense" interpretation of the problem was twofold: (1) you will not kill your husband or injure him if you leave the house to pursue some of your own interests, and (2) it is not a manifestation of anger or hate if you make realistic demands upon your husband even though he is ill with a heart condition. To summarize this case, Mrs. C was a 44-year-old woman, seen for a total of thirty sessions, once a week over a period of seven months. She had been married only 6 months at the time she applied to the clinic for treatment. Dissatisfied with what she termed her "incomplete sexual adjustment," she was seeking help at the suggestion of her husband who was in psychotherapeutic treatment and who had become unhappy with the marriage. At the initial interview with the psychiatrist, she complained that she had never experienced "vaginal orgasm," which turned out to mean no orgasm. Her first sexual experience occurred at the age of 30, and from that time until her marriage she had had five unsatisfactory sexual contacts, all with men younger than herself. She confessed feeling guilty over recurring thoughts during her marriage about her last boyfriend. She had no complaints other than her sexual dissatisfaction. She said, "I have anxiety about my husband's cardiac condition and am coming to therapy primarily to do everything to make our marriage a success."

The diagnosis made at the initial interview was "personality disorder with frigidity." Asked about her preference regarding a therapist, she said that she wanted a female analyst about 30 years old. The doctor felt she would do well with short-term therapy since it was obvious the patient was not motivated to work out her basic personality problems; rather it appeared that she merely wanted to be relieved of certain symptoms. (It is important to note that I did not take her story about frigidity at face value, thus taking it as a focus for treatment. Rather I went on to discuss the problem in its broader areas, finally discovering why she actually came to treatment and basing our work on what the common-sense factor was in relation to her *immediate situation.*)

Mrs. C was born and raised in a small New England town. She was medium of stature, with graying sandy-colored hair. She wore a hearing aid, which was well concealed; her face was plain, and she used little makeup. Her attitude during the first interview was one of utmost cooperativeness though she seemed ingratiating. One had the feeling that she was going into this therapeutic situation as if she were tackling spring house cleaning—a necessary job to be done, "so why not pitch in and get the task over with." She was the youngest of four children, with two sisters, 5 and 10 years older than herself and a brother seven years older. She was one of a pair of twins, but both her twin and her mother died of an infectious disease when the patient was a year old. She described her father, a Protestant minister, in glowing terms: a "wonderful, kind man loved by the whole town." Her home, to her, was a cultural mecca in which music, art, and literature were enjoyed. She herself was an accomplished pianist. There was no further elaboration about her sisters and brother or her feelings toward them. Her father, she said, had remarried, and she described her stepmother as a "wonderful mother to the children and a wonderful wife to her husband." Her father and stepmother, she said, had died eight years ago, and the patient felt a great loss, particularly at the death of her father. She then focused on her relationship with her husband, and it was decided that this was where she wanted the help.

Beginning the first interview with a long, circumstantial history of her masturbatory activities, she led up to her sexual relationship with her husband. She spoke with little apparent conscious guilt. Interspersed in this account were comments of thinly veiled hostility toward her husband, such as "I worry about his heart during intercourse." "My husband thinks his penis is too small." "My husband and I never discuss his dying." She *outlined numerous complaints that her husband had about her that he said he hoped would be eliminated by treatment.* He objected, for example, to her twirling her hair, picking at her face, and monopolizing conversations. She expressed considerable concern over whether these habits could be eradicated, and she agreed with him that they must be annoying to live with. He had suggested that twirling her hair was connected with masturbation, and she wondered whether this was true; if so, would the therapist please get to the reason for it. She was delighted with the choice of "therapist" since she had wanted a woman to help her. She felt, she insisted, completely at ease. Throughout the interview, and at subsequent ones, she displayed an almost manic push of speech. She rambled rapidly so as to be almost irrelevant. This rapid speech combined with a happy, smiling, elated manner was suggestive of a serious personality problem. When the therapist asked her to describe her mood during the session, she replied, "I am sad that I met my wonderful husband too late."

A brief summary of her huspand's problem described him as a warm attractive man of superior intelligence. He had a severe reality problem inasmuch as he had had two coronary occlusions with resulting anginal pains. In addition, he had reacted to his physical problem by refusing to expose himself to gainful work. His purpose in seeking treatment at a clinic was to discuss this problem with a trained person. He was assigned to a psychiatrist.

At the second session the patient brought in a series of dreams, all carefully written down together with her associations to them. (She knew this was the thing to do when one was in therapy.) One of her dreams was, "There was a house with an attic, a second-floor room, and a big attractive downstairs room. The landlord decided to shut off the second-floor room, and the only entrance to the attic was by an upright ladder from the large room below. He erected this ladder." Her written associations were, "I immediately thought the second floor was my clitoris, and the downstairs room my vagina. The closing off of the main entrance and the erection of the ladder meant that I intend the clitoris reaction to come from the vagina rather than directly from outside. The focus of interest has become the vagina, or I want it to be so." The therapist made no attempt to interpret the patient's dreams, merely accepted her associations with this statement: "Your associations seem to tell a story."

Her association was to a vague feeling of being trapped, particularly by marriage, but this was expressed in a completely disguised form by contrasting her feelings toward her husband with that of a friend who felt depressed after marriage. This trapped feeling was an important "here-and-now" feeling. It had to do with her current situation according to this association. Although she was willing to discuss sex ad nauseam, she only *alluded* to the depression and the trapped feeling. Her discussion of sex, while having some relevance, was, nevertheless, being used in the beginning as a defense.

In effect, the patient's dreams served four major purposes: (1) they stimulated her childhood recollections (there were frequent references to childhood incidents), (2) they kept the therapist informed of the patient's anxiety and how she was handling this, (3) they revealed the nature of the transference with the therapist, and (4) they served as a stimulus for *the patient's associations, which were used in interpretations.* In other words, while dreams gave the therapist data, they were not probed or dealt with except to refer to the current relationship with her husband and to speak of her *feeling of being trapped.* It seemed apparent from the dreams that a borderline condition exisited. The actual sexual relationship was discussed in common-sense language. When the patient said that her husband felt his penis was too small, the therapist said, "He has self-devaluation tendencies. Is he afraid of sex, or of women?" This in a sense was a double interpretation or what I call a *projective interpretation,* for this same kind of feeling of inferiority was typical of her too as she soon told me.

During the next session the patient began a pattern of alternately discussing her husband and her father. Whenever she mentioned a feeling or an attitude toward her husband, she would immediately compare it with attitudes toward her father. If she mentioned her father first, she would then compare these feelings with those toward her husband. Since hostility toward her husband was so thinly disguised, the therapist directed questions around this area. Why had she married her husband? "He thinks it's so to take care of him. I wouldn't want to leave him alone. I'd take care of him. I felt no one would take him away from me because he is so sick. I have given up trying for the best things. I couldn't have an orgasm; I feared failure."

At the following session she began talking about what she called her "jealousy of attractive women," relating her feeling of inadequacy to having had a pretty, older sister. Then she launched into feelings of dislike for her stepmother. She felt that her stepmother had been hypercritical in many of her dealings with the townspeople. Immediately thereafter she confessed that she did not believe that the therapist was as pretty as she had thought she was during the first interview. At this point she presented three dreams: (1) "A play was being rehearsed between a boy and a girl. The manager thinks it is immoral and separates them. I thought it was silly of him"; (2) "I went to the ladies' room and discovered it was the men's room"; (3) "I am in bed and holding the landlady in my arms." The first dream seemed to the therapist to be an ego acceptable resistance dream. This led her to ask the patient if she felt that therapy might cause difficulty between her husband and herself. It seemed that she was coming to therapy because her husband was pushing her due to his complaints. Did she believe that the therapist was critical of her behavior? The patient replied that she had actually felt that the therapist might come between her and her father. This was both the first and last transference reference that was mentioned during the entire treatment.

There are always transference reactions in short-term therapy, and the therapist must decide with the help of the patient's dreams, fantasies, and other productions just what aspect should be interpreted. The interpretation should have a here-and-now emphasis with no particular reference to the past. If the patient mentions the past, there is no need to go deeply into the meaning of the past.

During the next session Mrs. C brought in lists of complaints about her husband. She realized that she was repulsed by his numerous illnesses. She spoke of fearing that she might choke him while he dozed under the influence of sleeping pills. Similarly, she verbalized feelings of hostility toward her father. She felt that her father had caused her sexual repressions because of his religious and puritanical values. He imposed his values upon all of the members of his household.

Following these five sessions the patient remained away from therapy for three weeks due to infectious mononucleosis. Upon her return, she continued to exhibit the same rapid speech, and in one session she presented a variety of subjects. She talked about her husband's having gotten a job and then having lost it and expressed the notion that he was testing her to see if she was worried or not. She presented two dreams. In the first, her husband had turned into a fly; in the second, half an orange, stuck on the wall, was attracting and sucking in flies. She then talked about her husband's resemblance to his degenerate half-brother, who had raped his own daughter. Realizing, as she talked, the irrationality of any such connection, she then read off a list of what she considered shameful acts that *she* had committed in her childhood. She finished with a discussion of her father's demands for compliance from everyone around him. *[Her discussion of her father's actions was an indication of implied demands for acting out on the part of her father and her own fears that she might act out in some perverse way using her husband as the projective object.]* The therapist mentioned the patient's *guilt feelings* and said that she might even have guilt about talking about her husband and her father as she was doing. It seemed, said the therapist, that she felt trapped by her father's values as she now felt trapped by her husband's illness. She was staying at home a great deal, isolating herself from her friends and giving up music and other interests.

In this and the following sessions in which there were always numerous areas of interpretation, the therapist emphasized only those problems involving her realtionship with her husband—their social relationships as well as their sexual life.

Mrs. C's problem consciously emerged as she expressed that *she felt deprived socially because her husband hesitated to leave his home.* It was obvious from her talk in the sessions that she felt trapped in the house with her husband and was deprived of the company of others—her social life was nil. Her husband's phobias kept *her* trapped as well as himself. She felt guilty if she wanted to leave the house without him. They were angry at each other in the kind of closeness they were forced to have. The patient's dreams, however, dealt with her sexual problem. They were interpreted to mean that she seemed to have some fears regarding her own sexual aggressiveness, as if she might destroy her husband in some way. She picked this up enthusiastically, recalling a fear that she might injure, if not break off, her husband's penis were she not to control herself in intercourse. At this point the major content and direction of therapy changed from expressions of hostility toward her husband and father to one of talking about her intimate sexual feelings. This shift was ushered in by a discussion of a homosexual relationship she had had when she was 27 years old, which consisted of mutual masturbation with a woman with whom she had shared an apartment. She revealed this with much guilt, and the therapist responded with some educative material explaining the prevalence of certain kinds of masturbatory experiences, especially among girls and women who fear rejection by men.

The content of the next two months of therapy, eliminating circumstantial details, brought out many fearful obsessive thoughts. She spoke of having been frightened for years of being raped by men and of occasional thoughts that someone would put a hypodermic needle into her in the subway and cart her away to a white slave market. It was with some anxiety and guilt that she discussed her feelings of repulsion when her father kissed her on the mouth when she was a young woman. Treatment of these obsessive thoughts, which were also fantasies, consisted of discussing them as symptoms of a great fear of men sexually, and of her father in particular. Such fears, she was told, often preclude any real sexual relaxation and enjoyment. She confided her feelings of distaste for her husband's sexual advances. She then spoke for the first time of her notion that she might have injured herself through masturbation. She feared also that she might learn to be happy sexually without men. She had some nightmares, but the anxiety was not too intense as illustrated by these dreams: "I am supposed to shoot a gun at someone. A snowball comes out." "My husband, a woman, and I live together. I see an auto crash over a bridge. Actually I expected to see the crash, but apparently there was none, and the occupants were unharmed." "I fell off a cliff and nothing happened."

These dreams seemed to indicate a greater control over her feelings and fears of violence. They also seemed to the therapist to be an indication that she might be less fearful of making certain kinds of realistic demands on her husband and that the therapist would support this kind of behavior—not her hostility but her realistic demands. The therapist made the following interpretation: to make realistic demands is not being hostile. Shortly after this she began to experience orgasms.

In the session before her first orgasm she revealed a dread that she would urinate if she were to relax and enjoy intercourse. She recalled her disgust at her first discovery that men both urinate and have sex with the same organ. The following session she burst into the room saying, "I had three orgasms." She then described the following dream, which was the only one she could remember during the interval between sessions: "There is a scene in the mountains with a church; the building hangs precariously on a cliff." The rest of the discussion in the session was spent in describing the pleasure of her sexual accomplishment, the feeling of freedom which she now experienced, and the ability she had displayed in arguing with and expressing resentment openly toward her husband; this seemed to have released her in her feelings. She could see that her anger did not really injure her husband or herself. The therapist mentioned that she might now wish to become more mobile socially. If her husband did not care to go out, for example, perhaps she could go with a friend occasionally. It might be safe to leave her husband for an evening.

With the removal of the symptom of frigidity, the patient felt that the goals in treatment were accomplished, although her relationship with her husband was far from a good one. She continued, however, with the treatment for two more months. She focused on her attitude toward her husband, the therapist encouraging her to engage in her own cultural and social interests, art and music and social relations with other women.

A slowing of speech was apparent, and her dreams seemed to indicate a further reduction of her habitual fears. The following dreams illustrate this: "I am in a railroad station, I went to the ladies room. There were five men there [this is the number of men with whom she had had sexual contact]. I accepted them as having some right to be there." The second dream was, "I am 15 and at home kissing a boy. I felt that my stepmother would not disapprove." At this point she no longer assumed a protective role toward her husband; she began to make realistic demands of him. The effect of this change was that he did find a job. His severe anginal attacks greatly decreased. At the same time she no longer restricted her own activities by martyrizing herself for him. She began to take up her cultural interests again. She resumed attendance at concerts and the theatre, and went back to her piano playing, perfecting it to a point where she gave a recital.

Shortly before the termination of treatment she presented the following dream: "I am in a church with my father, I realize that I don't have the right handle to my umbrella, so I go into a new house where I find the right handle. Then I discover that I am not in church but in a political meeting, and that the man is not my father but my husband. I am very happy about the whole thing." During the last month of treatment the patient seemed to be handling her problems of daily living assertively. At her suggestion and with the agreement of the therapist, she felt that it would be a good time for her to stop coming to sessions and to try things on her own. A three-year followup via telephone showed the outcome to have been favorable.

In speculating what happened here it would appear that somehow—even though I happened to be older than her prerequisite for a younger woman therapist, I was able to establish a relationship with the patient that was not too frightening, one in which she could talk about the situation without developing overwhelming anxiety and where she was accepted in spite of her aggression and perverse habits. She was thus able to take what the therapist said to her with a minimum of anxiety and could therefore focus on her symptom of frigidity and her wish to become free to follow some of her own interests and desires, even though these did not coincide with her husband's concerns. She felt less trapped by the marriage and thus had better feelings for her mate. She was not motivated originally for therapy; she came primarily because her husband was complaining about her habits. Her wish was to be relieved of the burden of guilt that she felt in having so much hostility toward her husband. As her guilt abated through talking, she was able to go on with the marriage. The therapist never suggested areas for her to explore, and never made interpretations that would force her to look deeper into her unconscious. Only those problems which she herself raised were discussed. In terms of what was accomplished, it seemed that she worked through to a manageable degree, by what might be called "conscious insight," her sexual disgust for and her hostility to her husband. She also appeared to have touched upon enough of her oedipal conflict (insofar as she verbalized that her feelings for her father were interfering with her relations with men) to enable her to get along with her husband with some measure of relaxation.

The relationship between the therapist and the patient was kept on a positive level; transference was not permitted to build up to irrational proportions; the reality situation was focused on at all times; the content of the interviews was related to stress factors with which Mrs. C wished to deal. No attempts were made to open up facets that she herself had mentioned but that would require probing. The problems tackled were those she presented and could discuss openly. While no encouragement was given her to bring in dreams, she did this on her own, feeling that this was what was done in therapy, and her dreams were utilized as guidelines to conscious feelings. She was given common-sense interpretations with respect to certain aspects of the dreams. The negative transference was largely ignored except for the interpretation that touched upon the possible hostility that she feared the therapist might have toward her, based on a fear that the therapist might act like the stepmother. (This was actually a projective therapeutic technique for dealing with the patient's fear of her own hostility, using the stepmother and the therapist as the projective objects.) The projective technique was organized around the possibility that the patient was identified with some of the hostile attitude of the stepmother and the controlling father. The patient's sense of being controlled by the husband's illness was reminiscent of her being controlled by the father and some of her rage toward the husband was transferential. The patient feared the therapist would be like the stepmother, but in the end the stepmother, according to the patient's dreams, did not interfere with her sexual relations with her husband, an interference that she projected from the attitudes she felt her father and her stepmother displayed in actual life. We may theorize that the projective therapeutic technique touched upon enough of her repressed feelings and thoughts so that she was able to resolve some of the transference feelings by differentiating the therapist from the father and the stepmother.

The therapist was careful not to become too deeply involved with the patient's sexual material, which was in a sense being used by the patient at that time as a defense. The material was meaningful, however, and revealed much about the patient's sexual anxieties, her fears of being rejected sexually, her anxieties about her sex role, her need for assurance, her feeling of being trapped and injured by a man, her feleing that she may have injured her self, and so on. The interpretations were made around the general theme of her feelings of being trapped and her fears of her own aggression. When she was able to get angry at her husband because of his nagging and express her anger rather than hold it in, she felt released.

CHAPTER 11

Illustrative Sessions

This chapter contains primarily illustrative sessions to which I have referred throughout the book. The cases in point emphasize special problems that arise at different times in treatment. Characteristic resistances will be seen in these sessions. Some instances demonstrate a working-through process to a greater or lesser degree.

Maurice Belk

Maurice Belk was a particularly resistive patient. He came to me after having been with a doctor who used behavior-therapy techniques. The patient originally went to this psychiatrist because he had a "break" when one of his best friends died of a heart attack. The "break" did not require that the patient be hospitalized, but it seemed to me from the descriptions that he gave me in his early interviews, which are given below, that his fear and "hysteria" went beyond that of simply a neurotic reaction. He took two weeks off from work. During that time he reorganized his office and set up what appeared to be a hospital-like atmosphere in an office next door (in a small hotel) to his actual office.

Maurice works for a multinational organization as a "supersalesman" and an account executive in the field of advertising. He is remarkably intelligent despite the fact that he has had very little education (never having finished high school). He has been successful economically. After the "break" inspired by the death of his friend, he began to feel that he should not work so hard, and he went into what one might call a semiphobic state. He hired his brother, a bachelor who was not "doing so well," to live in the hotel near the patient's office and to be his private employee. He gives the brother directions as to what to do. The brother handles the details of the patient's work, and the patient does the "head work." He conducts his business from this hotel room, i.e., his "private hospital," and he gets very angry when people need to see him in the main office. The patient has had what I feel are mild psychotic attacks when he has to talk with the "big boss." He feels that the company wants to fire him (which may have some substance because it is inconvenient to deal with him since he has removed himself from the main office). He feels his superiors are unreasonable in wanting him to move back to the office. He is secretive about the role of his brother; the bosses in the main office do not know that his brother is working on their business. When he has to talk to the "big bosses," the patient is very angry and goes into an "episode." He "lets off steam" by returning to his hotel-room office and ranting to his brother about how miserable the bosses make him, how they would like to "give him the boot," how the office staff are inefficient, and how life in general is almost unbearable. He has stomach pains, for which he takes medications, and goes to bed for several hours. When he begins to recover, he gets up and goes home, where he often has a fight with his wife. On many occasions, after his talks (bouts) with the bosses, he goes to the races before he goes home.

He complains bitterly about his wife, and her attitude toward him. He feels everybody is a drain on him. He is the big "supporter"—wife, brother, son, and so forth, but they think little of him and his needs. Nobody really cares that he is in pain most of the time and that he nevertheless must work and carry a big financial burden. They want, want, want—but they never give.

His fantasy of himself is that of an all-giving, providing, dutiful person whose skill and acumen are used constantly to keep the members of his family in luxury—an exploited person who gets no thanks but only complaints and heartache, and misunderstanding. These complaints are manifestations of his general feelings toward others. He is guilt ridden, yet he is angry all of the time at the people who are close to him and at others with whom he must deal. He represses and denies all knowledge of his own controlling tendencies, his grandiosity, the need to be considered a great man despite the fact that life was "not kind" to him when he was child. Like Lisa (Wolberg, A., 1973, pp. 208-209) he denies his sadistic and revengeful role with people and sees himself only as the helper, the all-good person. He acts out his controlling, grandiose, and exhibitionistic sides. He often has an upset that puts him back to bed whenever he has to deal with a person who "gives him an argument," i.e., in addition to the bosses, a customer or a detail man, or any other person who disagrees with him in any way. He does not attack people openly but revenges himself secretively. Just as he has his upsets in the hotel room, he has them at home if anyone "crosses him." The following session (his one hundred and twentieth with me) illustrates many aspects commonly seen in a borderline patient, particularly the patient's use of projective identification and the acting out of a transference in the session.

Pt.   How do you do? Are you ready for me? *[He has come to the door of my office and sees me typing. I usually go out into the waiting room to usher patients into the office, but Mr. Belk seldom waits for me to do this. He often acts out in some way, going out into the kitchen for a drink, or bringing flowers and going to look for a vase, etc. He announces that he will go to the bathroom and then be in for the interview. His appointment was changed from the day before because it was a minor holiday and the patient wanted to stay home. I had changed to the next day without any comment. The patient is very manipulative and has a poignant need to control situations. He comes to the door again.]*

Th.   Come in.

Pt.   I was thinking about how I can't stand frustration. *[He becomes extremely angry when he feels frustrated and he is easily frustrated.]* I can't stand it when things move too slowly, and I can't stand it when I'm trying to get through to people when they are not listening. Is Schwartz back? *[I had referred the patient's 21-year-old son to Dr. Schwartz for treatment.]*

Th.   Yes, he is.

Pt.   Yes, the frustration.

Th.   Tell me about that. What was the frustration about? [Uses Bert as the PO—projective object.]

Pt.   Well, yesterday at the club I asked Bert *[the patient's brother who is in the patient's employ]* how things are going downtown and he started to talk. I wasn't too interested anyway, but I'm standing there with him and I have to talk about something. So I asked him—and he starts to talk—slowly. If he had something interesting to say, I wouldn't be so mad, but anyway he starts to talk and he says in this slow way, "We—did—this and we—did—that." It's nothing—and I'm standing there and I can't stand it; I want to get out, to withdraw, and then I start to react. *[The patient shows anger at most people he talks about. He never says anything good about a person, being always critical.]*

Th.   You're so impatient waiting for him to say something, and anyway after he says it you are not interested. *[The patient is very detached and self-centered.]*

Pt.   Yes, that's right. And again people don't listen. They don't want to be taught. They ask you and then when you tell them something, they don't listen. *[He is always the teacher. This is also a projection since he has a deaf ear to almost anything the therapist says because he is so defensive. Does he think of the therapist as a teacher? The answer is "yes."]*

Th.   Yes, that's very frustrating.

Pt.   What is that? They ask you and they don't want to change; they're not listening when it means that they have to change. *[A projection.]* And about Manfred *[his son]*—I told him to call Dr. Schwarz; he'll be mad.

Th.   Yes, well, we call that "resistance." It interferes with communications. You mean Manfred didn't want to call. *[I am using a projective therapeutic technique, Manfred being the object instead of the patient.]*

Pt.   Oh, yes! You can't get through to the person. It's these three things today that are bothering me: *frustration, impatience,* and *people not listening when you say something to them when they ask you.* In business and socially the same thing all over. I've been thinking that I was angry at my wife. I took her out to dinner, *but she was complaining so much.* I want to hear something pleasant; something helpful and good; something nice, but she says: "Why does Bertie call you about business every evening? Can't you talk to him during the day?" She gets mad at that, complaining [he has this very characteristic]. She likes to relax; do nothing; have nothing going on—just relax. Sometimes you have to think. Bert asked me to figure something, but I was so tired I said I can't think. I guess it is nice not to work in the evening, not to think of business. But my wife complained, so the next night I didn't take her out to dinner. I stayed home; I could have taken her out, but I didn't, I didn't want to hear that complaining. [What the patient seems to be doing is punishing his wife for complaining, i.e., criticizing him.] As you know, business is lousy, so yesterday I was trying to figure some things out, and then I go into some kind of dream state. While I'm thinking all the time about business, I'm thinking about Manfred [his son who is in treatment with Dr. Schwartz] and the girl he goes with—about whether they'll get married. I'm imagining that they will, and so forth. Or I think about women. I have been trying to read that book that you recommended to me—trying to get through it. It says that woman's role is to have a family, too. Well, I don't think that way; I'm more practical—there are other things a woman can do. But my wife doesn't think so. She's lazy. She doesn't do a thing. Lays around all day or goes shopping. What do you think Schwartz will do?

Th. Oh, you mean that Dr. Schwartz would want Manfred to pay for the appointment that he avoided because of the holiday? He didn't call up?

Pt. Yes, and Manfred won't like that! But I can't be involved in that.

Th. That's right; you shouldn't. [He is telling me here that Manfred is like him. He acts out and does not want to be thwarted by any kind of restriction or penalty. That would make him very angry.] But Manfred will be very angry if Dr. Schwartz wants him to pay for the appointment.

Pt. Yes. With me, action is better than thinking. If I'm thinking and thinking, then that's no good. I have to act; then I feel better. Any thoughts that go on things that have to be done, then action; otherwise, I'm trying to control myself and fighting myself. It's like standing at attention and blotting out everything, not to act. [His idea of action is often to act out, although this is not always true. At work he has excellent business judgment and he gets good results. I believe at this point, however, he is talking of his need to act out.] I think you can see that I can go through many sessions and never talk about feeling. [This theme had started several sessions before when the patient had told me that the language in psychoanalysis is not always the best and most precise. He believes that when people talk about feeling it leads to nowhere because what they should talk about is "function."]

Th. That's what you mean by "function," you mean the way something operates or works. And you mean action. [He denies feeling.]

Pt. Yes, the action—or the reaction.

[It seemed to me that the patient was in resistance because he sensed that in therapy his actions, i.e., some of his acting-out actions, would be restricted and inhibited and he does not like this idea. He says that actions help him relieve his anxiety. He does not believe that his withdrawal tendencies are ways of avoiding reality. Actually, his withdrawals are ways of avoiding the tension he feels in having to deal with people. When he avoids by going to the races, he gambles, and this relieves his tension and his depressed feelings.]

Th. Yes. But I thought what you were saying was that you go into these dreams states, or thinking states. You think of work, women, the races, and then you find you are too far in and you look for something to pull you out because it kind of scares you. A voice contact will pull you out.

Pt. I see that you are always talking about feelings. Now, in golf, for example, there are teachers and teachers. Some are good, and they get to you. *(He gets up and walks around the room as he talks.)* Some people can get just the right word, and then understanding comes and the person can change. If the golf teacher says "turn," then you are likely to do this (he illustrates with a slow half-turn); if he says "pivot," then you do this (he illustrates by keeping one foot in place and turning faster on one foot); but if he says "twist," then you do this, and it has a different meaning *(twisting his body fast and kind of jerkily and swings).* Now, if he means "pivot," when he says "twist," then it is not clear, and the individual is going to learn the wrong thing. I think it is the same with feelings. I notice you are writing, and you use the word "feeling" all the time. It's hard, though, because people don't want to listen to long explanations. They want short words that mean a lot—they don't have the patience to listen to an explanation. How do you get home to people when they have no patience to listen? Now, people tell me that I'm too good to people; and then I try to act differently, but after a while I go back to the old way, and I'm too good because that's the way I have to function. I know the people don't want to listen to me when I try to explain something in the way of a few sentences. I've done it, and they don't listen. They want "yes" or "no," or something short; they want it in telegraphic form. Now what is that? *[He reminds me here of my patient Lisa who had told me that she is a helper—always doing things for people. I take this to mean a kind of ideal-ization of masochism and a denial of the sadistic side of the sadomasochistic problem.]*

Th. Well, I still think it is what we call "resistance." They don't want to bother to listen; they want change, but not if they have to do anything about it. When they find out what's involved, they don't want to go through the trouble.

Pt. I guess so. Well, to go back to the "feeling" and the "function." You say: "How do you feel about that?" Or you say *(looking at a paper where I had written out an interview and reading),* "How did you feel in the dream?" you say here. My other analyst said to stop thinking and analyzing. How did I feel then? What did I feel next? Going on, trying to think out every single angle—you can get lost in that.

Th. Yes, you can. That is right; you become preoccupied with it. *[His other analyst felt that he used analysis as an obsessional defense and cautioned him that this was a masochistic way to use analysis.]*

Pt. To use "function" as against "feeling" you would say, "How did you func-tion in the dream, or what was your reaction in the dream?" But we don't want a physician word—a word that makes you feel about physical things; we want to get away from physician words. We're looking to find the reaction that is created in the dream—or what action did the dream create? And did it have anything to do with your functional activity? What you want to know is whether it interfered with the functional activity. This is especially true for people who have psychosomatic pain. *[He suffers from stomach pains and tension, and his doctor, he claimed, thought that he had arthritis. One doctor felt that he might have an ulcer, but all physical examinations seemed to be negative. He gets short of breath when he is upset.]*

Th. Well, I thought that in psychosomatic pain you could think of it as coming from fear, for example—but that is a feeling. But, I see what you mean, and I think that you are right; for it is the function, the action, or rather the inhibition of function that is bothersome.

I am trying to explain his phobiclike activities—an interpretation of what a symptom might mean. He moved into the hotel room next door to his office so that he could rest when he felt he needed to. This is to avoid a heart attack like his friend had. In his private retreat he does not have to cope with the regular office routine, nor does he have to see the "big bosses" much. They do not like the way he works because he takes a great deal of time out to go to the races, to play golf, and to go boating in the summertime. He takes frequent vacations—to Florida, to Puerto Rico, to health spas, and other vacation spots. Nevertheless, he earns good money for the business and for himself, and he has investments in the stock market; so that he has enough money to enable him to live on a high scale. He complains bitterly about the money that is spent; yet he encourages his son to be "sporty," to have cars, boats, to go to the races, to gamble, and so forth. He has money for gambling himself and thinks of this as just another sport. He always says that he keeps this within bounds and never loses more than he should, but this, of course, is not true.

Pt. Fear shouldn't bring on psychosomatic pain—fear is a feeling. The word "feeling" should only be used in relation to a doctor that is asking an individual how he feels so that he can find out where the pain is. Now, a horse doctor is even smarter. The horse can't talk and so the doctor can't say, "How do you feel?" He has to find out some other way. *[This subtle and humorous hostility I ignore.]* That is the important thing. *[Here again we are dealing with the patient's need to deny a relation between emotion and physical reactions and the fantasies that are connecting links to the present and the past.]*

Th. But can't fear inhibit function, and can't then the person have pain from inhibiting his function? He becomes tense and his muscles go into little spasms, and he feels somatic reactions, physical feelings, or, better, he has "physical reactions," to use your words, and then he can have pain.

Pt. Well, yes; but you don't have to emphasize feelings. The reaction, perhaps, and the inhibition of function, yes, but we're not dealing with a social habit that has to be changed—a pattern that has to go like being a drunkard or being a homo—some habit that you have to change. Most of the people that come to you do not have to change. Most of the people that come to you do not change social habits. They are not criminals, not murderers, not delinquents. They are being treated for "function," or for inability to function. As long as someone can function, that person will not be immobilized. I was talking to Bert and telling him that we should study arithmetic and seriously learn how to figure a parley—get an authentic method, some general principles. You see, as long as I function, I will be free of pain, but when I am restricted, I will get pain. That's what you release a person for in therapy—so that he can function and not feel pain. If you inhibit his function, you'll get chemical reactions and he will have to live on pills. *[This apparently is to justify his acting out even though he seeks help for the consequences of his acting out.]* I think if you could get this down, it would help in the whole field of psychiatry. I am trying to get it into words that are clear. Do you think that I can teach you? *[This is an example of his grandiosity.]* It is a good feeling when you—er, no, I don't want to use the word "feeling"—when you have done something and you know that it is right; that it is good; it is a good reaction.

Th.   You feel it in your bones. *[Both the patient and I laugh because the therapist has used the word "feeling."]* That's a habit to say "feeling" like that.

Pt.   It certainly is. Well, that's my lesson for the day—how do you talk to people, communicate to them so that they hear what you are saying. Can you help me with that? What is that when you can't communicate because the other person isn't listening? And does that have to happen every time that people have to learn something? Does the teacher have to go through that?

Th.   Well, yes. In learning there is always the problem of resistance. It is well known that almost every time a person has to learn something, he puts up resistance.

Pt.   Well, perhaps you can teach me about that, if you have some further information about it.

James Weber

James Weber is a psychologist who came to therapy as part of his requirements to receive a certificate that would "legitimize" him as a psychotherapist. He had already attended a "legitimate" psychotherapy school in the Midwest but felt that he could not practice as he wanted to (he had, he avowed, a perfectionistic trend and he also had what was called a "dependency problem" but what I saw as a sadomasochistic problem). The fantasies that James repressed were violent. Only occasionally would they be revealed (like the tip of the iceberg) in his power fantasies, the need for excessive riches and for political and economic power. He would live with girls he liked, but, he insisted, he could marry only a wealthy beauty. He would say that his present girlfriend is more gifted psychologically than he; she can get along better with people; he is withdrawn and cannot "give out" the way that he should. It is difficult for him to establish relationships with people; usually he does not like people. He will, he claimed, never be a good analyst because of his detachment. He gets irritated at patients, and he envies patients who get better and make a lot of money, and so on and so on. He will never be able to work out his problem of withdrawal and detachment. Therefore, he will have to have supervision all his life—someone who can judge whether he is doing the right thing. If he could have been a medical doctor (he flunked out of medical school twice), he would have never been in the psychology business where he has to deal with people. He resents being in the position. A doctor can "hide out." If he were a doctor, he would be a specialist where he would have to have as little contact with people as possible, and so on and so on. This same problem was evident in the case of George Frank Quinn, a physician in the field of roentgenology. He too said he could use his specialty to get away from having to deal with people and their problems. Underneath these two had fears of being destructive to people, and they needed a person or a situation that would "hold them in check" or "monitor them" constantly to see that they did not use their professions to injure people. They both had homosexual fantasies, which George occasionally used to act out. James never did act these out. He would "torture" his girlfriend by withholding sex for weeks at times, and during these periods he would have homosexual fantasies. He had a tumultuous relation with his girlfriend, she always anticipating masochistically that he would change, but he had no intentions of marrying her. The following session illustrates some transference manifestation and the dynamics of sadomasochism.

Pt.   Monday, in the morning when you were away, I had a dream where I was in bed with you and I was kissing you and you said: "That's nice." I was thinking that most of my patients have so many problems day-to-day and they have to talk about these problems. They don't have any time for going into things deeply. Some time ago I was sort of anxious. I let out a yelp in my sleep. I had a dream. I was in my home in Charlestown and I was playing a game with my mother. I was coming through the house. I was going to sneak up on her and scare her; my mother was in the kitchen and was going to prepare something. Then just before I went around the bend, I saw this monster and it frightened me so! *[Therapist, mother, monster—the patient reveals some of his innermost conflicts and his fears of retaliation if he were to express his anger.]*

Th.   What were your associations to the dream?

Pt.   Oh, it was the kind of kissing you do with your girlfriend. My girlfriend represents you. You represent my girlfriend. I want you to like me, to mother me; to be like my girlfriend is to me in the sense of taking care of me.

Th.   You say that I liked it in the dream. I say, "It's nice." What is it that I like?

Pt.   You like a relationship with me.

Th.   What kind of a relationship?

Pt.   Nonanalytic relationship. I don't think that's true, do you?

Th.   Well, yes and no. We are supposed to have an analytic relationship. Is it a wish that you'd rather not have an analytic relationship, that you'd rather not work out the problems?

Pt.   No, I guess not.

Th. It's a possibility.

Pt. Am I particularly resistive?

Th. Well, you do have resistances, probably related to closeness—that is, fears of closeness.

Pt. The associations to the dream would be more appropriate—like when I was studying for my doctorate. While studying, I would get something from the refrigerator, or I would go to someone to get attention, or I'd start playing a game like with my girlfriend. For example, I'll play up to her. Or we'll be sitting together and I'll suddenly make—a—sort of a kind of a teasing relationship—I'll sort of...

Th. You'll do what?

Pt. Let's see what will I do? I'll sort of tease her like I'm going to strike her. I'll—oh I'll—if I have a towel I'll act as if I'm going to hit her with the towel. If we're sitting on the couch, I'll curb the blow but act as if I'm going to hit her—teasing—a way that I handle aggression. When I do that, I feel I want to get close to her—and I have to act "as if" I'm violent. Some kind of an eruption—something that has to come out quickly. I have to do something suddenly to get close to her or to love her, and so it's a sort of—I'm not angry at her—an eruption of feeling. I'll also suddenly—maybe—I'll suddenly grab her and kiss her, or hug her. But sometimes I do feel it as a way of handling angry feelings. I'll tease her verbally rather than arguing with her, I'll tease her. [*This teasing game is an example of the patient's sadomasochism. He actually has very little sex with her.*]

Th. Did your mother act that way with you?

Pt. No. My associations are also, maybe she'll change. She won't play with me anymore—she'll be different—she'll be controlling—she'll become more like my father. My mother—my mother, like you, would do things for me any time I wanted anything. My girlfriend is there for me. She lives for me in a way—like you. [*The projection onto the therapist as an idealizing, all-giving maternal person is obvious. But it's a mother who enjoys a sadomasochistic relationship with him.*] I had another dream, or a part of the same dream. I was yelping too. I was going through the house at home. I was going to scare my mother, and I met someone who was dressed as I was and I was scared. It turned out it wasn't my mother but my girlfriend. There were other dreams. I remember one: A cemetery—old broken-down tombs—opened tombs. I went down a staircase. There was a place for two caskets, but there weren't any caskets there. Everything seemed to be in a state of decay—like a murder mystery. As I was going down, I met a boy with a cub scout uniform. He was running as I was coming out. I was startled to see him.

And another dream. I was in the house of a friend—a mutual friend of my girlfriend—Peruvian. After we had been away on a weekend—bamboo walls— and we were—sort of like an oriental thing. The walls were live bamboo shoots that had been planted along the.... That reminds me of another dream I had years ago—childhood dreams. Going down the stairs into this basement where there were a lot of boxes. And a very vivid dream I had as a child. A man was chasing me; he was on a motorcycle—heavy—I was walking down the street. I ran—then I noticed he was behind me. He was actually chasing me. He wasn't just on the street. As I ran, he was in hot pursuit. I ran into my driveway. I had the sensation of not being able to run fast, and I had the sensation that the motorcycle man was breathing down my neck. He fell off the motorcycle, and I ran into the house and slammed the door. Houses meant my mother, and some kind of safety. The motorcycle is a sexualized image. Then in the dream I was like people who feel they can't get away— they feel ambivalent— caught between running and not running.

I had another dream years ago—7 . . . 8 . . . 9 years old, two or three times, a motorcycle dream. Then another at 14, 15, 16 years of age, a later dream. I dreamed I was in a—er—er in a—er—some sort of in a room and—er—that—er—I—was—er *(silence one minute)* I was er—er—er—I don't know whether there were other people there or not. I was in this room. I was having intercourse—some sort of sexual activity—in a closet—and this woman turned out to be my mother. But it was grotesque because there were snakes in the closet. I thought of this dream today because I was talking to someone about Kleinian theory. I thought about this dream before, but I didn't tell it because it was so sick—so schizophrenic. Very often my mother would dress in the bedroom, off the bathroom. The house is so ill arranged—my mother if she was dressing, she'd say, "Wait a minute." Sometimes when I'd come through to go to the back part of the house, into the kitchen, or up to a back door to go to the outside—it's the custom in my family that you never use the living room or the dining room unless you have company; anyway, I'd see her. Sometimes I have a dream about snakes fighting. Well, Kleinian—mother having incorporated the father's "penis" orally. The child sees all sorts of things in oral-incorporating terms; he gets the idea that in intercourse the parents are having some sort of oral experience. It's born in him—the infant from 3 to 6 months—it's born in him if he wants to get—he wants the mother's body for himself—he still feels he has to fight the father's penis—the snake. Oh, I don't know!

This is an example of using theory as resistance. The patient knows that what he is saying in relation to theory makes little sense but he does relate today to his sexual problem. He does have a sexual problem. He tells me that he has no feeling in sex (the problem explored by Dince and Green, pp. 127, 157), but he has homosexual fantasies that do stimulate him. His "oedipal guilt" is obvious. But what does the oedipal guilt mean? In practical terms it means he cannot sustain sexual feelings with a woman, yet he idealizes the woman. He identifies on a conscious level with his father, yet he raves against what the father's attitude has done to him. He does not "hate" the father [a doctor], however; he "admires" him. The father is respected, but hides out and gets away with his neurotic behavior in his professional role as a doctor. Doctors are revered even if they are sometimes crazy. The patient wanted to be a doctor so that he would not have to deal with his neurotic personality, would not have to get into therapy. But he failed in his attempts. His father would be full of scorn if he knew that his son was in therapy. The patient has often referred to the scornful attitude of the father—the father has contempt for weakness, and having to be in therapy is a form of weakness, according to the father. The patient says he has never told his father that he needed psychotherapy, but many times he has made comments that leads me to believe that the father knows or suspects that this is true. Neither the father nor the patient would verbalize about the therapy to each other. The sadomasochistic adjustment to the father has made the patient have some hatred toward both father and mother, yet he idealizes them as he does his girlfriend. This is a defense against his rage and his fear of retaliation. He fears being hostile to the therapist, but he would like to attack directly. Instead he acts not by reporting the hostilities between therapists, or the hostilities of other therapists toward the present therapist as in the following excerpt.

Portion of Another Session with James Weber

Pt.   *(He comes in, smiles, and goes to the sitting position to talk about cases—he turns the analytic situation into a supervisory session.)*

Th.   I was wondering why we have this problem; Freud would say it's a transference problem. Do you have feeling about the couch? What are you feeling about being in therapy?

Pt.   *(He tells of a patient.)* I have this paranoid schizophrenic patient, and he acts in this distant way—he's resistive and I don't know whether... *(he drifts off and stops talking).*

Th.   Whether, what...

Pt.   Well, I'm uncomfortable with him—perhaps he shouldn't be here. *[An identification with a paranoid patient who is resistive, hostile, antagonistic, etc. He will make the analyst want to reject him.] (Pause)*

Th.   We did accept him, didn't we? *[He is referring to our clinic.]*

Pt.   For some reason I'm thinking of the doctor in Dallas. *[One of the patient's former therapists.]*

Th.   The one who got angry at you and told you to buzz off?

Pt.   Yes—he said, "Watch what you say to people because you may be insinuating something that...." He was incensed at what I said—he didn't take it as a transference feeling.

Th.   He told you to watch what you say; you might be insinuating something that isn't true? *[This is a reference to a real experience he had when he expressed negative feelings toward a former analyst.]*

Pt.   Yes.

Th.   He hadn't worked out *his* paranoid feelings?

Pt.   I try to put all my patients on the couch. But I like to have them sit up occasionally. I remember what Freud said—he didn't want to have to look at patients and he didn't want to have them watching his every facial expression. I let them sit up if I think they have paranoid feelings for reality testing.

Th.   Uh-huh.

Pt.   But when they're on the couch, I sort of miss them in a way. I can see their reactions better sometimes when they're sitting up—but I miss them. Separation anxiety? *[Actually, this could mean that he would feel desolate and lonely if he did not have a sense of being related to a schizophrenic person. I take this to mean he needs a sadomasochistic relationship and he would be extremely anxious if he were threatened with a breakup of this kind of relationship as a consequence of psychotherapy, i.e., if he were to*

*work through his identification with the paranoid schizophrenic and re-
lease himself from the sadomasochistic relationship.]*

Th. That's a different feeling from what you used to say you felt toward patients—you used to talk about anger; you used to get angry at them *[the other
side of his sadomasochism].*

Pt. Yes—it's less distracting. If they're on the couch, they look at my face.

Th. You mean they turn their heads to look at you? What do they see in your
face? *[This is what the patient does with me when he is on the couch.]*

Pt. They may see me frown or be angry at them, or I may smile and they might
think I'm making fun of them—that is, the sicker patients.

Th. Uh-huh. They wouldn't take a smile to mean a good feeling toward them,
would they?

Pt. No—well, I don't know. I guess they might feel threatened or ridiculed.
Anyway, if they're on the couch I feel freer—then I don't have to worry about
that—it makes an added burden on me if the patient is sitting up. I was
thinking about Asya; she said that in individual therapy she never confronted
her father transference and when she got into a group—the male group leader
was a good mother. She said that when she walked into her first group session, there she saw her father in one of the members—then she started to deal
with it.

Th. What does this mean for you and me? Perhaps when you make a mother out
of everyone, that means you don't have to deal with your feeling about father.
Dealing with your father is very difficult—you often say it's impossible.

Pt. Yes, that's true!

Th. I'm not your mother after all. But you act with me as if I'm your
mother—protecting you.

Pt. No, but your behavior is more like my mother's behavior than Dr. Chandler's
behavior, for example. *[Dr. Chandler is his group therapist.]*

Th. In what way?

Pt. Well, he confronts!

Th. Does that help you work out your father transference?

Pt. No, if I don't talk in a group, it means I want to avoid working out my father
transference—that's what we thought.

Th. That may be correct . . . . So why don't you talk in the group . . . . Break up
that father transference; why don't you want to break it up?

Pt. Well, I feel I'm closer—a few more ropes—I am beginning to talk—I feel I'm
about to break into it.

Th. Then it's a good idea to talk, talk, talk . . . in the group.

Pt. I feel all I can do is take in—I can't produce anything—I can't give out. I
was terrified in school; if anyone would call on me, I couldn't say anything.

Th. You can only take in and not give out. You are afraid to talk, to say
anything?

Pt. Well . . . .

Th. You can't speak—anything else?

Pt. I can't think of anything to say . . . . I think I could be a group leader but
not a co-therapist—the competition I couldn't stand. I can be a group leader
and a group therapist alone in the group. In the boy's club I can talk in the
group. In classes I can talk if there's a structured presentation. *[In the boy's
club he is doing a community project using group discussion techniques with
boys who have problems tending toward delinquencies.]*

Th.   That doesn't explain to me why you can't give out, spontaneously.

Pt.   Because I'll feel competitive.

Th.   Well, who doesn't.

Pt.   Then people will compare me . . .

Th.   They might, of course—but I know you'll compare. That's for sure, you'll compare yourself with others, and unfavorably too. You have a masochistic fantasy when it comes to thoughts of competition.

Pt.   I'll compare—I can't think of anything—I'll start thinking how good what the other person is saying is, and I won't have anything to say.

Th.   Really, you act out the masochistic fantasy when you think of competition. I'm not sure that you mean competition. Sometimes I think you mistake self-assertion for competition. And for you to be competitive is like you're hurting someone—or, at least, you are courting hostility on their part if you're competitive. It's probably some feeling you used to have with your parents. You used to feel that way in sessions talking about your clients. How did you work that out? The patient was always better than you, smarter, more verbal, healthier. I was always better too.

Pt.   Well, when my supervisor finally drummed it into me that if the patient said something detrimental to me, it is *his* transference feeling and I don't have to feel that he's right if he says I'm not helping him; for instance, this is counter-transference if I think he's justified.

Th.   Somebody had to tell you that—you didn't know that yourself?

Pt.   I feel that if the patient says I'm not a good therapist, that it means I'm not good.

Th.   I wonder what that means to us. I wonder what *my* patient is thinking about me?

Pt.   Oh, not that!

Th.   Well, it seems you must think I'm a better supervisor than analyst. The mother will take care of you—keep your ego operating by all this support . . . Do you have any feelings like that here?

Pt.   Yes. I also had a fantasy that my father would like another son—some other son better than me. I feel in the group that the group will judge me—they won't appreciate what I have to say; they'll think that what I have to say is stupid. I'm always comparing: Could I do this? Could I do that? Oh, that was stupid! Gee, that was better than *I* could think! Also the group will force me to do what I don't want to do. If I'm with one person, he isn't so likely to put as much pressure on me. I won't have to play baseball. I can influence one person to do what I want to do.

Th.   Like you do with me here—a mother transference. It's a mother situation—you can manipulate your mother; you can manipulate me.

Pt.   Yes, but the group—they'll make me do something I don't want to do . . .

Th.   Like what?

Pt.   Play baseball. *[He always talks about having gotten out of playing baseball as a child.]* I did not want to get into the game because I felt awkward. *[He was the last chosen. It may be that he does not want me to pressure him to get out of his detachment, or to change, or to work through his transference feelings.]*

Th.   Why didn't you want to play baseball?

Pt.   It's a competition.

Th.   What's wrong with that? What's wrong with competition?
Pt.   I never did anything competitively—I mean voluntarily—never played games or anything—except a few simple games that weren't tests of my intelligence.
Th.   You never did anything voluntarily? Competitively?
Pt.   Well, if you go to school . . . .
Th.   Yes—yes—and after you got into graduate school -- that was voluntary, wasn't it; that was competitive. I think there's nothing more competitive than graduate school.
Pt.   No, it wasn't in a manner of speaking.

As we have noted, James originally was in medical school and flunked out twice, but he still talks about wanting to be a doctor. He thinks of the doctor as being the superior and powerful one in the mental health field and the psychologist, which he is, and social worker, which I am, as underlings. He also thinks of a doctor as one who can be emotionally unstable and can hide out in the profession. He often talks of this in relation to general medicine and feels that if he could have gotten through medical school he would not have gone into the psychiatric field and been forced to become a therapist. Could it be that his father—a doctor—is a compulsive neurotic and never worked out his problems; but nevertheless he is a well-known respected doctor in his community. The patient wishes he could be in a similar situation and not have to work through his problem as is required in this particular training program. His father "gets away with it." Why does he have to be confronted with his emotional problems when his father does not have to deal with his neurosis?

Th.   In what manner of speaking? Who was doing the choosing? If you went to graduate school, graduate school isn't competitive?
Pt.   I was doing the choosing, but I had no choice. I couldn't be a doctor, and I didn't want to become an automobile mechanic. Oh . . . I don't know!
Th.   Are you trying to pin the responsibility for your going to graduate school on someone else?
Pt.   Well, remember I flunked out of medical school.
Th.   Why do you want me to remember that?
Pt.   Because there was competition.
Th.   Don't tell me that psychologists aren't competitive!
Pt.   Oh, yes, they are—what you said about Dr. Chandler. [*I am also a psychologist as well as a social worker and Dr. C is a psychologist.*]
Th.   Oh, yes, you said that I'm competitive with him. I would be interested in knowing what he was saying that interested you so much because it aroused my competitiveness.
Pt.   Oh, about narcissism, primary and secondary narcissism, how the ego represses. He was talking about repression and homosexuality.
Th.   What was he saying?

Pt.   Oh, about the—he doesn't—the homosexual doesn't want an object; he wants a part object.

Th.   Doesn't want a relationship; Oh, you said an object—only a part object.

Pt.   He can attach to any number of people. The person is not looking for a relationship. It's a fantasy relationship that's involved. A real relationship, I mean.

Th.   He wants a part object? Not a real relationship?

Pt.   Yes a penis is a part object—not a whole person—it's cathected because it's symbolic. It's symbolic of masculine strength, and behind that is the breast. The way narcissism is involved—the homosexuals often chose partners who look like themselves. They imagine each is the other, and they are loving themselves—parenting themselves.

Th.   Performing the parental function—parenting themselves.

Pt.   It's a fantasy.

Th.   What fantasy?

Pt.   Getting themselves mother love, father love—loving the other person as they wished their father or mother had loved them.

Th.   You say you do that with your girlfriend. She comforts you—you do that for each other. You are more interested in that than in the actual sexual act?

Pt.   Well, he says that sometimes homosexuals will—they all have the fantasy. Each one would imagine that he was the other and that he would be loving himself....

Th.   This is a sort of masturbatory equivalent?

Pt.   He didn't say that.

Th.   I was wondering . . . *[The patient seems to be groping for some kind of self-understanding. Because of this I shall interpret didactically.]*

Pt.   What do you mean?

Th.   Well, it's the acting out of a fantasy, and there is a sexual element in the fantasy—you say love. In homosexuality there is sex—a kind of sex—but it is a sex that is narcissistic or the concentration is on the self . . . the self—satisfaction is the thing. One is not stimulating another to respond but is stimulating one's self in fantasy. I think there are other elements too. There is the idea that the person is himself and yet is a parent acting in a certain way toward himself. I think of it as a parent. I think Freud said that in homosexuality the individual uses himself as object, but to my mind he sort of becomes the parent. And as I see it there is a caricaturing effect—he becomes an object of derision, I think -- a "whole object" not a part object of derision. His whole person is degraded, and humiliated. Its very complicated . . . . Well, I guess time is up and I guess we have to stop. It's a very complicated business.

Pt.   Oh-hum, oh yes!

Th.   I was also wondering what would happen if you criticized your father in any way.

Pt.   Oh, I'd never do that!

Th.   Not even in your mind?

Pt.   Well . . . I told you my mother always told me never to do anything to upset my father because he'd take it out on her.

Th.   Oh yes, I remember that! Well, we have to stop for today, but I wonder what this all means in relation to us. Perhaps I'm partly your father as well as your mother. It's very complicated.

Portion of Another Session with James Weber

In this session he has talked about a case of a man who has had sexual relations with his daughter. This is the first time that the subject of perversion has come up. We do not know what this means in relation to the sexual life of the patient, but one can be sure that it has meaning in relation to the patient's sexual activities. The borderline's relations with a member of the opposite sex has some significance in the overall picture of what he thinks of as a sexual perversion. Not being able to respond adequately to the woman is one manifestation of his difficulty. Having undue need for stimulation or foreplay is another. Kurt Blau, for example, expressed his problem of a perverse sexual trend by acting out with one of his patients. He had many fantasies about another young woman at work with whom he wanted to have sexual relations, but he never did. The whole problem is a function of Kurt's feelings about his mother, whom he considered to be inhibited sexually but who was "good looking" and sexually attractive, and his aunt, who was much more outgoing and overtly sexual but was married to a "German-like" punitive, strict, rigid, but fair and independent person as contrasted with his father who was a passive "mother's boy." Kurt's sexual fantasies were of all sorts of foreplay that might consciously give him the kind of sexual stimulation he felt he needed in order to perform. He wanted his wife to be very active in stimulating him and then he became very passive while he stimulated her. Kurt and James each introduced the problem of sexual perversion in his own unique way. James kept saying that he would never marry unless he could find a beautiful rich girl who was willing to put up with him. The discussion of perversion, as mentioned, came up in the following session.

[When James came into the room for his session, he talked of his appointments. He wants to cancel one. He has been coming three times weekly. I agree that we might cancel one.]

Pt.   If I'm here next year, we'll have to change the schedule.

Th.   Yes. *[In a series of meetings he has spoken of talking with therapists in the Group Department who were helping him with his resistance. They urge him to get away from me, his analyst, and to transfer to another. He feels guilty about this but would like to get away from me rather than work our problem through. These group therapists seem to be in competition with me and they are belittling me as a therapist.]*

Pt.   Uh-huh *(silence)* er, er...

Th.   What—er—are you thinking?

Pt.   *(Silence.)* I had a case of a patient today who was telling me about his liberal ideas but he's very conservative in his behavior. He's shy; he has trouble being outgoing.

James, who is himself very conservative, tells about his patient who has liberal political feelings. The patient has a mother who is restrictive and guilt provoking. He feels like murdering her, but he does not. He just beats his hand. (James feels like murdering his mother and father and me, but he obsesses about small matters instead of talking about his feelings.) James' patient's father is passive. James then talked about his patient's own liberal attitudes about sex; he feels anyone should do anything they want in sex. James and I talked about how this contrasts with his patient's actual behavior. The patient spoke of once having a girlfriend who was a close friend of the family. He could not have any sexual play with her; he was too guilty. We also talked about what that meant and that he, the patient, was saying that she's a "pure" girl. He would "insult" her if he made an advance; in any case, he could not because she is too close to his family. He obviously holds himself in; he feels he would like to free himself but he has aggression and self-assertion fused.

Th.	Why should she consider it an insult if he made a sexual advance?
Pt.	I was thinking my hang up was... *(a long pause)*...
Th.	Your hang up was what?
Pt.	If the girl didn't like him, she could have rebuffed him—he would be hurt. *[In transference he is afraid that if he gets close, he will be rebuffed and he would be hurt by that. He will take it masochistically.]*
Th.	Well, some girls are hurt if you don't make a sexual advance.
Pt.	Yeah.
Th.	But this whole thing is too much like incest, he thinks—and anyway if a rebuff came you'd be hurt if you were the person.
Pt.	I said to him she is too much like your sister. I also said some people might have sexual feelings toward a sister and they couldn't act on them; but this girl wasn't his sister. He was saying she is too close to his family. But because of the relationship between his and her parents he probably sees himself as being put down. They do have a sadomasochistic relationship—the man the loser...
Th.	Uh-huh.
Pt.	But he said if the job aspect—it might have a repercussion—and his best bet is to find a girl not close to his family. It's almost as if he feels that it's like incest. You're right, and it's as if you're hurting the girl, insulting her.
Th.	Sexual guilt. Where did he get so much guilt? He must have gotten the idea that for him to do anything like that was wrong. He feels he has to go away and find a girl who is not so close to home.
Pt.	Maybe he thought if he wanted something, it was bad.
Th.	Now, he equals closeness with...
Pt.	Yes.
Th.	Was his mother withdrawn—not close?
Pt.	No, she was like the prototype, controlling, strong, masculine.
Th.	Well, she could be like that and not close.
Pt.	Yes, she's not capable of being close—didn't give.

Th. Is he aware that he didn't get much affection? Is he aware what his feelings were? Is he aware of his feelings about you? *[This is a reference to the transference—and there is an implication that there are similarities between him and me and between him and his patient.]*

Pt. We didn't discuss that.

Th. He couldn't have gotten much affection from either parent; his father was passive, castrated, and his mother ...

Pt. To identify with his father he'd have to ...

Th. He apparently does identify with his father—passive—but sort of withdrawn too.

Pt. He had a brother who was very active in left causes—he went to England. He told the mother to go to hell. He couldn't put up with the mother's controls—the brother got away.

Th. Maybe the boy can refuse to be controlled by his mother and yet not have to flee the country....*[This is a suggestion that one might stay in analysis and change and not have to flee.]*

Pt. Yeah.

Th. He can change and still live in the same country...

Pt. Dr. Chandler is very strong in dealing with this kind of problem. He gets very indignant about a person controlling other people. He says; "Well, why didn't he hit back!" *[He is contrasting me and my technique with Chandler, who along with the group is trying to wean him away from me.]*

Th. How old was this person who was in this situation?

Pt. All his life. Right from the start until today.

Th. He was controlled all his life—uh-huh.

Pt. Yes....After he got older, he should have produced some controls in his parents' attitude toward him. This patient does seem to be doing very well though. He's not had any sexual experience with his daughter lately. *[The patient had engaged in incest.]*

Th. Good, if he has been able to control that.

Pt. Yes—I think he's . . . doing well. Dr. Chandler says he probably sees sex as very sadistic. He sees sex as getting close enough to the woman to hurt her. He must learn, he must gain some recognition that he is destroying his daughter—taking out his feelings on his daughter. Well, he had displaced his feelings to his daughter. He feels sexually inadequate. Chandler says this is schizophrenic—his wife and his child are both in treatment. He does peculiar things. By the way, I led some discussion in the Group Therapy Conference last weekend.

Th. That sound like a good thing.

Pt. It seems that my patient has better relations with his wife. But he feels he has very little sexual drive and he's tired. He thinks his wife wants it and he tries to please her, but he wants to have less sex. But he's more interactive with his family, feels more fatherly toward his daughter.

　　For a time, he was a pedophiliac—he had an experience with some kinds, an experience outside the family. His child is to him like any woman. He had fantasies at a very young age. He saw his mother's legs open—her genitals. He had sexual fantasies about his mother and his grandmother. His fantasy was more sadistic.

Th. You don't know what his fantasies were....

Pt.   Yes, his fantasies were that a woman was being very open with him. He pleases her and she pleases him and they get along. *[This is like his dream about me that he revealed in the former session.]*

Th.   The fantasy is a reaction to deny.

Pt.   Yes.

Th.   Denying what the real situation was?

Pt.   Yes.

Th.   There are lots of parents who do have sexual play with their children, just as blatant as this man. Others are more secretive, but, nevertheless, it's just as disturbing to the child.

Pt.   His son needed some sexual advice the other day, and he gave what I thought was very good advice.

Th.   Yes.

Pt.   He seems happy—he feels better—he's freer with me. He had a dream not too long ago—about having intercourse with his daughter. Not actual intercourse—but he was—in the dream—she was resisting—he had told me originally that the daughter enjoyed it.

Th.   Before, when he first told you about it?

Pt.   Yes.

Th.   His guilt has been reduced, I guess, and his relationship with his daughter is not on such an acting-out level.

Pt.   Yes, and he has more intercourse with his wife. Before he had less intercourse with his wife.

Th.   Uh-huh. *[James often loses interest in sex and goes for one or two months without approaching his girlfriend. When she asks for sex, he evades the subject.]*

Pt.   He feels fatherly toward his daughter. They go out together as a family. They go out together as a family, and he feels different. His sexual appetite has decreased. He hasn't such strong sexual feelings any more.

Th.   Does he enjoy sex with his wife?

Pt.   Sometimes...he says usually he's too tired. He says that a lot of his sexual performance is for his wife. He has these other feelings, but he's less tense. *[The other feelings are for his daughter and for the pedophiliac with whom he would like to act out.]* Sometimes he wants intercourse; he enjoys it.

Th.   Some of this pattern sounds like somebody I know.

Pt.   Yes, yes, my sexual drive is weak. I have this problem with women.

Th.   Do you feel angry at her, your girlfriend?

Pt.   Sometimes—but then sex with her is not stimulating.

Th.   Are you disgusted with her?

Pt.   I don't think so. It's just not stimulating.

Th.   Do you think of things to stimulate yourself?

Pt.   Sometimes—yes—I think of men.

Th.   Do you feel guilty with women—like you are imposing on them, I mean violating them?

Pt.   Not consciously.

Th.   How do you feel right now?

Pt.   Sort of exhiharated and exhausted, and a little put down and a little ashamed.

Th.   Those feelings are complicated.

Pt.   I guess so.

In this portion of a session the patient, Seymour Daird, talks of his ambivalence toward women, his need for them and disgust with them. The transferential aspects of his feelings are obvious.

Pt. Hello, I have to tell you that your slip is showing; is that a hostile remark?

Th. Well, not necessarily. Do you feel that it is meant to be hostile?

Pt. Yes, I guess so. I know that people say those things often. People tell each other if something is wrong with their clothes.

Th. Yes, it's sometimes thought of as being helpful.

Pt. When I do it, I think it's hostile—probably ambivalent.

Th. Well, perhaps. Are you angry at me?

Pt. No, not at all. Perhaps I should have been angry when I realized that you are using my record for teaching purposes; but I was not. I might even have been a little flattered.

During a group session on the previous night in which the patient was present, I had asked him if I could use a dream from one of his individual sessions that he had given me, for it seemed to fit into the session and the content of the dreams and fantasies of the other patients in the group, that is, with what they were discussing at that moment. I recalled the dream, where the patient had felt he was going to have a baby and would suffer with pain. The patient had denied the dream, said that he did not remember. I had mentioned that often when I recall one of the patient's dreams, he tells me that it must be someone else's dream, that I am mixing him up with some other person.

Pt. But I can't remember my dream last night—I can remember only part of it. That keeps me confused.

Th. That keeps *us* confused.

Pt. *(Laughs.)* Yes, my confusion is funny; I'm always feeling that I don't know what the rules are, how I'm supposed to act. I never know what the score is. It's as if some grown-up is always keeping me in a state of confusion. Then I feel inadequate. Then behavior-wise, I never know what to do, how to act, what the rules are, what the score is. I cast aside the only rules that they had to offer, that is, religious rules, and then I don't accept other rules, either. In fact, I don't know what the other rules would be. *[I interpret this to myself to mean that he knows what rules his parents used when they raised him, but he has been trained to deny those rules and to think that they were not in force, deny and dissociate them from his mind; for the parents do not want to accept the responsibility for training him in these neurotic ways. He must deny, and analysis tends to break into such denial and dissociative defenses. But I do not interpret this to him at this point. He is not yet able to handle this emotionally.]* Well, one part of my dream was mathematical. I can't remember that part of the dream. In the other part, I was looking at a scene on a stage, like the movies. *(Pause.)* *[Dissociation and derealization.]*

Th. You were looking at a scene.

Pt. Yes, well, no—because I was really looking at the audience, but it was like the movies. Half of the audience was decrepit, grotesque; and I remember thinking in the dream that we must be living in the Space Age, and these deformed creatures are part of that era of this Buck Rogers kind of existence.I wasn't so sure that one could have much contact with them; but then there was half the audience that didn't seem grotesque.

After the group session last night I went to Broadway to a delicatessen where I often go for a sandwich; no, for hot dogs—specials—and for a pastrami sandwich. It is a dreary place, and many of the customers wear skullcaps, but the man who runs the place seems like a good fellow, a nice guy. Things are high there—a bottle of soda costs more than it should but I don't mind that; I know things are high, so I don't resent it too much because the food is good. As I walked from this restaurant, I was going to go to the movies. I was just going to kill time; I don't really care about the movies. These neighborhood movies are getting to be just a hangout for degenerates—dishevelled-looking people.

Th. Are those the degenerates of your dream?

Pt. Yes, I guess so. I finally walked to 116th Street, and when I got home, I was annoyed with Jack *[a friend]* because he was wasting his time. The Oscar business! I was wondering who was more immature—Jack or me. I was wasting time, too; I was listening to music—just sitting doing nothing but listening. Then Jack walked in, and he turned on the television. I felt like telling him to turn the thing off—those Oscars don't mean anything—just commercialism. But, why should I be so dictatorial, like my father? *[He has never given me a true picture of his father; I am much clearer about his mother and her personality.]* However, I really felt like killing him. I really wouldn't let myself think of hitting anyone—let alone killing them—except in self-defense. My Freudian censor operating—what is it—my superego?

Th. Oh, yes. Your morals, or your code of ethics.

Pt. As I was waiting for the elevator today coming here, I had that feeling again, "Oh, what's the use!" I still think in those terms sometimes—that I'm wasting time. I have a quick feeling of disappointment that I'm not satisfying any need here. I'm still seeking to satisfy some neurotic need.

Th. Such as what?

Pt. Every once in a while I think of Jane coming up to New York. Even if this would be a temporary thing, it would be some excitement. I still think that I have this idea. And I apply it here, too. I say, if I didn't do this today, what would I do—it would be too boring. Coming here helps to break up the day. I'd rather do this than go to the office to do work. What I'm getting out of it, I don't know. In terms of neurotic needs, it's like going to the movies. I've managed to spend a few hours some place. I've some guilt in thinking that I'm not accomplishing anything. Because after any given session, I can't point to anything and say, "Now I feel better!" I don't think that I'm yet oriented to the long working out of anything and the slow acquisition of something new and solid. I want results quickly. On the other hand, I feel that it's necessary to spend a long time if one wishes to work out anything real—of value. I don't feel that I have the patience. Actually, there are certain things that can be learned quickly. I have this problem about music—or I used to when I was studying. I would have to learn a concerto. Some people would learn it in a week. I, on the other hand, would give myself a period of three months. I'd estimate that if I learned it in three months, I would be doing well. My goals are much too conservative. I anticipate this long time; then I don't try to make it shorter. I just reach these goals with difficulty.

Th. You think this pattern operates in the analysis, too?

Pt. Perhaps.

Th. And in dancing, too. I remember how you told me that you simply couldn't learn dancing. You were awkward, couldn't control your movements; and you couldn't keep step, had no rhythm in spite of the fact that you are a trained musician.

Pt. Well, I had no rhythm in music either; I had the same trouble in playing the violin. I always had to practice the rhythm; it didn't come naturally to me. I have to go slowly because that's the way things are.

Th. You have to go more slowly than other people.

Pt. Well, not more slowly, but I have to be average. I'm a little afraid of being fast.

Th. Why are you afraid of being fast?

Pt. Partly because I'll be sloppy—too many mistakes; I don't trust myself to do the thing right, so I have to take a long time to check and double check. I don't absorb. I just keep forgetting. I don't absorb.

Th. That's how you feel about me, too, isn't it—that I don't absorb—that I forget from one session to another what you have said—that I get your dreams mixed up with the dreams of my other patients?

Pt. Oh, yes! I do. I feel sometimes I'm in incompetent hands. I know that isn't true, but often I feel it.

Th. In the group you felt that I might have mixed you up with another patient and gotten the dream of another person.

Pt. Yes. I do the same in mathematics—fitting something into a mold. This has been my way. I see it, and then I don't see it. I think about it and see it and then it slips away, and I don't see it at all. Then, finally, I get it, and finally it becomes set and I have it. But, in the beginning I have to put it into some frame of reference with which I'm familiar. While I was listening to music last night, I was lying flat on my back and I kept wondering who was sicker—Jack or me. I felt, "He's still in an age where he has to be intrigued by show business." The night before, I had seen a few moments of Greta Garbo playing in "Grand Hotel." She played the role of an aging ballerina. She was turning her head around in a narcissistic manner. In that moment, I thought of Dulcey.

Dulcey is Professor X's married sister with whom Seymour had an affair. Prof. X and his mother seemed to encourage this affair because the sister was so unhappily married. In the beginning the sister held out the hope that she would leave her husband and marry the patient, but this was never forthcoming. It was because of this that the patient finally gave up the affair reluctantly, and he had fantasies of this woman steadily during the period of his analysis. It has been only in the past few months that he has not been obsessed with fantasies of Dulcey. Prof. X also has a pattern of holding out promises to girls—he often promises to become engaged to a girl but usually asks her to keep it secret. In this way, he keeps the girl on the string, so to speak, while he has an affair. Sometimes the girl realizes finally that this is only a come-on and that he has no serious intentions. Recently, Prof. X was secretly engaged to a girl, and he was leaving town for six months to serve on a committee which is being financed by the government to study a certain problem in engineering. Everybody knew that Prof. X was leaving town except the girl who supposed she is engaged to him. The patient feels that this is a form of cruelty, but nevertheless he identifies with Prof. X in the sense that he too has trouble with his feelings toward women. For example, he sees Sally on a regular basis, and recently, he says that their sexual relationship has become more pleasant and more successful, but he cannot think of getting married or of having a relationship where he would see Sally every day. He keeps his dates on a once-a-week basis, and his sexual relationships on a once-or-twice-a-week schedule. He usually takes Sally out once a week. He has feelings of revulsion when he is with women too long. He has revulsion at physical contact, and he feels very critical when he becomes too close. He finds fault with the woman's looks; and usually he feels that she is dirty, unclean.

Pt.   Dulcey used to pose and Charles *[Prof. X]* always moves his head around in a "cute" pose as if the world is a mirror. My first impression was that this is Greta Garbo; this is the way she is as a person. Directors and actresses know these things and I don't. They can abstract movements that can typify these things; ballet choreographers, too, have to know these things. Without knowledge of these things, they could never make these kinds of representations.

Th.   It's the understanding of the kinds of people these are—what their motivations are and what their behavior means?

Pt.   Yes. And it's knowing it on an emotional basis; maybe they are not consciously aware of these things on an emotional basis. These are things I don't know. I have thought that I'd like to take ballet lessons—to learn to dance ballet. Then I think that most of the men are homosexuals, and I feel hesitant. I'd get a lot of enjoyment taking ballet—more control of my body. Is that a homosexual idea? A homosexual wish? The fact that I'm homosexual? I don't feel entirely masculine. As I become aware of movement, however, there is more sense to the dance—this feeling of the dance has more sense to me now that I let myself see these movements. It's the same with music. I allow myself to hear more. What has this got to do with the grotesque types? It reminds me of the women who are pushing 60. They've lived a hard life; they have hard faces; and their faces become masks—a hard life—a person's life does leave marks on their faces.

Th.   The marks or the masks look like what?

Pt.   Wrinkled, rouged up a bit, full of terror and greed, hardness of a kind—I can't quite describe them—a little bit frightful; to my way of thinking, somewhat deformed. About 80 percent of the women on the West Side that I see on the streets, or going into the stores, or the movies are like that. They have this appearance—I don't know whether it's me or them!

Th.   Do you actually know women like that?

Pt.   I don't think so. Well, maybe some of the women who go to my uncle's house—they're like that. I see them but I don't know them. I don't like them—well, I mean they have those characteristics of hardness and so forth.

Th.   What about me? Do I impress you as being like that?

Pt.   *(He gets up off the couch and looks at me long and hard and seriously.)* No, not really; you don't impress me that way at all. But I can be very critical of you.

Th.   Sometimes when you call yourself critical you are being helpful at the same time—like the way you told me that my slip was showing.

Pt.   Yes, I have been critical of you; earlier I was much more critical. I had many things I didn't like. It's that about the teeth, remember.... You did get a replacement and I don't notice it now, because it is a good one, but it makes me feel that you are lacking—like I used to have dreams about losing my teeth; something is gone irrevocably. Then I used to hate hair on faces. I still do, and I used to see hair on your lip.

Th.   That's true; I had it removed by electrolysis.

Pt.   Well, actually it wasn't that bad. It wasn't a mustache or anything—not that bad. I'm overcritical. Does that hurt?

Th.   What?

Pt.   The electrolysis.

Th.   Well, a little, not much.

Pt.   The point is that I always come here partly for neurotic reasons; and when I'm dissatisfied with the reasons—when I don't receive the neurotic stimulation, I don't like it and I feel dissatisfied. Then I feel I'm wasting my time. But I do feel better, and in many ways I act better, so I guess we're accomplishing something.

Th.   We have noticed in the past that you did feel toward me somewhat as you did toward Dulcey. That you would wish me to talk against my husband, or that you would see me as a woman who wants to be relieved of my husband, or to complain about him. And then you have had sexual fantasies that were similar to the sexual acts you had with Dulcey.

Pt.   Yes, we've been over that so many times, and I don't think of it much any more.

Th.   Perhaps thoughts of Sally have replaced thoughts of Dulcey.

Pt.   Maybe. Oh, well, tomorrow is another day!

Th.   Yes.

Louise Woll (164th Interview)

Pt.   Hello. *[I sit in a chair and on the couch there are papers, but the patient hesitates to sit in a chair. I remembered that for the past two sessions the patient had been on the couch.]*

Th.   Are you going to use the couch today?

Pt.   Well, yes; last time I thought that you said I had done good work on the couch.

Th.   Yes, that is true.

Pt.   When I was anxious this morning, I thought maybe it was because I was thinking about using the couch. But, I'm not sure.

Th.   We never figured out why you didn't want to use the couch before—what your fears were.

Pt.   No. I think I figured out what my anxiety was about. *[Yesterday morning, Don, her husband, did not feel well; and when he took his shower, he vomited.]* Don thought that maybe he had an upset stomach because we had attended a bar mitzvah over the weekend and he had had too many Manhattans and too much food. Don went to work, but then he called me saying that he was coming home because he felt sick; he had chills. I told him to come home immediately.

I don't know why, but he didn't come home right away, and then I started to do something that I used to do almost continuously—I began to worry that he had had a heart attack. This used to be a worry that never left me. But for a long time I have not felt this way. But yesterday the obsession came back in full force. I knew that something was wrong—something neurotic. But I feel that I have learned something about why I have had that obsession all these years.

At one time this was a constant fear with me that my husband would have a heart attack; for a good many years I had this constant fear. It was accompanied with a panicky feeling—a feeling of anxiety. When he finally came home, I insisted that we call a doctor even though he didn't want to. Secretly, I wanted to rule out a heart attack. He had a temperature of 102, and he had chills, and I insisted.

That night I had a dream. I had been reading an old copy of the Bulletin *[the leaflet of the Community Lecture Series of the Postgraduate Center]*. I thought at first that the dream was inspired by my reading these articles in the Bulletin. There was a review of an interview with you entitled "Who Are You?" In the article you said that people have a built-in desire to do things and to be something, and they usually know what they want to do, but there are many reasons why they don't do what they want, and it is usually associated with their problems with their parents. I started thinking about my transgressions as a child. Why did I do the things that I had done? How is it possible that I, myself, could have done those things? I felt like a split personality; one-half was the person I am, that I have become, and the other half what I was as a child; the two are entirely opposite. I know that you can't be split, but *early me* doesn't seem to be *me* at all—it was not me—I was split off from it—I didn't accept it as part of me. And yet, I told myself yesterday, *it was me*, I know that it is impossible to dissociate yourself from part of yourself; yet that is what I have been doing all these years. I am me and that was me. Then I wondered whether it is ever possible really to know why one does things like I did. Is it ever possible to know really? To accept that this is a part of me—perhaps this would help me to find out why I did those things, if this is possible. I'd be able to have a greater esteem of myself—if I could do this.

Th.   Yes, the first step is to admit, to recognize that this was part of you and that there was some reason for your behavior. Presumably we can find out what those reasons were.

Pt.   I was thinking yesterday that it is *so painful* to talk about those things. When will I ever be able to discuss this matter? When will I ever be relieved of this awful feeling of shame? It just engulfs me! There are many things. Why can't I talk about them? I have talked about them before, but not to rid myself of these feelings—of this problem. While I was thinking all these things yesterday, I had a free association. I had an association about my neurotic feeling about Don getting a heart attack. I think that it is tied up with this feeling—my free association went something like this: If Don gets a heart attack, a fatal heart attack, I'll lose the only person who ever loved me. This is tied up with a feeling of not deserving anything. My fear has lessened.

My fear of being punished. I don't have this thought often, and it is diminishing to almost nothing; but yesterday when it recurred in such strength as to give me an anxiety attack, I felt anxious and faint and so upset for several hours; then I began to try to understand what was happening and what connections to the past were there. This need for punishment is tied up with my not being able to let myself do what I want to do—to be what I want to be—which, as you know, was to be an artist and to do designs as well as creative work. This obsession and this fear of Don's death is tied up with the feeling that I have had for many years—since childhood—that I don't deserve anything, that I can't have what I want, and express myself and be as good, or better than the next one.

Th.   You could do better than many artists.

Pt.   Yes, I guess I could, but that is not to be; I could, but I don't have the right to. Don used to say that he had to urge me to get things. I always would say: "Oh, I don't need that!" But, I don't feel that way any more. Perhaps that is why I didn't wear a wedding ring for several years. I never wore a wedding ring. I didn't have the rights and privileges that other people did. Then I was thinking about my mother and the fact that I have such a fear of driving a car. I have an unconscious fear that someone wants to crash into me—that someone wants to destroy me, and that I don't know how to protect myself. I'm still acting out—I still can't drive a car. While I'm aware of the aggression I have had, I'm aware of the anger toward my father—and with my mother, I wasn't aware of the full force of it; I was always trying to please her—still am to a certain extent. Well, anyway, I am aware of the anger, yet I'm still turning it on myself. [This psychosomatic symptom—she means the itching that had subsided in therapy for two years and had almost disappeared, but in the past year had returned to a point where she is sometimes almost beside herself—"is driving me crazy." The itching comes out under her arms, on her neck, around her waist, and around her thighs, and on her feet. She scratches until she is raw. When she scratches her feet, she becomes sexually aroused, but she is not conscious of the fantasies that she may have at that time; these are apparently repressed. Her sexual symptom of frigidity for which she came to treatment has in the past year been slightly reduced, and she had started to ask her husband for sex. He became very anxious when she did this, and he almost threatened to divorce her. He asked her not to continue with analysis and to "let sleeping dogs lie." He became very impotent when they would try to have sex. Formerly, he had had sex, and she had allowed herself to be "used" as a receptacle for him— never having any feeling at all and hardly moving her body during the sexual act. He would have a quick orgasm and the experience would be finished. She has been frigid all her married life, although during the early part of their marriage her husband used to try to stimulate her with fore-play and with manual manipulation of her clitoris. She never was able to respond. Patient feels that the symptom of itching began when her migraine headaches stopped, and she feels that the two symptoms are thus connected.]

The itching is a substitute for the migraine, a way of turning anger on myself. I'm not letting myself know of my sadistic feelings. I think this symptom keeps me from realizing how terribly hostile I am—or I would be—how sadistic I really am. I just don't let myself know of my sadistic feelings. I know that I have hostility toward my father, but I never realized the extent, I didn't realize how hostile I was—or am.

Then I was thinking about my mother. I think that I can see my mother's feeling toward me. My mother felt that everything I did was an act against her, and, that I did these things to her, she felt, because I had to keep paying her back.

The patient means here that this is the reason she has been her mother's slave all these years. Two years ago, the mother verbalized these feelings to the patient; her mother and father are still living and are over 80. Now they are both sick and infirm, but really there is nothing basically wrong with them. The father does not see too well, and the mother is always fearing a heart attack but never has had one. She is in very good health for her age. Under the impact of therapy, the patient expressed some of the resentment that she feels when the parents depend on her for everything—even though there are three other siblings who could as easily do things and the family can well afford maids. But the mother fights with the maids in a paranoid way, and the maids then walk out. The patient then feels that she must leave her own home and come into the parents' apartment to clean the place. The mother said that the patient owed work to her for what the patient had done in her youth. The patient was shocked to hear her mother say this, and was upset for several weeks. She was aware for the first time that the mother was consciously exploiting her and using the incidents of her youth to rationalize her actions or to excuse her feelings toward her daughter.

Pt.   Last night I was thinking that I can understand my mother. I was 14 1/2 years old when I was six months pregnant and my mother didn't know anything about it. *[The patient has spoken of these incidents before in the analysis, but not in this way.]* I can imagine that it was a great problem to her. She doesn't want to see her role in it, of course; but, practically speaking, she was presented with a great problem. She had to get an abortion for me. I asked her to take me to our family doctor and that was the first she knew about it—he told her that I was pregnant. I was afraid to tell her. But he wouldn't do anything about it because he thought it was too late, and he himself wouldn't do anything, anyway. So my mother took me to several doctors until she found one who would do an abortion. I don't remember the abortion at all; but I do remember an incident that fills me with shame when I was in the doctor's office. *[This incident, the patient had never mentioned before.]* My mother wasn't in the room with me when the doctor was examining me. I thought I was going to faint; he put my head between my legs so I wouldn't faint. I thought I was going to faint anyway. What happened then was that the doctor started to make advances to me. He put his arms around me; he wanted to kiss me; just exactly what he said, I don't know, but he was implying or asking why I wouldn't have intercourse with him. At the time that this happened, I felt that I was in love with the boy who had made me pregnant. I was shocked and upset when the doctor had this attitude toward me. I didn't feel that I was a whore; I felt that I was in love and that I was doing this for the boy. After this visit I became ill. After the abortion I became physically very ill and developed a temperature of 104. Then I learned that I had septicemia. I didn't know what the doctor did. I don't know of anything that was really done to me—if he actually did anything; either I didn't know it or I have repressed it. I don't know whether he did something to bring on the delivery, but, anyway, I remember that right at this time, while I was in the hospital—they had to take me to the hospital—I broke out with boils all over my thighs. I wonder if that has anything to do with my symptoms? I can understand my mother, as I say, but yesterday I realized that she was taking a terrible risk with my life—what was she trying to do, destroy me? In a sense, she didn't have any love for me; she was protecting herself and not worrying about my life. My life wasn't considered at all. She thought of this as a face-saving thing—I had done this to her—not what I had done to myself. Where could I have the feeling that I had any rights. Always my parents—not my parents, but her only her—it was that this had been done to.

The incident that happened to me a year later, when I was caught taking the trinkets off a counter—something was said the other night [she meant at the group therapy session]. Charlotte said that she cajoled and begged her parents to give her money, which she then used to buy things for girls. I remember now that these things that I took were not for myself—they were for gifts—to give gifts probably for the same reason—that if I gave somebody something, they'd like me. The reason for taking and for getting caught was for another reason—that's another matter—why did I have to get caught and go through all that humiliation? Was this a retaliatory thing to my parents for what they had done to me; was it to hurt them that I got caught? The result of this, however, was disastrous to me; I had to give up everything—my design school, my art career, and everything.

Th.   You had to give it up for all time?

Pt.   It seemed that way, although of course that was not so; but every time I have tried to go back to it, I have never been able to.

Th.   That was your punishment? Did you get caught as punishment, too?

Pt.   Perhaps that was it; I had to be punished for what I was doing to my parents and so I had to get caught. They degraded me so that it was terrible—in school, I mean.

Th.   I'm not quite sure that I have the sequence of events in my mind clearly. When did the stealing incident occur?

Pt.   Well, I first went into high school and my sister Alice would cut class. She was my older sister and I would go with them—with her and her friends. They would cut school on Wednesdays, for example, and go to matinees. They would sign notes for each other; we'd sign notes for each other and finally we were caught and put on probation—our parents were called to the school and we were disgraced. The principal talked terribly to me; said if I didn't stop, I'd be a forger and I'd end up in jail. They didn't expel me from the school; they discovered after looking at my records that I had an aptitude for drawing. And then I went to this other school—this school for design—I don't remember the name of the school—it was an art school and I loved it. It was on 57th Street. Then it was in this school that the incident of the trinkets came up and I had to leave school for good.

Th.   When was this in relation to the pregnancy?

Pt.   That was much earlier—I was 14 when I was pregnant—the stealing was later. I remember that I was in the hospital, there were Christmas trees. It was Christmas time when I had the septicemia, so I had the abortion, or the still-birth, or whatever you call it—so I was pregnant for six months—so I was pregnant in July.

[*The patient goes on to tell me of another pregnancy she had two years later. She mentioned that at the time she became pregnant the second time, her mother had left her in the city with her older sister and the family had gone to the country for the summer. The older sister had many episodes with boys but was never caught as the patient was. The sister was 18 at the time.*]

Th. What was your exact birth date again?

Pt. February 1904.

Th. So, actually, this was in 1918 [*the incident of the second pregnancy*].

Pt. Yes.

Th. And Clarence was how old? [*The boy who made her pregnant.*]

Pt. He was 19.

Th. Yes. He was 19 and you were 16?

Pt. I never thought of it's being 1918. I wonder if the war had anything to do with Clarence's attitude. I was in love with him—maybe he had to go to war—he didn't want to get married. Since that time, since I left art school, I have had a rope around my hands and a vise around my brain . . . I don't permit myself to do things.

Th. Yes, and that has been for a long time—since you were 15. And when was that in relation to the second pregnancy?

Pt. I was 15, but I guess after I left school. I have a very good feeling for color, and I know that I could do something with my talent. I could—I feel I could.

Th. You can't just let yourself go.

Pt. It seems not.

Th. You are afraid to express yourself?

Pt. I feel that this is all tied up with my own unconscious feeling that I'm not as good as anyone else, not as good as the next person.

Th. It's certainly not conscious; well, it is somewhat conscious. Have you been thinking recently about going to art school or doing some kind of art work? Is there anything else—does anything else go with this feeling?

Pt. How do you mean?

Th. Any other thoughts or feelings attached to this besides these feelings of un-worthiness?

Pt. Well, it's a feeling of being bad. Last night I had this feeling when I was thinking about this incident.

Th. What incident?

Pt. Well, what happened to me in my second pregnancy—I can't really under-stand that at all. Well, I was thinking that I was a murderer. It's a feeling of being bad; almost worse than committing murder—this was murder. Well, gosh, my mother tried to murder me, didn't she? I thought that—and the second time I completely cannot understand the dynamics of the second pregnancy.

Th. Did you think of the doctor?

Pt. Yes, of what doctor? You know what I said just a few minutes ago about be-ing a whore—in my mind it's almost worse than murder—in my feeling, this is worse.

Th. Are you thinking about the second pregnancy?

Pt. Yes, and also about having this senseless, meaningless affair with this doctor; worse than murder—being a whore. [*The affair she refers to occurred when she was much older, about 45. This doctor was her internist, and for some months she would go to his office and have sex with him. She still had no real feeling, but she felt excited, "not necessarily too sexually excited."]*

Th. Oh, you mean that you were thinking of the doctor that you had the affair with and not the doctor who did the abortions, or who made approaches to you?

Pt. Yes, I always had this doctor in my mind, too—always thinking of it—like an obsession.

Th. Yes.

Pt. Worse than murder—this must reflect my mother's feelings.

Th. How did you know what your mother's feelings about whoredom were?

Pt. About sex—I know how she felt.

Th. Well, what about whoredom?

Pt. One thing puzzles me, when my father was caught and I became upset.

Th. When did you find that out? *[It was somehow revealed in the family that the father had been having an affair with the patient's female cousin who was a doctor.]*

Pt. I was about 18, not long after I was married. I think that the fact that my father had had this affair for ten years—my mother kept up a friendly relationship for years with my cousin *[the woman with whom her father had had an affair]*. My mother was friendly with her, she still is friendly; this is difficult to understand. This is difficult for me to understand; it's as if she had given permission for this affair.

Th. Uh huh!

Pt. That she had condoned it.

Th. Uh huh! *[I believe here that the patient is about to make a connection, if not in this session, then in the next few sessions with the mother's and father's behaviors and her own acting-out patterns in the first sixteen years of her life, and perhaps with the later affair with the internist. The patient's scratching and itching may have had some connection with the physical parts of her body that were involved in these various sexual episodes.]*

Pt. And she probably did—since sex was nothing she desired—a wife had to endure sex being married to a beast; and all men are beasts! Quote! We talked about my mother's feelings about sex before. It wasn't anything that she recommended. You said how did I know what my mother's feelings about whoredom were? I had some associations.

Th. To my question?

Pt. Yes. I wonder if the fact that she was a doctor, and then the first doctor and the second doctor. Does this have any meaning to me? I don't know! I keep asking myself whenever I think of it, what were my motivations? Were these things that I did all part of a self-destructive pattern? Well, they were certainly destructive to me! I know that adolescents are very moody, but I think that I was an especially moody girl. I'd be very exuberant and then I'd have depressed feelings and ask myself, "What am I living for? What is life all about?" I was thinking all my life, "Why wasn't I born a man!" All my life, "How much better it is to be a man than a woman!" And it's only in the last two years that I have felt differently.

Th. That certainly should be of great significance to you. Your father's and mother's behavior in relation to his affair.

Pt. *(She gets up from the couch.)* Do you think that I'm doing better on the couch? I think that my anxiety last night was that I'd have to talk about these things, and my fear all along, and one of the reasons why I felt so anxious was that I'd lose control of myself and talk about these things—if I were on the couch.

Th.   That is perhaps the reason why you feared the couch; you feared letting yourself go. Letting yourself express these ideas.

Pt.   Yes. Well, I feel as if I'm getting somewhere—I'm not sure where.

Th.   Yes, I think you are. You seem to feel that the affair you had later in your life with the doctor had something to do with the experience you had with the doctor you went to as a child—the one who did the abortion—and you are suggesting that your father was "acting out" in some such fashion too, and that with both you and your father your mother has a definite role to encourage this kind of behavior.

Pt.   Yes—I'm so confused.

Th.   I wonder who those doctors represent to you.

Pt.   I don't know—the answer is always parents.

Th.   You have no particular thoughts or feelings about it?

Pt.   No, not this minute.

Th.   I was wondering also whether you were not identifying with your mother. You felt she was trying to injure you and you were in jeopardy—you said that maybe the fears represent your own aggression.

Pt.   Yes.

Th.   But we do not know what is in the present that set all this off?

Pt.   No.

Th.   I was wondering whether it was that you want to paint or go to art school? Have you been thinking about it?

Pt.   Yes—oh, yes!

Th.   Recently?

Pt.   Yes, the other day—I was thinking that I resent being a volunteer in a mental health agency and I like art better.

Th.   But you didn't want to say anything about it.

Pt.   Yes—that's it, I guess.

Th.   Will you go to art school?

Pt.   I don't know.

Th.   Will you start painting?

Pt.   Yes, I think so.

Eventually, the patient did start painting, and within one year she had a show—but this was about one year after she left treatment.

Maxine Diaz

In this portion of a session Maxine tells me indirectly of her anger and of how she defends against it in many ways; then she becomes more direct but defends against dispelling the rage.

Pt.   I had a dream, these dreams, I was anxious to talk about them. I was sorry I

	missed the session, but it was important, I had to stay at the meeting, the budget meeting. I had to testify at the meeting to justify the money for my department.
Th.	Oh, I see. I guessed that was something you couldn't help. What were the dreams?
Pt.	The dream was at night, walking on a road with a lot of people, we were all walking on this road until we got to this country store. Then people entered the store. I was walking in the mud, it was dark and muddy. I went out again (I guess alone), but I didn't really seem alone—but I was and I was carrying a big stick. I was told to carry a big stick to defend myself. With the stick I could push my way along and defend myself. I heard all these footsteps. I couldn't see anything and was fearful.

(The other dream) Fall leaves, many colors [*this is a recurrent dream*]. I could hear the sound of the leaves. There were crocodiles, made of paper cardboard—I've had many of these cardboard dreams. It was then raining. I was naked. Oh, I'm sorry, I was not naked; I was wearing a short-sleeved summer dress, with a towel over my shoulder, brown socks, and no shoes. I felt people were looking at me because of my clothes. It seemed like it was the University of Puerto Rico—and I was then walking around and it seemed like the university. Looking at a picture of the sons of Goya—and the painting was worth $120.

Th.	Did you say Goya? Like Goya the painter?
Pt.	Yes, Goya, sons of the painter. The children looked stern and gypsylike—like "gone"—like a fantasy or reverie—and the picture was worth $120. Those are the dreams.
Th.	What were your associations to these dreams? What about the first one?
Pt.	Well, first it seemed like the place was on a plantation in Puerto Rico where I did field work—the dark, no electricity—the country store. And it also reminds me of some of the places in Paris, some of the streets in Paris.
Th.	What streets?
Pt.	In the Algerian quarters. I often walked there. I got lost...
Th.	Well, if you walked there often...
Pt.	I didn't get lost; I went there often. Well, I guess it reminded me of Harlem and of the Puerto Ricans in New York—and of myself in New York; I guess I can't afford to dream of myself in New York. I've no stomach for that in New York—my life. On Saturday, I had an insight. Saturday I realized I was married to Charles. I'm his wife, he's my husband, I had insight.

Well, Saturday I was taking a nap and when I woke up Charles was lying next to me and then when I told him that I realize I'm married to him—I'm really conscious of our relationship. He said "It's taken you almost four years." I said; "Well, your mother hasn't realized it yet! You shouldn't blame me for taking only four years." He said: "Well, I'm glad you feel the way you do!"

When I was married to Pedro I felt that it was something if a man was willing to date me—that he was interested in me as a woman. I had no choice—the marriage was not anything I had any responsibility for. This is not the first time I have had revelations of this kind—I had unique and wonderful feelings, in Scotland, that Charles is a person I really trust. Last month he made me feel I come first in his life—I am really important in his life.

Th.   You feel you haven't had that relationship before. That's good to have.

Pt.   No, never.

Th.   What about here? In this relationship, do you constantly have to be on guard because of fears?

Pt.   Yes, why did I have the setting of Palmas Altes? There I was surrounded by people who were very close to me—at the same time I could not feel close. The people in the community symbolized the kind of relationship I could not have. But I wanted to be close; I had never seen people like that. *[She has ignored my reference to transference or to her feelings about me.]*

Th.   Did you want to be with somebody because you were afraid? Can you tell about the feelings you had? You said you were not responsible for the marriage! Did you feel you had to be on guard? What feelings did you have?

Pt.   I don't know, but I had just become 21; I had been sheltered all my life I didn't dare to drink the water there, nor eat the food. The scarcity frightened me. I was afraid. I didn't know how to behave. I was afraid of the rats—afraid of crabs, afraid of bugs—and if I heard rats chewing and crying outside my hut, I became more terrified. *[She is talking about the location where she was sent to do field work when she was working on her Ph.D.]*

Th.   Did each person have a hut?

Pt.   No.

Th.   Oh, you lived with a family?

Pt.   No, I didn't live with a family, but if they offered me food when I was in their hut, I was afraid to take it because of dysentery.

Th.   You didn't live with a family?

Pt.   No, I had a hut to myself.

Th.   You said you didn't know how to behave. Maybe that's one of the reasons you got married—your fear—you were afraid to live in the hut by yourself, you didn't know how to behave. Is that why you married Pedro? You were away from your protective family, and you needed protection? That's a different kind of relationship than you have with Charles.

Pt.   I was really lonely. In Chicago, I was not lonely in Chicago. I had many friends. I had never seen people like those in Palmas Altes.

Th.   In Chicago you had friends—both male and female? So you didn't feel the need for marriage.

Pt.   Yeah.

Th.   What do you think the dream means?

Pt.   The darkness—a whole period in my life—which still continues—isolation, depression. I have to organize my aggression against others whom I distrust because I don't know where I'm going.

Th.   You continue to have such feelings?

Pt.   Yes, that's why I think I can say that I block; I'm so blocked, my experience doesn't represent awareness.

Th.   Your former experience was that you did not allow yourself to be aware of many things?

Pt.   My present life—in my experience, I'm unaware. I still have this habit.

Th.   Even if things are obvious, you're unaware—even if things are obvious?

Pt.   That's right. I'm so detached I don't see. I'm blinded to recognition.

Th.   When did you have that dream?

Pt.   Thursday.

Th.   What was happening Thursday?

Pt. Thursday I was very upset. I feel I have to leave my job and it is stupid to leave when for the first time I could get some satisfaction in working, some research to my name, and some papers. My problem is should I give this up or should I stay until I get the thing done—the research. Sometimes the aggravations are such that I feel like giving the whole thing up. I was very angry Thursday.

Thursday, Paul told me the budget director turned my proposition down. The reason that I can't have the raise is that I do not function as a chief research scientist since I was doing a lot of administration I was very angry at that. Also they had turned down the other positions I requested for assistants. I had to leave my work at the university and write a statement. With all the things I have to do I also have to be bothered with this nonsense. I have to write a statement why this should be this way and then go and defend it before the budget hearing—I was so furious I could kill everyone dead. I could hardly write or breathe, I was so angry.

Th. Well, I don't blame you at all for being furious.

Pt. But I was in such deep rage, it was frightening. And I had such physical reactions—I wanted to walk twenty miles, I wanted to go away, I wanted to kill.

Th. Who do they represent to you?

Pt. Don't say that! They represent themselves! It's not true—I should be angry, but not to have such a terrible reaction. It was not my mother, nor my father. *[Denial.]*

Th. Were you ever conscious of having such feelings as a child toward your parents?

Pt. Never.

Th. You must have repressed all those feelings.

Pt. Yes—of course—but I remember being angry—but, really, I guess afraid. It has not spoiled my relations with men *[denial]*. I remember as a child liking men. In high school a boy fell in love with me; he acted awkwardly he never spoke with me about it. In grade school, in parochial school, I had a boyfriend; I liked him very much. In the university there was a boy whom I thought was a god. I know the man I was angry at—my brother; and the male servant who exposed his genitals to me; and my father—my own father, not my foster father.

My problem was that as a child I felt I was very ugly and that they could never really love me. At the University of Chicago there was a handsome boy who liked me, and I flirted with him. I was not afraid of him.

Th. The symbol is danger, harm will come to you, fear of danger—fear of being hurt if you're close to someone. You need a big stick.

Pt. Well, I was never afraid of rape, if that's what you mean. I was not a good sex partner when I first married, but that improved. I was just inexperienced and afraid, and I felt ugly. I know whom I was afraid of as a child—it was not in the relationship with boys. This does not mean that I was not afraid, that I wasn't afraid of the man. I was afraid of my mother, her sister, my cousins, my brother, my uncle, my father, two other cousins, my father's brother, the bad man servant we had, of authoritarians that would crush me by giving me orders and who would punish me if I disobeyed them.

The dream seemed to be in Puerto Rico, where I had friends, where I liked my peers for the first time.

Th. Cardboard—why cardboard?

Pt.   Snakes, alligators, toads, crabs are the same to me. I dream of them all.

Th.   What are your associations?

Pt.   Awfully big, vicious or tame, and scared of their death!

Th.   Why are you scared of their death?

Pt.   Before they die they will kill me—they're more desperate when they're dying.

Th.   They represent things that are potentially harmful to you if you disturb them in any way?

Pt.   They can harm me, hurt me.

Th.   You were talking in the context of a phobia, as if these animals represent dangerous people. We don't know who the people were.

Pt.   Once I had a dream of a big crab, when I was in the group—a big crab coming to get me—my father—the association was to my father.

Th.   A long time ago—when you were little—did you have any conscious fears of rape?

Pt.   No.

Th.   Did you have fears of the anger of men—of your father?

Pt.   No.

Th.   Then maybe it's reversed—maybe you have a fear of your own anger toward men.

Pt.   I wouldn't know. You see, my actual exposure to boys was good; there was a boy, sweetheart in the fourth grade, another boy in the sixth grade. I thought he was beautiful. My cousins, they hit me.

Th.   And in the sessions here you may be afraid of your own anger—your own fears of what would happen in closeness. I was wondering about the $120—what would that refer to?

Pt.   I don't know—nothing that I can think of.

Th.   I suppose it could be a sum that you paid—paid it for something.

Pt.   Yes.

Th.   To me.

Pt.   No.

Th.   Perhaps you fear I would be very angry if I knew what you do—or perhaps you are angry at me.

Pt.   No, I can't think of it that way.

Th.   Just that your anger frightened you when you realized how intense it was at work?

Pt.   Yes, yes.

Th.   I remember the long walks you used to take through the city here. You told me about those long walks. You must have been discharging a lot of pent-up anger through physical means, if the dream has any significance in relation to your anger.

Pt.   Oh, yes, I did that even a few months ago.

Th.   Perhaps you feel that people are like the snakes and the toads—that if you disturb them or ruffle them they will fear that you are trying to kill them, and they'll kill you first. Therefore, you need a big stick. Your associations seem to mean that the big stick is aggression—aggression to safeguard you against aggression. But your husband makes you feel accepted. No matter what you do, he accepts you.

Pt.   Yes, yes.

Th.   So you wouldn't need a big stick when he's around.

Pt.   Yes, yes.

Th.   What about *me*—how do you feel here?

Pt.   I feel safe enough.

Th.   But I mean perhaps you have transferred feelings to me—that I may turn on you and injure you!

Pt.   No conscious thoughts like that. You may not be helping me, but no thoughts that you'll injure me.

Th.   Who would I represent—if you did feel that way?

Pt.   I don't know.

Th.   Are you angry at me?

Pt.   No.

Th.   But you're not sure that I'm helping you.

Pt.   Well—I still have this intense anger, an overreaction to people and things and I don't seem to be able to reduce it or eliminate it. It makes me fearful, and we haven't done anything yet to make me get over it.

Th.   So you are angry about that.

Pt.   Not too angry really—but I would like to be less angry. It takes a lot out of me—I'm done in, exhausted. I have this overreaction; why can't I be a little angry and then get over it?

Th.   You feel you just keep on with the anger long after the situation is past?

Pt.   Yes, I could kill, that's so bad.

Th.   Well, you're not killing anyone even if you feel like it.

Pt.   Yes, but I don't want to feel that way.

Th.   That's understandable. I think you resented the side of the research problem where you had to spend the time writing up a justification and then going to defend it. You feel that if you want something, you should have it without such a hullabaloo.

Pt.   That's right.

Th.   The bureaucracy—authoritarian—is the bureaucracy authoritarian? And you got so angry because they were trying to control you—they were controlling you by making you leave your work at the university and making you defend yourself. And when you get angry, you become afraid of your anger. You feel if they see you are angry, they'll punish you by not giving you what you want and need.

Pt.   I guess so. Oh well. I wonder if this will help me be less angry.

Th.   Perhaps, I don't know, perhaps.

Perhaps one of the most difficult aspects of treating the borderline patient, using a theory of defense rather than a developmental concept, is the matter of making an interpretation at a point where the patient will listen and accept the interpretation without too much resistance. The patient will say, "My other therapist told me that a long time ago, but at the time, I had no idea what he was talking about. It meant nothing to me." Or the patient may say to me, "Well, why didn't you tell me that a long time ago? Why have you waited all this time?" My obvious reply is, "I did not think you would accept what I said." Some patients will say that they heard a lecture or they read a book and in the book they learned so and so about themselves. This may be the exact statement that I have made several times, but when I said it, the patient was not listening.

Conclusion

With our new understanding and the adapting of the theory set forth in this volume to the dynamics of the borderline, the therapeutic process will be more understandable and the therapist will be less likely to have counter-transference reactions. When knowledge is on a firm ground, both the patient and the therapist benefit, and the therapy is more likely to proceed to a satisfactory conclusion. Each patient will manifest his problems in a unique way. How the therapist will utilize the emerging dynamics will reside in his particular style of operation. I have indicated ways of functioning that I have found useful and that have been confirmed by some of my students and supervisees. It is my hope that this material will inspire readers to report their experiences with patients which will add to our knowledge about a syndrome that continues to intrigue us with its complications and challenges.

References

Aichorn A: (1925) Wayward Youth. New York, Viking, 1945

Alexander F: The neurotic character. Int J Psychoanal 11:292-311, 1930

Alexander F: Psychoanalysis revised. Psychoanal Q 9:1-36, 1940

Alexander F: Fundamentals of Psychoanalysis. New York, Norton, 1948

Alexander F, French TM, et al: Psychoanalytic Therapy. New York, Ronald, 1946

Allport GW: The historical background of modern social psychology, in Lindzey G (ed): Handbook of Social Psychology, Vol I. Cambridge, MA, Addison-Wesley, 1954, pp 16-17

Angel E: Observations on the units of differential developmental diagnosis. Issues Ego Psychol 3:16-21, 1977

Arlow JA, Brenner C: Concepts and the Structural Theory. New York, International Universities Press, 1964

Asch SE: Effects of group pressure upon the modification and distortion of judgment, in Guetzkow H (ed): Groups, Leadership and Men. Pittsburgh, Carnegie Press, 1951

Asch SE: Social Psychology. Englewood Cliffs, NJ., Prentice-Hall, 1952 (1st printing), 1965 (8th printing), Chap 16

Avnet HH: Psychiatric Insurance. Financing Short-term Ambulatory Treatment. GHI-APA-NAMH Psychiatric Research Report. New York, Group Health Insurance, 1962

Bales RF: Interaction Process Analysis: A Method for the Study of Small Groups. Reading, MA, Addison-Wesley, 1950

Bales RF, Borgatta EF: Interaction of individuals in reconstituted groups. Sociometry 16:302-320, 1953

Bales RF, Strodtbeck FL: Phases in group problem-solving. J Abnorm Psychol 46:485-495, 1951

Balint M: (1937) Primary Love and Psychoanalytic Technique. New York, Liverwright, 1965, Chap. V

Baumwoll E: Transnational Research Newsletter of Postgraduate Center for Mental Health (New York), Fall-Winter 1979. (*Report on Borderline Research*)

Benne KD, Sheats P: Functional roles of group members. J Soc Issues 4:41-49, 1948

Betz BJ: Experiences in research in psychotherapy with schizophrenic patients, in Strupp HH, Luborsky L (eds): Research in Psychotherapy, Vol 2. Washington, DC, American Psychological Association, 1962, pp 41-60

Bieber I: A critique of the libido theory. Am J Psychoanal 18:52-68, 1958

Bion WR: Differentiation of the psychotic from the non-psychotic personalities. Int J Psychoanal 38:266-275, 1957

Bion WR: Experience in Group and Other Papers. New York, Basic Books, 1961

Bion WR: Attention and Interpretation. London, Tavistock, 1970

Bouvet M: Oeuvres Psychoanalytiques, Vol 1. Paris, Payot, 1967

Boyer L, Giovacchini P: Psychoanalytic Treatment of Characterologic and Schizophrenic Disorders. New York, Science House, 1967

Brenner MH: Mental Illness and the Economy. Cambridge, Harvard University Press, 1973

Breuer J: (1895) Studies in the Hysterias. Case Histories (Anna O.) S.E. 2:45

Brinkley JR: Low dose neuroleptic regimens. Arch Gen Psychiatry 36:319-326, 1979

Caplan F: The First Twelve Months of Life. New York, Grossett & Dunlap, 1973

Cartwright D, Zander A (eds): Group Dynamics: Research and Theory. New York, Harper & Row, 1968

Chess S: Developmental theory revisited: Findings of longitudinal study. Can J Psychiatry 24:101-112, 1979

Chessick R: Intensive Psychotherapy of the Borderline Patient. New York, Aronson, 1977

Clark LP: Some practical remarks upon the use of modified psychoanalysis in the treatment of borderline (borderland) neuroses and psychoses. Psychoanal Rev 6:306-316, 1919

Dashiel JF: Experimental studies of the influence of social situations on the behavior of individual human adults, in Murchison, CA (ed): Handbook of Social Psychology. Worcester, MA, Clark University Press, 1935, pp. 1097-1158

Clark University Press, 1935, pp. 1097-1158

De Casper AJ: The "mommy tapes." Early perception. Science News 115(4):56, 1979

Delboeuf, JLR: Le Magnetisme Animal. Paris, Bailliere, 1889

Dennis W: Infant development under conditions of restricted practice and minimum social stimulation. J Genet Psychol 53:149-158, 1938

Dickes R: The concepts of borderline states: An alternative proposal. Int J Psychoanal Psychother 3:1-27, 1974

Dince PR: Partial dissociation as encountered in the borderline patient. J Am Acad Psychoanal 53:327-345, 1977

Druck AB: The role of didactic group psychotherapy in short-term psychiatric settings. Group 2(2):98-109, 1978

Duncker K: On problem-solving. Psychol Monogr 58(5), 1945

Durkheim E: Le Suicide (1897). Suicide: A Study in Sociology (rev ed). Simpson G (ed); Spaulding J, Simpson G (trans). New York, Free Press, 1951

Eder MD: Borderland Cases. University Med Rec (London) 5:1-10, 1914

Eibl-Eibesfeldt I: Love and Hate, the Natural History of Behavior Patterns. G. Strachen (trans). New York, Schocken Books, 1974

Eigen M: On working with "unwanted" patients. Int J Psychoanal 58:109-121, 1977

Eisnitz AJ: Narcissistic object choice, self-representation. Int J Psychoanal 50:15-25, 1969

Eissler KR: Notes upon the emotionality of a schizophrenic patient, and its relation to the problems of technique. Psychoanal Study Child 8:199-251, 1953

Eissler KR: Goethe, A Psychoanalytic Study 1775-1786, 2 vols. Detroit, Wayne State University, 1963

Erikson EH: Ego development and historical development. Psychoanal Study Child, 2:359-396, 1946

Erikson EH: Childhood and Society. New York, Norton, 1950

Fairbairn WRD: An Object-Relations Theory of the Personality. New York, Basic Books, 1954. (First published in 1952 as Psychoanalytic Studies of the Personality)

Fenichel O: (1934) On the psychology of boredom, in Collected Papers of Otto Fenichel. New York, Norton, 1953, Vol 1, pp 292-302.

Fenichel O: The Psychoanalytic Theory of Neurosis. New York, Norton, 1945

Fintzy RT: Vicissitudes of a transitional object in a borderline child. Int J Psychoanal 52:107-114, 1971

Foulkes SH: Introduction to Group-Analytic Psychotherapy. London, Heinemann, 1948

Freedman, BJ: The subjective experience of perceptual and cognitive disturbances in schizophrenia. Arch Gen Psychiatry 3:333-340, 1974

Freeman TA: Some aspects of pathological narcissism. JAPA 12:540-561, 1964

REFERENCES

345

French TM: Psychoanalytic Interpretations. Chicago, Quadrangle Books, 1970
French TM, Fromm E: Dream Interpretation. New York, Basic Books, 1964
Freud A: (1930) The Ego and the Mechanisms of Defense. New York, International Universities Press, 1946
Freud A: Normality and Pathology in Childhood: Assessments of Development. New York, International Universities Press, 1965
Freud A, Dann S: An experiment in group unbringing. Psychoanal Study Child, 6:127, 1951

(References to Freud, S. E., in the text, except where otherwise indicated, are found in The Standard Edition of the Complete Psychological Works of Sigmund Freud, *London, Hogarth, 1953-1974.)*

Freud SE: (1887-1902) The Origins of Psychoanalysis. Letters, Drafts, and Notes to Wilhelm Fliess. New York, Basic Books, 1954, p. 197
Freud SE: (1893) On the psychical mechanisms of hysterical phenomenon, 3:26-39
Freud SE: (1899) Screen memories, 3:301-322
Freud SE: (1900) The material of dreams—memory in dreams, 4:15-16, 20
Freud SE: (1900) The interpretation of dreams, 4:149-150
Freud SE: (1909) Family romances, 9:236-241
Freud SE: (1909) Notes upon a case of obsessional neurosis (Rat man), 10:226, 237-238
Freud SE: (1911) Notes on a case of paranoia, 12:70-73
Freud SE: (1913) Editor's note (to), the disposition to obsessional neurosis, 12:315-316
Freud SE: (1913) The disposition to obsessional neurosis: A contribution to the problem of choice of neurosis, 12:320
Freud SE: (1914) On the history of the psychoanalytic movement, 14:3-66
Freud SE: (1914) On narcissism, 14:69-102
Freud SE: (1915) The unconscious, 14:161-215
Freud SE: (1916 [1915]) On transience, 14:305-307
Freud SE: (1916) Some character types met with in psychoanalytic work, 14:311-315
Freud SE: (1916) Those wrecked by success, 14:316-331
Freud SE: (1917) Mourning and melancholia, 14:239-258
Freud SE: (1917) The libido theory and narcissism, 16:412-430
Freud SE: (1917) A childhood recollection, 17:150
Freud SE: (1919) A child is being beaten, 17:177-204
Freud SE: (1920) Beyond the pleasure principle, 18:14-17
Freud SE: (1920) The psychogenesis of a case of homosexuality in a woman, 18:147-172
Freud SE: (1921) Being in love and hypnosis, 18:111-116
Freud SE: (1923) The ego and the id, 19:3-66
Freud SE: (1923 [1922]) Two encyclopaedia articles, (A) Psycho-analysis, 18:235-254; (B) The libido theory, 18:255-259
Freud SE: (1924) Loss of reality in neurosis and psychosis, 19:182-187
Freud SE: (1926) Inhibitions, symptoms and anxiety, 20:75-174
Freud SE: (1927) Fetishism, 21:149-157
Freud SE: (1930 [1929]) Civilization and its discontents, 21:59-145
Freud SE: (1931) Female sexuality, 21:231, 238
Freud SE: (1933) New introductory lectures in psychoanalysis, 22:3-182
Freud SE: (1937) Analysis terminable and interminable, 23:211-252
Freud SE: (1938) An outline of psychoanalysis, 23:141-207
Friedman DD: Toward a unitary theory on the passing of the oedipal conflict. Psychoanal Rev 51:38-48, 1966
Furst SS: Psychic Trauma. New York, Basic Books, 1967

Geleerd ER: Some observations on temper trantrums in childhood. Am J Orthopsychiatry 15:238, 1945

Geleerd ER: Borderline states in childhood and adolescence. Psychoanal Study Child 13:279-295, 1958

Geleerd ER: Two kinds of denial: Neurotic denial and denial in the service of the need to survive, in Schur M (ed): Drives, Affects, Behavior, Vol 2. New York, International Universities Press, 1965

Giffin J, Johnson AM, Litin EM: Specific factors determining anti-social acting out. Am J Orthopsychiatry 24:664, 1954

Giovacchini PL: Characterological aspects of marital interaction. Psychoanal Forum 2:8-14, 1967

Giovacchini PL: Tactics and Techniques in Psychoanalytic Therapy. New York, Science House, 1972

Goldberg A (ed): The Psychology of the Self: A Casebook. New York, International Universities Press, 1978. See also The Postgraduate Center COLLOQUIUM, Dec 1978

Goldstein MJ, Jones JE: Adolescent and familial precursors of borderline and schizophrenic conditions, in Hartocollis P (ed): International Conference on Borderline Disorder, Topeka, Kansas, 1976. New York, International Universities Press, 1977

Gorvey JE: The negative therapeutic interactions. Contemp Psychoanal 15(2):288-337, 1979

Green A: La nosographie psychoanalytique des psychoses, in Doucet P, Lauren C (eds): Problems of Psychosis, Vol 1. Amsterdam, Excerpta Medica, 1969

Green A: The borderline concept; A conceptual framework for the understanding of borderline patient's suggested hypothesis, in Hartocollis P (ed): Borderline Personality Disorders: The Concept, the Syndrome, the Patient. New York, International Universities Press, 1977, pp 15-44

Greenson RR: The struggle against identification. J Am Psychoanal Assoc 2:200-217, 1954

Grinberg L: Projective identification and projective counter-identification in the analysis of group, in Wolberg LR, Schwartz EK (eds): Group Therapy 1973: An Overview. New York, Stratton Intercontinental Medical Book, 1973

Grinker R (ed): Toward a Unified Theory of Human Behavior, New York, Basic Books, 1956

Grinker RR, Werble B: The Borderline Patient. New York, Aronson, 1977

Grinker RR, Werble B, Drye RC: The Borderline Syndrome: A Behavioral Syndrome of Ego Functions. New York, Basic Books, 1968

Gunby P: The abused youngster in twilight years. JAMA 241:18-19, 1979

Gunderson JG: Major clinical controversies, in Gunderson JG, Mosker L (eds): Psychotherapy and Schizophrenia. New York, Aronson, 1975, pp 3-21

Gunderson JG, Carpenter WT, Strauss JS: Borderline and schizophrenic patients: A comparative study. Am J Psychiatry 132:1257-1264, 1975

Gunderson JG, Kolb JE: Discriminating features of borderline patients. Am J Psychiatry 135:792-796, 1978

Gunderson JG, Singer MT: Defining borderline patients: An overview. Am J Psychiatry 132:1-10, 1975

Guntrip H: Personality Structure and Human Interaction. London, Hogarth; New York, International Universities Press, 1964

Guntrip H: Schizoid Phenomena, Object Relations and the Self. New York, International Universities Press, 1968

Gurnee HA: Comparison of collective and individual judgments of fact. J Exp Psychol 21:106-112, 1937

Haley J: Changing Families; A Family Therapy Reader. New York, Grune & Stratton, 1971

Haley J: Problem-Solving Therapy: New Strategies for Effective Family Therapy. San Francisco, Josey-Bass, 1976

Harlow HF: Learning to Love. New York, Ballantine, 1973

Harlow HF: Love and Aggression. Kittay Lecture at Academy of Medicine, New York City, Oct 31, 1976. A response to Kittay award. Report in APA Monitor, Dec 1976

Harlow HF, Harlow MK: Social deprivation in monkeys. Sci Am 207(5):137-146, 1962

Hartmann H: Internationale Zeitschrift fur Psychoanalyse, XXIV, 1939. (Partly translated in Rapaport D: Organization and Pathology of Thought. New York, Columbia University Press, 1951)

Hartmann H: Comments on the psychoanalytic theory of the ego. Psychoanal Study Child. New York, International Universities Press, 5:74-96, 1950

Hartmann H: Ego Psychology and the Problems of Adaptation. New York, International Universities Press, 1958

Hartmann H: (1950) Psychoanalysis and Developmental Psychology. Essays on Ego Psychology. New York, International Universities Press, 1964

Hartocollis P (ed): International Conference on Borderline Disorders. Topeka, Kansas, 1976. New York, International Universities Press, 1977

Harvey OJ (ed): System structure, flexibility and creativity, in Experience, Structure, and Adaptability. New York, Springer, 1966, pp 39-65

Heath RG: Electroencephalographic studies in isolated-raised monkeys with behavior impairment. Dis Nerv Sys 33:157-163, 1972

Heimann P: A contribution to the reevaluation of the oedipus complex. The early stages, in Klein M et al (eds): New Directions in Psychoanalysis. London, Tavistock; New York, Basic Books, 1955

Heimann P: Comment on Dr. Kernberg's paper. Int J Psychoanal 47:254-260, 1966

Henle P: Exploring the distribution of earned income. Monthly Labor Review (U.S. Dept of Labor, Bureau of Labor Statistics) December 1972, pp 16-27

Hoch PH, Polatin P: Pseudoneurotic forms of schizophrenia. Psychiatr Q 23:248-276, 1949

Hoffding H: Outline of Psychology. London, MacMillan, 1891

Hoffding H: (1910) Human Thought. See International Encyclopedia of the Social Sciences. New York, MacMillan, 1968, pp 440-442; Encyclopedia of Psychiatry, Psychology, Psychoanalysis and Neurology, Vol 5. New York, Van Nostrand Reinhold, 1977, p 388

Homans GC: The Human Group. New York, Harcourt Brace Jovanovich, 1950

Hughes CH: Borderland psychiatric records: Pro-dromal symptoms of physical impairments. Alienist & Neurologist 5:85-90, 1884

Jackson DD: An episode of sleep-walking. JAPA 2:503-598, 1954

Jackson DD: The question of family homeostasis. Psychiatr Q Suppl Part I 31:79-90, 1957

Jackson DD: Guilt and the control of pleasure in schizoid personalities. Br J Med Psychol 28:433-434, 1959 (a)

Jackson DD: The managing of acting out in a borderline personality, in Burton A (ed): Case Studies in Counseling and Psychotherapy. Englewood Cliffs, NJ, Prentice-Hall, 1959, pp 168-189 (b)

Jackson DD: Family interaction, family homeostasis, and some implications for conjoint family therapy, in Masserman J (ed): Individual and Family Dynamics (Science and Psychoanalysis, Vol 2). New York, Grune & Stratton, 1959, pp 122-141 (c)

Jackson DD: Bibliography, in Wolberg LR, Aronson ML (eds): New York, Stratton Intercontinental Medical Book, 1977

Jackson DD, Bateson G: Social factors and disorders of communication. Some varieties of pathogenic organization. Research Publications of the Association of Research in Nerv Ment Dis 42:270-290, 1964

Jackson DD, Yalom J: Conjoint family therapy as an aid to intensive psychotherapy, in Burton A (ed): Modern Psychotherapeutic Practice. Palo Alto, CA, Science and Behavior, 1965, pp 81-97

Jacobson E: The self and the object world: Vicissitudes of their infantile cathexes and their influence on ideational and affective development. Psychoanal Study Child 9:75-127, 1954

Jennings HH: Leadership and Isolation: A Study of Personality in Interpersonal Relations, 2nd ed. New York, Longmans Green, 1950

Johnson AM: Sanctions for superego lacunae of adolescents, in Eissler KR (ed): Searchlights on Delinquency: New Psychoanalytic Studies. New York, International Universities Press, 1949

Johnson AM: Juvenile delinquency, in Arieti S (ed): American Handbook of Psychiatry, Vol 1. New York, Basic Books, 1959

Jones WA: Borderland cases, mental and nervous. Lancet 38:561-567, 1918

Kagan J: The form of early development. Arch Gen Psychiatry 36:1047-1054, 1979 (a)

Kagan J: Overview: Perspectives in human infancy, in Osofsky JD (ed): Handbook of Infant Development. New York, Wiley, 1979 (b)

Kellerman H: Group Psychotherapy and Personality. New York, Grune & Stratton, 1979, pp 27, 116, 209

Kernberg O: Structural derivatives of object relationships. Int J Psychoanal 47:236-253, 1966

Kernberg O: Borderline personality organization. J Am Psychoanal Assoc 15:641-685, 1967

Kernberg O: The treatment of patients with borderline personality organization. Int J Psychoanal 49:600-619, 1968

Kernberg O: Factors in the psychoanalytic treatment of narcissistic personalities. J Am Psychoanal Assoc 18:51-85, 1970 (a)

Kernberg O: A psychoanalytic classification of character pathology. J Am Psychoanal Assoc 18:800-821, 1970 (b)

Kernberg O: Borderline Conditions and Pathological Narcissism. New York, Aronson, 1975

Kernberg O: Object Relations Theory and Clinical Psychoanalysis. New York, Aronson, 1976

Kety SS, Rosenthal D, Wender PH, et al: The types and prevalence of mental illness in the biological and adoptive families of adopted schizophrenics, in Rosenthal D, Kety SS (eds): The Transmission of Schizophrenia. New York, Pergamon, 1968, pp 345-362

Kety SS, Rosenthal D, Wender PH, et al: Mental illness in the biological and adoptive schizophrenics. Am J Psychiatry 128:302-306, 1971

Kibel HD: The rationale for the use of group psychotherapy for borderline patients on a short-term unit. Int J Group Psychother 28(3):339-358, 1978

Klein M: Notes on some schizoid mechanisms. Int J Psychoanal 27:99-110, 1946

Klein M: Narrative of a Child Analysis. London, Hogarth, 1975

Klein MI: Notes on the seduction theory. Bull Menninger Clin (in press)

Klein MI: On Mahler's autistic and symbiotic phases: An exposition and evaluation (in press)

Klerman G: Age and clinical depression: Today's youth in the 21st century. J Geront 31(3):318-323, 1976

Kohlberg L: Development of children's orientations toward a moral order. Vita Humana, 6(1-2):11-33, 1963

Kohlberg L: Development of moral character and moral ideology, in Hoffman ML, Hoffman LW (eds): Review of Child Development Research. New York: Russell Sage Foundation, 1964, pp 333-431

Kohlberg L: A cognitive developmental analysis of children's sex-role concepts and attitudes, in Maccoby EE (ed): The Development of Sex Differences. Stanford, CA, Stanford University Press, 1966

Kohlberg L: Moral education. Newsweek, March 1, 1976, pp 74-75A

Kohler W: Gestalt Psychology. New York, Liverwright, 1929

Kohler W: Dynamics in Psychology. New York, Liverwright, 1940

Kohut H: Forms and transformation of narcissism. J Am Psychol Assoc 14:243-272, 1959

Kohut H: The Analysis of the Self. New York, International Universities Press, 1971

Kohut H: The Restoration of the Self. New York, International Universities Press, 1977

Kohut H, Seitz PFL: Concepts and theories of psychoanalysis, in Wepman JM, Heine RW (eds): Concepts of Personality. Chicago, Aldine, 1963

Kris E: On the vicissitudes of insight. Int J Psychoanal 37:445, 1956

Laing RD: The Divided Self. New York, Pantheon Books, 1970, pp 100-112

Laurance WL: Men and Atoms. New York, Simon & Schuster, 1962

Leuba JH: Introduction a l'etude clinique du narcissisme (Introduction to the clinical study of narcissism). Rev Fr de Psychoanal 13:456-500, 1949

Levy DM: Body interest in children and hypochondriasis. Am J Psychiatry 12:295-315, 1932

Levy DM: The Early Development of Independent and Oppositional Behavior, Midcentury Psychiatry. Springfield, IL, Thomas, 1953

Lewis J, Sarbin TR: Studies in psychosomatics. The influence of hypnotic stimulation on gastric hunger contractions. Psychosom Med 5:125-131, 1943

Lidz T, Fleck S, Cornelison AR: Schizophrenia and the Family. New York, International Universities Press, 1965

Lipschutz DM: Combined group and individual psychotherapy. Am J Psychother 2:336, 1957

Litin EM, Giffin ME, Johnson A: Parental influence in unusual sexual behavior in children. Psychoanal Q 25:37-55, 1956

McCarley RW, Hobson JA: The neurobiological origins of psychoanalytic dream theory. Am J Psychiatry 134(11):1211-1221, 1977

Macfarlane JW: From infancy to adulthood. Child Educ 39:336-342, 1963

Macfarlane JW: Perspectives on personality consistency and change from the guidance study. Vita Humana 7:115-126, 1964

MacHovec FJ: Hypnotic recall in psychogenic fugue states: Two cases. Am J Clin Hypn 23(2), 1980

Mack JE (ed): Borderline States in Psychiatry. New York, Grune & Stratton, 1975, pp 135-138

Mahler MS: A study of the separation-individuation process and its possible application to borderline phenomena in the psychoanalytic situation. Psychoanal Study Child 26:403-424, 1971

Mahler MS, Furer M, Settlage CF: Severe emotional disturbances in childhood, in Arieti S (ed): American Handbook of Psychiatry, Vol 1. New York, Basic Books, 1959

Mahler MS, Pine F, Bergman A: The Psychological Birth of the Human Infant. New York, Basic Books, 1975

Mason AA: The suffocating super-ego, in Grobstein J (ed): Do I Dare Disturb the Universe. New York, Aronson, 1979

Masterson JF: Treatment of the Borderline Adolescent: A Developmental Approach. New York, Wiley, 1972

Masterson JF: Psychotherapy of the Borderline Adult. New York, Brunner/Mazel, 1976

Masterson JF: Personality of the borderline adult: A developmental approach. Weekly Psychiatry Update Series (Princeton, NJ) 52:2-5, 1977

Masterson JF, Rinsley DB: The borderline syndrome: The role of the mother in the genesis and psychic structure of the borderline personality. Int J Psychoanal 56:163-177, 1975

Meltzer D: The Kleinian Development, 3 parts. Perth, Scotland, Clunie Press, 1978

Menninger Foundation Conference: (Sandoz Pharmaceutical Company, Hanover, NJ) 6(1):134, 1969

Merton RK: Social Theory and Social Structure. New York, Free Press, 1957

Meyer LB: Concerning the sciences, the arts—AND the humanities. Critical Inquiry 1:163-217, 1974

Milgram S: Obedience to Authority. New York, Harper & Row, 1973

Miller JG: Living systems: Basic concepts. Behav Sci 10(3):193-237, 1965

Miller NE: The frustration-aggression hypothesis. Psychol Rev 48:337-342, 1941

Miller NE: Theory and experiment relating psychoanalytic displacement to stimulus-response generalization. J Abnorm Soc Psychol 43:155-178, 1948

Modell AH: Primitive object relationship and predisposition to schizophrenia. Int J Psychoanal 44:282-292, 1963

Modell AH: Object Love and Reality. New York: International Universities Press, 1968

Modell AH: A narcissistic defense against affects and the illusion of self-sufficiency. Int J Psychoanal 56:275-282, 1975

Money-Kyrle RE: Normal counter-transference and some of its deviations. Int J Psychoanal 37:360, 1956

Moore BE, Fine BD: A Glossary of Psychoanalytic Terms and Concepts, 2nd ed. New York, American Psychoanalytic Association, 1968

Moore TV: The parataxes: A study and analysis of certain borderline mental states. Psychoanal Rev 8:252-281, 1921

Moreno JL: Who Shall Survive? A New Approach to the Problem of Human Interrelations. Washington, DC, Nervous & Mental Disease Publishing, 1934

Muller-Braunschweig C: Desexualization and identification; Being in love; Hypnosis and sleep; Notion of direction. Clark LP (trans). NY Med J 13:385-403, 1926

Muller JP, Richardson WJ: Toward reading Lacan: Pages for a workbook. Psychoanal Contemp Thought 1(3):325-372, 1979

Nadelson T: Borderline rage and the therapist's response. Am J Psychiatry 134:748-9, 1977

Noy P: The psychoanalytic theory of cognitive development. Psychoanal Study Child 34:169-216, 1979

Odier C: Anxiety and Magic Thinking. Schoelly ML, Sherfey MJ (trans). New York, International Universities Press, 1956

Ornstein PH (ed): The Search for the Self: Selected Writings of Heinz Kohut: 1950-1978, Vol 1. New York, International Universities Press, 1978

Penfield W: Memory mechanisms. Arch Neurol Psychiatry 67:178-198, 1952

Penfield W, Roberts L: Speech and Brain Mechanisms. Princeton, NJ, Princeton University Press, 1959

Piaget J: The Child's Conception of Physical Causality. New York, Humanities Press, 1951

Piaget J: The Origins of Intelligence in Children. New York, International Universities Press, 1952

Piaget J: (1937) The Construction of Reality in the Child. New York, Basic Books, 1954

Piaget J: The genetic approach to the psychology of thought. J Educ Psychol 52:275-281, 1961

Piaget J, Inhelder B: The Growth of Logical Thinking from Childhood to Adolescence. New York, Basic Books, 1958

Piaget J, Inhelder B: The Early Growth of Logic in the Child. New York, Harper & Row, 1964

REFERENCES

Plutchik R: The Emotions: Facts, Theories and a New Model. New York, Random House, 1962

Plutchik R: Emotions, evolution and adaptive processes, in Arnold M (ed): Feelings and Emotions: The Loyola Symposium. New York, Academic Press, 1970

Pruyser P: What splits in "splitting." Bull Menninger Clin 39:1-46, 1975

Rangell L: The borderline case: Panel reports, scientific proceedings. JAPA 3:285-298, 1955

Rangell L: Aggression, oedipus and historical perspective. LJPA 53:3-11, 1972

Rapaport D: A theoretical analysis of the superego concept, in Gill M (ed): The Collected Papers of David Rapaport. New York, Basic Books, 1967

Reich A: Narcissistic object choice in a woman. J Am Psychoanal Assoc 1:22-44, 1953

Rey JH: Intrapsychic object relations: The individual and the group, in Wolberg LR, Aronson ML (eds): Group Therapy 1975: An Overview. New York, Stratton Intercontinental Medical Book, 1975, pp 84-101

Rickman J: A survey: The development of the psychoanalytical theory of the psychosis, 1894-1926. Br J Med Psychol 6:270-294, 1926

Rickman J: The development of the moral function, in The Yearbook of Education, 1949-1952. London, Evans, 1951, pp 67-68

Rinsley DB: An "object" relations view of borderline personality. Paper presented at the International Meeting on Borderline Disorders. Sponsored by the Menninger Foundation and the National Institute of Mental Health, Topeka, Kansas, March 1976

Rinsley DB: Borderline psychopathology: A review of etiology, dynamics, and treatment. Int Rev Psychoanal 5:45-54, 1978

Riviere J: On the genesis of psychical conflict in earliest infancy. Int J Psychoanal 17:395-422, 1936

Robbins MD: Borderline personality organization: The need for a new theory. J Am Psychoanal Assoc 24:831-853, 1976

Rosenfeld HA: Considerations regarding the psycho-analytic approach to acute and chronic schizophrenia. Int J Psychoanal 35:135-140, 1954

Rosenfeld HA: Psychotic States. London, Hogarth, 1965

Rosse IC: Clinical evidence of borderline insanity. J Nerv Ment Dis 17:669-674, 1890

Rosner S: Problems of working-through with borderline patients. Psychother Theory, Res Prac 6:43-45, 1969

Rossner S: On the nature of free association. J Psychoanal Assoc 21:558-575, 1973 (a)

Rossner S: Free association and memory. J Psychother Theory Res Prac 10:278-280, 1973 (b)

Sarbin TR: Role theory, in Lindzey G (ed): Handbook of Social Psychology, Vol 1. Cambridge, MA, Addison-Wesley, 1954

Schaefer R: Aspects of Internalization. New York, International Universities Press, 1968

Schaffer H: Objective observations of personality development in early infancy. Br J Med Psychol 31:174-183, 1958

Schilder P: Psychotherapy, rev ed. Bender L (ed). New York, Norton, 1951

Scholz F: (1887) Sleep and Dreams. Jewett HM (trans). New York, 1893, pp 20, 57-58, 67-134

Schwartz DP: Psychotherapy, in Shershaw JC (ed): Schizophrenia Science and Practice. Cambridge, Harvard University Press, 1978

Science News: The brain and emotions. 112(5):74, 1977

Science News: Crime: Who is the real victim. 115(2):25, 1978

Science News: The "mommy tapes": Early perception. 115(4):56, 1979 (a)

Science News: Brains: The younger, the better. 116(5):89, 1979

Searles HF: Transference psychosis in the psychotherapy of chronic schizophrenia. Int J Psychoanal 44:249-281, 1963

Segal H: Some aspects of the analysis of a schizophrenic. Int J Psychoanal 31:268-278, 1950

Segal H: A note on schizoid mechanisms underlying phobia formation. Int J Psychoanal 35:238-241, 1954

Segal H: Depression in the schizophrenic. Int J Psychoanal 37:339-343, 1956

Segal H: Introduction to the Work of Melanie Klein. New York, Basic Books, 1964

Selye H: The Stress of Life. New York, McGraw-Hill, 1956

Settlage CE: Narcissistic and borderline personality disorders. JAPA 25(4):815, 1977

Shapiro ER: Research on family dynamics: Clinical implications for the family of the borderline adolescent, in Fensterheim SC, Govacchini PL (eds): Adolescent Psychiatry, Vol 6. New York, Basic Books, 1978

Showes WD, Carson RC: The A-B therapist "type" distinction and spatial orientation: Replication and extension. J Nerv Ment Dis 141:456-462, 1965

Sifneos PE: Short-term Psychotherapy and Emotional Crisis. Cambridge, Harvard University Press, 1972

Simmel G: (1908) The Sociology of George Simmel. Wolff KH (ed & trans). New York, Free Press, 1950

Spitz RA: The psychogenic diseases in infancy: An attempt at their etiologic classification. Psychoanal Study Child 6:255-275, 1951

Spitz RA: The primal cavity: A contribution to the genesis of perception and its role for psychoanalytic theory. Psychoanal Study Child 10:215-240, 1955

Spitz RA: No and Yes: On the Genesis of Human Communication. New York, International Universities Press, 1966

Spitz RA, Cobliner WG: The First Year of Life. New York, International Universities Press, 1965

Spitzer RL, Endicott J, Gibbon M: Crossing the border into borderline personality and borderline schizophrenia. The development of criteria. Arch Gen Psychiatry 36:17-24, 1979

Spotnitz H: Modern Psychoanalysis of the Schizophrenic Patient: Theory of the Technique. New York, Grune & Stratton, 1969

Stern A: Psychoanalytic investigation of a therapy in the borderline neurosis. Paper read at New York Psychoanalytic Society, 1937. Psychoanal Q 7:467-489, 1938

Stoller RJ: A further contribution to the study of gender identity. Int J Psychoanal 49:(Parts 2-3):364-369, 1968

Stroufe AL, Waters E: The autogenesis of smiling and laughter: A perspective on the organization of development in infancy. Psychol Rev 83(3):173-189, 1976

Sullivan HS: The Interpersonal Theory of Psychiatry. New York, Norton, 1955

Szurek SA: Notes on the genesis of psychopathic personality trends. Psychiatry 5:1-6, 1942

Szurek SA, and Johnson, AM: The genesis of anti-social acting out in children and adults. Psychoanal Q 21:323-343, 1952

Szurek SA, Johnson AM: Etiology of anti-social behavior in delinquents and psychopaths. JAMA 154:814-817, 1954

Thomas A, Chess S: The Dynamics of Psychological Development. New York, Brunner/ Mazel, 1980

Time magazine: Psychiatry on the couch. April 2, 1979

Trevarthan C: Conversations with a two-month-old. New Scientist 62:230-235, 1974

Ungar G: Molecular mechanisms in learning. Perspect Biol Med 11:217-233, 1968

U.S. News & World Report: Public officials for sale. February 28, 1977, p 36

Volkan V: Primitive Internalized Object Relations. New York, International Universities Press, 1976

Waelder R: Das Freiheistproblem in der Psychoanalyse. Imago 20:467-484, 1934

Waelder R: Basic Theories of Psychoanalysis. New York, International Universities Press, 1960

Weakland H: The "double-bind" hypothesis of schizophrenia and three-party interaction, in Jackson DD (ed): The Etiology of Schizophrenia. New York, Basic Books, 1960

Weissman MM: Depressed women: Traditional and non-traditional therapies, in Claghorn JL (ed): Successful Psychotherapy. New York, Brunner/Mazel, 1976

Weissman MM: Depressed parents and their children: Implications for prevention, in Noshpitz JD (ed): Basic Handbook of Child Psychiatry. New York, Basic Books, 1979

Wender PH: The contribution of the adoption studies to an understanding of the phenomenology and etiology of borderline schizophrenics, in Hartocollis P (ed): Borderline Personality Disorders, Topeka, Kansas, 1976. New York, International Universities Press, 1977, pp 255-269

Wertheimer M: Gestalt Theory. New York, New School for Social Research, Graduate Faculty of Political and Social Science, 1944

Whitehorn JC, Betz BJ: Further studies of the doctor as a crucial variable in the outcome of treatment with schizophrenic patients. Am J Psychiatry 117:215-223, 1960

Winnicott, DW: Transitional objects and transitional phenomena. Paper read before the British Psychoanalytical Society, London, May 1951

Winnicott DW: Transitional objects and transitional phenomena: A study of the first not-me possession. Int J Psychoanal 34:89-97, 1953 (a)

Winnicott DW: Symptom tolerance in paediatrics. Proc Roy Soc Med 46:675-684, 1953 (b)

Winnicott DW: Metapsychological and clinical aspects of regression within the psychoanalytic set-up, in Winnicott DW (ed): Collected Papers. New York, Basic Books, 1958, pp 278-294

Winnicott DW: Ego distortion in terms of the true and false self, in Winnicott DW (ed): The Maturational Processes and the Facilitating Environment. New York, International Universities Press, 1965

Winnicott DW: Playing and reality. Roche Report 6(6), 1969

Wolberg AR: The borderline patient. Am J Psychother 6:694-710, 1952

Wolberg AR: The psychoanalytic treatment of the borderline patient in the individual and group setting, in Hulse W (ed): Topical Problems of Psychotherapy, Vol 2. New York, Karger, 1960, pp 174-197

Wolberg AR: Patterns of interaction in families of borderline patients, in Riess BF (ed): New Directions in Mental Health, Vol I. New York, Grune & Stratton, 1968, pp 100-177

Wolberg AR: Intensifying the group process in psychoanalytic group psychotherapy. Psychiatr Ann 2(3):70-73, 1972

Wolberg AR: The Borderline Patient. New York, Stratton Intercontinental Medical Book, 1973

Wolberg AR: The contributions of Jacob Moreno, in Wolberg LR, Aronson ML (eds): Group Therapy 1976: An Overview. New York, Stratton Intercontinental Medical Book, 1976, pp 1-15

Wolberg AR: Group therapy and the dynamics of projective identification, in Wolberg LR, Aronson ML (eds): Group Therapy 1977: An Overview. New York, Stratton Intercontinental Medical Book, 1977, pp 151-181

Wolberg LR: Hypnoanalysis. New York, Grune & Stratton, 1945 (1st ed), 1964 (2nd ed)

Wolberg LR: Hypnotic phenomena, in Abramson HA (ed): Problems of Consciousness. Transactions of the 3rd Conference. New York, Josiah Macy, Jr., Foundation, 1952, pp 76-106

Wolberg LR: The Technique of Psychotherapy. New York, Grune & Stratton, 1954 (1st ed), 1967 (2nd ed), 1977 (3rd ed)

Wolberg LR: Short-term Psychotherapy. New York, Grune & Stratton, 1965

Wolberg LR: Psychotherapy and the Behavioral Sciences. New York, Grune & Stratton, 1966

Wolberg LR: Handbook of Short-term Psychotherapy. New York, Stratton Intercontinental Medical Book, 1980

Wolff KH (ed & trans): The Sociology of George Simmel (1908). New York, Free Press, 1950

Woug N: Clinical consideration in group treatment of narcissistic disorders. Int J Group Psychother 29:325-345, 1979

Zeigarnik B: Uber das Behalten von erledigten und unerledigten Handlungen, Psychologische Forschung, 9:1-85, 1927. Also: Zeigarnik effect, in Wolman BB (ed): International Encyclopedia of Psychiatry, Psychology, Psychoanalysis and Neurology, Vol 11, 1977, p 465

Index